Classical Memories/Modern Identities
Paul Allen Miller and Richard H. Armstrong, Series Editors

Postmodern Spiritual Practices

THE CONSTRUCTION OF THE SUBJECT

AND THE RECEPTION OF PLATO

IN LACAN, DERRIDA, AND FOUCAULT

Paul Allen Miller

THE OHIO STATE UNIVERSITY PRESS
Columbus

Copyright © 2007 by The Ohio State University.
All rights reserved.

Library of Congress Cataloging-in-Publication Data
Miller, Paul Allen, 1959–
  Postmodern spiritual practices : the construction of the subject and the reception of Plato in Lacan, Derrida, and Foucault / Paul Allen Miller. — 1st ed.
    p. cm. — (Classical memories/modern identities)
  Includes bibliographical references and index.
  ISBN-13: 978-0-8142-1070-3 (cloth : alk. paper)
  ISBN-10: 0-8142-1070-8 (cloth : alk. paper)
  1. France—Intellectual life—20th century. 2. Plato—Influence. 3. Lacan, Jacques, 1901–1981. 4. Derrida, Jacques, 1930–2004. 5. Foucault, Michel, 1926–1984.
  I. Title.
  DC33.7.M539 2007
  194—dc22
                                        2007015287

This book is available in the following editions:
Cloth (ISBN 978-0-8142-1070-3)
CD-ROM (ISBN 978-0-8142-9147-4)

Cover design by Dan O'Dair
Type set in Adobe Sabon

The paper used in this publication meets the minimum requirements of the American National Standard for Information Sciences—Permanence of Paper for Printed Library Materials. ANSI Z39.48-1992.

*For Carl Rubino and Wendy McCredie
and the summer we read Hegel.*

"The true human body is the bones and marrow of the realm beyond consciousness and unconsciousness. Just raising this up is the study of the way."

Dogen (1200–1253 CE)

Contents

Acknowledgments ix

Chapter 1 Introduction: Remaking the Soul:
           Antiquity, Postmodernism, and Genealogies of the Self   1

Chapter 2 The Modernist Revolt: History, Politics, and Allegory,
           Or Classicism in Occupied France   27

Chapter 3 Historicizing Transcendence:
           Antigone, the Good, and the Ethics of Psychoanalysis   61

Chapter 4 Lacan, the *Symposium,* and Transference   100

Chapter 5 Writing the Subject:
           Derrida Asks Plato to Take a Letter   133

Chapter 6 The Art of Self-Fashioning, or Foucault on the *Alcibiades*:
           Caring for the Self and Others   178

Chapter 7 Searching for a Usable Past   227

Appendix   Queering Alcibiades: Persius on Foucault and Halperin   231

Works Cited   237
Index   261

Acknowledgments

Like all books this one has many beginnings. One of its most important, however, took place in the office of Professor Wolfgang Haase at Boston University in the winter of 1998. Professor Haase generously invited me to be a plenary speaker at that summer's meeting of the International Society for the Classical Tradition in Tübingen. He then asked what I would like to speak on. I said "the classical roots of poststructuralism." I remember thinking to myself as I left his office, "boy you've really done it this time. Now you've got to write this thing. You don't know a thing about it." There followed several months of feverish work. The resulting address and later article, "The Classical Roots of Poststructuralism: Lacan, Derrida, and Foucault" (*International Journal of the Classical Tradition* 5.2 [1998]: 204–25), was in many ways the first draft of a book I might have never written otherwise. I thus owe a deep debt of gratitude to Professor Haase for the confidence he showed in a newly minted associate professor from a modest university in west Texas.

In the ensuing years, numerous friends and colleagues have provided emotional, intellectual, and moral support for this project. Sharon Nell and Micaela Janan both read the entire book in draft form and provided crucial help with clarifying obscure formulations, eliminating errors, and unknotting tangled webs of argument. Victoria Wohl read and offered sound advice on chapters 3 and 4. Jill Frank did the same for chapters 3 and 6. Mary Ann Friese Witt provided invaluable advice on chapter 2, as did Peter Burian on chapter 3, and Chuck Platter on chapter 6. David Wray, who identified himself as one of the readers for The Ohio State University Press, gave the manuscript a detailed and acute reading, and the final result is inestimably improved by his extraordinary care. The other anonymous reader provided additional sound advice, and Eugene O'Connor was a wonderfully supportive editor. All remaining errors and infelicities are thus stubbornly my own.

This book could not have been written without the generous support of a sabbatical provided by the University of South Carolina and a grant from the National Endowment for the Humanities. I owe a debt of gratitude to both. The year I was able to devote to research and writing was one I will always cherish.

Finally, I must thank my teachers, in particular Carl Rubino, who first showed me that the greatest classicists were not those who had simply accumulated the most information, but those who also reflected on their practice in a sustained and sophisticated manner. I also owe an unpayable debt of thanks to my long-suffering wife, Ann Poling. Really, honey, someday I'll slow down. And to you, Sam, the boy with the Mohawk who asks about Plato, all I do is really dedicated to you.

Chapter 3. section 3, appears with the permission of *Phoenix*. Chapter 6, section 1b, first appeared in the journal, *Foucault Studies*, and is reprinted here by permission.

Chapter 1

Introduction: Remaking the Soul
Antiquity, Postmodernism, and Genealogies of the Self

> The soul, such as we still manipulate it and such as we are still encumbered by it, the notion, the image of the soul that we have—and which was not stirred up out of the succession of all the waves of our traditional heritage—the soul that is our concern in the Christian tradition, this soul has as an apparatus, as an armature, as a metallic stem in its interior, the by-product of Socrates' madness for immortality. We live with it still. (Lacan 1991: 125)[1]

> At a minimum, you know what I am talking about and put yourself in accord with it as best as you are able, with this economy I mean, from Socrates to Freud and beyond, all the way to us (understood and not). (Derrida 1980: 45)

> The "essay"—which must be understood as the attempt to modify oneself in the game of truth and not as a simple appropriation of others for purposes of communication—is the living body of philosophy, if at least it is still now what it was in the past, that is to say an "askesis," an exercise of the self, in thought. (Foucault 1984a: 15)

THIS BOOK argues that a key element of postmodern French intellectual life has been the understanding of classical antiquity and its relationship to postmodern philosophical inquiry. In it I concentrate on the works of Jacques Lacan, Jacques Derrida, and Michel Foucault. It would, of course, have been possible to choose others. The extent of the influence of antiquity on such luminaries of French postmodern thought as Gilles Deleuze, Michel Serres, and Emmanuel Levinas remains all but unexplored, while more work remains to be done on the feminists: Julia Kristeva, Luce Irigaray and Hélène Cixous.[2] Yet

---

1. All translations are my own unless otherwise noted.
2. I had originally planned to include the works of Irigaray and Kristeva. The constraints of space and time would not permit this, but I hope to return to them and Cixous in the future. See, however, Miriam Leonard's important articles on Irigaray's reading of Plato (1999), Cixous (2000a), and Levinas (2006). Her *Athens in Paris* (2005), although I have some narrow disagreements with it, is absolutely fundamental reading for anyone interested in classics and the classical tradition in postwar France.

Lacan, Derrida, and Foucault remain not only three of the most influential exponents of French postmodern thought in the Anglo-American world, but also, as our three opening quotations indicate, they demonstrate a substantial continuity of concern in their approach to the ancient world in general and to Platonic philosophy in particular.[3]

As we shall see, despite their well-known philosophical and theoretical differences, they all three turn to the ancient world not only to examine what Charles Taylor terms "the sources of the self" (1989), but also to find ways to historicize and modify it. This genealogy of modern forms of subjectivation in all three cases aims at the potential deconstruction and hence transformation of the structures of power, desire, and inscription out of which the modern subject is fashioned. And thus, while Foucault alone makes explicit use of the terminology, I will argue that all three present the encounter with antiquity as a form of "spiritual practice," and that the Platonic dialogues come to serve as the foremost emblem of that psychic labor. Moreover, inasmuch as all three conceive the subject, not as a freestanding entity, but as a knot or fold in a complex web of language, power, writing, and the law, then the ethical and spiritual work that begins under the aegis of Plato is for all three of necessity, though to different degrees and with different emphases, always already political. They demand a rethinking of the subject's relation to power, pleasure, and the institutions that seek to regulate and produce them: a genealogy of the subject of democracy, law, and the market so that a new politics, a new ethics, a new economy of desire, a new relation to the body and pleasure may be thought (Derrida 1994: 127–29; Foucault 1976: 208–10; Žižek 1991: 154–69). The stakes, then, of these three thinkers' encounter with the Platonic dialogues and the issues that surround them, I would submit, are of central importance not only to an understanding of postwar French intellectual culture and the interpretation of Plato, but also to the most basic ethical and political concerns facing us today. In a world in which religious fundamentalism has become increasingly the ideological correlate of a world seen purely as a collection of instruments for advantage, in which ecological disaster threatens, and in which the commodification of daily life has become the answer to the problem of desire, the question of the self's relation to itself, and thence to the good, has never been more urgent.

The classical, and specifically Platonic, foundations of French postmodern thought have been underappreciated especially in the Anglo-

---

3. On the possibility and limitations of reading contemporary philosophers in their collective relation to "les Grecs," see Derrida (1992: 254–58).

phone world in part because of a fundamental division in culture that has yet to be felt to the same degree in France.⁴ In the United States and the United Kingdom, until very recently, the concerns of academic philosophy and philology have had little in common. On the one hand, this is due to analytic philosophy's self-confinement to technical questions of epistemology, speech act theory, and the philosophy of science. As such, it has had little to say about the relation between antique and contemporary modes of thought. There have been, it is true, a number of attempts to read Plato from an analytic perspective (see notably Vlastos 1970; 1991; Irwin 1977; Fine 1992; and Kraut 1992) in which the Platonic text is reduced to its propositional content, but no efforts to read Platonic philosophy as a critique of modernity or as a moment in the construction of the very reason that makes analytic thought possible. Rare is the philosophy department in the Anglophone world where continental thinkers are taken seriously, and rarer still those where contemporary French readings of ancient texts would be considered matters worthy of serious *philosophical* consideration. On the other hand, blindness to the merits of postmodern thought is also due to Anglo-American philology's own parochial instincts. Ensconced within a nineteenth-century German model of *Altertumswissenschaft* that continues to exercise a surprisingly strong influence, only the bravest of classicists have made forays into philosophical, psychoanalytic, and other speculative modes of inquiry.

The result has been that postmodern French thought has largely been the province, neither of philosophers nor philologists, but of scholars of the modern languages and particularly those interested in modern and postmodern literature. These thinkers have produced important readings of contemporary French theory. Unfortunately, scholars whose specialties are in the modern languages typically lack the training or the interest necessary to appreciate what is at stake in these thinkers' engagement with the philosophy and literature of Greco-Roman antiquity. As we shall see, the works of Derrida, Lacan, and Foucault are often only truly understandable in terms of the complex dialogue that exists between these theorists. That dialogue, moreover, forms part of the larger cultural context in which these thinkers are situated, a context that assumes detailed knowledge of a tradition of literary and philosophical understanding unavailable to most Anglo-American scholars. The kind of profound classical culture that makes a figure like the great Comparative Indo-European scholar Georges Dumézil

---

4. See Leonard (1999: 154, 157–59, 162–63; 2000b: 47); P. A. Miller (1999).

easily cited and appreciated by figures as diverse as Foucault, Derrida, and Kristeva is simply not available to most Anglophone scholars. The notion of Jonathan Culler, Richard Rorty, or Hillis Miller having the same easy familiarity with the works of such American Indo-Europeanists as Calvert Watkins or Jaan Puhvel is all but inconceivable. Consequently, an entire idiom of thought, which these French thinkers simply assume, often remains opaque even to their most ardent enthusiasts.

Indeed, when these thinkers are taught in most American universities, it is normally in a course on critical methodology. They are taught as "theory"[5]: that is, as a body of abstract concepts that students can use to produce "readings" of texts. The result is a series of ahistorical abstractions that are directly "applied" to texts to which they have no explicitly articulated discursive or dialogic relation. We receive a Bakhtinian reading of Plato, a Jaussian response to Horace, a Derridean—followed by a de Manian—deconstruction of Catullus, and an Irigarayan interpretation of Propertius, as if the theories were so many interchangeable parts. In this fashion, concrete historical interventions into specific critical and philosophical debates too often become timeless truths that can simply be appropriated. The result is a perversion of these theorists' intentions since postmodern theory in general and poststructuralist theory in particular aims to criticize precisely the kind of transhistorical metanarratives into which their works have been transformed (Lyotard 1984). The deconstruction of the closure of western metaphysics thus becomes the reification of *différance* as a textual property (Derrida 1980: 536). The critique of the patriarchal subject comes to function as an abstract universal fully as phallic as the Symbolic structures it was designed to fight (Weed 1994: 101–2; Irigaray 1977a: 173, 178).[6]

Obviously, I am not saying that we cannot offer a Derridean, Bakhtinian, or Lacanian reading of a given text. I have been guilty of this on numerous occasions and will no doubt recidivate. What I am saying is that when we do so or when we teach our students to do so, we must act in full cognizance of the context of the conversation we have entered. We do not only apply a theory, we re-ply to it and to its interlocutors. To do so implies a knowledge not only of its intellectual presuppositions, but also of its historical and linguistic specificity.

5. For the analogous fate of Lacan's reception by the American psychoanalytic and psychological establishment as "theory—not as the articulation of a clinical praxis," see Malone (2000: 6).

6. For a good, if ultimately formalistic critique of this trend in recent literary studies, see Aviram (2001).

The problem in a nutshell is that theory per se does not exist. It is a disciplinary fiction. Having begun life in the American university system as "literary theory," it represented an attempt to come to terms with the rapid developments in linguistics, philosophy, psychoanalysis, the social sciences, and the formal study of literary and rhetorical technique that were known as structuralism and poststructuralism. In turn, these theoretical interventions, mostly centered in France, but drawing on traditions of linguistic and literary scholarship that originated in the former Soviet Union, Czechoslovakia, and Denmark, were often combined with the Hegelian Marxism of Frankfurt school critical theory, Georg Lukács, and Bertold Brecht.[7] The result, in the late sixties and early seventies, was a heady mixture of diverse traditions and focused debates. Comparative and general literature programs were at the center of this intellectual ferment in the United States. They combined a traditional interest in the definitional problems of literary form with the cosmopolitan and multilingual perspective necessary to engage these issues.

By the early 1980s, when I was a graduate student at the University of Texas at Austin, my Comparative Literature classes were often filled with English and philosophy students coming to study what they could not read in their own departments. Yet, by this point, the change had already begun. Jonathan Culler's *Structuralist Poetics* (1975) had translated the difficult insights of Roland Barthes, Ferdinand de Saussure, and Derrida into a utilitarian American idiom that made these abstruse works approachable. As Frank Lentricchia chronicled in *After the New Criticism* (1980), the potentially radical insights of Derrida, Lacan, and Barthes were during this same period rendered in terms that were cognate with the legacy of American New Criticism by the likes of Hillis Miller, Geoffrey Hartman, and, to a lesser extent, Harold Bloom and Paul de Man. By the end of the eighties, one no longer needed to know French to read Derrida, nor even know much about French intellectual history. One could remain equally ignorant of the role of Alexandre Kojève in the dissemination of Hegel and of the concrete contributions of Jean-Paul Sartre, surrealism, Georges Bataille and Maurice Blanchot to French philosophy, while being serenely uninformed about the traditions of French classicism.[8]

---

7. See Jameson's still seminal *Prisonhouse of Language* (1972) and *Marxism and Form* (1971) as well as such collections as Lucid's *Soviet Semiotics* (1977) and Kristeva's early Σημειωτικὴ (1969).

8. See Descombes (1980), Butler (1999), Stoekl (1992), and P. A. Miller (1999) *inter alia*.

Derrida's readings of Plato, Saussure, Freud, and Rousseau were so many examples of deconstruction, which could be reduced to a method. All discourse is structured around binary oppositions, we were told. These oppositions are hierarchical. The deconstructive reader demonstrates the reversibility and hence contingent nature of that opposition: *et voilà,* an article, a seminar paper, and in some cases even a career is born.[9] Of course, Derrida advocates nothing of the sort and is at pains to distance himself precisely from such facile appropriations (1980: 48; 1993a: 141, 151). The problem is that once literary theory has been reduced to a method, such appropriations are not only natural but necessary.

This book is a call not for a return to a time before theory, but for a recognition of what theory is. It is not a set of truth-producing methods that can be simply applied to texts to produce results, preferably publishable. What we call theory is a series of ongoing debates about the nature of meaning, texts, knowledge, and subjectivity that extend from the Platonic dialogues, through Aristotle to Cicero, Seneca, Augustine, Aquinas, Dante, and so on to the present. It is an ongoing set of conversations that can be entered at a variety of points. There are huge discontinuities, lacunae, and ruptures. Threads are dropped, picked back up, snapped, and woven into tapestries their spinners could have never anticipated. They are relativized by encounters with the warps and wefts of alien traditions and concepts. Nonetheless, each entry point in these conversations only has meaning to the extent that it is a response to a set of ongoing dialogues (Todorov 1984: 19; Voloshinov 1986: 11–12; Morson and Emerson 1990: 309; Holquist 1990: 167) and the moment we take a segment of that conversation out of context and elevate it to a timeless conceptual truth, the moment we crown it as "theory," we have robbed it of that which makes it most authentic.

Take a text such as Julia Kristeva's *Tales of Love.* If we merely extract from her readings of Plato, Plotinus, the *Song of Songs, Romeo and Juliet,* Baudelaire and Bataille a general theory of love that we can then apply willy nilly to other texts, we would do this rich book a vast disservice. We would completely miss that her reading of the *Symposium* not only complements Lacan's own (1991), but also includes direct replies to Derrida's reading of the *Phaedrus* (1972a) as well as to Foucault's final volumes of the *History of Sexuality* (1984a and 1984b), which featured

---

9. One of the most egregious examples of this kind of one size fits all deconstructive approach can be found in Hillis Miller's "Vast Gaps and Parting Hours" (1981) in which Aristotle, Sophocles, and Crabbe are reduced to an undifferentiated mass of deconstructive goo.

their own interpretation of these same texts (Kristeva 1983: 67–69).[10] By the same token, her choice to include a substantial reading of Plotinus is a clear answer to Irigaray's *Speculum,* which also in the context of a psychoanalytically grounded feminist critique of occidental philosophies of the subject offers both a substantial engagement with Plotinus and a lengthy reading of Plato. To do justice to the Kristevan text, it must be interpreted, then, not only in terms of its own theoretical assumptions but also in terms of how it positions itself relative to the larger debates in psychoanalysis, feminism, and philosophy then underway in France. At the same time, it demands of the reader a detailed knowledge of the Platonic and neo-Platonic tradition and of their central importance in modern French intellectual life. It is not enough, therefore, to know theory; one must be able to enter into the frame of reference that makes these texts vital responses to pressing questions.

Now, as noted above, the classical subtext of these debates has gone all but unappreciated as theory has become a deracinated set of methodologies. This is a challenge that neither classics nor philosophy departments have been prepared to meet. Thus, we are left with a situation in which Anglo-American classicists and ancient philosophers do not know the theory, and so cannot appreciate the scope and depth of the French poststructuralists' contribution to our understanding of the genealogy of Western thought, while the Anglo-American theorists do not know the classics and the role they play in French academic life. The result is a pernicious situation in which the study of antiquity reinforces its image of irrelevant antiquarianism by neglecting the very texts that argue most strongly for its continued importance, even as scholars of postmodernism fail to recognize the cultural context that produced their own models of thought; as a result, they often offer clichéd and obsolete opinions regarding literary texts from antiquity. This book begins to bridge this gap by offering detailed and theoretically informed readings of three of French postmodernism's chief thinkers, and their engagement with Platonic philosophy and the classics.

As my argument unfolds, it will become clear not only that Lacan, Derrida, and Foucault's knowledge of ancient literature is broad and detailed, but also that their understanding of Platonic philosophy is central to their theoretical projects and the debates that animated them (Wolff 1992: 234–35). Where conservative ideologues from Bloom (1987) and Bennett (1992) to Hanson and Heath (1998) have argued

---

10. The French original of *Tales of Love* (*Histoires d' amour,* 1983) was published before the last two volumes of the *History of Sexuality,* but Foucault was already lecturing on this material at the Collège de France. See for example Foucault (1994c).

that postmodernism represents a repudiation of classical culture and the humanist tradition that flows from it, this book will contend that such claims are a vast oversimplification. Indeed, the study of antiquity in France remains central to the culture's self-definition and to the theoretical and political debates that animate it to an extent almost unimaginable in the United States or the United Kingdom. It is invoked and contested equally by the right and the left, by members of the neofascist Front National, those of the Parti Communiste, and those of the center-right and center-left parties in between (Leonard 2000b: 69–74; 2004; Loraux 1996: 204–16). In addition, philosophy remains the defining discipline of the French academy, and Plato is at the center of the syllabus of its highest church, the Ecole Normale Supérieure, from which Foucault and Derrida both graduated (Leonard 1999: 162; 2005: 17; Bernstein 1990: 265, 270–72).

Thus, what in American life is often treated as an effete curiosity remains of burning interest to a significant portion of the French populace. When the center-right government of Jacques Chirac in 2004 proposed cutting the number of Latin and Greek classes offered at those secondary schools where demand was slipping, allowing ancient languages to become one educational option among others, there was an immediate uproar. The classical heritage of the nation, access to which, it was argued, was at the heart of the French republic's egalitarian ethos, was being sacrificed on the altar of "la rentabilité" ("profitability") (Romilly 2004: 15–16; Neveu 2004: 85; Schmidt 2004: 87, 92; Robert 2004: 100; Bayrou 2004: 116). A petition was circulated that gathered 70,000 signatures.[11] Political and academic foes, Jacqueline de Romilly and Jean-Pierre Vernant, two of the foremost living Hellenists in France, joined forces to demand that the minister of education withdraw the proposal. A rally was held at the Ecole des Hautes Etudes en Sciences Sociales at which academicians and intellectuals from across the political and disciplinary spectrum spoke against this unconscionable assault on what former center-right minister of education and recent presidential candidate François Bayrou termed "the spinal column of French and European culture" (2004: 118). The project was annulled for the coming school year, although at this writing it remains unclear what the final fate of the proposal will be (Appel pour le latin et le grec 2005; Informations Diverses 2005).

---

11. The text of the petition, sponsored by a number of different groups but most notably by the C.N.A.R.E.L.A (Coordination nationale des associations régionales des enseignants de langues anciennes) can be found in a publication compiling the speeches given at the May 15, 2004 rally, *Appel pour le latin et le grec 2004: 70,000 signataires* (2004: 7–9).

Most scholars of the ancient world in the United States, while sympathetic to their French colleagues' position, can only shake their heads in envious disbelief at the prospect of Greek being taught at the secondary level, of Latin classes not being required to have minimum enrollments, and of being able to mobilize thousands of outraged citizens to defend the centrality of the study of antiquity to republican education. Classics for large parts of the American public, for reasons of race, class, religion, and geographical isolation, has never been central to its self-definition.[12] By the same token, in the United Kingdom, while classics has had greater prestige, it has been deeply associated with the public schools, the ancient universities, and thus with traditional class divisions.[13] It is no wonder, then, that in Anglo-American culture the reception of French postmodern thought has all but completely ignored its grounding in the ancient world, since for many Anglophone scholars of postmodern theory, the study of the ancient world is at best an irrelevancy[14] and at worst a reactionary attempt to quash diversity through the imposition of a white, male, imperialist canon, which it sometimes is (Scholes 1992; Gates 1992; P. G. Allen 1992).

The one exception to this general rule is the case of Foucault and queer theory. Here the work of David Halperin has shown both sensitivity to the ancient texts and an important ability to relate Foucault's engagement with antiquity to contemporary political struggles. Halperin's work has been important in bringing Foucault to the attention of the classics community and in convincing the readers of queer theory to think again about Plato and the Stoics. Nonetheless, as I shall demonstrate in the appendix, Halperin fails to do justice to both Foucault's concept of "spiritual practice" and the ancient texts on which it is based.

12. Thus when I grew up in Kansas City, the North Kansas City school district not only did not offer either Latin or Greek, but there was also no public outrage at this. Many questioned the need for foreign language instruction at all.

13. See Eagleton's "The Rise of English," in idem, *Literary Theory: An Introduction* (1996: 15–46).

14. See Richlin on the presentism that characterizes the reception of Foucault's work on antiquity by American feminists (1998: 138–39, 165–69). A search of the *MLA International Bibliography* (2005) reveals that in the last thirty years, while a vast bibliography has accumulated on Irigaray's reading of Freud in *Speculum*, only four articles have been published on her equally extensive reading of the "myth of the cave." Not a single book or article has been devoted to Derrida's reading of the *Philebus* in *La carte postale* and only two make substantial mention of his reading of the *Timaeus* in *Khora*. This is despite 2,266 entries overall. Out of 1,631 entries overall, there are only six published books or articles that make substantial mention of Lacan's relation to Plato, and out of 1,602 total entries, there are none on Foucault's reading of the *Alcibiades* and only two published books or articles that make substantial mention of his relation to Plato.

Moreover, the case of Halperin and Foucault are much more the exception than the rule in the English-speaking world.

The story is very different in France. Here, in the hands of intellectuals such as Jean-Pierre Vernant, Pierre Vidal-Naquet, and Nicole Loraux, the study of the ancient world is not opposed or even ancillary to, but part and parcel of a radical intellectual practice.[15] As Loraux, Nagy, and Slatkin write:

> Many of today's leading figures in French Classical scholarship are paragons of modernity and or even "postmodernity" in the eyes of some fellow Classicists in other academic cultures. Such impressions can mislead, however, if they are tied to the assumptions that modern or "postmodern" perspectives in Classics are mere symptoms of an overall intellectual capitulation to ephemeral trends. It is clear that these same French Classicists consider themselves leaders, not followers, in modern and "postmodern" thinking. More important, they have been acknowledged as leading thinkers by such non-Classicist counterparts as Michel Foucault, Jacques Derrida, and Claude Lévi-Strauss. (2001: 2)

Far from representing an irrelevancy or a reactionary exercise in nostalgia, the study of the ancient world in France is often a form of radical estrangement and hence political critique. "The intellectual ambition of French Classics writ large is to define and redefine the whole world by resituating all of it historically within its past as well as its present" (Loraux, Nagy, Slatkin 2001: 2). Thus the very postmodern thinkers who many in Anglo-American classics would see as occupying the antipodes to the study of antiquity are the friends, colleagues, interlocutors, and dialectical antagonists of France's leading classicists.[16] The ancient world and Platonic philosophy, rather than being at the margins of Lacan, Derrida, and Foucault's projects, are, as we shall see, at their center. Postmodernism represents not the rejection of the classical tradition but precisely its revitalization as a living means of thought.

The postmoderns use classical models as a way to rethink the self and its limits, as a form of profound historicization of the subject and its modes of formation. For the postmoderns, we are never simply the heirs of a univalent antiquity, which nonetheless also bequeaths to us the very concept of thought as a formal exercise, i.e., as theory or philosophy

---

15. See Leonard (2000b: 70–71; 2004: 142–43; 2005: 2, 15–16); P. A. Miller (2004b; 2004c); and Nectoux (2004).

16. See for example Loraux (1996: 169–89) and Leonard (2005: 83).

(Derrida 1992: 262–69, 274). The postmodern encounter with antiquity is committed to history and indeed to objectivity to the precise degree that it is committed to difference, to seeing the ancient world not as our reflection or legitimation, but as the intimate other who is also always already part of the same, both different from and yet formative of our identity, and hence able to serve as a means of refashioning it. For Lacan, Derrida, and Foucault antiquity is a chance to think differently, to historicize and thus potentially recreate what it means to be a subject, to be human.[17] It serves simultaneously as a genealogical point from which to observe the creation of the present and as a mode of access to what Foucault labels *la pensée du dehors,* or "thought from the outside."

The concept of "la pensée du dehors" was first formulated by Foucault in 1966 in an article by the same name for a special issue of the journal *Critique* devoted to Maurice Blanchot. It was later reissued as a small book (1986). *La pensée du dehors* not only gives a perceptive and laudatory close reading of Blanchot's fiction and criticism, it also, on that basis, offers its own definition of the literary field as that which escapes the limits of the dominant mode of representation in a given culture.[18] The value of that field is not born of philosophical interiority. It is not the product of the depths of the self-reflexive Cartesian consciousness:

> It is a matter rather of a passage to the "outside": language escapes from the mode of being discourse—that is from the dynasty of representation—literary speech develops from itself, forming a network in which each point, distinct from the others, at a distance from even the closest, is situated in relation to all in a space that simultaneously holds and separates them. (1986: 12–13)

For the early Foucault, then, literature is not the depiction of a preexisting reality, nor the revelation of an already constituted consciousness, but the construction of a network of surfaces, of exteriorities, that concretize the void, the negative space that constitutes the very possibility of the enunciation of enunciation. Language is marshaled in such a way as to reveal, through the very density of its surfaces, the conditions of possibility of the speaking subject, and hence an outside of representation that is prior to the subject's birth at the moment of

---

17. Antiquity is, in Pierre Hadot's famous characterization of ancient philosophy, a source of spiritual exercises (1987), of technologies of existence.
18. This is Blanchot's concept of "l'espace littéraire" (1955).

the enunciation of its own existence. "The speech of speech leads us through literature . . . to that outside where the subject who speaks disappears" (1986: 13–14).

The "I" of the "I think" or the "I speak," which is thus posited through this enunciation, exists only within a constituted world of signs, of a socially operative and historically constituted system of representation. The literary event, however, is not a plumbing of this interiority, but the constitution through language of a thought of the "outside":

> This thought that holds itself outside of all subjectivity in order to reveal its limits as though from the exterior, in order to announce its end, to make its dispersion glitter, and to recuperate only its unconquerable absence; this thought that simultaneously holds itself at the threshold of any positivity, not so much so as to seize its foundation or justification but to find the space where it deploys itself, the void which serves as its place, the distance in which it constitutes itself and in which, as soon as one turns one's gaze there, its immediate certitudes are sketched—this thought, in relation to the positivity of our knowledge constitutes what one could call in a word "the thought from the outside." (1986: 16)

This thought from the outside, which early on Foucault conceived as a function of the aesthetic, is precisely what he programmatically seeks in the turn to antiquity as announced in the opening pages of volume 2 of the *History of Sexuality*: "the wager was to know in what measure the work of thought on its own history could free thought from what it thinks silently and permit it to think differently" (1984a: 15).[19] The turn to antiquity has as its aim to seize momentarily the void in which thought constitutes itself, the glitter of that which lurks beyond our immediate certitudes, a true *pensée du dehors*.

As we shall see, to think the possibility of such a "thought" is the overarching motivation behind the turn to antiquity of all three thinkers. Each, of course, expresses it in his own idiom. For Lacan, it is the ethical pursuit of a good beyond all recognized goods, beyond the pleasure principle, which is sought in his readings of the *Antigone* and the *Symposium* in his seventh and eighth seminars. For Derrida, it is the deconstruction of the closure of western metaphysics, as pursued in his encounters with the *Phaedrus* and the *Philebus*. And for Foucault,

---

19. On the relation between Foucault's opening programmatic statements in *L'usage des plaisirs* (1984a: 14–15) and his earlier reading of Blanchot, see Deleuze (1988: 87, 96–97, 113–14) and Vizier (1998: 74–75).

it is the possibility of a new ethic of self-relation as outlined in his commentaries on the *Alcibiades*, Plato's letters, and the Stoics.

It is worth our time to pause for a moment and examine more precisely how this philosopheme of "thought from the outside" manifests itself within the specific structures of Lacanian and Derridean thought. Such an examination will make clearer the political and ethical stakes of our project. It will also help us further define the specificity of the postmodern encounter with the ancient.

We turn first to Lacan, whose ethics, as elaborated in his seventh seminar, have been criticized by Miriam Leonard for being apolitical, overly aestheticized, and for seeking to replace the previous generation's existential philosophy of the authentic act with an "unconscious ethics of the 'real'" (Leonard 2005: 221, compare 13, 114–15, 124–25). While Leonard's work is extraordinarily useful and has had an important impact on my own, I would argue that such a characterization shortchanges Lacan. As will be seen in chapters 3 and 4, the good beyond all recognized goods, which is the object of Antigone's desire and of the ethics of psychoanalysis, is indeed located in what Lacan terms the Real. This is the realm beyond the contingent forms of our socially constituted Symbolic norms and our individual Imaginary projections. Yet, it is the concept of the Real, I would contend, that gives Lacan's thought its political and ethical edge by permitting the radical relativization of any given Imaginary or Symbolic ideological formation, and hence opening the possibility of a fundamental rethinking of one's relation with one's self (ethics) and with others (politics).[20] As Fredric Jameson notes:

> It is not terribly difficult to say what is meant by the Real in Lacan. It is simply History itself; and if for psychoanalysis the history in question here is obviously enough the history of the subject, the

---

20. For the concept that philosophy inscribes itself in the Real through altering the relation of the self to the self, see Foucault's course, "Le gouvernement de soi et des autres" (1983a) and my account thereof (P. A. Miller 2006b). It is not without significance to the present book that this course at the Collège de France centered on Foucault's reading of Euripides' *Ion* and of a series of Platonic texts. It was also a continuation of his 1981–82 course, *L'herméneutique du sujet* (2001), in which Foucault was seen by his audience as using a set of specifically Lacanian operators. For more on these courses and their relation to Derrida and Lacan, see chapter 6. What is important to note for now is that while these thinkers are often viewed as operating in mutually exclusive universes by their most ardent supporters, and while that view is reinforced by some of their own more polemical utterances—especially in the case of Foucault and Derrida—nonetheless the basic thesis of this book is that these thinkers are engaged in a constant, intense, and mutually conditioning dialogue and that an essential part of this dialogue is their relation to antiquity.

resonance of the word suggests that a confrontation between this particular materialism and the historical materialism of Marx can no longer be postponed. It is a confrontation whose first example has been set by Lacan himself,[21] with his suggestion that the very notion of the Symbolic as he uses it is compatible with Marxism. . . . (1988: 104)

Today, of course, the urgency of the confrontation between Marxism and psychoanalysis is less strongly felt than it was in 1977 when Jameson's essay was first published. Nonetheless, few would accuse Jameson of apolitical quietism, and however dated its terminology, what this passage does make clear is that there is no prima facie case for assuming that Lacan's turn to ethics and the Real precludes an effective theoretical engagement with history and politics (Leonard 2005: 124, 182). Moreover, as we shall see in chapters 3 and 4, it is precisely the turn to ethics, and hence to the *Antigone* and the *Symposium*, that makes real change—i.e., change that does not simply reproduce the structures of the given—thinkable, first on the ethical level (chapter 3), and then on the intersubjective and collective level (chapter 4).

Indeed, I would contend, the Real is indispensable to any concept of philosophy or of theory as critique, inasmuch as the Real is that which is unassimilable to the ideological norms of a given cultural formation.[22] As such, the concept of the Real, and its ethical correlate of "a good beyond all recognized goods," is that which logically makes the historical succession of cultural and linguistic as well as political forms and institutions thinkable, and hence renders their transformation possible.[23] The Real marks the point at which the Symbolic meets its own systemic negation (Copjec 1994: 9, 121), its principle of finitude or limit. This moment of negation is necessary to any meaningful concept of historical change, since it is precisely this moment that figures the possibility of otherness within the reigning positive system.[24] Without the negation of the Real, without this conception of the beyond of the Symbolic, the norms and systems of meaning that constitute the latter

21. Citing Lacan (1966g: 876; 1966h: 260–62, 287).
22. For a fuller discussion, see P. A. Miller (2004a: 6–16).
23. See Lacan (1975: 32–33) on Marx's insight that history is the possibility of completely subverting the function of discourse, hence history is that which demonstrates the contingency of a given Symbolic system and its consequent inadequacy vis-à-vis the Real. On Althusser's concept of history being based on Lacan, see Jameson (1981: 34–35).
24. See Žižek (1993: 23, 109); Jameson (1991: 5–6; 1981: 91, 95, 97–98; 1972: 193–94); Adorno (1983: 53, 140–43).

would absolutize themselves in a way that would allow no room to conceive of the radically other (Jameson 1981: 90–91; 1991: 405–6; Copjec 1994: 17, 23–24).

Indeed, as Derrida has written, the concept of the future, of the yet-to-come (*à-venir*), depends on the existence of an opening within the Symbolic that cannot be reduced to the categories of either knowledge or ignorance, but must be seen as a systematic heterogeneity, an absolute otherness that exceeds the reigning positive system. "This opening must preserve this heterogeneity as the sole chance of an affirmed, or rather re-affirmed, future. It is the future itself, it comes from the future. The future is its memory" (1993a: 68). From this perspective, then, the concept of the Real, of an absolute "outside," is far from representing a denial of history, or politics (Rabinovich 2003: 208; Armstrong 2005: 20, 132–34). It is rather what makes them thinkable in the most radical sense. The refusal of the given is a predicate for fundamental ethical and political change.

Moreover, it is because of this radical potential that Lacan, as Leonard notes, serves "as a fundamental frame for understanding the dialogue between psychoanalysis and the revolutionary politics of the post-'68 Parisian intellectual scene" (2005: 88; see also Schneiderman 1983: 28–29). And it is for this same reason that Lacanian psychoanalysis has provided the main theoretical impetus for the neo-Marxist politics of Slavoj Žižek and those associated with him. Likewise, as Toril Moi notes, Lacan represents the starting point for the feminisms of such important thinkers as Julia Kristeva, Hélène Cixous, Luce Irigaray, and Cathérine Clément (Moi 2002: 99).[25] None of this is to deny the reality either of Lacan's own personal political quietism (Lacan 1986: 214–15; Roudinesco 1997: 103, 114–15, 158–59)[26] or of his complex and often conflicted relationships with the French feminisms that took their basic terminology from him.[27] Rather it is to argue that there is nothing intrinsically anti-political or ahistorical in Lacan's theoretical formulations, and that a wide range of political thinkers have found them enabling, even if they have also sought to go beyond, answer, revise, and reinterpret them.

25. See also Weed (1994: 87–90) and Feher-Gurewich (2000: 364).
26. Nonetheless in May 1968 he signed a letter published in *Le Monde* along with Sartre, Blanchot, and others in support of the student uprising. He was subsequently forced to move his seminar from the Ecole Normale Supérieure to the Ecole Pratique des Hautes Études (Schneiderman 1983: 29; Cohen-Solal 1987: 459).
27. For an extended reading of Irigaray's intense dialogic relation with Lacan, see my "Lacan le con: Luce Tells Jacques Off" (2005b). See also Ragland-Sullivan (1986: 279); Benstock (1991: 206); Weed (1994: 97–98); and Luepnitz (2003: 230).

In sum, central to the radical political potential of Lacanian thought is his concept of the Real, which on the level of individual desire is, as we shall see in chapter 3, instantiated in Antigone's search for a good beyond those approved by the dominant Symbolic formation, metonymically identified with Creon and the *polis*. The formulation of this good, which constitutes a Lacanian version of the *pensée du dehors,* is precisely what is sought in Seminar 7, *L'éthique de la psychanalyse* (1986). By the same token, it is the resocialization of that good in terms of intersubjective desire that is explored in the following year's seminar on Socratic *atopia, Le transfert.* In each case, what the turn to antiquity makes possible is a radical historicization and estrangement of the subject's relation to itself and others.[28] And it is for this reason that Lacan's readings of Sophocles and Plato became not only cornerstones of French thought throughout the postwar period, but, as will be shown in the chapters that follow, they were texts that demanded specific and detailed responses from Derrida and Foucault as they too turned to problems of ethics, desire, and the subject.

In the case of Derrida, this response to Lacan will come in the form of close readings of both the *Phaedrus,* with its careful mapping of the relations between writing, the subject and desire, and the *Philebus,* with its complex interrogation of the nature of the good life in relation to fundamental epistemological and metaphysical categories. More specifically, Derrida pursues his own "thought from the outside" through what he terms a radical "genealogy." Deconstruction for him is not primarily an apolitical textual methodology but a fundamental critique of democracy as currently practiced.[29] It is pursued

---

28. See, however, Leonard's acute remarks on Lacan's failure fully to historicize his reading of the *Antigone* and the *Symposium,* particularly as concerns matters of sexuality and gender (Leonard 2005: 129, 172–73). It should be noted, nonetheless, that she is more forgiving of the misogynist and homophobic caricatures found in the work of Lacan's contemporary, Sartre (Leonard 2005: 3–4), owing to the more explicit political commitment of his later work. I am very supportive of her efforts to rehabilitate Sartre as an important intellectual force. See, however, the portraits of the self-loathing homosexual Daniel in *L'âge de raison* (Sartre 1981a) and the sadistic Lucien in "L'enfance d'un chef" (Sartre 1981b) as well as almost all the female characters in his novels, and the vivid evocations of softness, liquidity, and viscosity in *L'être et le néant* (Sartre 1943). Moi's reading of Sartre's relationship with Simone de Beauvoir is particularly enlightening from this perspective (1994). Both these monumental figures in the final analysis, despite the manifest importance of their work and the changes in their respective positions over long careers, reflect many of the most deeply ingrained biases of the France of the 1920s and 30s in which they came to maturity. This should not surprise us. In the end, however, we are looking not for saints but for thinkers who can provide us with usable tools.

29. Derrida feels very much that the charges of being apolitical that have been leveled at him are unfair (1980: 48).

by tracing the intellectual roots of modern democratic societies to certain concepts of origins, purity, kinship, the citizen, and the centered, self-present subject (Derrida 1994: 127–28).[30] He seeks not only to provide a demystifying genealogy of these terms, and thus open up the possibility of a radically different future, but also to offer a genealogy of the possibility of his own inquiry, a genealogy of the question of the future's relation to the past (Derrida 1993a: 68, 151). One primary way in which this genealogy is traced, Derrida argues, is precisely through a return to the Greeks, to the first chapter of the dominant occidental discourse that has sought to define the subject and its relation to itself and the other, i.e., philosophy (Derrida 1992: 260–67; Wolff 1992: 235; Loraux 1996: 169; Leonard 2006). That first chapter is, of course, nothing other than the body of texts transmitted to us under the name of Plato. As in the case of Foucault and Lacan, the turn to antiquity for Derrida is at once a political and an ethical act. It seeks through the estrangement of the present to create a space in which we can imagine a new future by means of a precise and focused exhumation of the past. It seeks to open a space of difference that only an archeology of antiquity in general, and Plato in particular, makes possible, opening new forms of the self's relation to itself, others, and power.

Finally, it is precisely this pursuit of a thought from the outside that separates the postmoderns and their use of antiquity from that of their great modernist[31] predecessors. While classical themes are a common and important part of the literature of the thirties and forties, as we shall see in an initial examination of dramas by Sartre, Camus, and Anouilh, these writers in their appropriation of the ancient past do not seek to historicize the present. The neoclassicism that characterizes much of the theater from this period is widely acknowledged. Yet these dramatists do not aim to produce a genealogy of morals that would simultaneously posit a distinct and historically situated beyond. For them, classical themes serve to produce allegories of the present through framing it in terms of a timeless classical horizon. This is as true of those who can trace their intellectual pedigree to the aesthetic assumptions of European fascism as of those who embrace the politics of the socialist left. To be schematic, where the moderns seek to identify

---

30. On the differences between Lacan's concept of the decentered subject and Derrida's, see Ragland-Sullivan (1986: 218).

31. I use this term for the generation of thinkers preceding the postmoderns. It is not generally used in this sense in French, but is common when speaking of Anglo-American literature of the same period and is useful for describing an analogous period of formal innovation and neoclassicism on the continent.

the present with the past, the postmoderns seek to rethink the present through an encounter with the otherness of the past (Hartog 2004: 53–54).

This is not to say that the postmoderns have a more developed concept of historicism *tout court* than do the moderns. As one of the readers of an earlier draft of this work observed, it would be absurd to argue that Lacan's philosophy of history is more articulated and systematic than Sartre's in the *Critique of Dialectical Reason*.[32] Nor is this my intention. My first concern in making this distinction between the modernist writers of the thirties and forties and their postmodern successors is with the modernist writers' use of antiquity. My contention is that the way antiquity is used in the theater of Sartre, Camus, and Anouilh differs fundamentally from the way in which it is used in Lacan's seminars, Derrida's readings of Plato, and Foucault's lectures at the Collège de France. Second, Sartre's later Marxist philosophy, to which the *Critique* belongs, differs sufficiently from his earlier existential theatrical and philosophical work that one cannot simply read back from the former to the latter (Aronson 1980: 183–84).[33] Third, even when Sartre returns to antiquity at the end of his theatrical career in his 1960s version of the *Trojan Women,* he proceeds not in the mode of estranging the present from itself through an encounter with the past, but in that of representing the present to itself through allegory. The *Trojan Women* is, in fact, an articulate and pointed denunciation of the Algerian War (Leonard 2005: 224–26). Fourth, in a very real sense historicism is not what is at issue, but History, as Jameson defines it. Traditional historicism sees an organic continuity between the present and the past, with the one evolving directly out of the other. It assumes we can trace a history of democracy, of the subject, of the homosexual, because we know what these things are and can therefore trace lines of descent, grand narratives, that move from the distant past to its inevitable culmination in the present or the future. This teleological style of narrative (in the mode of orthodox Soviet Marxism), which sees an essential identity between present and past, is precisely what the postmoderns reject as ultimately ahistorical in its fundamental refusal of difference, of an encounter with the outside, the Real (Lyotard 1984; Foucault 1994bb: 136–37; Shepherdson 1995: ¶ 4, 9; Leonard 2005:

---

32. Nonetheless, Lacan did speak highly of the *Critique* (1986: 266). See also Leonard (2005: 61–63).

33. I am not at this point going to venture into the debate over whether these two aspects of Sartre's work are contradictory or complementary. But it is clear that they are different. See Stoekl (1992: 84–142).

73–74). Traditional historicism, then, sees history as a form whose relation to time is closed, whose end is contained in its beginning (Frow 1986: 292–93; Morson and Emerson 1990: 292–93).[34] It is for this reason, in part, that Althusser singles out Sartre's *Critique of Dialectical Reason* for rebuke in the final chapter of volume one of *Lire le capital*: "Le marxisme n'est pas un historicisme" (1968: 150–84). And, it is precisely this same historicist reduction of difference that we see in the modernists' allegorical equation of present and past on the theatrical stage of the thirties and forties, as opposed to the more critical use of antiquity found in the lecture halls and seminar rooms of the postmoderns (Miller 2006b; Sharpe 2005).

It is this critical use, in turn, that Foucault evokes in the figure of Montaigne and his invention of the essay, which he cites as his philosophical paradigm for volume 2 of the *History of Sexuality*. Indeed, it is Montaigne's species of Renaissance self-fashioning that comes closest to capturing the postmodern relation to antiquity. The *essai*, as Foucault notes, is precisely the "attempt" to think differently, an open-ended experiment of thought on itself through a sustained investigation of its own history (1984a: 15). Lest Foucault's allusion to the form of the *essai* be thought too slight to support such a reading of his relation to Montaigne, in his lectures at the Collège de France from the same period, he makes it clear that Montaigne's focus on the "care of the self" was a direct product of the latter's encounter with antiquity, and that this encounter should be read in parallel with the topics of his own late work:

> Of course, you find in the sixteenth century an ethic of the self, as well as an entire aesthetic of the self, which is otherwise very explicitly related to what one finds in the Greek and Latin authors about whom I am speaking. I think that it would be necessary to reread Montaigne from this perspective as an attempt to reconstitute an ethics and aesthetics of the self. (2001: 240)

Foucault is not alone in this reading of Montaigne and his relation to ancient philosophy and to the "care of the self." His interpretation

---

34. The elaboration of a theory of "emergence" that could explain how new modes of personal or social organization could arise out of pre-existing forms, without being seen as already contained by those forms, and so effectively subsuming the emergence of the new within a vision of the given, was seen by Althusser as one of the central problems of both Marxism and psychoanalysis if they were to overcome their idealist roots. In this struggle, he saw Lacan as one of his principle allies (1996: 59–60).

reflects Pierre Hadot's position as well (1995b: 395, 413), while Derrida in *La politique de l'amitié* opens with Montaigne's citation of Aristotle's supposed dictum, "O mes amis, il n'y a nul amy," as the exergue under which he will pursue his readings of these thinkers as well as Plato, Nietzsche, Heidegger, and Schmit (1994: 18).

Indeed, for Montaigne the encounter with the ancient other constitutes a form of self-discipline or shaping whereby, through the practices of reading, self-observation, and writing, a "new nature" is formed (Nehamas 1998: 117–18, 123–24). There are numerous examples of this throughout the *Essais,* yet one need read no further than the sweeping opening period of Book 1, chapter 8, "On Idleness":

> As we see from lands left idle, that if they are rich and fertile, they abound in a hundred sorts of wild and useless grasses, and that if they are to be brought to good use, they must be subjected to, and certain seeds must be used for, our service; and as we see that women produce very well on their own lumps and pieces of formless flesh, but that in order to produce a good and natural generation one must work into them some other seed: it is the same way with our minds. If one does not occupy them with a certain subject that harnesses and constrains them, they toss about wildly here and there in the ill-defined field of their imaginings.
>
> Sicut aquae tremulum labris ubi lumen ahenis
> Sole repercussum, aut radiantis imagine Lunae
> Omnia pervolitat late loca, jamque sub auras
> Erigitur, summique ferit laquearia tecti.
>
> Just like when a tremulous light from the Sun or the image of the radiant Moon, reflected in bronze basins of water, darts wildly here and there, and then beneath the sky is carried up and strikes the paneled ceiling at the roof's top. (Montaigne 1972: 61, citing *Aeneid* 8. 22–25)

Montaigne's message here is clear. Lest the ministrations of the mind miscarry, the proper seed, a salutary otherness, must be implanted to give its rich fertility focus and to subject it to our use. The passage itself enacts this process of mental culture. The opening syntax is lush and meandering, at first evoking the untended prairie's riot of wild grasses, but as the sentence continues to uncoil its serpentine folds the prospect of unfettered generation gives rise to monstrosities, before suddenly coming into sharp focus just before the quotation from Vergil that distills into a single image the instability of the restless mind. It is the *Aeneid*, then, that provides the seed that turns the wild gyrations of the agitated spirit into a limpid aesthetic object, and that implicitly subjects Montaigne's spirit to the discipline of masculine use.[35] The self is cultivated through its encounter with the other, and the paradigmatic other for Montaigne, as for Foucault and the other postmoderns, is the intimate other of antiquity.[36]

Postmodernism is, then, not a rejection of humanism *tout court*, but of a particular nineteenth-century formation of humanist thought (Foucault 1966: 314–98), finding itself far closer to the humanism of the Renaissance than to that of the Romantics. It is, in fact, Montaigne's use of classical models and their historical limitations as a way to rethink the self and its limits that most directly anticipates the postmodern encounter with antiquity.[37] That encounter represents a renunciation neither of the classical tradition nor of history, but rather a profoundly historical relativization of the subject and its modes of self-formation. It is also perhaps this shift to a humanism of self-fashioning, as opposed to the existential humanism of the fully constituted Cartesian cogito, that explains the postmodern focus on Plato. For where modernist appropriations of antiquity focus on the tragic stage and present already formed characters for our inspection and potential identification, the postmodern focuses increasingly on Plato's dialectical process of question and answer, self-testing and reproof, desire and lack. The postmodern turn to a thought from the outside, to a refusal to accept the categories of the given even in the guise of the antique, therefore, recapitulates on a new level Plato's own critique of the seductive spectacle of the tragic stage: its power to overwhelm the critical faculty and so thwart a genuine care for the self. The importance of Plato, thus, represents a fundamental distinction between the postmodern appropriation of antiquity and the modernist appropriation as represented

---

35. Montaigne's gendering of this process could easily be the topic of a separate essay.

36. In a similar fashion, the *essai* "Our Affections Carry Themselves beyond Us" marshals Plato and Cicero to lead to the ultimately Socratic conclusion that "he who knows himself no longer takes another's affair for his own"; rather he loves and cultivates himself before anything else (Montaigne 1972: 38). This image of self-cultivation is precisely the opposite of that of the untamed field gone to seed. See also Zalloua's exemplary article on Montaigne's exploration of the concept of the intimate other in his essay "Of Friendship" (2002), in relation to Foucault's concept of the "care of the self" as well as Aristotle's and Cicero's writings on friendship.

37. See Greene's concept of "dialectical imitation" (1982: 45–47) and Auerbach's still seminal essay (1953).

by the neoclassical theatrical practice of the thirties and forties. Thus, even when the postmoderns turn their attention to ancient tragedy, as in the case of Lacan's reading of the *Antigone,* they do not present a modernized recreation of the dramatic experience, but a careful and methodical reading of the text from a defined perspective.

Postmodern Spiritual Practices begins with an examination of modernist uses of antiquity to establish the unique nature of the postmodern intervention. The remainder of the book is organized around a series of dialogic interactions framed by Lacan's seminars on the *Antigone* and the *Symposium* and Foucault's final turn to antiquity. There follows a chapter-by-chapter outline.

Chapter 2, "The Modernist Revolt: History, Politics, and Allegory, or Classicism in Occupied France" sets the stage for the later investigations. The postmodern turn to antiquity, as we shall see, is also a return to the territory of Sartre, Nietzsche, and Heidegger (Leonard 2005: 5, 223). After a brief introduction to the philosophical and historical context of France in the 1940s, this chapter will look at three emblematic uses of antiquity in French modernist literature. As noted above, these examples are drawn from the realm of spectacle and performance rather than philosophical commentary and philological investigation. Antiquity for these writers represents an open field of imaginative and allegorical possibilities, of ideal identifications with characters as diverse as Orestes, Electra, Antigone, and Caligula. It is a way of representing a present that, as we shall see, is simultaneously defined by the ideological impetus of fascism and yet beyond good and evil.

The first piece under consideration is Sartre's *Les mouches.* In this version of Aeschylus' *Libation Bearers,* the existential philosopher combines a variety of different versions of the Electra-and-Orestes myths, including those of Sophocles and Euripides, to create a meditation on the costs of freedom and responsibility. The political resonances of the portrayal of the people of Argos as complicit in their subjection to the tyranny of Aegisthus are particularly strong. The play was first performed in 1942 in occupied Paris and is self-consciously anachronistic. It refers to Zeus and Jupiter as separate entities, portrays Orestes as under the care of a Skeptic *paedogogus,* and compares the former's learning to that of the travel writer Pausanias. Through these devices, the playwright makes clear his allegorical intent.

By the same token, Camus's *Caligula* combines allusions to Suetonius with deliberate distortions of Roman history to present his own dramatization of the relation between freedom, tyranny, and the eroticization of power. Having debuted in 1945, *Caligula* not only reflects the introspection of postwar France, but is a clear meditation on what Mary-Ann Friese Witt (2001) has termed the "aesthetics of fascism" and the pursuit of the absolute.

It is this very problematic pursuit of an absolute that is beyond the compromises of bourgeois life that is at heart of Anouilh's *Antigone*. This last play will have the most direct influence on the postmodernist thinkers who are the subject of the current work. It also presents the most direct challenge to them, for the play problematizes the difficulty of separating the earlier fascist pursuit of an absolute beyond the bounds of bourgeois subjectivity from the later postmodernist pursuit of a "pensée du dehors." The latter concern becomes all the more troubling in light of the complicities, flirtations, and collaborations with fascism of other postmodern icons like Blanchot, de Man, and Heidegger.

Chapter 3, "Historicizing Transcendence: *Antigone*, the Good, and the Ethics of Psychoanalysis," examines Lacan's reading of the *Antigone* in his 1959 seminar, *The Ethics of Psychoanalysis* (1992). It argues that his interpretation of Sophocles lays the groundwork for his reading of the *Symposium* the following year. The result is a unified theory of the ethical subject of desire as the subject of psychoanalysis. These two seminars form a single movement in which the possibility of an ethics of pure desire is first posited, and then reimagined in terms of the analytic situation as modeled in the relation between Socrates and Alcibiades. Lacan's conception of psychoanalysis, as we shall see, is inseparable from his profound engagement with the language, history, and interpretation of the founding texts of western thought (Lacan 1986: 21). Nonetheless, antiquity in Lacan's texts, unlike in the dramas of the great modernists, functions not as an allegory of, but as a critique and challenge to, the present. It demands that we account for the historicity of both our science and our selves.

For Lacan, Antigone represents a model of subject formation precisely to the degree that she is one who rejects the good as understood by the dominant mode of the Symbolic embodied in Creon's decrees. Antigone's choice, her desire, is pure insofar as it rejects all claims of the Other to dictate its objects or form, and to that extent offers no positive model to be emulated, no pregnant past that can simply issue into the present. This chapter examines both Lacan's reading of the *Antigone* and provides a close reading of key passages from the tragedy itself, demonstrating not only the function of the play in Lacan's discourse but also the positive contribution that discourse makes to our understanding of the play.

Chapter 4, "Lacan, the *Symposium*, and Transference" argues that Socrates, like Antigone, represents for Lacan a kind of purity that exceeds the bounds of communally acknowledged goods. Socrates' *atopia*, as Alcibiades terms it (215a2), places him beyond the bounds of the order defined by the Athenian *polis*, and that singularity in turn is the basis of his purity. In the wake of his encounter in the *Antigone* with an ethics of self-creation that sought an authentic beauty and monumentality beyond all conventional representations, Lacan turned to Socrates and the *Symposium*. There, he sought a model for elaborating a theory of love as a response to the fundamental lack in our being that Freudian theory sees as the root of human desire.

Yet whereas in the *Antigone*, Lacan presents what is ultimately a tragic and highly individualistic analysis of the pursuit of a *jouissance* that is beyond the pleasure principle, the Socratic *elenchus* is a profoundly intersubjective process, which like analysis itself is dependent upon the social mediation of language. In this chapter, then, we examine not only Lacan's reading of the *Symposium*, but also the relation between that reading and the *Antigone*, and between the ethics of psychoanalysis and the problem of transference. Transference is the metaphorical process whereby, in the course of coming to understand the nature and origin of the patient's desire, the desire of the analysand becomes the desire of the analyst. This is exactly the process described in the *Symposium* by Alcibiades, when he discusses the seductive power of Socrates' elenctic discourse. Chapter 4 will examine this phenomenon not only by tracing Lacan's reading of the *Symposium*, but also by examining the seductive power of elenctic discourse as Socrates purports to demonstrate it in the *Lysis*. In the process, we shall see not only how a Lacanian reading illuminates this dialogue, but also how it can shed light on the analyst's reading of his primary text.

Chapter 5. "Writing the Subject: Derrida Asks Plato to Take a Letter," shows how the Platonic corpus, particularly those texts that interrogate the relation between desire and truth, and between love and transcendence, are a central concern for all the major figures in postmodernism (Zuckert 1996). The *Phaedrus* is a crucial text for Derrida, himself a frequent audience member at Lacan's seminars. With Derrida, though, the lens through which Plato is read is no longer psychoanalysis per se but philosophy. In "Plato's Pharmacy," the ambiguous figure of the *pharmakos/pharmakon* functions as the instantiation of the problematic status of writing, intentionality, and meaning that Derrida sees as structuring the subsequent western metaphysical tradition. Plato's aversion to writing is interpreted as symptomatic of a more general tendency in philosophy to banish the external and the material from the essence of meaning and value, or the *logos*. This Platonic attempt at metaphysical closure, at the creation of a finite system of fixed meanings beyond the contingencies of the merely material letter, can in turn be seen as parallel to the system of preexisting interpretations and conventionally recognized goods that Lacan views as the antithesis of what constitutes the ethics of psychoanalysis. Both the attempt to establish a closed logocentric universe and the potted analytic interpretation assume that meaning is finite and preexists the acts of interpretation and enunciation that make signification possible. In the last analysis, both are designed more to police the realm of possible meanings than to create new possibilities of self-creation and understanding.

While Lacan is not specifically mentioned in "Plato's Pharmacy," he is explicitly engaged in Derrida's next extended meditation on Platonic philosophy, *La carte postale*. In this text, it is precisely the formation of the subject and the question of origins that are at stake. Here Derrida interrogates both Freud's unacknowledged debt to the *Philebus*, and Plato's debt to Freud, in terms of both the act of writing and the set of relays and mediations of the written that he ironically dubs the "postal system." The addresser and addressee of communication in this system represent posts in an infinitely disseminated web of significations, whose very constitution under the images of law and limit was first consolidated in the same Platonic corpus that also envisioned its beyond. It is Lacan's decision to continue to operate within this system of hierarchical meanings that constitutes the burden of Derrida's indictment of him in the now famous essay from the same book, "Le facteur de la verité," or "The Postman of Truth." This chapter will ultimately argue that the *Philebus* offers us the possibility of mediating between the Lacanian and the Derridean positions, while also laying the groundwork for a moving tribute to Foucault in *La politique de l'amitié*, which sketches a particularly Derridean response to the problematic of power.

Among the postmoderns, it is Foucault's turn to antiquity that has received the most notice. In chapter 6. "The Art of Self-Fashioning, or Foucault on the *Alcibiades:* Caring for the Self and Others," we see his turn to the Stoics, which begins in 1970 with his praise of Gilles Deleuze's *La logique du sens* and which deepens with his subsequent engagement with Hadot's understanding of ancient *philosophia* as a mode of life rather than an abstract conceptual system. During the last years of his life, Foucault was primarily interested in the problems of ethical self-fashioning as Plato and the philosophers of the Roman Empire explored them. He thus began his 1982 course at the Collège de France, *L'herméneutique du sujet,* with a meticulous reading of the *Alcibiades* (2001).

For Foucault, the *Alcibiades* constituted, to paraphrase Olympiodorus, "the gateway of the temple." He saw in it the first and fullest theorization of an ethic of self-relation that was to constitute his primary object of interest in the last years of his life (2001: 46). For Foucault, the *Alcibiades* represented a model of self-relation that made possible the Stoic ethic of the care of the self in the first two centuries of the Roman imperial period (2001: 65). It was this latter form of self-constitution and cultivation that Foucault would directly contrast with the Christian model of confession and self-renunciation that he saw at the heart of modern technologies of disciplining and normalizing the self (2001: 242, 247). The Stoics, starting from Plato's initial model, offered an alternative form of self-relation both to the Christian archetype and to that described later and implicitly denounced in Foucault's middle works such as *Surveiller et punir* and *La volonté de savoir.* It was this alternative model on which Foucault concentrated during the final years of his life.

In this chapter, we examine Foucault's reading of the *Alcibiades* as part of his wider understanding of Plato and ancient philosophy as a whole. We do so first as part of his continuing dialogue with Deleuze, Derrida, and Lacan on the importance and interpretation of Plato in contemporary philosophy. We then look in more detail at the relation between his reading of the *Alcibiades* and his overall political and ethical project, before examining the dialogue itself.

We close with an appendix in which we compare Foucault's reading of the dialogue to that of the Roman satirist Persius. Persius' fourth satire provides an apt means of examining the limitations of Foucault's reading of ancient philosophy. It also provides a valuable way of testing the value of Foucault's appropriation by the advocates of queer theory, while allowing us to concretize his reading of the relation of Plato to the Stoics.

Chapter 2

The Modernist Revolt

*History, Politics, and Allegory,
Or Classicism in Occupied France*

[Charles] Maurras was a man of deeply authoritarian temper, who espoused the principles of classical order and hierarchy in every field of human activity. [. . .] He was anti-democratic and publicly anti-Semitic (later to be incarcerated for his association with the Vichy regime). His organization, the *Action Française,* encouraged student riots (through offshoots like *Jeunes Filles Royalistes* and the *Camelots du Roi*) against free thinkers and Jews. [. . .] Throughout his life, Eliot would continue to support Maurras, and his philosophy was to enter the fabric of Eliot's own concerns. (Ackroyd 1984: 41–42)

[Eliot's] respect for communism was far greater than for fascism; in fact in his commentaries in the *Criterion,* he suggested that it was the only practicable alternative to the Christian faith. (Ackroyd 1984: 171)

IT MAY seem odd to start a chapter that will focus on the use of classical themes and texts in the French theater of the 1940s with a pair of quotations on T. S. Eliot's lasting flirtations with the incipient French-inflected fascism of Charles Maurras[1] and orthodox communism (Ackroyd 1984: 41, 76, 143; Shantz 2004). Yet what becomes clear to any observer of modernist culture in Western Europe, and particularly in England, France, Italy, and Spain, is the predominance of two cultural phenomena: the rise of neoclassicism and the rejection of bourgeois liberal society from both the right and the left. And while these two cultural phenomena were not identical,[2] they are all but impossible to separate. For, as we shall see, the appeal to the classics in this context

---

1. Maurras himself never became a full-fledged fascist but was closely allied with nationalist forces that supported European fascism, and many of his younger followers went on to join explicitly fascist movements (Kaplan 2000: 5, 13, 17).

2. The futurists, the dadaists, and the surrealists were all critics of the commodification of culture, but rejected the return to the classics. By the same token, Giraudoux and Cocteau both wrote plays on classical themes but were revolutionaries of neither the right nor the left.

is, in almost every case, the appeal to a timeless universal against which the tawdriness of the fallen present stands to be judged. It is the appeal to a sublime transcendence whether through the will to power, the coming revolution, or some other, more individualized form of revolt. Thus Eliot at the end of the *Wasteland,* a poem ventriloquized by Tiresias himself, speaks of "These fragments shored against my ruins," the shards of tradition as a bulwark against the forces of disintegration.

The commodification of culture and the rise of market- and media-based democracies gave rise to a widespread sense of disenchantment among the writers, thinkers, and artists of the early twentieth century. That disenchantment was most generally responded to by a call for either a reactionary return to the hierarchies of the past, a nihilistic fascism, or some variety of socialist revolution, and often by a bewildering blend of all three (e.g., German national socialism, Spanish Catholic fascism, Italian futurist imperialism, Stalinist "socialism in one country"). The reification and rationalization of advanced industrial capitalism, in which standards of value vanished before ruthless quantification, and all that had seemed solid either melted into the air or lay shattered on the fields of Verdun, produced a widespread sense of alienation and a desperate search for authenticity.[3] The rejection of a world based solely on exchange value led to the search for a transcendent standard in which aesthetics, politics, and tradition would be as one. We are left with the image of Ezra Pound writing his *Cantos* while making radio broadcasts for Mussolini, moving from the beautiful evocation of the Odyssean *nekuia* in Canto I, to the indictment of usury in Canto XLV, to the support of Italian fascism.

In this environment, the classics for the great modernists ceased to function primarily as objects of philological and historical inquiry and came instead to serve as timeless myths or universal monuments. As Eliot says in his famous text on Vergil, "What is a Classic?" (1944):

> In our age, when men seem more than ever prone to confuse wisdom with knowledge, and knowledge with information, and try to solve the problems of life in terms of engineering, there is coming into existence a new kind of provincialism which perhaps deserves a new name. It is a provincialism, not of space, but of time; one for which history is merely the chronicle of human devises which have served their turn and been scrapped, one for which the world is the

---

3. On these points and what follows, see Silverman (2000: 32–33); Renaut (1993: 35); Stoekl (1992: 72–73); Johnson (1982: 275); Jameson (1981: 62–66); Eagleton (1976: 13); and McLuhan (1962: 275).

property solely of the living, a property in which the dead hold no shares. The menace of this kind of provincialism is, that we can all, all the peoples on the globe, be provincials together; and those who are not content to be provincials, can only be hermits. If this kind of provincialism led to greater tolerance, in the sense of forebearance, there might be something to be said for it; but it seems more likely to lead to our becoming indifferent, in matters where we ought to maintain a distinctive dogma or standard, and to our becoming intolerant, in matters which might be left to local or personal preference. (1957: 69)

The classical texts of Greco-Roman antiquity, Vergil in particular for the later Eliot, were to serve as the sources of this standard and dogma. They were transformed into allegories of the present rather than historical estrangements, ideal modelings of transcendence rather than critical genealogies (Michon 2003: 123; Witt 2001: 235; Freeman 1971: 48; Highet 1949: 520–40; Grossvogel n.d.: 18).

Fundamental to any study of the classical tradition in Europe during this period is Mary Ann Frese Witt's *The Search for Modern Tragedy: The Aesthetics of Fascism in Italy and France* (2001). Witt traces in detail the ways in which the classical heritage, as interpreted through Nietzsche's *Birth of Tragedy,* was called upon to provide new models of purity and grandeur in response to what was widely seen as the dissipation of bourgeois modernity. Theorists such as Georges Sorel, Edouard Berth, and Charles Maurras in France, as well as writers and critics such as Gabriele D'Annunzio, Luigi Pirandello, and Giuseppe Prezzolini in Italy, sought in Dionysian violence a cathartic antidote to the decadence of the bourgeois, Enlightenment order. They sought an ideal Nietzschean balance between the Apollonian forces of order and Dionysian transcendence in both art and politics (Witt 2001: 3–10).

Tragedy was the preferred genre of this classical *risorgimento* as it was theorized first in Italy by D'Annunzio as well as others close to the fascist movement and later in France (Witt 2001: 32–134).[4] In his 1933 *Nietzsche,* Thierry Maulnier, a disciple of Maurras, following a line of interpretation first put forward by Mussolini himself in his 1908 essay on the German philosopher, argued for the revival of a French tragic tradition that was grounded in Mediterranean culture. Such a renewed

4. While the Italians were the first to theorize this classical revival, following what they saw as the "Mediterranean" side of Nietzsche, the French were the first to put the revival into practice with their outdoor production of ancient tragedies in the theater at Orange in the 1890s (Witt 2001: 37–39).

tragic form would eschew the compromises of both traditional moral systems and bourgeois *bonheur* ("happiness")[5] in favor of a tragic grandeur that was beyond good and evil (Witt 2001: 138–46). This Nietzschean position became the norm in French dramatic thinking of the period and was adopted by both the left-leaning Sartre and Camus and by those with more right wing ties such as Jean Anouilh and Henri de Montherlant.

Maulnier's roommate at the Ecole Normale Supérieure, Robert Brasillach, was another disciple of Maurras. As Witt explains, for these two fiercely intelligent and deeply alienated young men, the rejection of bourgeois liberalism and the embrace of classical culture were inseparable from one another.

> From their teacher at the Lycée Louis-le-Grand, André Bellesort, they had received an induction to right-wing ideology through training in and admiration for the Mediterranean tradition of classical humanism as the central foundation of French culture. Although he was initially drawn toward Charles Maurras's cultural-political movement, the Action française, Brasillach eventually rejected its conservative royalist-Catholic tenets to explore the newer revolutionary movements. [. . .] Like Maulnier, Brasillach approached fascism through aesthetics, unlike him, he came to support it in politics. (Witt 2001: 148–49)[6]

In fact, Brasillach went on to become a prominent collaborationist cultural critic during the occupation. The editor of the pro-fascist newspaper, *Je suis partout,* in which the names and addresses of Jews and members of the resistance were printed in his front-page column, he was also the sole writer to be executed by the Free French government after the liberation (Kaplan 2000: 32). Appropriately, Brasillach began his career with a book on Vergil (1931), celebrating his "Mediterranean genius" in the approved Maurrassian style. His last work was a collection of translations from Greek poets in the days before the liberation of Paris, a book that featured strong pro-German sentiments (Kaplan 2000: 9–10, 71). His own theatrical output was small, centered on the figures of Seneca, Racine, Corneille, an anti-Semitic rendering of *Bérénice,* and Joan of Arc (Kaplan 2000: 40–41). He remained a figure of controversy, and admiration to some, even after his death. The preface

---

5. Is it an accident that it is the mention of this word that leads Anouilh's Antigone to resolve on death? See below.
6. See also Kaplan (2000: 3, 278).

to his plays, which make up one volume of his complete works, was composed by Jean Anouilh (1963), and they were edited by Maurice Bardèche, his brother-in-law. The latter, a literary and film scholar of no small repute, was the intellectual godfather of postwar European neo-fascism and the first person to deny the holocaust in print (Shields 2004; Witt 2001: 162; Kaplan 2000: 3–6, 220).

The involvement of Anouilh may come as a shock to those who are accustomed to viewing his *Antigone* as an inspirational piece of Resistance theater in which the idealist Antigone gives her life in defiance of the cynical dictates of a disillusioned Creon (Fazia 1969: 22; Archer 1971: 18–19). Yet, as we are arguing here, and as we shall see when we examine the play in more detail, the realities of the situation were a good deal more complex. *Antigone* was, in fact, very well received by the occupation authorities, and Anouilh worked without interruption throughout the war (Marcel 1959: 101; McIntyre 1981: 42; Witt 2001: 220–21, 227–28; Leonard 2005: 105–6). Moreover, Brasillach himself, following in the footsteps of Maurras, had explicitly admired Antigone and compared her to Joan of Arc—both of whom were the subjects of plays by Anouilh—noting that each possessed "the 'fascist' qualities of youth, insolence, and devout patriotism" (Witt 2001: 185, 219; compare Fowlie 1960: 119–20). The borders between resistance and collaborationist aesthetics were, in fact, porous and the writers often shared many of the same ideological and artistic assumptions as well as theatrical institutions (Kaplan 2000: 30–31; Leonard 2005: 217).[7] Such well-known themes as the absurd, the rejection of traditional bourgeois morality and religion, and the necessity for radical self-creation can be found in both the work of fascist writers such as Drieu la Rochelle and Christian Michelfelder and in the leftist existentialism of Jean-Paul Sartre and Camus (Witt 2001: 177–80, 194, 238). These themes are as a much a part of *L'étranger* as they are of *Les mouches* and *Antigone* (Marcel 1959: 101; Fowlie 1960: 116).

It is in this fraught political and ideological context, then, that we must examine the extraordinary flowering of classically inspired theater in the France of the 1930s and 1940s. Indeed, over a dozen leading French playwrights produced works on ancient or mythic themes in these two decades (St. Aubyn and Marshall 1963: 9; Freeman 1971: 49–50). The Parisian stage became a virtual reincarnation of the theater of Dionysus in fifth-century Athens, even as gangs of communist and

---

7. Thus the last theatrical piece Brasillach saw, the night before the August 19, 1944 Communist-led insurrection in Paris, was Sartre's *Huis Clos* (Kaplan 2000: 71).

fascist sympathizers fought in the streets, the surrealists issued their manifestoes, and a young Jacques Lacan published his dissertation and began clinical work.

The commercial theater in France during the early part of the twentieth century had been dominated by the *Théâtre du Boulevard*. With the emergence of figures like Giraudoux and Cocteau in his *Antigone,* however, there develops a new experimental theater with both high artistic ambitions and a strong classicizing bent. This movement sought in antiquity both a universal style and a truly French idiom, one grounded in a shared Hellenic and Latin culture and in France's own classical theatrical tradition as embodied by Corneille, Racine, and Molière. It sought in the classics a bulwark against the commodification of daily life and the uncertainties of European culture in the aftermath of World War I, the Russian Revolution, and the Great Depression (Contat and Galster 2005: 1259–60; Boucris et al.: 1998: 35–36; Brée and Kroff 1969: 3, 6–23; Grossvogel n.d.: 18). In the paradigm of classical Mediterranean tragedy, it hoped to find a cleansing catharsis if not Baudelairean "luxe, calme, et volupté."

In this chapter, I will look at three emblematic uses of antiquity in the French modernist theater: Sartre's *Les mouches,* Camus's *Caligula,* and Anouilh's *Antigone*. All had a significant impact on subsequent literature and thought, and are essential to understanding the context in which first Lacan, and later Derrida and Foucault wrote. Unlike the later postmodernist uses of antiquity we shall be examining in the remainder of this book, all three of my modernist examples are drawn from the realm of dramatic spectacle rather than analytic investigation. As opposed to being ways to historicize the subject, antiquity for these writers represents a field of imaginative and allegorical possibilities. We become Antigone and Creon, Orestes and Electra, Caligula and his assassins. Antiquity becomes a way of re-presenting the present.

1. *Les mouches:* The Tragedy of Freedom

> Being an individual human being is not like being an individual peach. It is a project we have to accomplish. It is an autonomy we forge for ourselves on the basis of our shared existence, and thus a function of our dependency rather than an alternative to it. (Eagleton 2003: 162)

> I wanted to deal with the tragedy of freedom as opposed to the tragedy of fate. In other words, the subject of my play could be summarized as follows: "the way a man comports himself in the face of an act he has

committed, for which he assumes all the consequences and responsibilities, even if the act otherwise horrifies him." [. . .] I wanted to take the case of a man who is free and yet situated, who is not content to imagine himself to be free, but who frees himself at the cost of an exceptional act, however monstrous it may be, because he alone is able to bring to it this definitive liberation in relation to himself. (Sartre 2005a: 76–77)

In Sartre's *Les mouches,* the Furies of Aeschylus' *Libation Bearers* and *Eumenides* have become flies feeding upon the bloodguilt of the people of Argos for the death of Agamemnon. In it, the existentialist philosopher combines a variety of versions of the Electra-and-Orestes myths, including those of Sophocles and Euripides,[8] to create a meditation on the cost of freedom and responsibility (Contat and Galster 2005: 1265). The choice of an ancient setting was in many ways natural. Sartre's acquaintance with the ancient world was anything but superficial. His knowledge of Latin and Greek was excellent. He had won prizes in translation at the *lycée* and during his preparations (*hypokhagne* and *khagne*) for the Ecole Normale Supérieure. Nor were these forays into philology merely academic exercises of only transitory significance; the ancients in general and ancient drama in particular would continue to be of interest to Sartre throughout his adult life. We know, for example, that he reread the works of Sophocles while in a German prison camp at the beginning of the war shortly before the composition of *Les mouches* (Cohen-Solal 1987: 51–53, 66, 158).

There is nothing surprising, then, in the fact that Sartre would turn to ancient tragedy for the theme of his first commercially produced theatrical work, nor that his last play would be an adaptation of Euripides' *Trojan Women.* Yet, while Paris in the early 1940s was awash in neoclassical tragedies and productions of the ancients, Sartre's play was no neo-Aristotelian drama in the manner of Giraudoux or of Cocteau's *Antigone* (Contat and Galster 2005: 1262–63). In the occupied Paris of 1943, it was intended as a call to arms, but one that, owing to its classical "disguise," was able to clear the German censors with little difficulty.[9]

---

8. Thus, as in Euripides' *Electra,* Clytemnestra is portrayed as in many ways a sympathetic and caring mother who regrets the murder of Agamemnon. See Act 1, scene 5 (Sartre 2005b: 19).
9. The whole question of how and why the French theater continued to function under the occupation and whether it was a tool of that occupation, a center of resistance, or, more likely, an unstable and constantly renegotiated mixture of both, remains a source of bitter controversy (Witt 2001: 16, 190). It is, however, a matter of record that Sartre sought and received permission from the Resistance to have *Les mouches* performed in occupied Paris (Contat and Galster 2005: 1268).

At this remove, the political resonances of the portrayal of the people of Argos as complicit in their subjection to the tyranny of Aegisthus seem unmistakable. The flies feed on Argos' bloodguilt. They represent the Furies of self-repression inflicted by the citizens upon themselves in the recognition of their own *jouissance* at the death of Agamemnon (Sartre 2005b: 5, Act 1, scene 1). The flies thus function as an allegory of the way in which many in France submitted to the guilty pleasure of fascist occupation.

> Jupiter: As for the people of Argos, the next day, when they heard the king howl in pain in the palace, they didn't yet say anything, they lowered their lids as their eyes rolled back in pleasure, and the whole town was like a woman in heat. (Sartre 2005b: 7, Act 1, scene 1)

The sadistic pleasure of the act is complemented by the townspeople's enjoyment in their submission, in their own reduction to an instrument of Aegisthus' power.[10] Accordingly, Jupiter describes one townswoman's listening to the king's final agony in terms that directly recall sexual penetration:

> Jupiter: You are old enough to have heard them, those massive screams that circulated through the streets of the city. What did you do?
> Old Woman: My husband was in the fields. What was I able to do? I locked my door.
> Jupiter: Yes, and you opened the window to hear better and you leaned over on your elbows behind the curtains, panting, with a strange tickling sensation in your loins. (Sartre 2005b: 7, Act 1, scene 1)

In this passage, the town is allegorized as giving itself over to the *jouissance* of power, to the enjoyment of its own subjugation (Copjec 2002: 213, 216–17; St. Aubyn and Marshall 1963: 19–20).[11] The sexualized citizenry melts into the position of the object.[12]

---

10. See Copjec (2002: 223–25); and Sartre (1943: 452–54).
11. Compare the following statement by Inès to Garcin in *Huis Clos* on occupying the position of object in relation to the gaze of the other, "Tu es un lâche, Garcin, un lâche parce que je le veux. Je le veux, tu entends, je le veux! Et pourtant, vois comme je suis faible, un souffle; je ne suis rien que le regard qui te voit, que cette pensée incolore qui te pense" ("You are a coward, Garcin, a coward because I want it. I want it, do you hear me, I want it! And yet, look at how weak I am, a breath; I am nothing but the gaze that sees you, but this colorless thought that thinks you") (Sartre 2005e: 126, scene 5).
12. As Mary Ann Friese Witt reminds me (*per litteras*), "This sexual aspect could be

Les mouches, which was first performed in 1943 in occupied Paris, is in many ways an allegory and biting satire of the Pétain regime and the hypocritical ideology of guilt and repentance it sought to impose on its defeated populace. As Sartre himself acknowledged, the play directly ridicules the government of Vichy and those who collaborated with it and with the occupation. It shows them reveling both in the slaughter of Agamemnon (prewar France) and in their guilt over that slaughter. Orestes from this perspective can be read more easily as a hero of freedom and of the resistance than as a Mycenaean Greek or a character from an actual fifth-century tragedy (Sartre 2005c; Sartre 2005d: 82–83; Contat 2005: xxiv–xxvii; Kaplan 2000: 28; St. Aubyn and Marshall 1963: 7). *Les mouches* is, in short, a very contemporary work and in no way an historical reconstruction. As Michel Contat observes, "Conceived as a play lauding the spirit of resistance by founding itself on a philosophy of freedom, *Les mouches* had nothing Greek about it except the reference to the myth" (2005: xxiv).

Nonetheless, the play is more than a simple cryptogram to rouse the resistance (Leonard 2005: 219). It is also a profound intertextual and philosophical meditation. It may not be completely Greek in spirit, but it borrows elements from Aeschylus, Sophocles, and Euripides, while being a direct response to the classicizing theater of the period and a treatment of Sartre's own philosophical concerns. The flies, as Sartre's evocation of the Furies, are not only symbolic of the shame and guilt, the profound sense of original sin that the Pétain regime sought to foster in Vichy and occupied France, they are also figurations of the people of Argos' own bad faith (Sartre 2005b: 5, 8–10, Act 1, scene 1; 54, Act 2, tableau 2, scene 8). They thus form part of Sartre's larger philosophical critique of the routine processes by which subjects delude themselves and so becomes unable and unwilling to assume the burden of their acts, and hence to exercise a meaningful, positive freedom (Sartre 1943: 85–90, 616–23; St. Aubyn and Marshall 1963: 17). The flies on this reading metaphorize the problematic of resistance in general, on the ontological and existential level, rather than merely embodying a more narrow and immediate political concern.

Moreover, while Sartre's inspiration for *Les mouches* can be shown to derive from a variety of sources and was part of the larger neoclassical revival discussed above, it is also a very specific and pointed response to Giraudoux's *Electre* (Contat and Galster 2005: 1258–61; St. Aubyn and Marshall 1963: 8–10; Marcel 1959: 179). It was in the

---

related to Sartre's (unfortunate) tendency in writing about collaboration after the war to equate collaborators with feminized homosexuals who found *jouissance* in submission to the power of the occupiers."

latter that the term *mouches* was first used of the Furies (Giraudoux 1982: 600, Act 1, scene 1), although not in a sustained fashion but merely in a passing ironic sense. In many ways, the difference between Giraudoux's pesky coquettes, whom the gardener refers to as "flies," and Sartre's bloodsucking insects, feeding on the guilt of Argos, stands for the larger divergences between these two plays. It will be worth our while to take a moment to examine more closely how these two authors treat this same mythic complex, both to reveal the originality of Sartre's text and to give a better sense of the neoclassical context in which he, Camus, and Anouilh were working.

There is in fact a sense in which Giraudoux's work, while both a tragedy and a profoundly sophisticated work of art, remains an aesthetic vehicle of ironic distraction, rather than engagement. Where Sartre's Orestes will reject any notion of bourgeois or domestic contentment, including the opportunity to "teach philosophy or architecture in a large university town" (Sartre 2005b: 12, Act 1, scene 2), Giraudoux's gardener, who corresponds to the farmer in Eurpides' *Electra,* declaims that even amidst the murder and mayhem of tragedy, "life's sole aim is to love" (1982: 640, Entracte). Clearly, this statement in the context of the play as whole cannot be taken as a straightforward declaration of fact. Yet it is anything but merely sarcastic. The irony is perhaps best caught in the following speech by Electra. In it, we see both a denunciation of bourgeois happiness as hypocrisy and resignation, a move which is common to all the texts we are examining in this chapter, and the simultaneous evocation of that happiness as offering a moment of utopian deliverance, however compromised it may be:

> Spouses, sisters-in-law, mothers-in-law, all of them, when their husbands in the morning no longer see anything through their swollen eyes but purple and gold, it's they who rouse them, who offer them coffee and hot water, the hatred of injustice and the contempt for meager happiness [*bonheur*]. [. . .] And they watch their awakening, And the husbands, even if they have only slept five minutes, they have regained the armor of happiness, satisfaction, indifference, generosity, appetite. And a patch of sunlight reconciles them with the blots of bloods. And a bird's song with all the lies. (Giraudoux 1982: 651, Act 2, scene 3)

Electra's contempt is manifest, but the attractions of happiness, generosity, sunshine, and bird song are not so easily to be discounted. The choice between a fierce hatred of injustice and a resigned contentment is not straightforward in Giraudoux's eyes. It is, instead, further problematized at the play's end. There Electra's insistence on "truth" and "justice" so incapacitates Aegisthus that he is unable to lead the resistance to an army of Corinthian invaders with the result that the city of Argos is sacked. Her justice leads to destruction.

A bit of bad faith, in the end, may not be more than we can stomach, as Giraudoux the professional diplomat knew only too well. Thus, where Sartre's Orestes[13] will offer Argos the possibility of liberation through a single authentic act for which he assumes full responsibility, Giraudoux's *Electre* offers truth as a purification, but also as a massacre. The latter's encounter with antiquity presents neither a call for political resistance nor a means of radical self-transformation, but rather exemplifies an ironic and sophisticated resignation. Nothing could be less Sartrean (Contat and Galster 2005: 1262), and *Les mouches* is not only a riposte to its predecessor but also a rebuttal.

This intertextual dialogue, in turn, is key to understanding the nature of Sartre's relation to antiquity in the play. The encounter with the ancients, for him as well as for Giraudoux, is not a moment of estrangement from the present. *Les mouches* is in fact best read as a response to its own political, aesthetic, and intellectual context, far more than as an encounter with the otherness of antiquity in the manner of the poststructuralists. Indeed, for all its classical machinery, *Les mouches*, like many of its neoclassical counterparts, is self-consciously and ironically anachronistic (Contat and Galster 2005: 1274).

We can point to a number of examples. First, although the play is set in Greece, the father of the gods is referred to by his Latin name, "Jupiter." The one time "Zeus" is invoked, he represents Orestes' lingering belief in the possibility of a moral absolute, before the discovery of his own freedom. Zeus is prayed to as a transcendental principle that could reveal to Orestes the nature of the good, *le Bien,* at a point, however, when he already finds himself beyond good and evil ("A présent je suis las, je ne distingue plus le Bien du Mal" ("At present I am worn out, I no longer distinguish Good from Evil"), (Sartre 2005b: 38, Act 2, tableau 1, scene 4). To the extent that he represents a firm distinction between these poles, the Zeus addressed by Orestes is opposed to the cynical and conniving Jupiter, the "god of the flies and of death," who works hand in glove with Aegisthus to keep the people of Argos enslaved to their guilt (Sartre 2005b: 3, Act 1, scene 1; St. Aubyn and

---

13. Compare the beggar's description of Orestes in Giraudoux's play, as one whose real life was to "smile [...] to laugh out loud, to love, to dress well, to be happy" (1982: 644, Act 2, scene 1).

Marshall 1963: 11–12). Yet, Jupiter in fact is nothing more than brute nature, the realm of being-in-itself (Sartre 2005b: 63, Act 3, scene 3), to use the vocabulary of *L'être et le néant,* which was written at the same time as the play (Cohen-Solal 1987: 185). He only has meaning to the extent that human beings grant it to him. Gods and kings are a way for people to avoid looking at the emptiness inside themselves, a figuration of bad faith (Sartre 2005b: 45–51, Act 2, tableau 2, scenes 5–6; Curtis 1948: 10).[14] Aegisthus has power from Jupiter only so long as the citizens of Argos recognize it, only so long as they remain enmeshed in the warm bath of guilt in which they languish and luxuriate. As Electra says, "They love their ill, they need a familiar wound that they carefully cultivate by scratching it with their dirty nails" (Sartre 2005b: 35, Act 2, tableau 1, scene 4). Thus, when Orestes prays to Zeus he asks for a sign of whether he should accept his fate with "resignation and abject humility." Jupiter then produces one by having a boulder at the mouth of the cave shine with a miraculous light. But Orestes refuses to accept it as intended for him, and in the moment of that refusal he first becomes both truly Orestes and truly free, "The light [. . .]? It's not for me; and no one any longer can give me orders" (Sartre 2005b: 39, Act 2, tableau 1, scene 4). One will search in vain for an analogous passage in Sartre's ancient or neoclassical predecessors.

This is an antiquity that never existed, but one clearly constructed to be a reflection of the present. Witness passages such as Act 2, tableau 1, scene 1, where a mother admonishes her son before sending him off to attend the rites of the dead. He is told to be careful of his tie, to be "good and [to] cry with the others" (Sartre 2005b: 24). Self-inflicted guilt and bourgeois conformity are central topics in this text and obsessions of the period. They were hardly the concerns of Aeschylus.

In a similar vein, Sartre portrays Orestes as under the care of a Skeptic *paedogogus*, although the *Oresteia* is set in the Mycenaean period.[15] He also compares the learning of the *paedogogus* to that of the travel

---

14. There is a slight inconsistency concerning this matter within the play. In Act 2, tableau 1, scene 3, when Electra dances to prove that the dead have no hold and that the people of Argos need not live their lives sunken in shame, Jupiter utters a spell and a boulder, which had blocked the entrance to the cave, rolls noisily against the steps of the temple. This causes the priest to say, "oh cowardly and too easily swayed people, the dead avenge themselves." The crowd promptly returns to a state of naive credulity (Sartre 2005b: 32). This would seem to be an example of what Lacan would later term "the answer of the Real": a contingent encounter that is provided with a *post hoc* logical consistency and hence meaning (Žižek 1991: 29–30; 1989: 170–71).

15. As David Wray observes to me, this is not per se different from Euripides' inclusion of characters using sophistic rhetoric in tragedies set in the Homeric age.

writer Pausanias from the second century CE (Sartre 2005b: 11, Act 1, scene 2). As in the case of Jupiter, this is no character from an ancient tragedy. Indeed, the *pédagogue* represents more the smug enlightenment self-assurance of Madame Bovary's petit bourgeois apothecary, Homais, than the skeptical philosophy of Pyrrho, Sextus Empiricus, or any of their disciples. As the *pédagogue* says of the people of Argos:

> How ugly they are. See, Master, their waxy complexion, their hollow eyes. They are dying from fear. That's the effect of superstition. Look at them; look at them. And if you need any further proof of the excellence of my philosophy, consider then my rosy complexion. (Sartre 2005b: 25: Act 2, tableau 1, scene1)

The complacent self-assurance of this bourgeois, academic philosopher may well be a worse form of delusion than the self-abasement of the people of Argos. The freedom that this philosophy offers, like that of the neo-Kantianism that dominated the French academy when Sartre was a student, is purely negative and abstract (Sartre 2005b: 11–12, Act 1, scene 2; St. Aubyn and Marshall 1963: 16–17). It is not the freedom of a concrete individual, rooted in a particular situation, which Sartre advocates. It is not that of one who performs an act for which he or she is ready to assume the consequences, and for whom those consequences, however heavy, are the signs of that freedom (Contat and Galster 2005: 1262; Marcel 1959: 186). It is instead a form of bad faith.

Tragedy for Sartre, then, offers not a way of thinking about history, of estranging the formation of the subject through an encounter with the intimate other of Greek history and culture per se, as will be the case for the poststructuralists, but rather it functions as a sublimation of the present into the realm of the timeless so as to imagine a single act of transcendence: Orestes' murder of Aegisthus and Clytemnestra (Fowlie 1960: 172). That act, moreover, far from abstracting Orestes from the realm of the concrete and the immediate, will root him in it (Aronson 1980: 181–82).[16] He seeks through it not an abstract or negative freedom, but a form of embodiment: "I hardly exist: of all the ghosts that gnaw through today, none is more ghostly than I." He is not the fated avenger of Agamemnon's murder found in Aeschylus, Sophocles, and Euripides, but a strictly contingent one who, through coming to recognize that contingency, his "thrownness" in Heideggerian terms, thereby

---

16. Compare Sartre (2005b: 12–13, Act 1, scene 2).

gains the means to come to a real and substantial freedom (2005b: 37, Act 2, tableau 1, scene 4).[17] Freedom and authenticity consist not in the denial of our "thrown"[18] nature—of our temporality, our finitude, and our intersubjectivity—but precisely in their assumption (Sartre 2005a: 77; Zuckert 1996: 46; Silverman 2000: 34).

> Orestes: Listen, all these people who tremble in their darkened rooms surrounded by their departed, suppose that I assume all their crimes. Suppose that I wish to merit the name, "stealer of remorse," and that I take on myself all their guilt [. . .]. Say then, on that day when I will be haunted by regrets more numerous than the flies of Argos, by all the regrets of the city, will I not have become your fellow citizen? Will I not be at home among your high bleeding walls, as a butcher in his red apron is at home in his shop among the bleeding beeves he has just skinned. (2005b: 40, Act 2, tableau 1, scene 4)

Yet that assumption is always immediate and existential, it does not engage history as a profoundly decentering, impersonal process (Eagleton 1996: 56–57). It is, in a word, dramatic. The double murder of Aegisthus and Clytemenestra produces a moment of ecstatic freedom. Orestes and Electra for a brief instant are united in a *jouissance* of blood. Orestes declares:

> We are free, Electra. I seem to have brought you to birth, and I have just been born with you; I love you and you belong to me. Yesterday I was still alone and today you belong to me. Blood unites us doubly, for we are of the same blood and we spilt that blood. (Sartre 2005b: 53, Act 2, tableau 2, scene 8)

Yet this momentary clearing that the authentic act inaugurates, this rupture in the consecrated order of things (Marcel 1959: 187), immediately becomes the site of determination as the consequences of that act are genuinely assumed. Electra retorts, "Free? I certainly don't feel free. Can you make it that all this has not been? Something happened and

---

17. For an excellent analysis of Sartre's complex relationship with Heidegger, see Renaut (1993).

18. See *Being and Time* I.6, "To Dasein's state of Being belongs throwness; indeed it is constitutive for Dasein's disclosedness. In throwness is revealed that in each case Dasein, as my Dasein and this Dasein, is already in a definite world and alongside a definite range of definite entities within-the-world. Disclosedness is essentially factical" (Heidegger 1962: 264).

we are not free to undo it" (Sartre 2005b: 53, Act 2, tableau 2, scene 8).[19] But this is precisely the essence of freedom and the authentic act. The member of the resistance who assassinates a Nazi official not only remains an assassin, but may well cause the death of countless innocents in reprisals, as Sartre himself recognized (2005d: 82–83; Kaplan 2000: 46). Yet it is only in the willingness to assume those consequences, to recognize and accept them, that the possibility of real self-determination in the broadest and most philosophical sense becomes possible (Marcel 1959: 183). As Orestes says in response, "Yesterday I walked aimlessly on the earth, and thousands of paths fled beneath my feet. [. . .] Today, there is only one and God knows where it leads: but it's my path" (Sartre 2005b: 53, Act 2, tableau 2, scene 8).

At the end of the play, Orestes is able to offer freedom to the people of Argos through his willingness to assume their responsibility for avenging the death of Agamemnon. He thereby transforms the abstract and academic freedom that characterizes the *paedogogus*'s philosophy into an embodied act. His "crime" becomes the grounds of a potential collective liberation (Fowlie 1960: 171), but one that we have little reason to believe will actually occur, given both the passivity and bad faith of the Argive populace and the radically individualistic nature of freedom as Sartre has Orestes define it. On the one hand, the people of Argos, as we have seen from the beginning, maintain a profoundly sensual cathexis with their guilt and oppression. Their wound is their object of desire. Orestes' acceptance of his crime, of its naked criminality without seeking the excuses of law or shame, is precisely what they cannot accept (Sartre 2005b: 69, Act 3, scene 6). On the other, Orestes' act of situated freedom, while grounding him in the world of concrete historicity, immediately alienates him from the very community to which it is addressed (Aronson 1980: 183).[20]

The free man is "an exile," someone who has ripped a hole in the order of things, who has refused the reigning realm of positivity in the name of a situated act of negation, but who can rely on no canons of nature or of existing morality to justify his action (Sartre 2005b: 64–65, Act 3, scene 2). His act and the world exist in a relation of strict opposition, not as part of a complex network or system of situated differences. Consequently, that act's negativity is almost instantly recuperated in the realm of the Sartrean "in itself," the inert existent. As Electra herself notes, this is a freedom that is all but indistinguishable

---

19. On Electra's inability to assume her act and her need for the cathexis of guilt embodied by the Furies, see Sartre (2005b: 59, Act 3, scene 1) and Aronson (1980: 182).
20. See also Champigny (1982: 44–45).

from its opposite: "Can you make it that all this has not been? Something happened and we are not free to undo it." Orestes offers to the people the possibility of their own political and existential liberation, but he cannot offer it as anything more than a pure negation, which they are unable and unwilling to accept, lest it be reintegrated into the reigning realm of positivity, and become just another form of bad faith. This is perhaps what Michel Foucault had in mind when he later referred to Sartre's "intellectual terrorism" (Macey 1993: 429). We are faced with the stark choice of meaningless but free self-responsibility, through knowing crime, or bad faith, self-deception, and sensualized slavery.

In the end, Orestes' act becomes a triumph of the individual will rather than a true, collective, political act, and this is, of course, the ground on which Sartre's play rejoins the terrain of his modernist and neoclassical *confrères:* for there is nothing in the act itself of killing Clytemnestra and Aegisthus, or in the logic of the act, that necessarily distinguishes it from an analogous gesture of revolt deriving from a fascist orientation. In itself, this is no necessary condemnation: for it was not the revolt per se that was unjustified but the authoritarian and genocidal regimes that ensued. Sartre's recognition, however, of this fundamental ambiguity at the heart of his philosophy of the act would lead him, first, to the failed attempt to produce an ethics based on the ontology of *L'être et le néant* (Contat and Galster 2005: 1272; Aronson 1980: 181; Marcel 1959: 179), and later to his own idiosyncratic embrace of Marxism in *La critique de la raison dialectique* (Renaut 1993: 153). In the end, in the absence of a transcendental law or principle, it was the turn to history and not just historicity that would be called to judge. In a world beyond good and evil, the project of radical self-fashioning, of an ethics of self-creation, could, it seems, have no other ground (Renaut 1993: 218–19).

Indeed, as different as the two approaches may be, and as stark as the opposition between them may have been painted by Foucault and others, both the modernists and the postmodernists find themselves addressing a very similar set of questions: What kind of ethics is possible? What concept of the self's relation to itself is possible in a world that no longer offers transcendental guarantees? How do we offer resistance to the forces of identity, homogenization, and commodification, to all those forces that in Lacan's words ask us to cede on our desire? How do we distinguish our acts of resistance from those of our fascist brothers? Where the modernists seek to answer these questions on the level of the act, the postmoderns will answer them on the level of the concept (Macey 1993: 33; Foucault 1994cc: 764–65): through a systematic interrogation of the construction of the basic categories of subject, self, and other that make the act possible. Where the modernist model is that of dramatic display, the postmodern will be that of analysis, the *essai*, and the subversion of the sovereign subject.

2. *Caligula:* The Logic of the Absurd

> You never believed in the sense of this world and you deduced from that the idea that all things were equivalent and that good and evil were defined as one wished. You supposed that in the absence of all human or divine morality the only values were those that ruled the animal world: violence and trickery. You concluded from this that man was nothing and that one was able to kill his soul, that in the most outrageous adventures the task of the individual could only be the quest for power, and his morality, the realism of conquests. And in truth, I, who believed I thought as you, hardly saw any argument with which to oppose you, except a violent desire for justice that, in the end, seemed to me as little reasoned as the most immediate of passions. (Camus, *Lettres à un ami allemand,* 1965a: 240)

> Men too secrete the inhuman. In moments of lucidity, the mechanical aspects of their gestures, their pantomime void of sense renders ridiculous all that surrounds them. A man talks on the telephone behind a glass screen, we don't hear him, but we see his pointless mimicry: we ask why is he alive. This discomfort before the inhumanity of man himself, this incalculable fall before the image of what we are, this "nausea" as a contemporary author calls it, is also the absurd. (Camus, *Mythe de Sisyphe,* 1965b: 108)

The pattern is set: for the modernists, antiquity will serve as an allegorization of the nature and cost of the authentic act. Implicit is the assumption that there can be no authenticity without revolt, without a refusal to accept the universe as bequeathed to us. This is as true for Sartre's Orestes as it is for Camus's Caligula. The problem, of course, as Camus acknowledges in his fourth "Lettre à un ami allemand," is that it is just as true for the fascist's will to power as his own humanist revolt. Each perceives the inhuman and the contingent as not merely accidental but as a necessary part of the human. The act is precisely a gesture of remaking the world that at once acknowledges this facticity, the thrown nature of human existence, and takes it as the ground of its own self-construction. The question is what kind of construction shall that be. As the First Patrician in *Caligula* says of the numerous rapes, thefts, and murders that he and the other aristocrats have suffered at the hands of their artist emperor, "Are you going to put up with this? As far as I'm concerned, my choice is made. Between running the risk and this intolerable life of fear and impotence, I have no hesitation" (Camus 1962a: 32, Act 2, scene 1). *Caligula,* then, poses the question of whether it is possible to make a response to inhuman cruelty in an absurd world that is not itself simply a mechanical, and thus ultimately inhuman, reproduction of the already given. In a world beyond good and evil, who is more deluded, Caligula or those who finally assassinate him? Thus, in both its subject matter and philosophical atmosphere, *Caligula* is a play that is very much typical of French theater in the 1930s and 1940s as well as of the ideological and political complexities and complicities of its historical context (Freeman 1971: 38–39, 48). And while Camus himself was more directly involved in the resistance than Sartre, he too had no difficulty publishing during the occupation and was considerably less convinced of the morality of executing Brasillach and other collaborationists than were Sartre and de Beauvoir, owing in part to his opposition to the death penalty (Todd 1996: 284, 292, 394–95; Kaplan 2000: 74, 195–98, 216–17). Lines had to be drawn, but the question was always where and how?

What is most important to note from our point of view, however, is not the individual and perhaps accidental ideological complicities that necessarily occur in any conflict, but the larger theoretical concerns and how they relate to the uses to which antiquity was put by the modernists as opposed to their poststructuralist successors. For the central point to observe is that so long as contingency, historicity, and facticity are viewed as the simple dialectical others of the subject, as that which ultimately must be overcome in a higher synthesis through the authentic act, then real history cannot emerge. The past can only be an allegory of the present's will. This distinction is crucial, for there are numerous overlaps and points of contact between the poststructuralists and Camus and Sartre, not the least of which is a common affinity with Heidegger whose own Nazi past was never explicitly renounced (Renaut 1993: 35). As we shall see, then, when we come to Lacan, Derrida, and Foucault, they too seek to elaborate a post-Nietzschean ethics of self-creation, to seek a good beyond all socially recognized goods. But that moment of self-creation is never simply opposed to the given, is never simply a break with the past or an assumption of contingency, but it is also a moment of enjoyment, an acknowledgment of the erotics of power, that simultaneously creates itself and gives itself over to that contingency. Foucauldian "power and knowledge," the

Derridean "signifier and signified," the Lacanian "Real and Symbolic" are never opposed to each other as subject and object, being and negating (*l'être et le néant*), but instead exist as a series of "folds" (Foucault), "knots" (Lacan), "exchanges" (Lacan), and "disseminations" (Derrida). The imagery here is important. Rather than a series of oppositions, which ultimately mirror each other and place a premium on identity (*le même*),[21] poststructuralist metaphors emphasize networks, interdependence, complex systems, overdetermination, and difference. History from the poststructural view, therefore, is never simply an allegory of the present, its re-presentation, but always its intimate other, the opaque kernel that lies at its heart and operates its dispersion (Žižek 1991: 36). It is only by coming to terms with that otherness qua otherness, that a genuine ethics of self-creation, a real spiritual practice, an authentic politics can be formulated that is not predicated on either the eternal reproduction of the same or its dialectical complement, the annihilation of the other.

Camus's *Caligula* is, then, anything but a straightforward historical drama. It is a high stakes existential wager that combines a careful reading of Suetonius with deliberate, calculated distortions of Roman history.[22] Published in 1944 and having debuted as an immediate hit on the Paris stage in 1945, *Caligula* in many ways reflects the introspection of post-occupation France and is a clear meditation on what Witt terms "fascist aesthetics" through the pursuit of the absolute (Freeman 1971: 35–36).

Moreover, while Camus's direct knowledge of classical culture was less than Sartre's—his Latin was average and he had no Greek—he too had an abiding interest in antiquity,[23] even writing his thesis for his *Diplôme d'études supérieures* in philosophy on Augustine and Plotinus (Todd 1996: 98). The play owes its origins to a 1934 university course, which Camus took in Algiers, on the Roman emperors. In it, he read Caligula's biography by Suetonius in the original Latin (Todd 1996: 52, 64). Nor was this, in fact, his first exposure to the topic. We know that Jean Grenier, Camus's philosophy professor in his final year of the *lycée* (1932) and a lifelong influence, had spoken of Suetonius' *Life*

21. On the related problems of the mirror and identity in interpretation, and the call for a mode of deconstruction that, while not denying reflection, seeks to multiply its facets, see Irigaray (1974: 27, 167–69, 178).

22. Thus in Act 1, scene 2 (1962a: 11–12), the character Cherea makes a clear allusion to Nero, the emperor after Claudius, Caligula's successor. We know from earlier drafts that this was a deliberate anachronism and not simply a mistake (Quilliot 1962: 1752).

23. Thus the character of Sophocles' Oedipus is cited as one of the figures for the formula of "absurd victory" in *Le Mythe de Sisyphe* (1965b: 197).

of Caligula and Nietszche's *Birth of Tragedy* to the young student on several occasions. We also know from an early essay of Camus's appreciation of Grenier's *Les îles,* which itself features a distinctly Nietzschean reading of the Suetonian text (Camus 1965c and 1965d; Quilliot 1962: 1740–41; Freeman 1971: 50–52). Given this background and the atmosphere of neo-Nietzschean classicism that dominated the French theater of the thirties and forties, the creation and production of *Caligula* could hardly be considered a surprise.[24]

The earliest notes for the play date from 1937 and it went through repeated drafts before the first published edition in 1944 (Quilliot 1962: 1733; Todd 1996: 352). A revised edition was subsequently published in 1947 and the play underwent a final revision in 1958.[25] The Suetonian life of this most depraved of emperors clearly struck a chord with Camus's deepest interests, and he would even go so far as to sign his satirical articles in *Combat* using the *nom de plume, Suétone* (Grenier 1987: 119–20).

Caligula, like both Orestes and Antigone, rejects bourgeois happiness in favor of an uncompromisingly logical, but ultimately inhuman pursuit of a transcendence of the existing order of things (Camus 1962a: 78, Act 3, scene 6). This pursuit is not irrational but beyond the scope of humanity as commonly understood: "I am not mad and in fact I have never been so reasonable. Simply, I suddenly felt a need for the impossible. Things as they are no longer seem satisfying" (Camus 1962a: 15, Act 1, scene 4). Caligula is not insane, but rather he alone unites the dream of a radical transcendence with the power to bring it about (Camus 1962a: 24, Act 1, scene 9). He represents precisely the force of an implacable logic in an absurd universe that knows no transcendental ground. In that universe, all human actions become ontologically and thus morally equivalent from a metaphysical perspective (Todd 1996: 297; Sprintzen 1988: 75; Curtis 1948: 30–31). As Cherea says, Caligula must be killed "since he cannot be refuted" (Camus 1962a: 35, Act 2, scene 2).

---

24. Camus's early writings are also suffused with a sense of Mediterranean humanism and its roots in the classical world. See *L'envers et l'endroit* (1965e) and *Noces* (1965f).

25. The 1958 version is now considered the definitive one and forms the basis for the text published in the Pléiade edition (1962). Our primary concern is with the play as published in 1944 and produced in 1945, thus when it was contemporary with Sartre's *Les mouches* and Anouilh's *Antigone*. While variants should be noted, for our purposes their significance is limited. As Sprintzen observes, "The last two major revisions, those of 1947 and 1958, do not radically alter the structure and dynamics of the play" (1988: 66). What is most significant to observe is that Caligula remained a figure of fascination for Camus from at least 1934 to 1958 as did the Nietzschean context in which the initial encounter with Suetonius and the emperor occurred.

It is precisely this point concerning the emperor's perverse logical rigor to which Gabriel Marcel refers when he writes that *Caligula* is "purely and simply the theatrical transposition of the absurd man as he is defined in *Le mythe de Sisyphe*" (1959: 165). Marcel has in mind passages such as the following, "[in a passion for the absurd] there must be an unjust, that is to say logical, mode of reasoning. It's not easy. It's always simple enough to be logical. It's almost impossible to be completely logical" (1965b: 103). Caligula is precisely the "unjust," logical man, who reasons all the way to the end, who does not balk at the consequences of his conclusions. Of course, the resemblance between the play and Camus's more formal exercise in "absurd reasoning" is in no way accidental.[26] Camus had not only written *L'étranger, Le mythe de Sisyphe,* and *Caligula* all at the same time, but he had initially hoped that Gallimard would publish all three simultaneously as his "three absurds" (Todd 1996: 241, 261, 274–300).

Nonetheless, the three texts are not identical. Indeed, while Camus clearly identifies himself with the passion of the absurdist hero in *Le mythe de Sisyphe,* most critics would be loath to claim that there is a similar direct identification with Caligula (or for that matter with the affectless and ultimately murderous Meursault).[27] Nonetheless, that identification is precisely what is at stake in Marcel's notion of *Caligula* as the theatrical transposition of *Le mythe*. Moreover, the problem of this identification with evil or with the criminal is precisely the very one noted in the passage quoted at the beginning of this section from the *Lettres à un ami allemand* ("And in truth, I, who believed I thought as you, hardly saw any argument with which to oppose you"). In this collection of fictitious letters, which were clandestinely published during 1943 and 1944 in resistance periodicals and then collected after the war, Camus tries to clarify what separates the resistance fighter from his Nazi counterpart, not on the basis of nationality, but in terms of foundational ideological and philosophical assumptions. Nonetheless, as the above quoted passage indicates, the difference can seem surprisingly small. In a world denied all transcendental guarantees of meaning and value, Camus the absurdist can do no more than oppose an irrational "passion for justice" to the cold-eyed logic of his fictitious Nazi interlocutor, a logic that is, as we have seen, the distinguishing feature of both the absurdist hero of the *Myth of Sisyphus* and of Caligula himself (Freeman 1971: 47–48).

26. Part 1 of *Le mythe* is entitled "un raisonnement absurde."
27. Freeman (1971: 43–44) argues that Caligula represents a novel solution to the problem of the absurd by attempting to universalize the nonsensical relation between the self and world. In so doing, however, Caligula is simply being "completely logical."

Caligula's project is, in fact, to be completely and uncompromisingly logical "jusqu'à la fin" ("all the way to the end"): for what he has discovered in the death of his sister, Drusilla, is not personal loss, but the loss of meaning, the absurd (Freeman 1971: 37–38):

> Caligula: I also know what you think. Such foolishness over the death of a woman. No, it's not that. [. . .] That death is nothing, I swear to you; it is only the sign of truth [. . .]. It's a very simple and lucid truth, a bit stupid, but difficult to discover and hard to bear.
> Helicon: And what is this truth, Gaius?
> Caligula: Men die and they are not happy. (1962a: 16, Act 1, scene 4)

The world, in short, is indifferent to the lot of human beings, and yet we cannot bear to face the absurdity of our desire that it should be otherwise. All of Caligula's seemingly random cruelty is designed to drive home this simple pedagogical lesson:

> Helicon: Come on Gaius, it's a truth that one lives with quite easily. Look around. It certainly doesn't stop them from enjoying their dinner.
> Caligula: That's because everything around me is a lie, but I want us to live in the truth. And I have precisely the means to make them live in the truth. For I know what they lack, Helicon. They are deprived of knowledge and they lack a teacher who knows what he's talking about. (1962a: 16, Act 1, scene 4)

What Caligula's violence threatens, then, is not just the senators' lives and property, but the very possibility that those lives might have meaning (1962a: 34, Act 2, scene 2). This is why he, like the philosopher, must be killed: for he bears the most deadly virus of all, self-knowledge. The confrontation with the absurd is unbearable and yet liberating, not because it brings with it a sense of loss, but the final loss of loss (1962a: 105, Act 4, scene 13).[28]

Caligula, thus, like the Nietzschean theorists of neoclassical French tragedy, Maulnier and Brasillach, seeks purity (1962a: 102, Act 4, scene 13) and absolute clarity:

> You see I have no excuses. Not even the shadow of a love nor the bitterness of melancholy. I have no alibi. But today I am freer than

---

28. Compare Camus (1965b: 99–118).

I have been in years, liberated as I am from memory and illusion. (*He laughs with real emotion.*) I know that nothing lasts! (1962a: 106, Act 4, scene 13)

Caligula thus becomes a "god" by transcending the bounds of human reason and fashioning an identity that is beyond illusion and beyond sense, and thus is truly free (1962a: 69, Act 3, scene 2). What offends is not the enormity of his crimes, but their self-avowed absurdity. Yes, he is a murderer, a thief, a rapist. But these are normal instruments of policy throughout the world, whether in Stalin's Russia, Hitler's Germany, Srebrenica, or Abu Ghraib. Yet, however, horrible these acts are in themselves, they are always committed ostensibly in the service of a greater good. What makes Camus's Caligula so powerful is the complete lack of pretence. His violence makes no sense and that is its point and what from one perspective makes it so liberating. It is grounded in the absurdity that is the ultimate foundation of the human condition. It offends not in its violence, but because it reveals that absurdity (Sprintzen 1988: 70–71). In point of fact, as Caligula himself observes, the enormity of his crimes pales in comparison to those committed in any so-called reasonable war:

Caligula: If you knew how to count, you would know that the least war waged by a reasonable tyrant would cost you a thousand times more than the whims of my fantasy.
Scipio: But at least it would be reasonable and the essential is to understand. (1962a: 36, Act 3, scene 2)

In the end, this is what makes Caligula such an attractive figure to Camus. He reveals the nakedness of power and in that makes a mockery of it. There is no justification for his crimes and hence no way to convince us of the reasonableness and the necessity of carrying them out (Todd 1996: 392).

For Caligula, like Orestes, true freedom is not the abstract liberty to make personal choices, but rather represents a fundamental and concrete breach with the existing nature of things. He seeks nothing less than to remake the universe, or at least our relation to it:

Caligula: And what good is there in ruling with a firm hand, how does this astonishing power serve me if I cannot change the order of things, if I cannot make the sun set in the East, suffering decrease, and men no longer die? (Camus: 1962a: 27, Act 1, scene 11)

Such a desire is madness, but only such madness can authorize the truly authentic act. Caligula is beyond good and evil, and from this position of the Nietzschean superman he sets out to teach the patricians the nature of their own subjection:

> Caesonia: There is good and evil, that which is great and that which is base, the just and the unjust. I swear to you that all this will not change.
> Caligula: My will is to change it. I will grant to this century the gift of equality. And when everything will be all flattened out, the impossible will finally be on the earth, the moon in my hands, then, perhaps, I will be transformed and the world with me, then finally men will not die and they will be happy. (Camus: 1962a: 27, Act 1, scene 11)

Only when there is nothing to live or die for, will death's sting be lost, and the need for delusion transcended. Only in the recognition of the absurdity of our relation to the world does a radical self-transformation become possible. This is Camus's and Caligula's wager and the ground on which they meet (Camus: 1962a: 25, Act 1, scene 10).

Caligula, then, represents not a moment of self-estrangement, but precisely a hyperbole of the self that only the distance of antiquity permits. In Rome of the early empire, in the megalomania of the young emperor, Camus found the ideal conditions for a radical assertion of the self, an almost pure subjectivity released from all constraints. Caligula is free from the social and behavioral fetters that would have constrained the actions of even the most sociopathic contemporary Frenchman. At the same time, he operates outside the ideological categories that would have framed and interpreted even the emperor's behavior in first-century CE Rome. This is not to say that Camus departs radically from his sources with regard to the basic plot. In point of fact, he follows very much the sequence of events in Suetonius, including the young emperor's strange relations with his sister, his fixation on the moon, his fondness for contemplating himself in the mirror, and his assassination. The crucial differences are not in the specific actions or even the particular characters but in the explicit reflections on those characters' motivations. Suetonius provides a chronicle of lurid depravity—rapes, murders, the abuse of senators and their wives. It is gossipy and sensationalistic. His emperor, though, has no inner world. Camus's Caligula is one who has not only discovered the absurdity of man's relation to the universe, but he is also one who is determined to follow the consequences of that intuition to their logical end. He is not Suetonius' madman but the hero of a particular vision of the absurd that the distance of antiquity serves to reveal. In the end, however closely Camus may hew to Suetonius' line, however factual the account of Caligula's crimes may be, this Nietzschean emperor will always necessarily be an allegory, rather than an estrangement, of the self.

3. *Antigone:* "Pour personne, pour moi"

> M. Henri: My dear boy, there are two races. The members of one race are numerous, fertile, happy, a great wad of dough to knead. They eat their sausage, make their children, use their tools, count their pennies, in good times and bad, despite wars and epidemics, till old age sets in. These people are meant to live, everyday people, people you don't imagine dead. And then there are the others, the nobles, the heroes. Those that one can easily imagine laid out, pale, a red hole in their head, one minute triumphant with an honor guard the next between two policemen as the case may be: the cream of the crop. Hasn't that ever tempted you? (Anouilh 1942: 440, *Eurydice*, Act 2)

> With her cult of youth and refusal to grow old, her resounding "no" to everything resembling bourgeois mediocrity and "happiness," her ideal of "purity," her notions of the superiority of her "race," her courting of danger and death, her rejection of "politics" and law, and her guiding principle of irrationality, the character of Antigone reverberates with themes dear to French fascism since the 1930s. (Witt 2001: 226)

It is Caligula's problematic pursuit of an absolute, a logic, that is beyond the compromises of bourgeois life that is also at heart of Anouilh's *Antigone*. This last play, via Lacan's reading of the Sophoclean original, will have the most direct influence on the postmodernist thinkers who will occupy us in the latter part of this book. It also presents the most direct challenge to them: for the play problematizes the difficulty of separating the earlier fascist pursuit of an absolute, beyond the bounds of bourgeois subjectivity, from the later postmodernist pursuit of a *pensée du dehors*. The latter concern becomes all the more troubling in light of the complicities, flirtations, and collaborations with fascism of postmodern icons like Maurice Blanchot, Louis-Ferdinand Céline, de Man, and Heidegger (Stoekl 1992: 173, 233–60). Nonetheless, the costs of avoiding these complicities must not be underestimated either. For what are the alternatives to maintaining some vision of a radical critique of the existing order, of enlightenment rationality and the bourgeois economic model of man? Are we not then doomed to choosing between a suffocating positivist dystopia and a fascist utopian beyond? Are we not doomed to a choice between the impossibility of fundamental change—"Keep working: as for desire, better luck next time" (Lacan 1986: 367)—and a beyond that is not only beyond the pleasure principle, but directly embraces the death drive in the most literal and tangible sense? The rejection of a *pensée du dehors* as inherently authoritarian, if not homicidal, is also the surrender of thought itself as the radical project of rethinking the very concept of the human, the social, and the structures of power and domination they entail.

In many ways, such concerns seem far removed from the aesthetic world of Anouilh. He rejected the title of master thinker in favor of that of simple artisan (Fazia 1969: 28; Vandromme 1972: 17). In so doing, he sought to distinguish his work from that of both the fascists who claimed him (Witt 2001: 192–93, 216–17, 220–21, 227), and from the likes of Sartre and Camus with whom he was often compared (Grossvogel n.d.: 8–9,12, 35n.3; Fazia 1969: 139). Yet, in spite of his modest claims, *Antigone* is no simple theatrical exercise. The fact is that Antigone, like many other of Anouilh's characters, embraces a suicidal search for purity and an exacting rejection of bourgeois compromise. These twin traits place his work squarely in the middle of the ideological and aesthetic debates of the period (Grossvogel n.d.: 11; Vandromme 1972: 100, 109).

The *Antigone* not only enacts a pursuit of nobility and grandeur, squarely in line with Maulnier's Nietzschean aesthetics as well as with Anouilh's own quite conservative views, but it also directly thematizes that pursuit as the essence of the tragic form (Fazia 1969: 27). As the chorus says:

> It's clean, tragedy. It's calm. It's certain [. . .]. In tragedy, one is tranquil. First, one is among intimates. Everyone is innocent, in the end. It's not because one kills and the other is killed. It's a question of distribution. And then above all, it's calm, tragedy, because you know there is no longer any hope, foul hope; you're caught, you're finally caught like a rat [. . .]. In a drama, you debate because you hope to escape. It's ignoble, it's utilitarian. Here, there is no justification. This is for kings. (Anouilh 1946a: 165–66)

Antigone's regal rejection of all forms of compromise, her search for purity, which like that of Caligula is ultimately "a higher form of suicide," is thus at one with the neoclassical vision of tragic aesthetics

(Todd 1996: 352). There is no negotiation, no compromise, no commerce between competing goods, no arguments offered in their favor. The tragedy of fate is both cruel and calm. Antigone serves simultaneously as a self-conscious allegory of the play's own dramaturgical practice and of tragedy's role as a permanent protest against the mediocrity of modern society (Gignoux 1946: 102).

Her position is, in fact, characteristic of Anouilh's other mythical and semi-mythical heroines (Curtis 1948: 34). She represents a poetics of death. Thus, Jeannette in *Roméo et Jeanette* rejects both her father's peasant vulgarity and her sister's smug bourgeois conformity for the poetic suicide of wading into the ocean in her wedding dress (Anouilh 1946b). Similarly, in 1941's *Eurydice,* the act of living does not affirm the value of existence but rather represents the loss of transcendent simplicity through the compromises entailed in daily life. Happiness becomes an alibi for vulgarity:

> Orphée: Live, live! Like your mother and her lover perhaps, with sweet nothings, with smiles, with forgiveness and then good meals, after which one makes love and everything is in order. Ah no! I love you too much to live. (Anouilh 1942: 468, Act 3)[29]

Tragedy, however, offers a way beyond utilitarian impurity, beyond a happiness that can only be conceived as conformity (Fazia 1969: 29–33). The Dionysian stage serves as an ironic platform for the sublime. Antiquity in this vision becomes a means of simultaneously allegorizing the fallen nature of the present and of dreaming of its transcendence. Antigone's singular act of refusal, her "non" to Creon's offer of life on his terms, is not the defense of an articulated set of beliefs, principles, or commitments; rather it represents the dream of a return to a moment of pre-Oedipal purity, a dream in which the image of Antigone's very antiquity symbolizes a lost childhood of the soul (Vandromme 1972: 61, 95). This is not Caligula's fallen empire, but the vision of a tragic Hellas beyond the dreary compromises of Creon's politics and Rome's depravity.

In fact, Anouilh's *Antigone* was one of various versions of the story, including an adaptation by Thierry Maulnier, that were staged during the war, both in occupied Paris and Vichy. The subject matter was anything but *verboten* and, like neoclassicism in general, was actively promoted by the occupation authorities (Steiner 1984: 147, 192–94;

---

29. See also Anouilh (1942: 465–66, Act 3, and 498–99, Act 4).

Witt 2001: 218–19). Nor did the *Antigone*'s fascist subtext go unnoticed. The clandestine resistance periodical, *Les lettres françaises,* in its review immediately stigmatized Antigone's nihilism as the first step toward fascism, and on this basis it unfavorably compared Anouilh's *Antigone* to Sophocles'. Anouilh's play, however, received generally favorable reviews from the collaborationist press (Witt 2001: 227–28).

The differences between the two plays are in fact anything but trivial, even though on the level of plot the stories are essentially the same. The atmosphere and the stakes, however, are completely different. Where Sophocles' tragedy is characterized by a complex interplay between the individual wills of Antigone and Creon, their traditional obligations to their families, genders, and the *polis,* and their religious obligations to the gods of Olympus and the underworld, Anouilh focuses almost exclusively on questions of the will. The unwritten laws of the gods of the Sophoclean underworld, the original play's air of piety and mystery, are quickly disposed of. In their stead stands Antigone's empty self-assertion, devoid of any communal sacral aura, a denuding which the modern play's systematic anachronism—its allusions to coffee, automobiles, and the working-class status of the guards—only serves to underline (Anouilh 1946a: 137; Grossvogel n.d.: 18, 37n.1; Steiner 1984: 293).

The crucial passage in which this denuding occurs is worth citing at length. In it Creon first demonstrates the absurdity of Antigone's religious and moral pretexts. He then asks why did she really defy his edict. Why did she sneak out in the middle of the night with nothing but a child's toy bucket to scoop a few pitiful handfuls of sand over her brother's rotting corpse? The passage is unparalleled in Sophocles' text. And in many ways her response is typical of the period. If one were to pose the same question to Orestes in *Les mouches,* as he leaves the stage alone, assuming the burden of Argos' guilt unbidden and unaided, abandoned by Electra and the people of Argos—"why did you slay Clytemnestra and Aegisthus, for whom did you do it?"—he almost certainly would have been forced to make the same answer, "Pour personne, pour moi." He did it not for the people of Argos—they didn't want it—but for himself, so he could be free.

> Creon: Do you really believe in this burial according to regulations? In your brother's shade being condemned to wander forever if no one throws a little dirt on the cadaver along with the formula of the priest. Have you already heard them recite it, the priests of Thebes, their formula? Have you seen these poor tired employees abbreviating

their gestures, swallowing their words, doing a slapdash job on one corpse so they can move on to the next before lunch?

Antigone: Yes, I've seen them.

Creon: Haven't you ever thought that if that was someone you truly loved lying in that box you would start to shout immediately? Screaming for them to be quiet, to leave?

Antigone: In fact, I have thought that.

Creon: And now you are risking death because I refused your brother this ridiculous passport, this monotone mumbling over his corpse, this pantomime which you would have been the first to be ashamed of if I would have had it played? It's absurd.

Antigone: Yes, it's absurd.

Creon: Why did you make this gesture then? For others, for those who believe in it? To rouse them against me?

Antigone: No.

Creon: Neither for others, nor for your brother? For whom then?

Antigone: For no one. For me. (Anouilh 1946a: 177–78)

Antigone here lies bare, stripped of all religious, transcendental, or political pretences. Later Creon will even demonstrate that both brothers were traitors who plotted against their father and were little better than common thugs. He doesn't even know which corpse is which. His decree was not based on virtue but raw political expediency (1946a: 187–89; Vandromme 1972: 104–6). Antigone's act, then, was an empty gesture, devoid of positive content, at least as conventionally understood.

Antigone, however, admits the absurdity of her choice, just as Caligula glorifies in his (Curtis 1948: 39; Gignoux 1946: 100–101). In the end, she seeks to fashion an identity out of that absurdity. She does not resign herself to it in the manner of Creon, but rather takes it as the grounds for an aesthetics of existence, in which the embrace of her own emptiness becomes the grounds of her subjectivity (Grossvogel n.d.: 61n.2; Gignoux 1946: 109; McIntyre 1981: 44–45, 53–54). To this extent, her position is no different from that of Sartre and Camus, or for that matter of Lacan in the *Ethics of Psychoanalysis* and of the late Foucault. Hers too is a post-Nietzschean ethics and aesthetics that is beyond good and evil. What is different, however, is precisely her refusal of difference, her worship of purity. This we find in neither Sartre nor Camus, let alone their successors.

Camus's *Caligula,* in fact, is not a tragedy in either the Aristotelian or the Anouilhian sense. It presents neither a single completed action leading to a catharsis of pity and fear, nor a regal sense of pure determination. The emperor's assassination does not lead to the repose that comes from the rejection of "foul hope," but rather constitutes a first and necessary step toward envisioning another kind of life, one that goes beyond, but nonetheless incorporates, the insights produced in Gaius' pedagogy of the absurd. It is the first step toward the resigned stoicism of Tarrou in *La peste,* a chastened philosophy that, while rejecting all knowledge of transcendental values, nonetheless embraces the other and affirms a will to resist the crush of death:

> With time I have simply perceived that even those who were better than others were not able to stop themselves from killing or allowing killing because it was part of the logic in which they lived, and that we weren't able to make a move in this world without risking killing someone. Yes, I've continued to be ashamed, I've learned this, that we're all in the plague, and I've lost my sense of peace. I search for it still today by trying to understand them all and by being nobody's mortal enemy. I know only that it is necessary to do what is necessary to no longer be a carrier of the plague and that in this alone can one hope for peace or, failing that, a good death. (Camus 1962b: 1425)

The Camus of *La peste* accepts the messiness of existence, the necessary heterogeneity that comes with life, without denying the suffering that follows in its wake.

Similarly, *Les mouches* offers not the repose of the classical tragedy of fate, but the unsettledness of human liberty. Orestes may depart alone, but his freedom has been won only by assuming his relation to others and by carrying that responsibility with him. Rather than an ethics of purity, Sartre will embrace the necessity of having dirty hands. Yet as the later play by that same name reveals (*Les mains sales*), the embrace of our obligations to the other, of the political, never relieves us of the weight of the existential choices we must make if we are to assume the burden of authenticity, never replaces our ethical self-relation (Sartre 2005f). Whom we may love, whom we may kill, for what we would choose to die, and for what we would choose to live—these are questions whose burden must always be fully assumed and which can never be answered in principle but only by the irretrievable act. This *is* the tragedy of freedom: it only exists in the fabric of determinations that binds us to the other, that creates us from our own necessary impurities. We fashion ourselves from the very transgressions of our immaculate essence. Thus, in the end, it is only in the recognition of the self's necessary constitution in relation to the other, to history and hence difference, that it is possible to envision a self-fashioning that is not simply a triumph of the will. The creation of that self is predicated, not on the subjugation, but rather on what Lacan will call "the desire of the other."

Antigone's self-fashioning in purity, however, constitutes a pre-Oedipal narcissism that cannot be breached. Like Caligula, she rejects "happiness" and the bourgeois compromises that it implies (Witt 2001: 223):

> Creon: Get married quickly Antigone, be happy. Life is not what you think. It's a water that young people let run through their open fingers without knowing it. Close your hands, close your hands, quickly. Hold on to it. [. . .] You are going to scorn me all the same, but to discover this, you will see, it's the laughable consolation of growing old—life—it is perhaps nothing more than happiness [*le bonheur*].
> Antigone: *murmurs, a confused look.* Happiness . . .
> Creon: *suddenly a bit ashamed.* A poor word isn't it?
> Antigone: *quietly.* What will be my happiness? What happy woman will little Antigone become? What economies will she have to make, day by day, to snatch away in her teeth her little shred of happiness? Tell me to whom will she have to lie, to smile, to sell herself? Who will have to die while she turns away? (Anouilh 1946a: 190–91)

In her world there can be no dirty hands. Antigone demands an absolute purity and will not cede on her desire: "I do not want to be modest and content myself with a small morsel if I behave myself. I want to be sure of everything today and that it should all be as beautiful as when I was little—or I want to die" (1946a: 193).

As in the case of Caligula and Orestes, real, substantial, freedom—as opposed to its pale abstract imitation in a bourgeois philosophy of rational choice, the consumerist calculus of economic man—can only be achieved through the act, through an intervention in the world that does not simply repeat the existing order, and hence has no prior justification in that order (Grossvogel n.d.: 35 n. 3). This is the existential and surrealist *acte gratuit,* every bit as much as it is the fascist embrace of the pure act *en soi* and *pour soi* (Marcel 1959: 103). Anouilh's Antigone, therefore, unlike Sophocles', performs her act for no one and nothing other than herself ("Pour personne. Pour moi."). It is her affirmation of the very absurdity of her act that renders her free while Creon remains a slave to the causal chain of contingency and utility that eludes his control. Antigone puts a stop to this chain through her "non," but Creon, by assenting to the existing order, by saying "oui," will never stop paying, will never remove himself from a system of exchange that always demands more (1946a: 183; Grossvogel n.d.: 21).

Here, then, we see the true function of Anouilh's use of deliberate anachronism throughout the play: his allusions to cars, coffee, and cigarettes; the production in modern dress. Anouilh's *Antigone* takes place beyond history, beyond the accidental determinations of sheer contingency, and so exists in a space where absolute freedom and tragedy can be envisioned and allegorized in the present. The price paid for this purity is a complete severance from history and consequential action. Where Camus in *Caligula* and Sartre in *Les mouches* recognize the price paid for freedom envisioned as the opposite of historical determinism, Anouilh wholeheartedly embraces this severance from history as the predicate of Antigone's aesthetics of existence. Camus and Sartre in their succeeding works continue to search for an authentic mode of action in the world, and so continue to pose explicit problems of ethical agency and political action. Anouilh, however, will seek precisely to remain "un bête du théâtre." Paradoxically, it is his *Antigone* that would have the most immediate effect on the postmodern turn to antiquity: it was impossible for Lacan at the end of the 1950s to pose the problem of the ethics of psychoanalysis, through a reading of Sophocles' *Antigone,* without Anouilh's version haunting the lecture hall as well.

4. Conclusion

In 1959, Jacques Lacan in his seminar would focus his attention on the *Antigone* and the ethics of psychoanalysis. This choice was motivated neither by simple antiquarian curiosity nor Lacan's famed eccentricity. As he points out in his lectures, he is hardly the first to have observed the centrality, from at least the time of Hegel, of Sophocles' tragedy to the ethical tradition in the West. Moreover, ethics in 1950s France was a fraught topic. A formal philosophical ethics was one of Sartre's great unfinished projects, and in time became intimately associated with the latter's increasingly close relationship with Marxism and the Parti Communiste Français. Moreover, the larger question of what one owes oneself and what one owes others could not be broached in postwar France without also broaching the less abstract questions of one's relation to the resistance and the occupation during the war. The question of the resistance, in turn, also necessarily brought into play one's relation to the Parti Communiste, which had played a leading role, and therefore to both Marxism and Stalinism. The choice to read *Antigone*, then, with Anouilh's play as well as the struggle to claim it for both the resistance and the collaborationists still fresh in mind, was in no way an innocent one.

Lacan, of course, does not baldly pose his question in terms of collaboration versus resistance, ideology versus authenticity, or Marxism versus fascism versus Gaullist nationalism. He asks instead, How can the subject pursue a good that is not simply a reproduction of the assumed range of goods sanctioned by the dominant ideology and therefore not an ethical choice at all, but a species of quietism and conformism? How can the subject pursue an object of desire, which is not recognized by society's Symbolic norms, and hence beyond the economic calculations entailed by a strict adherence to the pleasure principle? In the process of posing these questions to the *Antigone*, he offers his own original reading of not only the play, but also of the good and its relation to beauty, thereby providing a forceful if largely oblique rebuttal to Anouilh through Sophocles. That rebuttal, in turn, takes a stand on the same ground as Orestes in *Les mouches* against the sensual cathexes of fear and bad faith that lead us ever to cede on our desire, without, however, Lacan's endorsing Sartre's ontology of the subject.

Indeed, for Lacan these questions of the subject, of the act, and of the beautiful can never be posed in the abstract or by themselves. They always necessarily entail the problematic of desire, and desire for Lacan, as we shall see, can be conceived only in terms of the subject's relation to language, the Other, and the Real. In short, it is always already deeply intersubjective and social. My desire is necessarily the desire of the Other in both the subjective and the objective sense of the genitive. I desire both the Other and what the Other desires. I desire to be its desire. Thus the problem of ethics, as one of the desire for the good (*le bien*), can never be posed in abstraction from the pre-existing, historically determined set of obligations and expectations that define our relation to the Other and hence our desire for the Other. This interrogation of the constitution of our desire as the desire of the Other is in turn precisely the subject of Lacan's eighth seminar, *Le transfert* or *Transference*, on his reading of the *Symposium*. It is this interrogation, moreover, that fundamentally distinguishes the ethics of psychoanalysis from the final emptiness of Orestes in *Les mouches,* the murderous absurdity of Caligula, or the blind self-assertion of Anouilh's Antigone. In the seminar on transference, the fundamental psychoanalytic relationship between analyst and analysand is reread in terms of that between Socrates and Alcibiades. The Platonic process of dialogue, self-testing (*elenchus*), and clarification as to the true nature of the object of our desire becomes the model for a psychoanalytic practice in which the ethics of not ceding on one's desire becomes part of the larger set of relations between self and other, without which desire itself could not exist.

There is, in sum, a distinct difference between the modernist and the postmodern approach to antiquity, as exemplified in the different ways Lacan and Anouilh approach the *Antigone.* Yet the basic problem of how to formulate an ethics remains markedly similar: how does one fashion a relation of the self to itself, and so to others, that is neither a mere repetition of the dominant ideology, and hence an act of bad faith, or a cruel assertion of its impossibility. The post-Nietzschean, post-Marxian, and post-Heideggerian world of the existentialists on this level remains in many ways that of the poststructuralists as well. The answer for Lacan and for those who come after is not simply a return to antiquity, but a reading of antiquity as the intimate other, as that which structures our self-relation without ever being identical to it.

Central to this Lacanian endeavor is the turn to Plato and the focus on the Socratic form of question and response, proof and refutation, dialogue and desire. By the same token, it is precisely through his readings of the *Phaedrus* and the *Philebus* that Derrida, in turn, will make his response to Lacan and to the larger problem of the subject and its status in the history of western metaphysics. Lastly, it is the question of the relation of ethics to knowledge, to desire, and to the form of the dialogue that will structure Foucault's own analysis of the *Symposium,* the *Alcibiades,* and Plato's seventh letter, and hence his rejoinder, through these analyses, to both Lacan and Derrida.

There are, *in fine,* a series of definite, if complex and overdetermined, genealogical relations that can be traced from the concerns of the neoclassical tragic stage of Paris in the forties to the lectures given by Foucault at the Collège de France in the early 1980s. Those relations, however indirect they may be, pass explicitly through Lacan and Derrida. It will be the work of the rest of this book to make those relations as clear as possible, without reducing their complexity, and thus to define the central importance of antiquity in general and Plato in particular for understanding postmodern French thought.

Chapter 3

Historicizing Transcendence

Antigone, *the Good,*
and the Ethics of Psychoanalysis

If Aristotelian philosophy is difficult for us to conceive, it is because it has to be thought in a manner that never omits that matter is eternal, and that nothing is produced from nothing. On account of this, it remains stuck in an image of the world that has never permitted even an Aristotle—it is however difficult to imagine a more powerful mind in the entire history of human thought—to escape the enclosure that the celestial surface presented to his eyes, and not to consider the world—even the world of human relations, the world of language—as included in eternal nature, which is by definition limited. (Lacan 1986: 146)

Lacan rejects Anouilh's portrayal of Antigone as a "little fascist" hellbent on annihilating everything in her path. What he opposed is not the thesis that her deed destroys, but that it is conducted out of a pure will to destruction, for such a characterization overlooks the affirmation and the satisfaction from which her act derives its unstoppable force. (Copjec 2002: 41)

JACQUES Lacan is chronologically the first of the thinkers labeled poststructuralist. His seminars, begun in the 1950s, drew up to eight hundred people and influenced all the major thinkers of the 1960s, 1970s, and 1980s in France. One could agree or disagree with him, accept or reject his teaching, but one could not ignore his provocative rereadings of both the classics of western culture in terms of psychoanalysis and of Freud in terms of the history of literature, philosophy, and art.[1] Indeed, Lacan revolutionized the practice of psychoanalysis in France by reading Freud's corpus not as a manual of interpretation that provided potted answers to pre-existing questions[2] but as a grammar

---

1. On the influence of the seminars, see Schneiderman (1983: 28–30); on his multifaceted involvement with the major intellectual figures of the century, see Ragland-Sullivan (1986: 87, 91) and Roudinesco (1997: 31, 98–101).

2. Such an apriori style of interpretation is the problem with the psychoanalytic investigations examined by Lloyd-Jones (1985+) in his dismissive account of psychoanalysis's relation to classical studies. Lloyd-Jones is u+naware of Lacan's work.

Vernant and Vidal-Naquet's claim that psychoanalysis has made no contribution to the understanding of ancient tragedy (1981: 63–86), likewise fails to engage Lacan's reading

that made it possible to begin decoding the rhetoric of desire. Lacan was the first to apply the findings of linguistics to the study of psychoanalysis, and there was from the beginning a strong affinity between his work and philology. As Jean-Michel Rabaté observes, "Lacan not only stood out among his immediate contemporaries and colleagues in psychiatry as a philosopher who could read Greek and German fluently and who put to good use his knowledge of the classics, but also as someone who had the nerve and ambition to 're-found' a whole field" (2003a: 12).[3] For Lacan the study of the classics was never a mere

---

of the *Antigone*, though neither writer could have been unaware of the seminar, although it had been not been published at the time. Again, they are reacting to an article published by Didier Anzieu in Sartre's *Les temps modernes* (1966) that pursued a more traditional typological interpretation. For a fascinating discussion of the political motivations behind this assault, see Leonard on Vernant, Lacan, and Irigaray (2003). She also has important remarks to make on Lacan's disturbing suggestion that the incestuous desires voiced in the play can all be traced to Jocasta.

3. Lacan was also fluent in Latin, but this was common for anyone of his generation who had received a traditional education. He speaks knowledgeably of Ovid and does not hesitate to assign Cicero's *De natura deorum* to his auditors. He also shows clear knowledge and a lively appreciation of Wilamowitz (Lacan 1986: 183; 1991: 76, 191; Rabaté 2003b: xix).

There remain, nonetheless, disputes about just how good Lacan's Greek was. These often involve polemics with Lacan's literary executor and son-in-law, Jacques Alain Miller, who has vigorously prosecuted anyone who has sought to bring out alternative versions of the Seminars. It is thus often difficult to tell where the blame lies for mistakes in the Greek, with Lacan or his editor, since the original stenographic transcriptions of the seminars are unavailable for consultation and transcriptions of unauthorized recordings and personal notes are seized and destroyed as soon as they are published. Nonetheless, in their zeal justly to admonish Miller for his highhandedness, critics sometimes overstate the seriousness of the difficulties. See Roudinesco (1997: 423–24):

> When Miller published *Seminar VII (The Ethics of Psychoanalysis)* in the autumn of 1986, no one attacked him. His adversaries, stunned by the legal defeat of [an unauthorized seminar] preferred to remain silent for the moment. But this seminar was more defective than the preceding ones. Miller had probably foreseen the danger, for he had sought assistance from several people: Judith Miller had helped with the Greek references; he had turned to Franz Kaltenbeck for the German quotations. Three academics had done some research, and several friends had corrected the proofs. . . . He sent a copy of the book to Pierre Vidal-Naquet, with a dedication reading "To Moniseur Pierre Vidal-Naquet, who may wish to read the three lectures on 'Antigone,' this book, which would certainly have been sent to him by Jacques Lacan." Vidal-Naquet at once began to read the magnificent chapter on Antigone, and was taken aback to find at least two mistakes on every page. Not a single Greek term was correct, several quotations were wrong, there were many misprints, and none of Lacan's own serious mistakes had been spotted.

It is true that one can find numerous errors in the Greek, but it is certainly an exaggeration to say that not a single term is correct. While Miller clearly did not do Lacan a service by not having the Greek checked by a better-trained philologist (and one who

ornament, nor even a rhetorical field in which he hoped to find the master tropes of his discourse, but always, and very precisely, the genealogical ground on which he sought to refound psychoanalysis. The return to Freud (1966c) sought not to found a series of timeless truths, but the historical ground on which the present was constructed and by which it could thereby be deconstructed. It sought to "re-found" the subject in relation to the discrete forms of meaning that structured its desire. It is paradigmatic of Lacan's profound engagement with Greco-Roman antiquity, therefore, that in 1959, when searching for a model of pure desire for his seventh seminar, on *The Ethics of Psychoanalysis,* he chose as his model Sophocles' *Antigone.*

Lacan's reading of the tragedy represents the climax of a three-year engagement with the genre that had begun the year before with a reading of *Hamlet,* and would draw to a close the following year with an examination of Claudel's Coûfontaine trilogy (Leonard 2005: 109). Throughout this period there are also abundant references to the *Oedipus Tyrannos* and the *Oedipus at Colonus.* Nonetheless, it is the reading of Antigone as one who does not cede on her desire that is justly considered a masterpiece in psychoanalytic circles (Leonard 2005: 112; Loraux 2002: vii–xiv; Zupancic 2000: 174).

> Antigone presents herself as *autonomos,* the pure and simple relationship of a human being to that which it miraculously finds itself carrying, that is the rupture of signification, that which grants a person the insuperable power of being—in spite of and against

---

was not intimidated by Miller's ruthless manner of dealing with dissent), most of the errors are minor and involve issues such as misplaced accents or clear typographical errors (see 1986: 366). These problems can be annoying but seldom affect the basic value of Lacan's insights.

As for Lacan's "serious" mistakes, unfortunately Roudinesco does not provide a list. While not systematically seeking to catalog them, I have observed the following errata. Lacan's paraphrase of *Poetics* chapter 6 (1449b), *di' eleou kai phobou perainousa tên toioutôn pathêmatôn katharsin* ("accomplishing through pity and fear the purgation of such emotions") as "par l'intermédiaire de la pitié et de la crainte, nous somme purgés, purifiés de tout ce qui est de cet ordre-là," is perhaps tendentious (1986: 290). Lacan claims *atê* occurs twenty times in *Antigone,* when in fact it appears a mere fourteen times (1986: 305). He translates *ekhthra* (94) "inimité," rather than *ennemi* (1986: 306). More seriously, he attributes the chorus's description of Eros as *enargês blepharôn himeros eulektrou numphas* ("radiant desire from the eyelids of the well-bedded bride") (795–96) to Antigone, who enters only after the third stasimon is finished (1986: 327). It is true that Antigone will later be described as the bride of Hades, but in the current context the chorus's words constitute more an ironic juxtaposition than a direct description. None of these flaws, however, detract from the baseline value of Lacan's interpretation and can for the most part be easily accounted for by the routine imprecisions that occur in the course of oral teaching. It is important to remember that Lacan himself never prepared this seminar for publication.

everything—what he [*sic*] is. . . . Antigone all but fulfills what can be called pure desire, the pure and simple desire of death as such [i.e., of that which is beyond the pleasure principle]. She incarnates this desire. (1986: 328–29)[4]

Lacan's commentary on the *Antigone,* unfortunately, is not well known to English-speaking classicists. His allusive and convoluted style has proven a significant barrier to the dissemination of his work in the classics community, while his close readings of canonical texts have failed to appeal to many of his less learned, postmodern successors.

The following year, Lacan's seminar focused on Plato's *Symposium*. Socrates, like Antigone, represents for Lacan a kind of purity that exceeds the bounds of communally acknowledged goods. His *atopia,* as Alcibiades terms it (215a2), places him beyond the bounds of the order defined by the Athenian *polis,* and that singularity in turn is the basis of his purity (Lacan 1991: 18–19, 126–27; 1973: 287).[5] Thus, in the wake of his encounter with the *Antigone,* Lacan turned to Socrates and the *Symposium* to find a model for elaborating a theory of love as a response to the fundamental lack in our being that Freudian theory sees as the root of human desire.

The two seminars are widely acknowledged to form a pair (Leonard 2005: 167), and both Lacan's ethics and his reading of the *Symposium* became touchstones in later postmodernist debates. More often than not, these texts are uncited, but Derrida, Kristeva, Irigaray, and Foucault all respond to these seminal readings. The seminar on transference, as we shall see, grows directly out of the concerns broached in the ethics. Where the seminar on the ethics asks most fundamentally: What do we owe our desire? that on transference asks: What do we owe the other as both the cause and the object of that desire? The next two chapters, thus, constitute a continuous argument and were originally conceived as one. They have been divided for purposes of clarity and to simplify the exposition. Nonetheless, it is our contention that it is the *Antigone* that leads Lacan to Plato, and it is through Plato and the problem of ethics that Derrida and Foucault will respond to Lacan.

---

4. See also Moi (2002: 101): "If we accept that the end of desire is the logical consequence of satisfaction (if we are satisfied, we are in a position where we desire no more), we can see why Freud in *Beyond the Pleasure Principle,* posits death as the ultimate object of desire—as Nirvana or the recapturing of the lost unity, the final healing of the split subject."

5. On *atopia* as a trope in ancient philosophy, see Davidson (1995: 23) and Hadot (1987: 205; 1995b: 57).

The fact is that neither Lacan's work nor his subsequent influence can be fully appreciated without a sustained encounter with the works of antiquity that formed for him a constant point of reference. His concept of desire finds its roots in the Platonic corpus. His work on both love and transference, as Micaela Janan indicates, draws heavily on the *Symposium* and the *Phaedrus* (1994: 7–21, 144), and the Platonic concept of love as the effort to return to a lost—but somehow dimly remembered—unity figures prominently in much of his later work.[6] In fact, Lacan's conception of psychoanalysis is inseparable from his profound engagement with the language, history, and interpretation of the founding texts of western thought (Lacan 1986: 21). His much-vaunted return to Freud is also a return to the roots of Freudian thought. "Psychoanalytic theory, in order to be truly responsible for its concepts must account for its own historical emergence as it seeks to articulate its place in relation to the philosophical tradition which it inevitably inherits" (Shepherdson 2003: 117). In short, antiquity in Lacan's texts, unlike in the dramas of the great modernists, functions not as an allegory of, but as a critique and challenge, to the present. It demands that we account for the history of both our science and our selves.

Lacan's reading of Sophocles' *Antigone*, therefore, although on one level clearly a response to Anouilh's, never directly engages it. Rather, Lacan, with no small irony, observes that if, as Erwin Rhode claims, tragedians must pick a mythic subject yet portray it in a fashion consonant with the conflicts and prejudices of the present day, then Anouilh was correct to give us "his little fascist Antigone" (1986: 293).

There are, unsurprisingly, resemblances between Anouilh's Antigone and that of Lacan. Both reject bourgeois "happiness" and oppose to it a concept of purity and anarchic transformative desire. Both show the influence of Nietzsche's *Birth of Tragedy*, with Antigone associated with Dionysian transgression and Creon with Apollonian order. For Lacan, Antigone's choice, her desire, is pure precisely to the degree that it rejects all claims of the Other to dictate its objects or form. For Anouilh, that same alien otherness represents the mediocrity and alienation of the contemporary world.

So far, Lacan's Antigone is little different from her predecessor. But desire in Lacan can never be separate from the signifying chain of which it is both a part and a deviation (1991: 201–2; 1986: 143, 340). Antigone's desire can only be pure in relation to a historically specifiable

---

6. Lacan (1973: 119; 1975: 67–68; 1986: 341); Julien (1990: 112, 186); Janan (1994: 27); Halperin (1994: 48).

set of circumstances. It is embedded in the discursive possibilities of the moment. Tragic beauty for Lacan does not reflect but transcends the present. Antigone's negation is not made in the name of abstract purity or empty self-assertion, as in the case of Anouilh, but in the name of specific and determined claims of flesh and blood that are rooted in the grammatical and ideological structures of fifth-century Athens. The affirmation of her desire cannot be separated from the tragic fate of the Labdacids. She is the bride of Hades who will lie with her brother.

Anouilh's Antigone, however, defies Creon in the end "pour personne, pour moi." Hers is an egoistic desire that seeks personal transcendence of bourgeois morality, where Lacan's reading of Sophocles' *Antigone* detects an antihumanism that ultimately demands a transcendence of the structures of the ego per se (Lacan 1986: 319–22). For Lacan, Antigone represents an ethical model, a model of ideal subject formation, precisely to the degree that she is presented as one who rejects the good as understood by the dominant mode of the Symbolic embodied in Creon's decrees, i.e., by the law of the present. Her negation only makes sense in relation to Creon's concrete positivity, not some abstract principle of transcendence.

In the end, *Antigone* needs to be studied, Lacan claims, precisely because of what the play is: one of the central points in the western tradition of ethical and moral discourse. We cannot think about the choice of the good without thinking about Antigone and her choice of death, her "non," whether we know it or not (Lacan 1986: 285, 330; Žižek 1992: 77). In the same manner, we cannot understand the nature of our desire and the desire it provokes in others, without undertaking a reading of the *Symposium*. The transcendence, the *dépassement*, of our present impasse that psychoanalysis proposes is always anchored within the signifying chain out of which our collective discourse is fashioned.

1. Ethics, Beauty, and Transformation

> It is clear, I think, to all that what I am showing you here this year is able to be situated between Freudian ethics and aesthetics. (Lacan 1986: 190)

> There is no history without an internal limit within history itself, without an irreducible element, a negation that forbids the emergence of an outside of history. Again, this negation is able to be designated by its Lacanian name: the real. There is no arguing with the real, no negating it, since history depends on it. It is precisely because it cannot be negated that we

say it eternally returns or repeats [. . .]. Referring to the real as empty, Lacan underscores this fact that what returns is nothing but the negation that prohibits any exception to history (Copjec 2002: 96)

Lacan's choice of Antigone as his model for elaborating an ethics of pure desire is in fact variously motivated. First, there is the wish to respond to Anouilh. Second, there is the obvious interest of all facets of the Oedipus myth for psychoanalysis. Third, there is the centrality of Antigone to post-Hegelian reflection on the nature and foundation of our ethical substance. Fourth, there is the fundamental relationship that Lacan observes between the Freudian concept of catharsis and its Aristotelian precursor in the *Poetics*. Tragedy in general, therefore, and the *Antigone* in particular, Lacan argues, must occupy a central place in any satisfying psychoanalytic account of culture and ethics.

Accordingly, Lacan begins his commentary on the *Antigone* with an explication of catharsis as defined by the Stagirite.[7] The purgation of pity and fear, he notes, does not merely posit the representation of such emotions. Indeed, as he observes, Antigone herself exhibits neither. But rather the phenomenon of catharsis evokes the existence of a position that transcends both pity and fear, "a beyond of" conventional categories of emotion, which he in turn links with Antigone's unconditional pursuit of an object of desire that in itself is beyond the bounds of a normative or utilitarian reason (Lacan 1986: 285–90, 300, 372; Julien 1990: 112; Armstrong 2005: 270–71).[8]

Lacan, moreover, frames the whole of his investigation of the ethics of psychoanalysis and of the *Antigone* with a series of trenchant comments on the *Nicomachean Ethics,* which he admonishes his audience to read from end to end (1986: 30). The next year he would qualify this same work as a decisive step in the development of western ethical thought (1991: 14). One should not overinterpret these remarks, however. Lacan is anything but a strict Aristotelian. Aristotle's ethics, he contends, represent a practice of the self based on the reasoned pursuit of communally acknowledged goods in conformity with the reality principle. It seeks happiness in the context of what Lacan, and later Foucault, would label an ethos of mastery that was inextricably bound

---

7. The most commonly cited name in all of Lacan's seminars is Aristotle, followed by Descartes, Hegel, and Socrates. Sartre and St. Augustine also make notable appearances (Roazen 2000: 59). See also Rabaté (2003c: xiv).

 8. In *Rhetoric* 2.8, 1386a Aristotle indicates that pity and fear are mutually exclusive emotions. Tragedy thus creates a virtual space in which the impossible can be evoked and purged.

to the subject position of members of the Greek ruling class. For Lacan, Aristotelian ethics were concerned with the problematics of knowledge (*epistêmê*) and right discourse (*orthos logos*), not desire (*erôs, epithumia*) (1986: 13–14, 30–39, 338–39, 363; Buci-Glucksmann 1992: 365–67; compare Vlastos 1991: 205–6). As such, they were ultimately ill suited to provide an ethics of psychoanalysis, which is predicated on the ineradicably individual desire of each analyst's and analysand's encounter with the collective structures of language, kinship, and law. It is in this context that, after examining the alternative models of Kant and Sade, Lacan will offer *Antigone* as his paradigm for an ethics of self-transformation that transcends the historically and politically ordered realm of the pleasure principle, an ethics that thereby reveals the limits of any socially constituted notion of the good (Lacan 1986: 281; Julien 1990: 109). He will follow this the next year with a direct examination of the role the desire of the analyst plays in the analytic situation when he reads Plato's *Symposium* at the beginning of the seminar on transference, *Le transfert*. Thus in response to what he sees as an Aristotelian ethics of recognized goods, Lacan responds with an ethics of desire and self-transformation grounded in a reading of Sophocles and Plato in a psychoanalytic context.

For Lacan ethics is not a matter of virtue, self-improvement, or the pursuit of happiness, as found in the most common reading of Aristotle's ethics of *eudaimonia*.[9] For Aristotle, as Julia Annas notes, the end of every intentional act is the good and the final good is happiness, which, though it does not imply a rejection of necessary sacrifice or pain, does require an overall positive evaluation of one's life and material situation (Annas 1993: 30, 35–36, 38, 46, 367–68). To see happiness as Antigone's goal, even when most broadly construed, would be to strain normal usage to the breaking point. This is a view that is very difficult to square with Antigone's choice of deliberate death, whether in Sophocles' text or Anouilh's.[10] Ismene's combination of principled

---

9. For a more open-ended and dialectical approach, although certainly not a Lacanian one, see Frank (2005).

10. There is one interesting exception. Aristotle's discussion of the great-souled man or *megalopsychos* allows for someone who would not make pragmatic concessions, even at the risk of his own life, but would consider honor the supreme good:

> If, then, he deserves and claims great things, and above all the greatest things, he will be concerned with one thing in particular. Desert is relative to external goods; and the greatest of these, we should say, is that which we render to the gods, and which people of position most aim at, and which is the prize appointed for the noblest deeds; and this is honour; that surely is the greatest of external goods. Honours and dishonours, therefore, are the

resistance and pragmatic calculation seems much closer to the mark (Annas 1993: 96; Frank 2006; Goldhill 2006).

Of course, even from a Lacanian perspective, happiness, virtue, and self-improvement are not evils. But, unlike conventional psychotherapy, they are not the goal of analysis. They do not entail the fundamental self-transcendence and conversion that lie at the heart of the psychoanalytic cure (Copjec 2002: 44). The end of analysis is not to produce the "normalized," "well-adjusted" individual of late capitalist society, nor to overcome the analysand's resistances to the analyst's interpretations (Schneiderman 1983: 94). These are merely instances of countertransference and the imposition of the analyst's desire as a sovereign good with which the patient must identify (Lacan 1973: 176–77). Rather the end of analysis is just the opposite. It is to reveal the factitious nature of our Imaginary identifications, to disclose our subordination to, and acceptance of, relations of domination through our identification with certain images of existence, which are projected by the ruling instances of power in our personal and social lives, and with the illusory promises of satisfaction they offer. Analysis does not reveal the truth of a traumatic past (primal scenes, bad mothering, absent fathers) but the nature of our finitude. The realization of our desire, which analysis seeks to offer, is, therefore, a traversing of our fantasy constructions of a stable identity that itself would represent and reflect the desire of the Other ("if only I would just do X, then I would be loved by my spouse, my parents, my country, my god, etc."). As a consequence, this realization of desire represents a confrontation with our mortality and the Lacanian Real, the internal limit that guarantees the historicity and hence ultimately fictitious or "made" nature of all forms of Imaginary or Symbolic (i.e., coded, linguistic, socially constructed) identity (Lacan 1986: 351; Freiberger 2000: 225–26, 237–38; Luepnitz 2003: 232).[11]

---

    objects with respect to which the [*megalopsychos*] is as he should be. And even apart from argument it is with honour that [*megalopsychoi*] appear to be concerned; for it is honour that they chiefly claim, but in accordance with their deserts. (*Nichomachean Ethics* 1123b 15–24; Ross: 2001: 991–92)

The prime examples of great-souled men are precisely the heroes of epic to whom Antigone compares herself, but as the examples of Ajax and Achilles demonstrate their single-minded devotion to public virtue and honor can be a double-edged sword (Annas 1993: 116–17).

    11. Every formation of the Symbolic is unique, as is every point of insertion in it, and thus every relationship to its beyond (Ragland-Sullivan 1986: 230–31, 299–305; Clément 1975: 16). The Imaginary, the Symbolic, and the Real are not reified things, but a set of logical relations presumed by the existence of the speaking subject (Julien 1990: 213–14). The speaking subject only exists to the extent that it exists in language—defined as the total set of codes and syntagmatic relations that make articulated meaning possible—that

It is for this reason that Antigone comes to function as the ethical model. As Joan Copjec observes:

> Antigone's *Haftbarkeit*, her perseverance to the end or to the momentous conclusion of an act that will necessarily overturn her, is contrasted to the *Fixierarbeit* of Creon as conversion, or self-rupture to modern progress. This contrast lets us observe the difference between "acting in conformity with the real of desire" and acting in a self-interested way to preserve one's own continuity with oneself. The principle of *Fixierarbeit* is articulated by Lacan as: "Carry on working. Work must go on. . . . As far as desires are concerned come back later. Make them wait" (S VII: 315). *Work* here signifies something different, something opposed to the act insofar as work never concludes, it keeps going—or rather waiting. (2002: 45)

The ethical imperative, then, is to insist on desire even beyond the realm of goods, of *biens,* inscribed within the pleasure principle defined by bourgeois reality (Zupancic 2003: 179): for the realm of goods is not that of use, but exchange value. Freedom for it is defined by the ability to dispose of one's goods as one wishes and this includes the good that is the self. The realm of goods is the realm of the commodified self of social exchange. It is for this reason that Lacan says, "Le domaine du bien est la naissance du pouvoir" ("The domain of the good is the birth of power"), punning on the notion of the good as an ethical substance and as a commodity in social-symbolic exchange relations. The ethics of psychoanalysis, as modeled by Antigone, are beyond "the good" and hence also beyond evil every bit as much as they were for Sartre's Orestes and Camus's Caligula (Lacan 1986: 269–70; Žižek 1992: 77–78; Zupancic 2003: 175–76).

Ethical action, therefore, does not simply reproduce society's founding assumptions and our imaginary identification with those assumptions (Althusser 1971; Žižek 1992:12; Dowling 1984: 82–83). True ethical and moral action is creative. It introduces something fundamen-

---

is to say to the extent that it exists in the Symbolic (Althusser 1996: 72; Julien 1990 176; Moxey 1991: 990). It is only a subject to the extent that it can project an image of itself, by means of which it can come to identify with the meanings into which it is born: this realm of projection and identification is the Imaginary (Julien 1990: 48–49; Roudinesco 1997: 216). And finally that subject is finite only to the extent that neither its self-projection nor the codes against which it projects itself constitute the sum total of existence, that is to say, to the extent that the Real exists as that which is beyond the Imaginary and the Symbolic (Ragland-Sullivan 1986: 188; Lacan 1975: 85). No one of these logical relations, however, has any necessary or prescribed content in and of itself (Lacan, 1986: 114–19, 128–29).

tally new into the Real. It creates a space for our existence. The role of analysis is to make this act possible, not to make us comfortable with what already exists (Lacan 1986: 30). On this level, it is Oedipus himself in his self-inflicted blindness that can serve as our model:

> He does not know that in attaining happiness [*le bonheur*], conjugal happiness and that of his profession as king, as the guide of a happy city, he is sleeping with his mother. The question can be asked: what does this treatment that he inflicts upon himself signify? What treatment? He renounces that which held him captive. In truth, he was conned, duped, by his very access to happiness. Beyond the providing of goods and services [*service des biens*], beyond even his complete success in providing these, he enters the zone in which he searches for his desire. (Lacan 1986: 352)

And it is here that we find Lacan's ultimate objection to Aristotle: for Lacan the realization of desire can only be attained as an act of creation *ex nihilo*. It represents a fundamental transcendence of (and through) the given, which, as Lacan understands it, is a logical impossibility from an Aristotelian perspective.

> If Aristotelian philosophy is difficult for us to conceive, it is because it has to be thought in a manner that never omits that matter is eternal, and that nothing is produced from nothing. On account of this, it remains stuck in an image of the world that has never permitted even an Aristotle [. . .] to escape the enclosure that the celestial surface presented to his eyes, and not to consider the world [. . .] as included in eternal nature, which is by definition limited. (Lacan 1986: 146)

It is for this reason that Lacan will ultimately turn to Plato instead (Lacan 1991: 13; Zupancic 2003: 184): for, as we shall see when we examine Lacan's reading of the *Symposium* in chapter 4, the Platonic pursuit of the lost object, the Socratic *agalma,* is precisely a pursuit of what is not there. Hence, as Alcibiades learns to his discomfort, the dialectic of desire leads ultimately to a confrontation with the lack, the nothingness, at the heart of our being *(manque à l'être),* from which the object of that desire is created.[12]

---

12. Sartre had contended that it is this lack at the heart of being which propels us forward in the project of our existence (1943: 624–25). Such a vocabulary is central to post-Freudian analysis as well, as is exemplified in Lacan's deliberate echoing of Sartre's

This created object of desire or *agalma* that structures our existence is termed the sublime object and as such is the ground for the rapprochement between ethics and aesthetics cited by Lacan in the headnote to this section (Silverman 2000: 45).[13] The sublime object, to which, according to the seminar on the *Antigone,* the phenomenon of beauty[14] is intrinsically related, is that which is raised to the level of the Thing (Lacan 1986: 133). The Thing, here, refers to a concept first outlined by Lacan in this same seminar, *das Ding.* It is the ground of our being that is beyond Symbolic determinations and Imaginary identifications (Lacan 1986: 67). *Das Ding* is, then, the pre-object and, according to Lacan, it is the true object of Antigone's desire. It is that piece of the Real that is both in us and beyond us and therefore is the ground of our desire (Silverman 2000: 16; Žižek 1989: 208–9; 1991: 169). The Beautiful and the Sublime, then, become two aspects of the same Thing: the first representing the beyond of representation and the second representing the impossibility of that representation:

---

terminology (Lacan 1986: 229; 1973: 341; Ragland-Sullivan 1986: 43), and their common Hegelian and Heideggerian heritage (Butler 1999). But where for Sartre this lack at the heart of being is ontological, for post-Freudian analysis it is a fact of language: our lack is an effect of the castration we suffer upon entrance into the world of the Symbolic, that is of the a priori renunciation of plenitude all human beings undergo when we enter into the world of difference that makes articulated thought, and thus subjectivity, possible (Kristeva 1979: 11; Moi 2002: 99–100; Žižek 1992: 270). It is for this reason, I would argue, that post-Freudian psychoanalysis escapes the Sartrean strictures on the logical impossibility of repression. So long as the unconscious is seen as a substance in which ideas arise and are censored before they can come to consciousness, then the only way they can be censored is if they are already fully formed and known to exist by the subject. The subject thus becomes split against itself and can only engage in repression through a deliberate, knowing act of bad faith (1943: 85–90, 616–23). Such objections, however, hold no purchase on a conception of the unconscious as an effect of language. In the post-Freudian view, the unconscious is not a seething pit within, but precisely that portion of enjoyment that haunts the institution of the subject itself. It is the voice of the Other, i.e., the meanings and significations that constitute our unique subject positions in relation to the pre-existing world and thus escape our conscious control even as they are the fabric out of which consciousness itself is made (Lacan 1986: 42; 1973: 142, 167; Žižek in Hanlon 2001: 842; Ragland-Sullivan 1986: 221).

13. Interestingly, this is one of the areas of similarity between Aristotle's and Lacan's ethics. Aristotle describes virtuous action as being done for its own sake, because it is *kalon* or "fine, noble." One common translation of *to kalon*, however, especially in Plato, is "the beautiful" (*Nicomachean Ethics* 1115b11–24, 1116a 11, 1120a: 23–24; Annas 1993: 123, 370). Lacan's and Foucault's visions of ethics as a species of the aesthetics of existence, thus, has deep ancient roots.

14. Lacan thus collapses Kant's categories of the beautiful and the sublime, but as Sussman (1993: 36) points out, beauty in Kant is a "way-station between pure reason and the sublime." It presents the antinomies of pure reason: demanding the particular be apprehended within the universal, while maintaining its particularity. See also Sussman (1993: 28–29)

> Although the suprasensible Idea/Thing cannot be represented in a direct, immediate way, one can represent the Idea "symbolically," in the guise of beauty (in other words, the beautiful is a way to represent to ourselves "analogically" the good in the phenomenal world); what the chaotic shapelessness of the sublime phenomena renders visible, on the contrary, is the very impossibility of representing the suprasensible Idea/Thing. (Žižek 1992: 164)

The sublime object is not that which is caught up in the endless substitutions of Symbolically regulated exchange, but that which occupies a place beyond the quotidian satisfactions of the pleasure and reality principles (Lacan 1986: 131). This is also, as we shall see in the case of the *Antigone,* the place of death.

Freud defines the pleasure principle in his *Beyond the Pleasure Principle* (1961a) as one of the self-preservative or ego instincts. The reality principle is its reflex and represents our socially constructed picture of the world that places limits on our pursuit of pleasure so as to avoid unpleasure. The reality principle is, then, not beyond the pleasure principle but a direct outgrowth of it. It is a set of norms, codes, representations, and rules of conduct that are an immediate product of the Symbolic, Lacan's term for the world of regulated signifying practices (Lacan 1986: 42–43). Yet, the pleasure and reality principles are not all. Their attempt to constitute a closed totality always produces an inassimilable remainder. Freud's argument is founded on concrete observations of the repetition compulsions of traumatized World War I veterans and other examples taken from his case histories. Here he detected the existence of a drive for a kind of satisfaction that cannot be accounted for by our daily seeking of immediate pleasures or by the fact of our settling for the kind of substitute satisfactions the reality principle offers in their stead. This drive represents the search for an absolute, pure satisfaction that transcends the very bounds of our identity and threatens it with destruction (Eagleton 2003: 213; Žižek 1992: 48). Freud would eventually label it the death drive or Thanatos, as opposed to the pleasure principle or Eros.[15]

The sublime object is thus not that which is searched for within the existing protocols of knowledge (i.e., the reality principle), but that which is "found" or "created" while nonetheless inhering in the

---

15. It is Lacan's acceptance of the death drive that most decisively separates him from American psychoanalysis (Schneiderman 1983: 52–53).

Symbolic as a necessary moment of its own self-betrayal. It is worth quoting from the *Seminar* at some length on this difficult point:

> We come once again upon a fundamental structure, which allows us to articulate the fact that the Thing in question is, by virtue of its structure, open to being represented by what I called earlier ... the Other thing.
>
> And that is the second characteristic of the Thing as veiled; it is by nature in the finding of the object, represented by something else.
>
> You cannot fail to see that in the celebrated expression of Picasso, "I do not seek, I find," that it is the finding [*trouver*], the *trobar* of the Provençal troubadours and the *trouvères,* and of all the schools of rhetoric, that takes precedence over the seeking.
>
> Obviously, what is found is sought, but sought in the paths of the signifier. Now the search is in a way an antipsychic search that by its place and function is beyond the pleasure principle. For according to the laws of the pleasure principle, the signifier projects into this beyond equalization, homeostasis, and the tendency to the uniform investment of the system of the self as such; it provokes its failure. The function of the pleasure principle is, in effect, to lead the subject from signifier to signifier, by generating as many signifiers as are required to maintain at as low a level as possible the tension that regulates the whole functioning of the psychic apparatus. (Lacan 1986: 143)[16]

The repetitive structure of most TV series offers a great example of what Lacan means by "searching" within the pleasure principle. They do not present the found object that breaks the frame of representation, but seek to lead the viewer through an endless chain of substitutions, while assuring us that nothing has really changed. Matt Dillon always gets the bad guy. Lucy never gets to perform with Ricky. The *Friends* are always friends. Antigone, however, like Oedipus, becomes a paradigm of beauty and ethical insight when she enters the zone where death encroaches on life and, as a willing victim, goes beyond the pleasure principle (Lacan 1986: 290; Julien 1990: 114–15; Žižek 1992: 21). Her model cannot be understood by the dominant reading of an Aristotelian ethics of happiness, *le bonheur,* nor would she be subject to the Sartrean charge of bad faith.

---

16. I am here using Porter's translation (Lacan 1992: 118–19).

2. Lacan, *Antigone,* and the Ethics of Pure Desire

> The authentic act of self-realization is equivalent to 'die *sittliche Substanz*'—the 'ethical substance' or 'morality as substantive performance.' To enquire of the justification or compass of this ethical substance, to challenge its enactment in the name of external criteria, is vanity. Enter Creon. (Steiner 1984: 29; emphasis in original):
>
> καλόν μοι τοῦτο ποιούσῃ θανεῖν.
> φίλη μετ' αὐτοῦ κείσομαι, φίλου μέτα,
> ὅσια πανουργήσασ'
>
> Antigone: for me, it is a beautiful thing to die doing this. Dear to him I will lie with this dear one, having committed holy crimes. (lines 72–75)

Lacan notes that the *Antigone* itself has long played a central role in western ethical thought.[17] Indeed, he argues that the play forms part of our implicit morality whether we realize it or not (1986: 330), "I did not by some decree make *Antigone* a central point in the matter that concerns us, ethics. For a very long time this has been known, and even those who have not acknowledged its presence know that it plays a part in the discussions of the learned" (1986: 285). In the context of this evocation of the tradition of erudite, philosophically informed readings of the play, Lacan takes particular note of the famed interpretations offered by Hegel and Goethe. He remarks that Hegel is mistaken in his reduction of the conflict between Creon and Antigone to a mere allegory of the contradiction between the discourses of the *polis* and the *oikos* (1986: 276; Žižek 2004: 54).[18] In this objection, Patricia Johnson's psychoanalytic reading of the character of Antigone throughout the Sophoclean corpus echoes Lacan. Johnson notes that

---

17. See also Steiner (1984: 125, 138) and Oudemans and Lardinois (1987: 204).

18. In doing so, Lacan gives short shrift to how much his own interpretation owes to the history of Hegelian interpretations of this tragedy and considerably simplifies Hegel's view. See Copjec (2002: 31), "Historically situated at the very 'threshold of biological modernity,' as a contemporary of Bichat and the rest, Hegel considered Antigone's act from the point of death. Her deed, he argued, concerns not the living but the dead, 'the individual who, after a long succession of separate disconnected experiences, concentrates himself into a single completed shape, and has raised himself out of the unrest of the accidents of life into the calm of simple universality' (para. 452 [*Phenomenology of the Spirit*])." For a complete account of Hegel's various readings of the play, their significance, and later impact, see Steiner (1984: 28–42) as well as Oudemans and Lardinois (1987: 116). Peter Burian has recently argued that all oppositional readings of the Antigone can be ultimately traced to Hegel (2004, reported to me by Don Lavigne). On Hegel as the first to see the Greeks and Greek philosophy as the origin of modernity, see Leonard (2005: 148).

Antigone cannot be conceived of as the representative of the *oikos tout court* since her allegiance is exclusively to the male members of the household. Thus she rejects her sister even when Ismene offers to share Antigone's punishment although she did not share the crime (Johnson 1997: 369–72).[19]

Lacan also objects to Hegel's positing of a final reconciliation between the two competing discursive modes at the play's end (1986: 292). Antigone's splendid isolation in her choice of death presents her as a figure whose ethical act can never be recuperated by the civic discourse, of which Creon perceives himself as the sole legitimate representative (Lacan 1986: 300–1; Žižek 1989: 117; Copjec 2002: 15; Leonard 2005: 113–14). To that extent, Lacan's reading is closer to Goethe's which posits—not an opposition between two abstract principles—but a conflict between a representative of the state who oversteps his bounds and tries to force even the dead to conform to the norms of civic life, and the victim, or rather the agent, of an all-consuming passion (Lacan 1986: 297).[20]

Indeed, as Lacan notes, Antigone's decision to defy Creon and bury Polynices is an act that consciously seeks death. She makes no effort to defend Polynices' actions nor denies Creon's argument that Eteocles and Polynices should not be accorded the same honors (Lacan 1986: 290, 323–25; Guyomard 1992: 106; Benardete 1999: 6).[21] Her choice takes her beyond the realm of rational calculation and the collective norms of satisfaction it implies, beyond the Freudian pleasure and reality principles, beyond an Aristotelian concept of the good (Lacan 1986: 78, 281; Žižek 1991: 25; Julien 1990: 109). Hers is a stance that transcends the comfortable binary oppositions that structure our daily social and moral lives.

Because her choice of death cannot be understood according to strictly rational calculations, and she makes no attempt to justify it within those norms,[22] Antigone cannot be read as representing a simple

---

19. For another recent psychoanalytic account of tragedy that makes mention of Lacan, though not of his commentary on the *Antigone*, see Caldwell (1994).

20. Lacan's reading is closely paralleled by that of Segal (1995: 132).

21. See Johnson (1997: 374) on "the excessive, or at least self-destructive, nature of her attachment to Polynices in *Antigone*, observed by every reader of the play."

22. As David Wray observes to me, in ancient thought, and particularly among the later Stoics, suicide was not per se an irrational choice, depending upon one's situation. He also observes that Antigone's learning of her incestuous parentage might well have been considered so great a dishonor that suicide, as Jocasta's case shows, was not unthinkable. Nonetheless, the text offers no such justification and dramatically the *Antigone* takes place several years after the original revelation, thus she has been living with this knowledge for quite some time. Moreover, the chorus itself at line 220 declares anyone who desires death

antithesis of freedom to tyranny, or of the individual to the state (Lacan 1986: 281; Žižek 1989: 116–17; 1992: 77–78). In fact, as she acknowledges, she had chosen death before Creon's decree against the burial of Polynices had been promulgated, and she defines herself to Ismene as one already belonging to the realm of the dead: σὺ μὲν ζῇς, ἡ δ' ἐμὴ ψυχὴ πάλαι / τέθνηκεν, ὥστε τοῖς θανοῦσιν ὠφελεῖν ("You live on! My soul has long since died so that it might serve the dead") (ll. 559–60; see Lacan 1986: 315, 326; Guyomard 1992: 106). Admittedly, Kamerbeek and Jebb refer these lines back to 69 through 77 and accordingly date Antigone's symbolic death to her decision to violate Creon's edict. Such an interpretation is designed to smooth out the most disturbing aspects of Antigone's declaration: *death* was not her desire; she simply enacts a pious wish to see her brother buried.[23]

But there are problems with this strategy of containment, which consistently asks us to resolve moments of psychological tension or textual indeterminacy in favor of a normative model based on the utilitarian calculus of the pleasure principle.[24] First, it ignores the literal content of the line. *Palai,* "long since" (Griffith 1999: ad loc.), would not in most

---

to be *môros,* "a fool." It would be interesting to speculate, however, on what a Lacanian reading of the Younger Cato's suicide might look like and how much it might resemble his analysis of the *Antigone.*

23. Burial of the dead was a complex and controverted issue in fifth-century Athens. The practice of collective burial of the war dead in democratic Athens, as testified to by Pericles' funeral oration in Thucydides and Plato's *Menexenus,* represented a transfer of responsibility from the family, where mourning rituals were primarily the responsibility of the women of the house, to the state, which was a masculine arena. An unburied corpse was thought to pollute the household as a whole and members of the family were under an affirmative obligation to address the matter. The house or *oikos* was also the traditional aristocratic seat of power as opposed to the democratic *polis.* One purpose of the burial legislation was to take the power and glory traditionally associated with aristocratic warfare (*kleos*) and to transfer them to the *dêmos* as a whole. In addition, the bodies of felons were normally left unburied in Athens. Finally, there is a version of the Seven against Thebes myth told by Euripides in the *Phoenecian Women* in which the Thebans leave the bodies of the seven unburied, and Theseus, the great Athenian culture hero, personally sees to their proper burial. The issue of burial, then, crystallizes a number of the structuring ideological oppositions around which the play is built: *oikos* versus *polis* (as Hegel saw); male versus female (as Creon repeatedly asserts); democratic versus aristocratic rule; Athenian versus Theban; and the law versus transgression. See Knox (1982: 39–41); Oudemans and Lardinois (1987: 98–101, 113, 162); and Tyrell and Bennett (1998: 27, 47–48, 62, 139–40).

24. Or what Oudemans and Lardinois term the categories of "separative thinking" (1987: 43, 233 and passim). On the "plasticity" and "open syntax" of Sophocles' text, which allows for multiple readings, see Tyrrell and Bennett (1998: 67–68). It is not so much that the "commonsense" reading of lines 559–60 is necessarily wrong, as that it should not be privileged and allowed to suppress other textually founded interpretations in the name of a normative (and hence inherently anachronistic) notion of what Sophocles "must have meant."

cases mean "earlier that same morning"—as it must if it refers back to the passage cited by Kamerbeek and Jebb—but "long ago" as David Grene translates (1992: 183).[25] Second, this more soothing interpretation of 559–60 advocated by Kamerbeek is in seeming contradiction with the express content of lines 460–62 where Antigone says that she knew she would die, even if Creon had not issued his edict, and that if she died before her time, so much the better:

θανουμένη γὰρ ἐξῄδη, τί δ' οὔ;
κεἰ μὴ σὺ προυκήρυξας· εἰ δὲ τοῦ χρόνου
πρόσθεν θανοῦμαι, κέρδος αὔτ' ἐγὼ λέγω.

For I knew very well that I would die—why not—Even if you had not made your pronouncements; but if before my time I will die, I will count it as a gain.[26]

Antigone seeks death not because of Creon's decree, but almost in spite of it. Thus Jebb glosses line 461, "Even if thou hadst not proclaimed death as the penalty of infringing the edict" (1900: ad loc.). Antigone has, in fact, "long since" been dead. That is her nature, as indicated by her very name: "she who is *against,* or *in place of, generation,*" i.e., the reproductive force of life (Benardete 1999: 18, 199). Thus, in death, she is portrayed as the bride of Hades, the culmination of her *erôs* (654, 806–16; Griffith 1999: 52).[27] Likewise Haemon's final embrace of her expires in an ejaculation of blood.

ἐς δ' ὑγρὸν
ἀγκῶν' ἔτ' ἔμφρων παρθένῳ προσπτύσσεται·

25. Kamerbeek (1978: ad loc.) cites Jebb's commentary for arguing that *palai* here must have the less common meaning of "not long ago," where Jebb writes, "i.e., ever since she resolved to break the edict." Nonetheless, in Jebb's actual translation we find "my life hath *long* been given to death" (1900: ad loc.; emphasis mine). See also: Fagles (1982: 88), "I gave myself to death long ago"; and Watling (1947: 141), "My heart was long since dead." It seems clear that Kamerbeek and Jebb both are struggling in their commentaries against what they see to be the normal reading of the line. It is the implication they find intolerable, not the Greek. Woodruff is perhaps best, allowing the possible ambiguity of *palai* to show through (2001: 24), "Already my soul is dead."

26. "In contrast to Creon's crass mercantilism (221–22, 1035–39nn.), Ant. uses the term to mean 'a true benefit'" (Griffith 1999: ad loc.).

27. As Loraux notes (1987a: 37–38), virgins led to their death in tragedy are routinely referred to as "brides for Hades. In the shared understandings of social life, death is a natural metaphor of marriage because, in the course of the wedding procession, the young girl renounces herself." In tragedy in general and in the Antigone in particular, however, this metaphor becomes literalized. See also Ormand (1999: 93).

καὶ φυσιῶν ὀξεῖαν ἐκβάλλει ῥοὴν
λευκῇ παρειᾷ φοινίου σταλάγματος·
κεῖται δὲ νεκρὸς περὶ νεκρῷ, τὰ νυμφικὰ
τέλη λαχὼν δείλαιος ἔν γ' Ἅιδου δόμοις.

> Still conscious he enfolds the maid into his soft embrace
> And panting shoots forth a sharp stream
> Of drizzling crimson on her white cheek.[28]
> Corpse lies with corpse, wretchedly receiving
> Its marriage rites in the house of Hades. (1236–41)

Antigone dies a virgin whose marriage (like Haemon's) is consummated in death (Oudemans and Lardinois 1987: 144, 183–84; Segal 1995: 128). Creon's edict provides but the moment in which her desire is realized (Benardete 1999: 72–73). She is in fact the inconceivable monster whose existence the chorus had denied in response to Creon's initial threat: she is the one who desires (*erâi*) death, who is beyond the pleasure principle (line 220; Oudemans and Lardinois 1987: 168).[29] "She is the 'so terribly voluntary victim' who does not know either fear (*phobos*) or pity (*eleos*), unlike Creon who will experience fear—but not till the end" (Loraux 2002: x, citing Lacan 1986: 290).

Her desire for that which lies beyond the pleasure principle is precisely what Lacan helps us see when he famously refers to Antigone as one caught between the two deaths: the Symbolic and the Real. Antigone has "long since" died the first death. Since she accompanied her father into exile, she has in effect been the servant of the dead, shut off from communal Symbolic life and immured within the closed world of her family (Butler 2000: 60):

> Oh tomb, oh bridal chamber, oh hollowed out
> Ever-wakeful home, where I journey
> To those who are mine. (891–93)

---

28. "The sexual associations are strong (esp. after ἐς . . . ἀγκῶν' . . . παρθένῳ), as the fatal 'marriage' is finally consummated (cf. 1240–1)" (Griffith 1999: ad loc.). The conventional ethical reading of the play as a conflict between the rights of the individual or the family and the state can make no sense of this scene. Only a reading that squarely faces the symmetry of death and desire can account for this climactic image.

29. On the necessary association of love and death for Antigone, see Segal (1990: 195, 200) and Tyrrell and Bennett (1998: 98). On Dionysus and Eros as the ruling deities of the play, see Vernant and Vidal-Naquet (1981: 17).

The first death is that to meaning, the second to being. It represents an annihilation beyond punishment and beyond redemption: in Lacan's Heideggerian terms, it is a loss of one's individual being ("the ontic") and a rejoining of Being per se. One may, in fact, always die one death without the other (Lacan 1986: 291, 341, 353–54; 1991: 120; Žižek 1992: 43; Butler 2000: 48–49). Thus, as Žižek notes, Napoleon on Elba did not know he was already dead (1991: 44), and, as I have argued elsewhere, Ovid in Tomis did and hoped for resurrection (Miller 2004a: chapter 8). Antigone, however, both knows she is dead and desires death (the second) nonetheless.

It is in fact her exclusion from the Symbolic community, her Symbolic death that "imbues her character with sublime beauty" and raises her to the level of the Thing, according to Lacan (Žižek 1989: 135; Žižek 2004: 54; see also Lacan 1986: 327; 1991: 154). In her embrace of the Real, she traverses the very *atê,* the sinister daimonic force,[30] that marks the impassable barrier between the Symbolic and the Real, the human and the divine, intelligence and folly, the law and its transgression.[31] Lacan here joins Butler and casts an interesting light on the views of some of Sophocles' most distinguished classical readers. *Atê* is variously translated as "devastation," "disaster," "curse," "ruin," and "madness" (D. Allen 2000: 88; Oudemans and Lardinois 1987: 135). It appears fourteen times within the play, making it one of the tragedy's most important recurring themes. Moreover, as the chorus in the second stasimon makes clear, *atê* is that which defines the curse of the house of the Labdacids (line 593; Lacan 1986: 306–7; Tyrrell and Bennett 1998: 81). It finds its representation in the combination of superhuman power and *hubris* that defines an Oedipus who insists upon his desire for insight to the point of blindness, exile, and ultimately death (Knox 1988: 6–16; Segal 1988: 140; Vernant and Vidal-Naquet 1981: 81–119). It is also the blind rage of Polynices and the attack of the Seven against Thebes. It is Antigone's sublime choice of death before the decrees of Creon. As the chorus sings, "There is nothing outstanding in the life of mortals outside *atê*" (lines 613–14).

> Finite beings can only exist by permanently using their finite power against the dangers of destruction, which is nevertheless inevitable. This is precisely the position of Antigone and Creon at the end of

---

30. In Empedocles' *Purifications,* the soul is pictured as a *daimôn* wandering in the field of *Atê.* See Vernant (1965: 1.120).

31. See: Lacan (1986: 329; 1991: 133); Žižek (1993: 115–16); Vernant and Vidal-Naquet (1981: 11–12, 52); and Aeschylus, *The Suppliant Women* 470.

the play.... In the *Antigone* the cosmic order is revealed in its duality. It is part of this order that finite beings transgress their limits and are destroyed. Divine order is also disorder. (Oudemans and Lardinois 1987: 203)[32]

Atê marks this border or limit, which is also that between the two deaths, the realm designated by the sublime object as that of *das Ding*, of which all true ethical action must partake if it is not to be a simple reproduction of the existing relations of domination (Lacan 1986: 347; Žižek 1991: 25; Copjec 2002: 43).

As Judith Butler puts the case (and it is worth quoting her at some length):

> For Lacan, to seek recourse to the gods is precisely to seek recourse beyond human life, to seek recourse to death and to instate that death within life; this recourse to what is beyond or before the symbolic leads to a self-destruction that literalizes the importation of death into life. It is as if the very invocation of that elsewhere precipitates desire in the direction of death, a second death, one that signifies the foreclosure of any further transformation. Antigone, in particular, "violates the limits of *Atè* through her desire" (277). If this is a limit that humans can cross only briefly or, more aptly, cannot cross for long ... She has crossed the line, defying public law, citing a law from elsewhere, but this elsewhere is a death that is solicited by that very citation. She acts, but acts according to a command of death.... (Butler 2000: 51)

In fact, Butler and Lacan are merely glossing what the chorus itself tells us at 622–25, "the bad sometimes seems to be the good to that man whose mind a god turns toward *atê*, but one may live only the slightest time beyond *atê*" (see Lacan 1986: 315, 322–23). Antigone, therefore, by insisting upon her desire beyond the second death, traverses the veil of *atê* and achieves a sublime beauty that is unable to be accounted for by any strictly rational calculation of costs and benefits nor assimilated to a universal Symbolic, and hence normative, maxim of ethical conduct (Butler 2000: 53). Her authenticity cannot be separated from her transgressive desire.

Finally, although Kamerbeek and Jebb wish to see in Antigone's declaration that she is long since dead a reference to her resolution to bury

32. See also Goold (1988: 158).

Polynices, not to a more disturbing sense that she is already dead and that Creon's edicts therefore are but the occasion for realizing the desire that forms the core of her being, the passage they point to is every bit as disturbing as the implications they seek to avoid:

Antigone: καλόν μοι τοῦτο ποιούσῃ θανεῖν·
φίλη μετ' αὐτοῦ κείσομαι, φίλου μέτα,
ὅσια πανουργήσασ' (lines 72–75)

Antigone: for me, it is a beautiful thing to die doing this. Dear to him I will lie with this dear one, having committed holy crimes.

The incestuous overtones of these lines, though widely denied, are too self-evident to require extensive elucidation (Bernadete 1999: 13; Butler 2000: 17; Wohl forthcoming: 12). As Griffith judiciously notes, "The unusual double repetition in 73 (for the simple *polyptoton*, φίλη μετὰ φίλου) emphasizes the bond of φιλία (cf. 81 φιλτάτωι...) and the physical closeness of the two bodies (cf. 1240 [Haemon's last embrace])" (1999: ad loc.). The embrace of the dead Labdacid brother can no more be free of sexual overtones than can Haemon's spurting blood on Antigone's cheek. Thus, Vernant and Vidal-Naquet's claim that when Antigone "scatters dust over the corpse of Polynices, [she] is not prompted by an incestuous affection for the brother she is forbidden to bury: she is proclaiming that she has an equal religious duty to all her dead brothers" represents an extraordinary moment of textual insensitivity by two of the twentieth century's most gifted interpreters of Greek culture (1981: 77–78).[33] Antigone is a maid who refuses to leave her family and join that of her husband. She consistently ignores or rejects the demands of exogamy and conflates the categories of kinship and love. To say in a fit of literal mindedness that the scattering of dust on Polynices' corpse does not signify a desire to have intercourse

---

33. But see also Kamerbeek (1978: ad loc.), "It is certainly preposterous to read an incestuous intention into the words, whatever insinuation may be heard in some utterances of Creon's." One always wonders when someone forbids you to interpret a text in a manner to which they have just drawn your attention about the motivation for such a police action. Again there is no argument about the meaning of the Greek, only about the licit and illicit inferences one can make from the text's content. Compare *sugkoimâmai* (= *sun* + *keimai*, for which *meta* + *keimai* is an obvious periphrasis) at Sophocles, *Electra* 274; Euripides, *Phoenecian Women* 54; Aechylus, *Agamemnon* 1258; and *sugkoimêsis* at Plato, *Phaedrus* 255e. No one would think to argue for a non-erotic reading in these passages, although the literal import of the word is the same as that of *meta* + *keimai* in the passage under discussion.

with her brother is both reductive (who said it did?) and a manifest attempt to ignore the consistent incestuous imagery and themes that saturate this and other scenes in the tragedy, as well as the Theban cycle as a whole.³⁴ Rather, as Judith Butler points out, Antigone is one who was born into a conflation of the positions that anchor the most elementary of Symbolic codes, the bonds of kinship and their corollary, the incest taboo, and as a result she is from the beginning tainted by its transgression and hence beyond the Symbolic per se (2000: 18–22). She is sister, daughter, and aunt simultaneously. She is, in fact, long since dead: she has no unambiguously recognized place within the Symbolic from which she can make her claim to legitimacy, to a law that will be recognized by all.

Creon, then, does not so much represent the tyrant who forces Antigone to make an impossible choice between life and freedom, but rather he is the inflexible embodiment of the civic norms that her pursuit of a desire beyond the bounds of those articulated within the realm of common life both requires and transcends. Her choice thus represents a pure ethical act that is shaped neither by the banality of a self-interested selection among communally recognized goods nor the self-loathing of conforming to a code that is both recognized and despised (Julien 1990: 112; Žižek 1992: 77). Such an ethical choice, as Lacan implicitly acknowledges, is Kantian in its devotion to a pure concept of duty, but psychoanalytic in its predication on a highly individualized desire that cannot be generalized, with regard to its content, into a universal ethical maxim of the kind that Kant required (Lacan 1986: 68, 365–66).

Antigone's choice, her desire, is pure precisely to the degree that it ultimately rejects all claims of otherness and encloses itself in what Patrick Guyomard, in his critical response to Lacan's reading, sees as an incestuous narcissism. For this latter-day French psychoanalyst, it is Creon's bitter ability finally to learn from his mistakes, rather than Antigone's suicidal purity, that presents the real ethical model (1992: 45, 52, 62–64, 75). But for Lacan, it is the beauty of Antigone's choice of a good beyond all recognized goods, beyond the pleasure principle, that gives her character its monumental status and makes her a model for an ethics of creation as opposed to conformity (1991: 13). It is for this reason that he cites Antigone's self-comparison to the ever-weeping, petrified Niobe, another princess encased alive in stone—as the central axis around which the play turns (ll. 823–33). In this one image

---

34. Oudemans and Lardinois (1987: 112–13, 167, 172); Zeitlin (1990: 149); Ormand (1999: 90–92); Benardete (1999: 9, 62, 97–98).

we see brought together the themes of beauty, monumentality, and death in a singular apotheosis of tragic transgression (Lacan 1986: 311, 315, 327). Beauty for Lacan represents the perfect moment between life and death, a moment both articulated by and beyond time and desire, a moment whose true achievement can only be imagined as the incarnation of a pure desire beyond any recognizable object.[35] For Lacan, then, as will be the case for Foucault in his turn to antiquity, the search for an ethics leads above all to an aesthetics of existence, to the search for the beautiful life (Foucault 1994d: 415; 1994c: 617).[36]

Not to cede on one's desire, Lacan's formula for Antigone as an ethical model, is not therefore to absolutize the object of one's desire into a timeless good, but to recognize the nature of desire as a situated lack that points beyond itself (1986: 368, 370). To not cede on one's desire is the conscious affirmation of finitude, and hence of contingency, as the condition necessary for the sublimation and transcendence of that contingency.[37] In other words, for us to go beyond the bounded nature of our position within the world of Symbolic law, i.e., beyond the pleasure and reality principles, we must die to the subject position that defines what *we* are (1986: 328–29). Like Antigone, we too must be "long since dead": for in affirming our desire we affirm both our necessary situatedness and our capacity to go beyond it.[38] Creon's dictates make possible Antigone's desire to transgress them, and Antigone's affirmation of her desire can only point beyond the law by recognizing that it is defined and bounded by the law. If Antigone were an innocent, blithely unaware of Creon's edict, when she buried her brother, there would no tragedy, no transcendence. In more orthodox Freudian terms, the death drive is necessarily implicated in the pleasure and reality principles even as it points beyond them.

True ethical action does not simply reproduce the Symbolic law. It introduces something new into the Real. It creates a place for our existence. Analysis is the prelude to moral action as such, because it is what makes our desire, as a relation to the law, visible. Antigone's "no," then, stands as a demand addressed to Creon's law, to what Lacan defines

---

35. See Lacan (1986: 291, 344; 1991: 15, 154); Julien (1990: 114–15); Žižek (1989: 135); Copjec (2002: 218); and Oudemans and Lardinois (1987: 188–90).

36. See note 13.

37. See Renaut 1993 on Heidegger and Sartre's conception of finitude as the condition for the subject's self-transcendence. Lacan was a greater reader of both.

38. In a sense, the affirmation of that capacity is what makes one already dead: for to posit the ability transcend one's subject position is already to stand outside it. This is precisely what Ismene cannot do. Of course, the moment we step beyond, a new position begins to form beneath our feet, lest we slide into irreversible psychosis or the second death.

as the Other, but her demand is only authentic in relation to that law (Lacan 1986: 30, 331). It projects an absolute transcendence that can only be founded upon the contingent. On a Lacanian reading, Creon is not opposed to Antigone, but the condition of her possibility.

3. Reading *Antigone*

> Whereas Creon's language and attitudes associate him with the aggressive, manipulative rationalism of the Ode on Man, Antigone appears as part of the human-dominated natural world. In her grief she is the mother bird lamenting her empty nest (ll.423–25), the hunted animal. She herself compares her fate to that of Niobe, fused with the organic process of nature . . . (ll. 826–27). (Segal 1990: 164–65)

> The reciprocal affection between parents and children on the one hand and brothers and sisters on the other represents the model of what the Greeks called *philía*. The word *phílos*, which has a possessive force corresponding to the Latin *suus*, denotes first and foremost that which is one's own, that is, for the relative, another relative close to him. Aristotle on several occasions and in particular when writing about tragedy tells us that this *philía* is based on a kind of identity felt between all the members of an immediate family. Each member of the family is an *alter ego*, a sort of double or multiplied self, for each of his relatives. (Vernant and Vidal-Naquet 1981: 76–77)

In its beauty, Sophocles' *Antigone* presents what Lacan defines as a "sublime object."[39] Our ethical obligation as readers and analysts is to be true to this object to the precise degree that it transcends all normative categories. As Antigone does not cede on her desire, neither can we assimilate her tragedy to a pre-existing set of critical categories, even psychoanalytic ones. This is an obligation to the text, but it is simultaneously an obligation to our own desire as readers, critics, and subjects: for the encounter with the sublime object is one that must shake us to our very core if it is not to be a factitious or mechanical exercise in the application of reassuring truisms. To meet our obligation to the sublime text we must go beyond the dictates of the pleasure and reality principles, beyond good and evil to encounter pure desire: the moment in which the canons of meaning shudder before their own beyond.

In many ways, this ethical obligation to beauty is met not by subjecting the text to a pre-existing theoretical model, but by the practice of

---

39. On Lacan's frequent conflation of the beautiful and the sublime, see note 14.

old-fashioned philology. We must closely attend to the play of meaning in the text and the ways in which it transcends our normative canons of the good, the true, and the beautiful, that is to say our day-to-day unreflective commerce with our larger Symbolic communities as defined by our profession, our ideological commitments, and our personal histories. The problem, of course, is that good, old-fashioned philology has almost never existed and what has passed for attention to the text has too often been an exercise in domesticating it to norms of intelligibility, canons of taste, and concepts of historical plausibility alien to the brute facticity of the text itself. We have submitted to Creon's laws rather than pursued the sublime object in all its strangeness. We have ceded on our and the text's desire in the name of utility, in the name of conformity to a reality principle that would predetermine the limits of our experience and its signification, in the name of *le bonheur*.

To demonstrate how this ethical (and hence philological) obligation to the text, and its own aesthetic transcendence of the already given, could be pursued in relation to Lacan's own proof text, therefore, I propose to pursue a close reading of the *Antigone's* opening lines, taking as little for granted as possible while allowing the unfolding of the alien, conflicting, and at times repetitive forms of meaning that inhabit these lines to proceed with a minimum of interference. Antigone's first sentence is addressed to her sister Ismene before dawn outside the royal palace. As is typical of Thebes on the Athenian stage, already we are in a space that is explicitly beyond the norm. Athenian women of good families were not to be found running about in the street in the middle of the night (Wohl forthcoming: 2). We begin thus in a place outside the law to announce an edict of the new *tyrannos,* Creon, and to seek the support of a woman and a sibling in its transgression:

Ὦ ΚΟΙΝΟΝ αὐτάδελφον Ἰσμήνης κάρα,
ἆρ' οἶσθ' ὅ τι Ζεὺς τῶν ἀπ' Οἰδίπου κακῶν
ὁποῖον οὐχὶ νῷν ἔτι ζώσαιν τελεῖ;
οὐδὲν γὰρ οὔτ' ἀλγεινὸν οὔτ' ἄτης ἄτερ[40]
οὔτ' αἰσχρὸν οὔτ' ἄτιμόν ἐσθ', ὁποῖον οὐ
τῶν σῶν τε κἀμῶν οὐκ ὄπωπ' ἐγὼ κακῶν.

---

40. See Gross's gloss "'(nothing) not without destruction'; since the accumulation of negatives gives the reverse of what Antigone means, K[amerbeek] reads οὐδ(ὲ) instead of the second οὔτ(ε), '(nothing) painful and (nothing) which is lacking destruction' but the sense is clear in any case" (1988: ad loc.). for a survey of the textual difficulties see Jebb (1900: 243–46).

Oh common wombmate, dear head of Ismene,
Do you know what if any of the evils from Oedipus
Zeus has yet to accomplish for the two of us still living?
For there is nothing painful nor without *atê*
Nor shame nor dishonor such as
I have not seen in your evils and mine.

The first two words after the initial vocative interjection are all but impossible to translate in anything approaching their original concision. They form a tautology whose harshness most translations smooth over (Watling 1947: 126; Grene 1992: 161; Woodruff 2001: 1). Jebb's, "my sister, my own sister" in no way does justice to the strange conjunction of these two words, reducing them to the recognizable sentiments of the nineteenth-century drawing room (1900: ad loc.).[41] Rather than seeking to find a solution to this problem, let us linger over these words, resisting the urge for an overhasty naturalization while paying close attention to their resonance with the whole of Sophocles' closely wrought text.

Koinon normally means something "held in common, shared." What is the shared thing, the thing held in common addressed here? On first hearing, it would appear to be the *autadelphon*, a kinship term, which here appears in its lengthened form rather than the more normal *adelphos*. While conventionally translated "brother" or "sister," as Benveniste has pointed out (1969: 1.220–21), Greek uses a periphrasis for male and female siblings, unparalleled in other Indo-European languages. *Autadelphon* literally refers to one of two or more people or things that have shared the same womb or *delphus*. The term thus names one of the play's central themes. Hence, Antigone will later refer to herself as one who does reverence to those who have shared the same entrails (*homosplanchnous sebein*, 511). The less common lengthened form, *auta-delphon,* underlines the literal content of the word and prevents its rapid assimilation to a purely conventional kinship term. It is an image of one flesh, inseparable in the womb and beyond (Segal 1990: 180; Leonard 2005: 127). Why, then, is *koinon* even necessary? Does it not merely repeat the idea inherent in *auto?* "Oh common same-wombed one" these opening syllables seem to cry. What same-wombed one is not common, is strange, is *unheimlich,* we might well ask? Moreover, the neuter, as Griffith notes, "may suggest also their 'common brother'": Eteocles, Polynices, or Oedipus

---

41. He is of course constrained by the bonds of Victorian poetic decorum.

himself (1999: ad loc.; see also Loraux 1987b: 173; Butler 2000: 18).

Indeed, it is same-wombedness that is at the heart of the Oedipal family romance. The self-enclosed world of the tauto-logy is precisely what opposes Antigone's obligations to family and professed love of death to the ordered realm of civic law and virtue that Creon proposes to inaugurate with his edict forbidding the burial of the rebel Polynices (Segal 1990: 179–81; Benardete 1999: 9, 97–98). Similarly, it is Oedipus's own discovery of an excessive sameness, of a strange commonality at the heart of his being, that will cast him beyond the bounds of civic life in the *Antigone*'s belated prequel (Butler 2000: 61). In fact, words that begin with the *auto-* prefix have a peculiar prominence throughout the play (Benardete 1999: 2; Wohl forthcoming: 18). Not only does *autadelphos* occur twice more (503 and 696) where it refers unambiguously to Polynices, but also, and perhaps most famously, Antigone herself is later referred to as *autonomos* (824), a reference to her being a law unto herself, a self-enclosed, self-legislating unity, who rejects the otherness of the law of the *polis*, of the Symbolic community in which intersubjective norms of human conduct are imposed and negotiated (Loraux 1987b: 165–67; Tyrrell and Bennett 1998: 104; Lacan 1986: 328–29).

But wait! Surely, I have committed the worst sort of howler. Only someone possessed of the most elementary Greek would fail to recognize that *autadelphon* is not a substantive but an adjective modifying the neuter *kara*. It turns out that I have been creating difficulties where none exist—all in the name of an extraneous theoretical agenda. Yet before we deliver ourselves over to premature self-flagellation, perhaps it would be best to ask whether the words yield themselves up to common sense quite as quickly as my interlocutor might claim. Perhaps, just perhaps, the original construction is not resolved quite so easily as it appears. First, the word *autadelphos* is always a substantive elsewhere in the play.[42] Second, while it would be incorrect to say that *koinos* can never mean "related by consanguinity" as Kamerbeek claims (1978: ad loc.), it is far from the most common meaning, and it is never used of things rather than persons, nor is it ever once used in Kamerbeek's sense elsewhere in Sophocles, even when referring to Antigone and her siblings. Thus, if we take *autadelphon* as an adjective, and translate

---

42. A search of the *Thesaurus Linguae Graecae* database reveals only six instances of the word in classical Greek, three of which are in this play.

literally, the result is something like that recommended by Gross in his commentary (1988: ad loc.), "shared ... real-sister head of Ismene." The image is grotesque. Even if with Gross we insert a parenthetical "in parents" after "shared," the result is only slightly less strange than imagining Antigone and Ismene as a two-bodied monster. *Kara,* it will be quickly added, is synecdoche for the person of Ismene, like Latin *caput,* and hence a term of endearment, not a reference to an actual head. Yet the translation, "shared" or "common same-wombed person of Ismene" is every bit as much an offense to our commonsense notions of independent personhood and individuality as that of a "shared (in parents) head," and, inasmuch as the emphasis is on their being one flesh, it is hard to keep the image of the "head" as head out of one's mind. Indeed, the more one struggles to construe the grammar of this line, the more it seems to cry out for a comma after *autadelphon,* so that *kara* stands as an appositive, rather than the substantive modified by the adjective, "Oh shared same-wombed one, head/person of Ismene."[43]

Nonetheless, before we adopt the truly old-fashioned philological expedient of an emendation, even one as unobtrusive as an extra comma, should we not ask ourselves if the crux we have ferreted out in this first line is not reflective of a deeper structure, one that stretches not only throughout this opening passage but also throughout the play as a whole? For the question of whether or not to insert a comma is in fact nothing less than the question of how to articulate the relation of shared flesh to the discrete personhood[44] of the two sisters and by extension to their two brothers, and to Oedipus, their father/brother. In this question, we find the entire dialectic that characterizes Ismene's relation to Antigone. The essence of that relation is embodied in the tension between the *koinon autadelphon* and the principle of individuation denoted by the proper name, Ismene, in line 1. That tension represents a conflict between an order of existence of finite, separate individuals, which is explicitly announced as masculine and civic in nature within the play and which Lacan labels the Symbolic, and an order of mutual reflection and fleshly interrelation, which the play casts

---

43. It is important to remember that the punctuation is a latter-day editorial convention and so, therefore, is the strict grammatical distinction it implies.

44. Although individuality is problematic in an ancient context, nonetheless, it is difficult to dispense with and hardly anachronistic. As Vernant observes, "Civic cult is attached to a concept of σωφροσύνη consisting of control, self-mastery, each being situating itself in its place within the limits assigned to it" (1965: 2.81). Nonetheless, this is clearly not the freestanding Cartesian *cogito,* but a notion of the individual as constituted by and within the community.

as feminine and domestic and which Lacan labels the Imaginary. This tension characterizes Ismene's simultaneous attempt to adhere to the norms of civic conduct through assuming the position designated for her gender by the law and her refusal to abandon Antigone even in the face of the law's condemnation and seemingly certain death (Vernant and Vidal-Naquet 1981: 1–6, 16; Oudemans and Lardinois 1987: 88, 233; Tyrrell and Bennett 1998: 76–77).

The structure of this double movement is very precisely embodied in the next two lines. Leaving aside the textual controversy concerning *ho ti* versus *hoti,* these two singularly difficult lines directly address Ismene concerning what sort of evil, out of those stemming from their father, Zeus has not yet brought to pass for the two of them who are still living.[45] On the one hand, line two seems to move firmly in the direction of the *principium individuationis,* with its verb in the second person and two proper nouns. There is a *you* who "knows." *Zeus* is the active agent of the finite verb *telei,* and *Oedipus* is the origin, if not the owner, of the evils brought to pass. On the other, this opening out of the closed incestuous world of common flesh and shared being into the world of intersubjective recognition and responsibility, of articulation before the law, already contains the seeds of its own negation. Who is this Zeus? The anthropomorphic force behind the name, as Griffith notes, seems particularly attenuated in these lines (1999: ad loc.). *Zeus* is less a proper name, denoting a discrete individual with articulable motives and desires, than synecdoche for an impersonal force, even as the oft noted hyperbaton, which shifts the name into a syntactically anomalous position (Kamerbeek 1978: ad loc.), foregrounds the very agency that seems to be lacking. Similarly, the phrase "the evils from Oedipus" at once names his acts (the evils he committed: parricide, incest, the curse laid upon Eteocles and Polynices), their consequences (the evils he suffered: exile, blindness, the mutual slaughter of his sons), and their origin in the curse of the Labdacids (Jebb 1900: ad loc.). In what sense, we must ask, are these evils Oedipus' and how are we to understand them in relation to the "we" who are "still living" and for whom they are "yet to be accomplished"?

This last question gains particular poignancy when we reflect upon the force of the duals, *nôin* and *zôsain,* in line 3. These are the first of what Griffith notes to be "a dense cluster of duals" throughout the

---

45. Like Kamerbeek (1978 ad loc.), I would contend that *eti* may be taken with either *zôsain* or *telei.* Indeed, I would argue for an *ex commune* construction.

play used to describe "murderous brothers, disunited sisters, sister and dead brother, dying bride and groom" (1999: ad loc.).[46] Extrapolating the conceptualization behind the duals to its logical conclusion, Antigone and Ismene are here conceived as a unit: not separate individuals, but one substance from a common womb, the womb that is the origin of Oedipus's evils (Wohl forthcoming: 15). It is Antigone's desire to assert and maintain these failed unities, to return to the oneness of the flesh and lie with her brother in the grave that fuels the central conflict of the play embodied in the countervailing forces of a transgressive oneness and an ultimately sterile and self-destructive logic of radical separation. As Charles Segal sums up:

> Even her dual form when speaking of herself and Ismene in the third line has its significance, for it repeatedly denotes the polluted fratricides ... and comes to mark a shift of allegiance on Antigone's part as she leaves the living kin for her bond to the dead. Creon's path is, of course, just the opposite: he insists on "difference" and carries it to its logical conclusion in the face of those bonds of sameness which the gods finally vindicate. (1990: 183)

Antigone is the *autognôtos* (875), the "self resolved," the *autonomos*, who cannot admit the other except as the *autadelphon*, the same-wombed, that is, as a member of a potential self-reflecting dual. The experiential reality of that dual, however, is characterized by the constant presence of *atê* defined paratactically in lines 4–5 as "pain," "shame," and "dishonor" that is, by the experience of a shared transgression of, and rejection by, the Symbolic law.

The force of the dual is explicable but not translatable. It asserts as an unarguable grammatical fact the existence of an intermediate category between the absolute identity of the one and the fundamental difference of the many: the self-reflecting two. In the Labdacids' tale of internecine murder and incest, of the two as the transgressive one or the one as the murderous two, this increasingly archaic piece of Greek morphology looms large. Throughout the play, it is self-consciously manipulated to achieve maximum effect. Thus Ismene, who attempts to occupy the impossible middle position between Creon's difference and Antigone's sameness, replies to Antigone's first speech:

---

46. Steiner's assertion that the dual only occurs at the play's beginning and therefore we cannot be sure of its significance is incorrect (1984: 113). Compare Loraux (1987b: 173–74); and Tyrrell and Bennett (1998: 44–45 and 78) on the significance of the dual.

ἐμοὶ μὲν οὐδεὶς μῦθος, Ἀντιγόνη, φίλων
οὔθ' ἡδὺς οὔτ' ἀλγεινὸς ἵκετ', ἐξ ὅτου
δυοῖν ἀδελφοῖν ἐστερήθημεν δύο,
μιᾷ θανόντοιν ἡμέρᾳ διπλῇ χερί· (11–14)

Not one story of those who are *dear*, Antigone, whether sweet or painful has come to me, outside of the fact that *we two* were stripped of *two brothers dying as a pair* on *one* day from a *double* hand.

The deliberate alternation between ones and twos is designed to draw attention to the dual as a fundamental textual signature of Oedipal incest and murderous strife, in contrast to both the normative individual of fifth-century Athens and the social collective of the *dêmos*, represented on stage by the chorus.

The unambiguous connection of the grammatical dual to the incestuous story that lies at the heart of the Oedipus tale, to the *atê* of the Labdacids, is made explicit, however, in Ismene's next speech:

οἴμοι· φρόνησον, ὦ κασιγνήτη, πατὴρ
ὡς νῷν ἀπεχθὴς δυσκλεής τ' ἀπώλετο,
πρὸς αὐτοφώρων ἀμπλακημάτων διπλᾶς
ὄψεις ἀράξας αὐτὸς αὐτουργῷ χερί·
ἔπειτα μήτηρ καὶ γυνή, διπλοῦν ἔπος,
πλεκταῖσιν ἀρτάναισι λωβᾶται βίον·
τρίτον δ' ἀδελφὼ δύο μίαν καθ' ἡμέραν
αὐτοκτονοῦντε τὼ ταλαιπώρω μόρον
κοινὸν κατειργάσαντ' ἐπαλλήλοιν χεροῖν· 49–57

Alas, consider, oh my *sister by birth*, how the *father*
to the two of us died hated and notorious,
for *self-revealed* crimes having torn out
his *two* eyes *himself* with his own *self-working* hand.[47]
Then the *mother* and *wife*, a *double* name,
Destroys her life with knotted ropes.
Third, two brothers on *one* day
The *wretched pair by killing themselves*
Accomplish a *common* fate *with each other's two hands*.

---

47. "αὐτοφώρων . . . αὐτὸς αὐτουργῷ χερί: cf. 1, 55–7nn. . . . αὐτόφωρος usually means 'detected in the very (αὐτο-) act': but here 'self-detected,' and perhaps also 'in an incestuous act'" (Griffith 1999: ad loc.).

The duals at the end of the passage come thick and fast. But throughout these closely packed lines, tragic fate is embodied by a shared flesh (*sister by birth, father, mother, brothers*) whose division into self-reflexive twos (*the two of us, two eyes, double name, two brothers, wretched pair, two hands*) resists the separation of the Symbolic law, the intervention of the third as represented by Creon's notion of communally defined goods and rule-based *philia*. These twos, these incestuous duals, in the end collapse into a self-reflecting identity (*self-revealed, himself, self-working, themselves, common*) that is ultimately indistinguishable from death itself (*killing*): "*Third, two brothers* on *one* day."

This tension between Imaginary reflection and Symbolic law is also embodied precisely by Creon's and Antigone's competing notions of *philia* articulated in the play's opening lines (Griffith 1999: 123; Goldhill 1986: 88–103). As David Konstan has made us aware, there are essentially two concepts of *philia* operative in classical Greece. These are an inheritance of a complex of values that, as Benveniste has shown (1969: 1.335–53), are predicated on an originary notion of the *philos* as being a person or thing intrinsically bound to the self—through ties of kinship, tribal and political loyalty, guest friendship, and/or companionship (Santas 1988: 8; Benardete 1999: 12–13). For this reason, the Homeric usage of *philos*, especially when applied to body parts, is thought to differ little from that of the possessive adjective. *Philos*, then, is most directly contrasted with *ekhthros*, that which is "outside, other, inimical" (Nagy 1979: 242–44; Goldhill 1986: 80–83). Thus Antigone ends her first speech (line 10) by asking Ismene if she has heard what evils are now approaching their *philoi* (i.e., Polynices) from their *ekhthroi* (i.e., Creon).

As Konstan observes, this use of *philos* to signify that which is part of the "same" is the primary sense in Homer, where the word is used exclusively in the adjectival form. And while certain types of interpretation may have gone too far in reducing the affective dimension of such ties to the purely functional, nonetheless archaic *philos* cannot be translated "friend" without serious distortion. The same is true for the abstract noun *philia* as it is used both in archaic and classical texts where the term "friendship" would be inadequate to those aspects of it that apply to kinship and other forms of meaning that imply a sense of shared being. In addition, however, Konstan argues that the classical period sees the emergence of *philos* as a noun explicitly used in contrast or coordination with kinship terms, meaning an "achieved relationship" of mutual loyalty and affection (1997: 1–67). This is *philos* as "friend."

Antigone defends the archaic view of *philia* as inextricably linked to an essential oneness, in which legal and Symbolic identity is secondary to the primal oneness of Being. For her the *philoi* are those who share the bonds of flesh and blood. She will lie *philê* with *philos* in Polynices' grave, not because his cause was just, not because of the existence of an "achieved relationship" that they have constructed between them, but because he is who he is (Lacan 1986: 324–25; Guyomard 1992: 42n.7). A husband, she says, or even a son, can be replaced but, with both parents in the grave, a brother is irreplaceable (lines 909–12).[48] That tear in the oneness of the flesh cannot be mended. There is no possible exchange or substitution, no way to fill this gap within the domains sanctioned by the pleasure and the reality principles. "Doing this," she says, "it is a beautiful thing to die."

For Creon, however, *philia* is a fully legal and rule-bound relationship. Its purpose is to promote the civic good and is firmly a part of the kingdom of *biens* of which he is the foremost representative (Lacan 1986: 300–1; Oudemans and Lardinois 1987: 164). Dearness for Creon is a function of submission to the law. As he argues in a speech that would be later quoted with approval by Demosthenes, and which represents what many in Sophocles' audience would have considered accepted truth:

> Whoever considers a friend or kinsman [*philon*] greater than his fatherland, I say this one to be of no account. For I—let ever-vigilant Zeus know this—would neither be silent seeing disaster [*atê*] approaching the citizens, instead of safety, nor would I ever count as a friend (*philon*) a man bearing ill will to my land, knowing this that when the city is safe we make friends [*philous*] for ourselves by sailing on a sound ship of state. (182–90)

Creon here represents a kind of civic-minded vision of *philia* that excludes all aspects of kinship, flesh, and enjoyment (Griffith 1999: ad loc.). He does not seek to traverse the veil of *atê* but to avoid it (even as he ultimately falls prey to it). His position is at once that of the new constitutional order in democratic Athens (Tyrrell and Blake 1999: 46–47; Oudemans and Lardinois 1987: 161; Knox 1982: 35, 38–39), and a totalitarian insistence on the law as law, without any grounding in family, tradition, or the immediacy of shared being (Steiner 1984:

---

48. On the textual controversies surrounding these lines since at least the time of Goethe, see Lacan (1986: 298); Tyrrell and Bennett (1999: 112–14); and Griffith (1999: ad loc.).

37; D. Allen 2000: 91–92). In the end, Creon refuses to recognize the world of enjoyment that supports and grounds the law and his desire. And that refusal leads to the destruction of his family and himself (Benardete 1999: 74–75; Tyrrell and Bennett 1999: 90–91). By the same token, Antigone's refusal to recognize the claims of the law, her pure desire to transgress the barrier of *atê*, leads her from the Symbolic death affirmed by the pleasure principle to the second death, which is its beyond. Her destruction is not the product of an error in judgment, *hamartia*, like that of Creon, but of a fundamental and uncompromising disposition toward Being.

In her insistence on her desire to the point of death, a desire that transcends all rational calculations of Symbolically determined utility, a desire that points beyond the pleasure and reality principles, she embraces the familial *atê* of the Labdacids. Like Niobe, she becomes both more and less than human, immortalized as a sublime figure of beauty in death, a figure of folly and awe. In the process, she becomes a profoundly ethical figure in her uncompromising singularity. At the same time, she points to the desire and obligation of the analyst to listen to the text, to be true to its indeterminacies and contradictions, its self-transcendence, its awesome foolishness. All Creon's rational calculations, while constituting the grid that makes this moment possible and necessary, can never fully account for it. They can only attempt to contain it within the constraints of a self-satisfied instrumental reason that when confronted with Tiresias' horrible truth sees only baseness, bribery, and bad faith. Creon remains blind until the awful moment when he is brought up short before the image of his son's dying body clasping the beautiful corpse of Antigone.

It is here, to this unthinkable abyss, that a true ethics of psychoanalysis leads. The talking cure as conceived by Lacan takes the analysand not to the world of facile adaptation and normalization, but makes possible the direct confrontation with the destitution of desire and the consequent embrace of Being:

> The question of the Sovereign Good has always been posed for man, but the analyst knows that this is a closed question. Not only does he not have what one demands of him, the Sovereign Good, but he knows there isn't any. Having led an analysis to its term is nothing other than to have encountered this limit where the entire problematic of desire is posed. (Lacan 1986: 347)

With freedom from the Sovereign Good, however, comes the possibility to realize one's desire in all its idiosyncrasies, to withdraw from an exclusively instrumentalized and utilitarian relation to the world, and to encounter a beauty that cannot be confined to immediate use. It is Antigone, according to Lacan, as sublime object who points the way to a pure desire, and so to a true spiritual practice, that can transform us, like Niobe, into something fundamentally awe-full and new. [49]

4. Conclusion: Ethics and the Other

> He yawned: he had finished his day; he had finished with his youth. Already certain tried and true ethical systems discretely proposed their services to him: there was clear-eyed Epicureanism, smiling indulgence, resignation, sober maturity, stoicism, each of which would allow him to taste minute by minute, like a connoisseur, his failed life. He took off his jacket; he began to loosen his tie. He repeated to himself as he yawned, "It's true, it's really true, I've come to the age of reason." (Sartre 1981d: 729)

> [Alcibiades] comes to ask Socrates for something that he does not know what it is, but he calls it *agalma*. Some of you know the use I made of this term a while back, I want to use it again, this *agalma,* this mystery that, in the fog surrounding the gaze of Alcibiades, represents something beyond all recognized goods [*biens*]. (Lacan 1973: 283–84)

Lacan's reading of the *Antigone* represents a crucial juncture in the complex network of affiliations that ties the work of Sartre, Camus, and Anouilh to the later Platonic turn of Derrida, Foucault, and Lacan himself. The central problem we are left with at the end of *Les mouches* and *Caligula* is how, in a world beyond good and evil, does a philosophy of the act create an ethics and a politics that is not a betrayal of its fundamental insight into the ungrounded nature of our being (and hence our freedom, our absurdity, and our nausea). How do we distin-

---

49. As Leonard observes, Derrida and Irigaray have both criticized the gendered nature of Lacan's reading. Irigaray objects to Lacan's complete neglect of the civil dimension of Antigone's discourse. Derrida notes that the ethics of desire cannot exist outside the political (Leonard 2005: 130–33, 140). As I have argued throughout this text, in the final analysis the ethical and the political cannot be separated, even if they are not identical. This argument will be extended in the next chapter. For a reading of the formula of "ceding on one's desire" that is neither confined to the exclusively ethical or the feminine, but directly addresses the politics of enjoyment from a queer perspective, see Zoberman (forthcoming). More damaging is Leonard's observation that there is no textual basis for Lacan's assertion that the *Antigone* supports his reading that Jocasta is "the active agent of Oedipus' incest" (2005: 128–29).

guish Orestes' act of murder from Caligula's, from that of the genuine fascist? This search for an authentic ethics, for a genuine relation of self to self and to others, is also that faced by the protagonist of Sartre's novel, *L'âge de raison,* the final lines of which are quoted above. Having come to a clear-sighted recognition of his fundamental emptiness, of his lack (*manque de l'être*), how does Mathieu move forward without succumbing to the allure of the various consoling fictions that present themselves either in the guise of ethical systems of the past or of the muted *bonheur* of the present? To accept a Stoicism or an Epicureanism *tout fait* is not to make an ethical choice but to fail to. By the same token, the rejection of bourgeois *bonheur*—of the narcotized happiness of compromise and bad faith, of forever ceding on one's desire—is indistinguishable on its own from the empty self-assertion of Anouilh's Antigone who seeks death "pour personne, pour moi."

The fundamental problem, then, faced by Lacan is how to establish an ethics of desire, of one's own unique relation in time, space, language, and society, to the lack at the heart of being. How does one establish an ethics of psychoanalysis, which is neither a naked assertion of the will to power nor a fundamental denial of our desires through assimilating them to a system of recognized goods—of moral commodities traded in the daily commerce between the pleasure and the reality principles? The modernist turn to antiquity, which sought in the allegorical equation of present and past to dramatize these questions, was of necessity unable either to solve or to transcend them because it was predicated precisely on that equation, on an effacing of difference. This is not what Lacan offers. Rather, through his reading of Antigone's desire for a good beyond all recognized goods—which is predicated on her unrepeatable relation to Creon and his edicts, to the *atê* of the Labdacids, to her incestuous parentage, and to the conflict between competing historical concepts of *philia*—Lacan seeks to create an ethics that neither conforms to a pre-existing moral system nor revels in an authoritarian solipsism. Beyond this duality of self-denial and pre-oedipal narcissism, the ethics of psychoanalysis is always and only realized in relation to a precise and historically located other. It demands and is the product of a particular unrepeatable narrative (Armstrong 2005: 86, 137–39). This psychoanalytic ethics of desire is thus necessarily also an ethics of difference. Antigone, like Freud's Dora or the Wolfman,[50] may serve as an example, but we cannot be her. Antigone's desire is authentic only to the extent that it is unique,

---

50. Two famous characters from his case studies.

and it is unique only in its simultaneous relation to and constitution by the Other (Creon, the *polis,* the Law, etc.).⁵¹

From this recognition, it is but a short step to Lacan's reading of the *Symposium,* for it is precisely the question of the relation between desire and the Other that is at stake in the eighth seminar, *Le transfert.* As Lacan makes clear above, Alcibiades' desire is conceived along lines directly parallel to those of Antigone: his search for the Socratic *agalma* represents a desire for a good "beyond all goods." Of course, Alcibiades, as one who has yet to embrace philosophy (*philosophia*) fully, does not understand that. He does not recognize his desire. He believes its object is something that is directly in Socrates' possession, that it is a good exchangeable with other goods. It will only be in Socrates' refusal to grant him that object that Alcibiades will have the occasion to recognize the true nature of his desire. For however fleeting a moment, Alcibiades, as a result of his intimate commerce with the philosopher, begins to analyze, and hence care for, his soul. He comes to have an inkling of the possibility of a good beyond those recognized by the agonistic world of the democratic *polis.* With that intuition, however, comes the simultaneous realization that he can stay in that world of competitive political honors (*philotimia*) only by stopping his ears, by rejecting Socrates' *atopia* in favor of the subject position Athens has bequeathed him, and thus by ceding on his desire.

> Still, I swear to you, the moment he starts to speak, I am beside myself: my heart starts leaping in my chest, the tears come streaming down my face, even the frenzied Corybantes seem sane compared to me. [. . .] [H]e makes it seem that my life isn't worth living! You can't say that isn't true, Socrates. I know very well that you could make me feel that way this very moment if I gave you half a chance. He always traps me, you see, and he makes me admit

---

51. This is the foundation of its empirical nature, of its status as History or the Real. As Richard Armstrong reminds us, Lacan in his insistence on this point is very Freudian. Indeed, it is precisely this insistence on the unique and the unrepeatable that separates psychoanalysis from the discipline of psychology and the other normative (and normalizing) social sciences:

> The importance of the empirical for Freud lies not in what can be replicated in the laboratory, but what is *experienced* between the analyst and the analysand: the phenomena of transference and resistance. (Armstrong 2005: 43; emphasis in original)

It is precisely the constructed nature of our experience as a relation with the Other (the analyst, father, the love-object, the Symbolic) that guarantees its profoundly historical and differential nature.

that my political career is a waste of time, while all that matters is just what I most neglect: my personal shortcomings, which cry out for the closest attention. So I refuse to listen to him; I stop my ears and tear myself way from him, for, like the Sirens, he could make me stay by his side till I die. (215e–216b; Nehamas and Woodruff 1997: 497–98)

Socrates' discourse thus represents a true "thought from the outside." It is literally without a place (*atopos*) in the world of the *polis*. Owing to its simultaneous focus on an absolute interiority (the self, the soul, the psyche) and an absolute externality (the forms, the one, the good, the beautiful), it exists beyond the bounds of civic ideology. In the *Alcibiades,* the *Symposium*'s prequel, Socrates, however, claims that it is only through philosophy, only through a genuine care of the self, that Alcibiades will eventually be able to be a true success in politics, because only then will he recognize the nature of the good and be able to seek it for his fellow citizens. (The *Alcibiades* will be a crucial text for Foucault.)

It is thus only through a love of wisdom (*philosophia*), only through a species of desire, that one can come to a real thought from the outside, that one can encounter a mode of thought and self-relation that does not simply repeat the founding prejudices of a given community and thus nullify ethical and political action. This "askesis," in turn, this "exercise of the self, in thought," as Foucault reminds us, is the true labor of philosophy (Foucault 1984a: 15). And, as we shall see, it is precisely in the complex and overdetermined nexus between philosophy, ethics, psychoanalysis, and the construction of the subject that Derrida and Foucault will respond to Lacan. These responses, in turn, will be made in terms of their own distinctive readings of the Platonic corpus.

Chapter 4

Lacan, the *Symposium,* and Transference

> Freud also observed overvaluation in the case of transference-love, when in the therapeutic situation there is "a transference of feelings onto the person of the doctor" though the situation in the treatment does not justify the development of such feelings. In the next paragraph Freud tells us that transference-love, somewhat surprisingly, occurs in the case of male as well as female patients (towards a male doctor). (Santas 1988: 121, citing SE XVI, 442)

> The internal contradiction of a morality of happiness, in which one aims only at the happy state of the subject, is that this prey flees us insofar as we search for it. If we pursue happiness, we are never happy. We obtain a bit of rest, a bit of peace, but only in the moment that we renounce the quest and transfer in some way our happiness into the happiness of an Other. However this Other is named—Justice, the Good, Duty, Moral Law, God—it is by losing oneself in it that one finds oneself again. (Festugière 1950: 332; uppercase in the original)

1. Why Antigone Must Read the *Symposium*

ONE OF the most disturbing things about Lacan's reading of Antigone is her absolute dedication to the obscene kernel of her enjoyment (*jouissance*), to *das Ding*. There is an asocial immediacy to absolute enjoyment, to pure desire, which while profoundly ethical—in the sense of representing an absolute dedication to the transformation of self, which the realization of a desire beyond the pleasure and reality principles requires—nonetheless also figures a rupture with the Symbolic order as we know it (Irigaray 1977b: 95). It is an ethics that demands the transgression of the law as its universal maxim (Lacan 1966f). This is a most peculiar ethics to say the least, and one that certainly does not seek to promote happiness as it is commonly understood. But, is such an ethics good? Could we, would we, want to live in a world peopled by Lacanian Antigones, a world of beautiful, but monstrous enjoyment, the world of the death drive (Žižek 1992: 134)?[1]

Maybe Guyomard is right in his critique of Lacan's reading. Maybe Creon should be our model (1992). At minimum, Lacan's interpretation provokes a number of questions. Does the choice of Antigone not ultimately rest on an ethical model of incest and self-destruction (Lacan 1986: 83)? Are the good and the beautiful to be equated if the pursuit of the latter leads not to calm repose but to the sublime depravity of Niobe turned to stone and Antigone's virginal bedding by Hades?

What happens, then, if we translate this ethics from the individual to the *polis* as a whole? As a model of collective action, would not the choice of Antigone represent precisely the very aestheticization of politics that Benjamin describes as the essence of fascism (1969: 241–42)?[2] And if so, does not Lacan's Antigone, therefore, in the last analysis rejoin Anouilh's? The *Liebestod* of Haemon with Antigone is, on this reading, only too Wagnerian, a love-death every bit as moral as Hitler's Nuremberg rallies and the suicide bomber hell-bent on paradise.

Such an interpretation, however, is an impoverishment of both Lacan and *Antigone*. It assumes that Antigone's *jouissance* exists without Creon and that her desire for death represents an ahistorical constant. It assumes that the law, and hence its transgression, is one and unchanging. In opposition to a monolithic present, it can offer only what Witt describes in Anouilh's case as "timeless worlds of the imaginary past, childhood or death: a kind of pre-Oedipal *jouissance*" (2001: 235). Yet, if such is the case, then, any drive toward aesthetic transcendence would be equally fascist, an assertion of the death drive in the name of beauty. Antigone's "non" would always necessarily, as in the case of Anouilh, lead to the affirmation of an empty will to power. Why does she defy Creon, bury her brother, and seek death? "*Pour personne, pour moi.*"

Such questions pose not merely an abstract theoretical problem, devoid of practical consequence, but one on which the bedrock questions

---

1. This question, I would argue, is as urgent for Sophocles' Antigone as for Lacan's. It is, of course, true that it is anachronistic in the extreme to assume that Sophocles proposed Antigone to his audience as an ethical model. But that is precisely the way she has functioned in the western imagination for the last two centuries. Lacan, on one reading, does little more than draw the necessary consequences of the status that Antigone already holds in our thought. If the results are disturbing, that is no reason to shoot the messenger.

2. Mussolini confided to the biographer Emil Ludwig that "'everything depends on dominating the mass like an artist' . . . his ambition was to make a dramatic masterpiece of his own life" (Witt 2001: 6).

of meaningful political and ethical action rest. For if we accept Guyomard's position that it is Creon, not Antigone, who presents the real ethical model, if we have determined that ethics is a process of choosing from the socially recognized goods sanctioned by the pleasure and reality principles as they exist under a given Symbolic regime, then we have necessarily foreclosed the possibility of not only a radical critique of the existing order, but also of any fundamental transformation of ourselves. Guyomard's reading of Lacan's interpretation of the Antigone poses precisely the problem that we outlined in chapter 2's investigation of the modernists: "Are we not then doomed to choosing between a suffocating positivist dystopia and a fascist utopian beyond?"

The fact is, however, that Antigone's desire has no sense outside the signifying chain that makes it possible and that articulates its demand for transcendence. Creon's edicts may not, as Antigone intimates, be the material cause of her desire "to lie dear with dear" in the arms of death, but nonetheless without them her demand would be an empty signifier devoid of content. What would Antigone be if there were no Creon? What could she possibly mean? Moreover, it is not the case that without Creon the content of her desire would be different, but the form would remain the same. Creon in a meaningful sense is but metonymy for the Law and for the Symbolic norms of kinship, exchange, and behavior that constitute the fabric of Greek society (Steiner 1984: 37; Segal 1990: 164–65). However, those norms never exist in abstraction (Butler 1990: 28, 55, 76). They never exist per se, but always as a historically specific set of signifying practices, of discrete unrepeatable speech acts that occur within a larger set of discursive norms that render them intelligible (Holquist 1990: 167; Voloshinov 1986: 167). This is what Lacan means when he says the big Other does not exist. The imagined totalization of rules and expectations that make up the Symbolic as a single coherent system, to which we must adhere in order to be recognized as subjects, has no reality except as a series of events that appeal to a diverse and often incoherent body of implicit rules and expectations that ground their intelligibility.[3] Creon is the synecdochic evocation of this Other whose ultimate nonexistence, yet tragic efficacy, the play lays bare, even as Antigone's desire can only be articulated in terms of a transgression of these very rules, which are always of necessity particular and historically determined.

Jouissance, the enjoyment that is beyond the pleasure principle,

---

3. See Lacan (1973: 228); Julien (1990: 155); Žižek in Hanlon (2001: 12); Žižek (1991: 77–78); and Ragland-Sullivan (1986: 299–300).

then, becomes the condition of possibility for the meaningful transformation of self and other, for the radical negation of what is. It is at once transgressive and the ground necessary for the creation of any authentic new regime of pleasure and its limits (Bataille 1957: 15, 43, 75; Janan 1994: 5). As Julia Kristeva writes:

> In our modern societies without any beyond, or at least with transcendence removed from this world (Protestantism) or reduced to dust (Catholicism in its present crisis), counterculture remains the sole refuge of *jouissance* because it is precisely an a-topia, a place removed from the law, a lock in the canal of utopia. (1979: 13)

Atopia, it will be recalled from the last chapter, is what characterizes both Socrates in his refusal of the unexamined goods (*biens*) of the traditional Athenian *polis* and Antigone in the purity of her desire (see page 64).

"Counterculture" is perhaps an unfortunate translation for Kristeva's "contre-société," with the image of drug-addled hippies and naive rock stars out to "change the world" that it necessarily conjures. Nonetheless, it should not be missed that it was precisely in the canalization and ultimate collectivization of new modes of *jouissance* that sixties radicalism made its most lasting contributions to postmodern society. Gay, lesbian, and women's liberation are all ultimately senseless except in their ability to posit forms of enjoyment that are beyond the law, that transgress the norms of phallic and partriarchal subject formation. Nor are such moments of atopia limited to explicitly sexual matters. The lives of the saints, the self-mortification of the desert fathers, monastic practices of all sorts, both Buddhist and Christian, represent fundamental attempts to transform and collectivize radically different forms of being in the world and the forms of *jouissance* they establish.[4] By the same token, the utopian socialist movements of the last two centuries posited radically different relations between the subject and the community of recognized goods, and hence new forms of enjoyment that demanded in turn new forms of intersubjectivity. Likewise, the surrealists, the dadaists, and other avant-garde artistic movements of the early twentieth century all posited fundamentally new forms of beauty, existence, and enjoyment.[5] Nor would any of these movements—

---

4. On the relation between *jouissance* and mysticism, that is as an encounter with being, with the not-all that escapes the Symbolic, and hence its relation to woman, see Lacan (1975: 66–71, 76–77); Luepnitz (2003: 228–29); and Janan (1994: 30).

5. On Lacan's relations with the surrealists as well as other members of the artistic

from the desert fathers to Queer Nation—have been possible without the violence, the obscenity, and the excess that, from the perspective of normative culture, defines radical transgression, and a true "thought from the outside."

Psychoanalysis and its ethics, from this point of view, are the enemies of all forms of quietism and resignation that, through the discourse of a master, seek to deny the passions. Psychoanalysis seeks to rouse them, to incite us to insist on our desire and not to settle for any substitutes, including normative sexual satisfaction (Jameson 1988: 44; Braunstein 2003: 107). Thus Žižek argues that Lacan's ultimate political goal was to produce an analytic collective whose discourse was sustained not by any claims of mastery or authority but by the very surplus of enjoyment that is the sign of the object of desire's relation to the Real. Psychoanalysis "asserts a violent passion to introduce a Difference, a gap in the order of being" (Žižek forthcoming).

Moreover, it is precisely in terms of the insistence on new forms of collective enjoyment that Antigone's claim, as Judith Butler observes, resonates with particular clarity today:

> [For this is] a time in which the family is at once idealized in nostalgic ways within various cultural forms, a time in which the Vatican protests against homosexuality not only as an assault on the family but also on the notion of the human, where to become human, for some, requires participation in the family in its normative sense.... [T]his is a time in which kinship has become fragile, porous and expansive. It is also a time in which straight and gay families are sometimes blended, or in which gay families emerge in nuclear and non-nuclear forms. What will the legacy of Oedipus be for those who are formed in these situations, where positions are hardly clear, where the place of the father is dispersed, where the place of the mother is multiply occupied or displaced, where the symbolic in its stasis no longer holds? (2000: 22–23)

The moment Butler describes is precisely one in which Antigone's desire has become collectivized, in which the relations between law, pleasure, kinship, and transgressive enjoyment have become directly and insistently problematized. Such a collective demand, however, is not able to be generalized into an ahistorical universal, nor is it conceivable

---

and intellectual avant-garde from the twenties on, see Roudinesco (1997: 31–32) and Rabaté (2003a: 18; 2003b: xix–xxi).

outside the particular structures that gave rise to it. The notion that all those who practice same-sex eroticism at any time or in any place have an inherent, inalienable right to participate in marital institutions based on modern Christian conceptions of heterosexual monogamy becomes ridiculous as soon as it is formulated in universalizing terms. At the same time, there is absolutely nothing ridiculous about the demands for gay marriage in the specific legal and cultural context of postmodern western society. Similarly, Antigone's demand, when abstracted from fifth-century concepts of family, *philia,* the proper relation of the individual to the *polis,* the status of women, and the broader cultural resonances of the myth of the Labdacids, may appear gratuitous and perverse. It gains its beauty and power, Antigone's sublime transcendence, only to the extent that its historical particularity is restored. Her *jouissance* is not pre-, but post-Oedipal, in all senses of the word.

Paradoxically, where this recognition of the historical contingency of Antigone's (and our) desire leads is to the recognition that *das Ding,* while logically prior to the subject's entry into language and the Symbolic, in fact has no pre-empiric existence. Rather it is always a retrospective construction of the "not all,"[6] of that which exceeds a given Symbolic formation and its grid of intelligibility (Silverman 2000: 16; Copjec 2002: 6; Žižek 2004: 60). If the cardinal ethical principle of psychoanalysis is not to engage in the self-betrayal entailed in ceding on one's desire, then the analyst's role is to assist in this retrospective reconstruction that leads the subject through her signifying chain, its own unique pattern of associations, recollections, slips, dreams, and interpretations to the realization of the lack that structures its being (Lacan 1986: 362, 368–71). The analyst's role is to assume the position of the Other, the principle of coherence that founds the system, to serve as a kind of placeholder guaranteeing that "the inconsistent string of 'free associations' will retroactively receive meaning" (Žižek 1992: 39).

This principle of coherence for which the analyst stands is ultimately the phallus,[7] the missing object that everyone wants to be or to

---

6. This is of course Lacan's term for the position of the feminine in the psychic economy as that which escapes the phallic totalization of the masculine Symbolic. As such, it represents Lacan's rereading of Hegel's dictum, said in relation to Antigone, that "woman is the everlasting irony of the community" (Hegel 1977: 288). The feminine for Lacan, however, unlike Hegel, is a position, under which he includes his own *Ecrits,* not a category of being. See Lacan (1973: 13, 53–71, 75); Irigaray (1977b: 106–7); Kristeva (1979: 15); Janan (1994: 30); Weed (1994: 89); Leonard (2005: 132–33). *Das Ding* ultimately occupies the place of the lost plenitude of a retrospectively posited unity with the maternal.

7. The fantasy of phallic plenitude has clear resonances with Aristotelian *eudaimonia,*

have, which, if present, would ground the system of Symbolic norms in the Real and thus close the gap between our Imaginary self-projections and our social and linguistic identifications. The phallus represents the desire of the Other, the *clef de voûte* that would supply this consistency (Julien 1990: 124; Janan 1994: 21; Luepnitz 2003: 226). But the desire that the phallus names is defined precisely as that which is missing, as the founding lack, difference, or gap that is required if the signifying system is to function. It is a signifier without equal precisely because it has no signified. The phallus literally means nothing.[8] It points to the impossibility of Symbolic closure, to there never being a last word, a meaning that would be completely adequate, bringing the process of signification and association to a close.[9] The analyst's role is to figure this lack and thus make possible the recognition and realization of the analysand's desire as a specific and unrepeatable relation to the signifying chain (Lacan 1991: 18).

The assumption of this position is called *transference*. In the analytic situation as formulated by Freud and Breuer in their *Studies on Hysteria,* at the same time the analyst becomes the object of desire, and his or her desire is also necessarily solicited. These two phenomena are known as *transference* and *countertransference* respectively. Lacan condensed these two inherently related notions into a single formulation, the "desire of the analyst," in which the genitive is both subjective and objective. They are at the center of his reading of Plato's *Symposium,* which opened seminar 8, *Le transfert* (1991), and which immediately followed his reading of the *Antigone* (7).

The conjunction of the ethics of psychoanalysis with the problem of transference is anything but fortuitous (Leonard 2005: 185). The analytic situation is precisely the moment in which the analyst's individual ideological and libidinal investments come face to face with those of the analysand who seeks understanding, liberation, and ultimately the realization of his or her own desire. The ethics of analysis demands a

---

as David Wray has pointed out to me. Lacanian ethics, however, seek to traverse the fantasy rather than to realize it. Lacan's continued use of the term phallus, even while denying that the phallus is the penis, is the source of controversy (Feher-Gurewich 2003: 194; Lacan 1982: 168). His usage is defended by some because it points precisely to the confusion of the penis with the phallus that founds patriarchy's long and sordid history. "Because I have a penis, I have a special claim to Symbolic power" (Ragland-Sullivan 1986: 283). Others contend the continued use of the term helps to perpetuate its reign (Tort 2000: 176–77).

8. As should be clear from this formulation, Lacan's concept of the phallus assumes the universality of castration (Luepnitz 2003: 227).

9. See Lacan (1986: 362; 1975: 40); Ragland-Sullivan (1986: 281–82); Plotnitsky (2000: 272); Braunstein (2003: 111).

radical openness to the desire of the other and a simultaneous refusal of a false objectivity, of a disavowal of our own inescapable demand (Chaitin 1996: 180–84).

More precisely, in the analytic situation, the analysand, through transference, metaphorizes the analyst, as the Other to whom the discourse of demand is addressed, into the place of his or her desire. The analyst comes to occupy the position of that desire and his or her refusal to comment directly on the associative chain of the analysand produces the surface on which the analysand in turn comes to recognize the nature of that desire. The danger comes in the possibility—indeed the necessity—of countertransference, that is, in the process whereby the analyst's own desires are solicited by the discourse of the analysand. Like Socrates in his relation with Alcibiades, the moment the analyst yields to these solicitations, the analytic situation is reversed and the doctor becomes the patient, the beloved the lover, and the chain of association short-circuits. By the same token, the moment the analyst refuses the countertransference, the moment Socrates refuses the affective bond, then all hope of Alcibiades' pursuit of the good is lost, the transferential relationship is broken (Lacan 1991: 185–86).

It is thus only through a profound knowledge of the nature of his or her own desire that the analyst can serve as the mirror for the analysand and countertransference be turned into a means of investigating, rather than satisfying or frustrating, the desire of the other. It is only through an understanding of the fundamentally empty nature of his or her desire that the analyst can serve in this role (Lacan 1986: 347–51; 1992: 127). That emptiness is not a void or absence, but a refusal of every fetish, a fundamental openness: the recognition of desire per se (Žižek 1991: 131; Feher-Gurewich 2000: 369; Freiberger 2000: 225–26). As Diotima teaches Socrates in the *Symposium*, *Erôs* (Desire) can never represent any specific good (beauty, wisdom, wealth, happiness), but can only be fully realized in the pursuit of the good per se. Transference, metaphoricity, and substitution are thus not means to an end, but inherent in the nature of desire itself (Julien 1990: 120). Like Socrates, the analyst must be able to lie on the couch with Alcibiades and arise in the morning unstained.

Transference, the search for a subject supposed to know, cannot be escaped (Žižek 1990: 168). The analyst is always desired and desiring. But the analyst must respond with a relentless and ascetic negativity[10] that reveals the illusory nature of each neurotic, fetishistic substitution,

---

10. In the sense of Adorno in *Negative Dialectics* (1983), see McCredie (1998).

without yielding to the temptations of countertransference, of imposing one's own fetishes, one's own object of desire, as a totalizing discourse of mastery. Analysis is both the product of and an answer to suffering. It demands an ethics of care (Silverman 2000: 29–50) and listening, a loving Socratic asceticism, and a relentless criticism of all attempts to arrest the discourse of desire, to normalize it, and to cede on its realization by accepting, as Cephalus does in *Republic* Book 1, the decreed range of acceptable social goods (*biens*) as the definition of our being (Blondell 2002: 168–73).

2. Socratic Therapy: Γνῶθι σεαυτόν

> Dialogue is, in a certain sense, already an exercise in death. For, as R. Schaerer [1969] has said, "corporal individuality ceases to exist at the moment in which it exteriorizes itself in the *logos*." . . . From the perspective of the story of the death of Socrates in the *Phaedo,* we see that the "I" that must die transcends itself in an "I," which is henceforth a stranger to death, because it identifies itself with the *logos* and thought. (Hadot 1995b: 110)

> Perhaps Plato's use of myth and image is an attempt to state something about the limits of reason, together with an insight into the consequences of this limit for ethical conduct. What if he is simply propounding what appears to be a metaphysics for the sole purpose of having it subverted in the destructive/interpretive act that transforms it into an ethical practice? Plato is well aware of what he is doing. He is engaged in something very like a Wittgensteinian "destruction," which recognizes the necessity of appealing beyond the system of cultural constructions of ordinary language in order to discover not a real entity, but the possibility—already implicit in the language of the crowd . . . of articulating another standard for our conduct than the parental, conventional, and theoretical constructs that hold us in the sway of their imaginary power. (Freiberger 2000: 242)

In this section, we shall examine the relation between Socratic and psychoanalytic practice, and their respective conceptions of desire. The Socratic *elenchus,* the process of question, answer, and refutation that lies at the heart of the Socratic dialectic as it is presented in the early and portions of the middle[11] and even late dialogues (Nehamas

---

11. I will continue to use this conventional distinction between the shorter, aporetical dialogues, and the longer more elaborate "constructive dialogues," though, as Blondell argues (2002: 10–13), there is no unambiguous proof that the shorter aporetical dialogues uniformly date to an earlier period than the so-called "middle dialogues." See also Annas (1993: 19).

1998: 72), is, of course, very different from the analyst's self-effacement. Indeed, Socrates' interlocutors are asked to do anything but free associate. Rather there is a relentless demand for definition as each succeeding approximation reveals the degree of delusion under which the various interlocutors suffer. As Socrates explains in the *Apology*, he roamed the streets of Athens trying to disprove the oracle at Delphi's pronouncement that he was the wisest man alive. This could not be true since the only thing Socrates knew was that he was empty, that he knew nothing. Surely, amidst all the wise poets, politicians, and craftsmen of Athens there were many wiser than he. Nonetheless, when Socrates came to question these people, time and again he found that although they possessed certain skills (*technai*), or had a knack for certain activities, they could give no rational account (*logos*) of either that knack or of themselves. Nor were they able to show that the possession of these skills in any way made them better, happier, or more just, yet every one of them considered himself to be knowledgeable. In the end Socrates concludes, much to his surprise, that the oracle was right: not because he possesses some special wisdom that he could dispense to others, but because he alone knows that he knows nothing. Nonetheless, this knowledge provides no satisfaction in and of itself. The pursuit of wisdom does not abate. To cease from asking questions would be to pretend to have an answer, to pretend that one possessed bounded determinate knowledge separate from the process of investigation that produced and uncovered it, to pretend to be a god (Hunter 2004: 86–87). But Socrates rejects this hubristic reification. His intention, therefore, is to continue questioning all those he encounters, both to try to find someone who knows more than he and, failing that, to lead others to the knowledge that they too know nothing (20c–23b; Ledbetter 2003: 114–16).

The goal of the *elenchus*, then, is to produce self-knowledge and hence to adhere to the precept carved over the entrance to the oracle at Delphi, "Know thyself," which, it turns out, is little more than a variation on the oracle's pronouncement that Socrates is the wisest of all men. Thus, one formulation of the self-knowledge produced by the Socratic dialectic is precisely a recognition of one's own emptiness in the Lacanian sense, an encounter with pure desire through the methodical exteriorization of the self in the *logos* by means of the emotionally charged situation of dialogue with a Socratic master.

> In the end, after having conversed with Socrates, his interlocutor no longer knows why he does what he does. He becomes conscious of

the contradictions of his discourse and of his own internal contradictions. He doubts himself. He comes like Socrates to know that he knows nothing. But by doing this, he takes a certain distance from himself, doubles himself, with a part of himself even identifying with Socrates in the mutual accord that Socrates demands of his interlocutor at each step in the discussion. (Hadot 1995b: 55)

Thus in the greater *Alcibiades,* Socrates presents himself as a suitor to the young aristocrat, and as an earnest of his love, leads the youth through a series of questions and answers to the realization that he is utterly lacking in self-knowledge, and hence of any real knowledge of matters of state.[12] Yet it is precisely this dialectic of question and answer, revealing the interlocutor's own emptiness to himself, that proves so seductive and all but irresistible. As Alcibiades says of his encounters with Socrates in his speech in the *Symposium,* which we have quoted before:

Whenever I hear his words my heart leaps more than that of Cybele's Corybantic priests,[13] and tears pour forth. I see many others also suffering these same things.... And still, even now, I am aware that if I were to wish to lend my ears to him, I could not hold out, but I would suffer the very same thing. For he forces me to agree that, although I am still greatly lacking, I neglect myself while busying myself with the affairs of the Athenians.[14] And so, I force myself to stop my ears and run away in flight, as from the Sirens, lest I grow old seated here by him. (215d–216a)

Alcibiades must choose between a career as a politician and a general and the siren song of philosophical self-knowledge. The *jouissance* that is the "love"—or, as Diotima makes clear, the "desire," *erôs*—of wisdom (*philo-sophia*) is, as in the case of Antigone, the encounter with a good beyond all the traditionally recognized goods of the Athenian *polis*—political accomplishment (*philotimia*) and personal fame (*kleos*)—beyond the pleasure principle.[15]

---

12. For a more thorough discussion of this dialogue, see chapter 6.
13. Worshippers of Cybele, depicted in Catullus 63, they castrate themselves in a ritual marriage to the Great Mother goddess. Alcibiades is thus unmanned in his devotion to Socrates, even as the effect of Socrates' discourse is compared to the orgiastic rites that accompany this mystical union.
14. Compare *Apology* 29d–e (Dover 1980: ad loc).
15. Hence, it is compared to initiation into the Mysteries (Hunter 2004: 92–93). On Alcibiades' *philotimia*, see Wohl (2002: 139–40).

That encounter is staged, and the desire realized, through the erotic reciprocity that characterizes Socratic discourse (Halperin 1990a: 270). Gregory Vlastos describes the peculiar mix of intellectual and erotic charge that makes up the Socratic dialectic as follows:

> That form of passionate experience invented by Plato, which should count as the original, and always primary, sense of "Platonic love," is a peculiar mix of sensuality, sentiment, and intellect—a companionship bonded by erotic attraction no less than by intellectual give-and-take. (1970: 39–40)

The give and take between master and student, lover and beloved has as its primary effect to reveal to the student/analysand the empty nature of their fantasy construction, i.e., of the system of goods around which they have organized their lives in conformity with the pleasure principle. This traversing of the fantasy is achieved primarily, not through Socrates' doctrinal declarations nor through the pronouncement of long and eloquent speeches in the manner of a rhetorician such as Gorgias or Hippias (*Gorgias* 449b–c, 461c5–462a10; *Hippias Minor* 373a; Blondell 2002: 40–41), but through the methodical examination of the interlocutor's discourse in the crucible of the Socratic *elenchus*.

A fine example of the process is delivered in the *Lysis*. Socrates is making his way from the Academy to the Lyceum, two of the three main *gumnasia* in Athens, looking for conversation partners and handsome young men. The *gumnasia* represented sites of general culture—physical, spiritual and artistic—in the Greek world. It is no accident that Plato and Aristotle would later set up their own formal philosophical schools in these two *gumnasia*. The *gumnasia* were also the places where men met to exercise in the nude and hence were the sites of many erotic encounters (*Symposium* 217b–c; Hubbard 2003: 3–4, 69, 163). Socrates runs into two young men, Hippothales and Ctêsippus. The former, we find out, is deeply, but unrequitedly, in love with the aristocratic young Lysis, composing poems and speeches in his praise, but all to no avail. Socrates informs him that this is wholly the wrong strategy. Praising young boys only makes them arrogant and does not encourage them to yield. Hippothales then asks Socrates to tell him what sort of *logos* one uses in conversation (*dialegomenos*) with a young man in order to become dear (*prosphilês*) to him. Socrates responds that it is difficult to say, but "if you were to wish to make him come into words (*logous*) with me, perhaps I would be able to show you with respect to what things it is necessary to converse with him (*dialegesthai*) in place of those that these men say you now say and sing" (206c4–7). I have chosen to translate this passage quite literally to bring out the ambiguities of the Greek. On the one hand Socrates says merely, if you invite him to talk with me I will show you how to converse with a boy. On the other, the passage is filled with the burgeoning technical vocabulary of Platonic philosophy[16] and can also be translated, "if he were to enter into the realm of the *logos* with me, I would be able to show you how to enter into a dialectical conversation with him [and then you would see how to become truly *philos* ("dear," "a friend") to the young man]." Thus, on the one hand Socrates offers a lesson in seduction, a kind of pederastic *ars amatoria*. On the other hand, what he really presents is an initiation into philosophy that is shown to fascinate these young boys in a manner analogous to Alcibiades. Hippothales accepts Socrates' offer to show him how to talk to boys.

After some brief preliminaries, Socrates enters into a dialectical conversation with the young men about the nature of *philia*. The end result, however, is "aporetical" (Robin 1964: 39–40; Derrida 1994: 179). This is a common feature of the early dialogues, in which what counts is the practice of the dialectic and "the transformation it brings. Sometimes the function of the dialogue is . . . to reveal the limits of language, the impossibility of communicating moral and existential experience" (Hadot 1995b: 105). In the case of the *Lysis,* what makes a man *philos* to another is never sufficiently defined. For the good man by definition cannot be deficient in any way. Thus he will not be a friend either to another good man, since he is self-sufficient, or to a bad man who can bring him only harm. Nor will a bad man be a friend to a bad man since a bad man is one who by definition cannot do good and so he will benefit neither from befriending another bad man, nor from being befriended by one. Likewise, the bad man, in so far as he is bad, will not love the good man and so will not befriend the good. The only possibility left open is that someone who is neither good nor bad would befriend the good, in so far as he or she suffers some evil and so has need of the good, just as a sick man has need of medicine. This last option anticipates Diotima's doctrine in the *Symposium,* in which Erôs is described as a *daimôn* because he occupies an intermediate position between good and evil, the beautiful and the ugly, the gods and men. Yet Socrates in the *Lysis* hesitates to accept this solution

16. The *Lysis* is often considered a relatively early dialogue, almost certainly written before the *Gorgias*, the *Republic,* and the *Symposium*, whose later discussions of dialectics and *philia* it nonetheless anticipates. See Vlastos (1970: 35–37).

unreservedly, for it seems to imply that the good is desirable, and hence truly good, only in the presence of evil. Or as Socrates says:

Ταῦτα μὲν γὰρ φίλου ἕνεκα φίλα κέκληται, τὸ δὲ τῷ ὄντι φίλον πᾶν τοὐναντίον τούτου φαίνεται πεφυκός· φίλον γὰρ ἡμῖν ἀνεφάνη ὂν ἐχθροῦ ἕνεκα, εἰ δὲ τὸ ἐχθρὸν ἀπέλθοι, οὐκέτι, ὡς ἔοικ᾽, ἔσθ᾽ ἡμῖν φίλον.(220e2–5)

These things are called dear on account of being dear, but in truth the dear appears to be wholly the opposite of this nature: for the dear has been manifest to us on account of that which is inimical, if the inimical should depart, it would most likely no longer be dear to us.

This line of reasoning would be tough sledding for most adolescent boys. The aridness of the dialectical argumentation here is striking. The repetitions of *philos* and *ekhthros* seem to empty the terms of meaning as though they were counters moved about on a mental chessboard.

In the end, other solutions for the problem of what it means to be a friend or dear are proposed, but none is completely satisfying.[17] Clearly, then, when Socrates is proposing the *elenchus* as a means of seduction, he is exemplifying his famous irony.[18] We are a long way

17. Socrates does manage to coax Menexenus, Lysis' cousin, into agreeing to the proposition that the lawful and sincere lover should be held dear (*phileisthai*) by his boy (222a6–b1). This seems primarily a joke designed to demonstrate the power of eristic argumentation to extort consent from young boys. One of the charges against Socrates, of course, was corruption of the youth. But unlike those sophists who specifically advertised the ability to make the weaker argument the stronger, Socrates concedes the specious nature of his argument (222e1–7) even as he demonstrates his superiority as an *erastês* to Hippothales.

18. Vlastos (1991: 115–17) argues that the *elenchus* is jettisoned by Plato in the *Lysis*, *Hippias Major*, and *Euthydemus* as he moves away from imitating Socrates and toward the establishment of a properly Platonic philosophy. The *Lysis* he argues presents but a pale imitation of the *elenchus* because the teenagers, unlike Callicles and Polus in the *Gorgias*, do not offer their own theses, but merely respond naively to Socrates' questions. It is often left to the latter then to demolish his own arguments. But Vlastos's position, while brilliantly argued, is clearly an oversimplification (Blondell 2002: 10–11). First, elenctic argumentation can be found throughout the corpus, even if at times it becomes less prominent or less intense. It clearly features in Socrates' interrogation of Agathon in the *Symposium*, Diotima's interrogation of Socrates in the same work, the last section of the *Phaedrus*, the *Philebus*, the *Meno*, the greater *Alcibiades*, and elsewhere to a greater or lesser extent. Second, the *elenchus* is not always as robust in the early works as Vlastos would have us believe. Ion in the dialogue that bears his name is certainly no better at argument than Lysis and Menexenus are in the *Lysis*. Third, as the seventh letter makes

from Ovid's seductive wit in this dialogue. The investigation of the nature of *philia* produces no firm conclusions, only dizzying exercises in dialectical argumentation that produce lines such as, ἕνεκα ἄρα τοῦ φίλου <τοῦ φίλου> τὸ φίλον φίλον διὰ τὸ ἐχθρόν ("Thus on account of the dearness of the dear, the dear is dear through the inimical") (219b2–3),[19] which would be of doubtful efficacy as a means of either seduction or persuasion.[20] Indeed, Socrates himself admits at the time to becoming "dizzied" or "drunk" from the convolutions of his own argument (216c5, 222c2).

And yet, oddly, his conversation with Lysis seems to have had the desired effect. The dialogue closes with Socrates saying:

> And so what might we still do with the *logos?* Or is it clear that there is nothing more to be done? And so now, we must, just like the sophists in court, ponder all that has been said. For if indeed neither the loved, nor the loving, nor the same, nor the different, nor the good, nor the familiar, nor any of the things we have gone through—there were so many I no longer remember—but if none of these is dear I no longer know what I might say.[21] (222e1–7)

The confession of aporia at the end of such an exercise might well be thought to dash all of Hippothales' erotic hopes, but it seems that Socrates' have been enhanced. In the final lines of the *Lysis,* as the others leave, Socrates turns and says to his two young interlocutors:

> Now, Lysis and Menexenus, we have become laughing stocks, both I, an old man, and you. For these leaving will say that we think ourselves to be friends of one another [or, *to be dear to one another*]—for I place myself among you—but we have not at all been able to say what a friend [or, *the dear one*] is. (223b4–7)

---

clear, which, whether accepted as genuine or not, derives from the early Academy (see chapter 6 for a fuller discussion), the primary means of philosophical instruction remained for Plato, to the end, elenctic discussion between friends (344b5; Szlezák 1999: 7). See the definition in Robin (1929: lxxii–lxxiii).

19. The text is Race's (1983).

20. One of the readers for the press suggested that the line was meant as an example of Gorgianic playfulness, but in the context of the dialogue as a whole, it smacks more of an exercise in logic chopping than of the clever deployment of the rhetoric of repetition.

21. The normal assumption is that *legô* is deliberative subjunctive (Race 1983: ad loc). Morphologically, however, there is no reason why it might not be indicative, in which case the final clause would be translated, "I no longer know what I am saying," a very Lacanian sentiment.

Whether Socrates has in fact become "dear" to the boys is left unclear, but it seems that others will think so, precisely because he has inserted himself into their midst. Collectively, they all will be ridiculous because they have become friends without being able to define what being a friend is. Yet in that they are no more ridiculous than other men, who, as the *Apology* demonstrates, regularly make claims to titles or status that they can neither define nor defend. Moreover, in emptying out the term *philos*, in reaching the point where they no longer know what it means, in having become "drunk" on the *logos*, they have very precisely gained an insight into their own natures, which those who laugh at them do not have. They now know that they do not know. How real the boys' insight is—whether like Socrates in the *Apology* they now know that, at least on this topic, they know nothing—will determine if they do, in fact, become the *philoi* of Socrates and of the *sophia* he seeks. This alone will decide if they have truly become bonded by a common desire, for which Socratic conversation is the unique and all but indescribable vehicle.

If that is indeed the case, however, what they would come to love in Socrates through the dialectic is something more and other than Socrates himself. If the *Lysis* demonstrates anything, it is that what we love (*phileô*) in the other is not the other as itself, but the other as the representative or vehicle of the *philon* ("the dear"). Thus, as Vlastos writes in his commentary on the *Lysis*, "to say of another person that he or she is what you really and truly love would be to lapse . . . into moral fetishism" (1970: 10n.25):

> Socrates . . . goes on to argue that just as we love the doctor for the sake of health, so we love health for sake of something else; hence, short of an infinite regress, there must be a πρῶτον φίλον, οὗ ἕνεκα καὶ τὰ ἄλλα φαμὲν φίλα εἶναι—a "first [i.e., terminal] object of love, for whose sake, we say, all other objects are loved" (219D), this being the only thing that is "truly" (. . . ὡς ἀληθῶς) or "really" (τῷ ὄντι) loved—or, more precisely that *should be* so loved. There is danger, Socrates warns, that "those other objects, of which we said that they are loved for *its* sake, should deceive us, like so many images of it" (219D2–4). So unless a man we loved actually *was* this πρῶτον φίλον, it would be a mistake to love him "for his own sake," to treat him, in Kant's phrase, as "an end in himself." We would then stand in need of a philosopher, like Socrates, to cure us by his dialectic, to break the illusion, and to make us see that what we "really" love is something else. (Vlastos 1970: 10; brackets in original)

The recognition and transcendence of this fetishism is what constitutes the real difference between Socrates' art of love and that of Hippothales. Hippothales desires the erotic possession of Lysis. His resort to encomia is not an effort to realize the boy's desire, but to enter into a relation of exchange in which Lysis will grant him his favors in return for the flattery proffered (Nightingale 1995: 109).[22] But Socrates becomes dear to the boys precisely insofar as he reveals that what they love *in* him is not what he personally has on offer, but something that is beyond himself, a *prôton philon,* that in itself cannot be described (219d2–4): the original dear Thing on account of which all else becomes dear. One can hardly imagine a more Lacanian formulation of love than that supplied by Vlastos himself: what we desire in the other is the encounter with that which is lacking at the heart of our being, the lost transcendental ideal that would render us whole and beyond the contingencies and compromises of Symbolic exchange and the pleasure principle (Žižek 1991: 169; 1993: 90; Lacan 1973: 119; Copjec 2002: 34). It is, in turn, this fundamental lack, the search for the original dear Thing, that as Diotima observes makes us human, because only the gods, as perfect beings, do not desire anything—even wisdom—and thus the gods (just like the wholly ignorant) are never *philo-sophoi.*[23]

The dialectic, then, is not an exchange relationship, as Alcibiades believes in the *Symposium* and as Hippothales hopes in the *Lysis.* It aims not at a simple *quid pro quo.* Rather, the give and take of the Socratic *elenchus* performed under the sign of *erôs* reveals both your position in, and the limits of, the reigning system of beliefs (*doxa*). In doing so, it does not offer a prefabricated wisdom (Hadot 1995b: 106), or one that can be detached from the process of intellectual intercourse in which it is born (*Symposium,* 208e5–209c7). The Socratic practice of the pursuit of wisdom ultimately aims at that which cannot enter into relations of exchange and substitution. "His wisdom is simply not negotiable" (Nightingale 1995: 59). It is precisely a *jouissance,* an ethical commitment, that like Antigone's is beyond the pleasure principle and thus beyond the very Symbolic means through which it is revealed (Žižek 1991: 36; Copjec 1994: 176–77). The master can prepare the student through a practice of intellectual rigor and purification, in which the intellectual and emotional fetishes (political ambition, vanity, sexual fixation) that stand between the student and the pursuit of wisdom are shown for the fragile and shoddy constructions they are,

---

22. Compare the Pergamene boy story in the *Satyricon.*
23. As Lacan observes, the gods inhabit the Real, the beyond of the Symbolic (1991: 58; Janan 1994: 62).

and the possibility of a beyond of the fantasy life they structure is envisioned, but he cannot produce or transmit the experience of that wisdom per se (Festugière 1950: 49, 191; Koyré 1962: 20; Blondell 2002: 100, 124). The student must leave the cave under his or her own power.

Nonetheless, an objection will be forthcoming, "This is a fine model perhaps for the aporetical dialogues such as the *Lysis,* the *Euthyphro,* and the *Ion.* In these dialogues, as in the *Apology,* the *elenchus* is but a means of revealing the delusion of others. But what of the great middle dialogues, such as the *Republic,* the *Phaedrus,* and the *Symposium* itself? There is most assuredly the elaboration of a positive doctrine in these dialogues, and the *elenchus* itself is often reduced to a mere mode of exposition."[24] This is not the place to engage the numerous assumptions that lie behind this response with the fullness they merit. It would take us too far afield from the nature and significance of Lacan's reading of the *Symposium.* Let it suffice to note first that, although there are undeniable stylistic and even doctrinal differences between those dialogues commonly labeled early and those labeled middle and late, at no time does Plato or Socrates simply lay out a set of propositions that are to be taken as true teaching. They are always open to the interchange of question and answer, and any given proposition must be able to marshal *logoi* in its defense (Diès 1941: xvi; Gadamer 1991: 2, 10–11; Annas 1993: 18; Szelizák 1999: 15–19, 42, 55–60, 108; Blondell 2002: 42). Indeed, the portrayal of Socratic questioning as a form of demystification rather than mere exposition—with *aporia* as its possible and even desirable end—is not limited to what are termed the early dialogues (Blondell 2002: 12–13), but is in fact explicitly thematized in such later works as the *Theaetetus* (187b–c, 210a–d) and the *Sophist* (230a–d). Moreover, Plato famously never speaks *in propria persona* in the dialogues, and to reduce Socrates to being a mere spokesman for Plato is highly problematic, since it ignores that in some dialogues he is clearly closer to what is presumed to be the historic Socrates (e.g., the *Apology*) than in others (*Philebus*), while in still others he has at best a minor role (*Sophist, Statesman, Timaeus, Critias*) or does not appear at all (*Laws*). This is not to say that Socrates does not frequently espouse ideas that are probably quite similar to Plato's and that the role of Socrates in this regard does not change from dialogue to dialogue. Nonetheless, the idea that in any given dialogue one

---

24. For more on this common division of the dialogues, see Vlastos (1991: 46–47) and accompanying bibliography.

could simply delete the name Socrates and write in Plato has no warrant (Koyré 1962: 18; Nehamas 1998: 87; Blondell 2002: 17–19). The notion that Socrates is merely the mouthpiece of Plato presumes that one has already abstracted a pure philosophical content from the text, which escapes all modes of figuration or rhetorical distortion, and that one can then take this pure meaning, which exists separately from any particular textual instantiation, and go back to the text and find it directly exemplified in Socrates and therefore claim that Socrates is the spokesman of that philosophy. Such a procedure, however, is not only illegitimate, since pure meaning apart from any vehicle of inscription never exists for human intelligence, but also circular, since the initial abstraction is then used to validate itself.

Second, when what appears to be positive doctrine is presented, it appears in mythological or allegorical forms that deliberately defy acceptance as literal truth. When asked to describe the good in the *Republic,* Socrates responds that he cannot, but he can say what it is like. This leads to the analogy between the good and the sun, which in turn leads to the myth of the cave. When Socrates describes the chariot procession of the gods before the forms in the *Phaedrus,* it is not only a manifestly mythological evocation of the transcendental realm, but it is in the context of a discussion of love, poetry, and other forms of divine madness. Moreover, it is inscribed within a self-conscious palinode to his previous speech, itself a response to Phaedrus' performance of Lysias' purported *tour de force* demonstrating that boys should only yield to those who do not love them. Lastly, when Socrates recounts Diotima's teaching on *erôs,* he not only disclaims personal authority— in a dialogue that already problematizes authorship and transmission by presenting itself as the report of a report of what had happened years earlier at Agathon's party (Hunter 2004: 26–27)—but he is also directly followed by the irruption of the drunken Alcibiades onto the scene, thus forbidding the image of true lovers ascending the *scala amoris* to the *prôton philon,* beauty itself, from being the last word on desire.

The ironic juxtaposition of Alcibiades' grotesque entrance and his subsequent praise of Socrates with Diotima's evocation of erotic transcendence creates a deliberate interpretive gap between these two textual surfaces that forces the reader to read each of these moments as an ambiguous figurative evocation (metaphor? metonymy? inversion? parody?) of the other. By means of this juxtaposition, the dialogue itself comes to function as a kind of Silenus box so that the incongruity of its rhetorical surfaces serves to project the possibility of an infinitely more precious depth, an *agalma* that lies deep within.²⁵ The Silenus box is, of course, the image that Alcibiades uses to describe Socrates himself (215a). Alcibiades' drunken speech, thus, not only functions as an ironic sequel to Diotima's vision of the beautiful in itself (*auto to kalon* 211d3), it also provides the reader with an interpretive model by means of which he or she might understand the relation of the speech to that which comes before. Yet by simultaneously evoking and performing the model of the Silenus box, the speech sets up an interpretive *mise-en-abyme*, as content and interpretive frame come to occupy the same rhetorical space. The result is an irresolvable difference between surface and depth that will not allow the fundamentally ironic relation between Alcibiades' grotesque immediacy and Diotima's abstract ideality to be resolved, but forces each reader to continue his or her own dialectic with the text and the interpretive community that surrounds it (Hunter 2004: 10–11, 129–30; Wohl 2002: 163; Nehamas 1998: 61–68).

Third, in so far as positive doctrine is presented in the middle dialogues, it is presented as an ontology of the forms, yet the exact nature of that ontology is far from a settled question, both in the scholarship and within the dialogues themselves. What is the relationship of the forms to each other and to actual empirical experience? What is their origin? How does their status as intelligible essences relate to the individual instances that manifest them and that, according to the method of collection and division as presented in the *Phaedrus* and the *Philebus*, constitute them (Zuckert 1996: 73; Nehamas and Woodruff 1995: xli–xlv; Boussoulas 1952: 8)? The appeal to the ontology of the forms, then, does not in fact provide a uniform and stable doctrine from which appropriate ethical, political, and aesthetic choices can be unreflectingly deduced. The forms, as presented within the dialogues, do not unproblematically dictate the nature of what is. Rather they force the interlocutors to probe the nature of what they understand as the intelligible bases of knowledge and experience, and challenge them to find an unambiguous warrant for their lives beyond the limits of existence acknowledged by the dominant discursive regime, i.e., the Symbolic (Hadot 1995b: 103, 120). What are the good, the beautiful, and the just, not as instantiated in any particular representation, but in themselves? How can we understand these concepts to be meaningful without reducing them to mere imitations of the accepted *doxa* and hence voiding them of any critical content? The doctrine of the forms, as

---

25. The effect becomes all the more profound when one begins to factor in the other speeches as well.

presented in the dialogues, invariably by means of myth, analogy, and fiction, does not represent the end of inquiry, but provides the spur to examine its conditions of possibility. The forms, as we shall see in our later readings of the *Phaedrus, Philebus,* and the seventh letter, function in the dialogues less as a final answer to the question, τί ἐστιν, from which all else can be deduced, than as a turn to philosophy, the *logos,* and the systematic questioning of all that is, in the name of a unity of being that both transcends and embraces the immediate (Festugière 1950: 184n.1, 187; Gadamer 1991: 82–83; Szelizák 1999: 49).

Plato's metaphysics, then, are far less the imposition of an authoritarian system *à la* Popper than a critique of what is (Hadot 1995b: 104–5; Foucault 1983a). They point far more to what is lacking in the present than to what must always and everywhere be the case.[26] It is precisely the gap between the world of sensual immediacy and the desire for transcendental completion, beyond the pleasure principle, that the doctrine of the forms articulates with admirable immediacy. As such, the distinction between the ironic figure of Socrates in the aporetical dialogues and the mythopoetic philosopher of the great middle dialogues is maybe more apparent than real, at least in terms of the existential demands placed upon the subject (Gadamer 1991: 4–5; Wallace 1991: xv–xvii).

The forms, in fact, articulate the irony of immediate existence, the necessary self-alienation of the unreflective life, as one pursues a satisfaction that remains forever elusive. They represent the same insistent demand for an account (*logos*) of the self and its claims to knowledge, on the level of Being, as Socrates does in the *Apology* on the level of subjective existence. It is the pure desire for this completion that Alcibiades misrecognizes as the beautiful *agalma* concealed within Socrates' Silenic exterior: making Socrates the possessor of a hidden substance that could then be passed in whole or in part to Alcibiades himself (Nightingale 1995: 123–27; Vlastos 1991: 36–37). In doing so, he not only fundamentally misrecognizes Socratic desire as an object that can be given in exchange, good for good, he also transfers his desire onto the person of Socrates as the reflection of his own fundamental lack.

In the end, the *agalma,* the beautiful icon that Alcibiades perceives beneath Socrates' grotesque exterior, is literally no Thing (Leonard

---

26. This is not to deny Plato's aristocratic sympathies, but as the Marxist critic Peter Rose observes, Plato's responses to the crises facing aristocratic culture, both in democratic Athens and throughout the Greek world, were never simple or monochromatic (1992: 331–69). See also Platter for a good concise articulation of both sides of this argument and an admirable presentation of how any simple argument for Plato as either reactionary aristocrat or cryptoprogressive is necessarily oversimplified (2005).

2005: 186). It is the gap marked by the loss of the first Thing, the *prôton philon,* and it is infinitely precious: for it is our relation to this desire (*erôs*), this lack, at the heart of Socrates that points us toward that transcendence of the fantasy self bequeathed by the realm of recognized goods that is the final project of both philosophy and Lacanian psychoanalysis. The *agalma,* thus, is the embodiment of that mediating relation of the human to the divine,[27] which Diotima defines as the daimonic, and whose primary instantiation within the *Symposium* is found in the myth of the birth of Erôs himself (Halperin 1994: 48; Robin 1964: 120). Moreover, it is this very daimonic nature that animates the desire we term *philo-sophia*: the concrete practice through which we come to know, and thereby to transcend, ourselves by means of a determined relation of erotic reciprocity and mutual dialectical testing, in the presence of a Socratic master (Wohl 2002: 164–65; Lacan 1991: 190–91; Robin 1929: xci–xcii). It is thus no accident that, as many commentators have noted, Erôs, the barefooted *daimôn* described in Diotima's speech, bears a striking resemblance to Socrates himself (Nightingale 1995: 129; Robin 1929: lxxx, ciii–cvi; 1964: 109–10), nor that Lacan reads the latter as a figure for the analyst.

3. Lacan reads the *Symposium: Le transfert*

> Socrates is the "precursor of the analyst" in so far as he says that he "knows nothing except what concerns desire" (*Symposium,* 177d). It is a question of *épistémé*,[28] of a knowledge concerning not only the discourse of those who speak *on* love, but also he who publicly speaks his love: Alcibiades. (Julien 1990: 118; emphasis in original)

> [Alcibiades] comes to ask Socrates for something that he does not know what it is, but he calls it *agalma*. Some of you know the use I made of this term a while back, I want to use it again, this *agalma,* this mystery that, in the fog surrounding the gaze of Alcibiades, represents something beyond all recognized goods [*biens*]. (Lacan 1973: 283–84)

As Jeffrey Carnes has noted, the *Symposium* is not only a natural choice for Lacan, but Aristophanes' myth reads as if it were made to order for the Parisian analyst.[29] In it:

---

27. Understood as those beings who possess in perpetuity the good and the beautiful and are therefore not affected by desire.
28. The accentuation in French of this Greek word varies from author to author.
29. On Lacan's frequent appeal to this myth, see Hunter (2004: 118).

> The impulse toward sex has its origin in the recognition of castration—of the loss (or impossibility) of fullness. Zeus, the phallic father, punishes and says "no" yet also gives us sex (while hiding his own desire). Indeed, this *coupure* or cut gives rise to the individual subject himself, who is a *symbolon*—a tally, a half of his former self, but also a *symbolon* in the sense of a signifier. This individuation, not freely chosen, is the source of sexual desire, a mark of our mortality and imperfection. . . . (Carnes 1998: 114–15)

It is Aristophanes, Lacan notes, who introduces the concept of the splitting of the subject, or *Spaltung,* which played a central role in Freud's etiology of desire (Lacan 1991: 108, 144; Carnes 1998: 115). Lacan goes on in his eleventh seminar, *The Four Fundamental Concepts of Psychoanalysis,* to develop Aristophanes' myth further by adding the concept of the *lamelle,* i.e., a "thin blade or membrane."[30] The *lamelle* represents both the effective agent that splits the initial dyadic unity of self and other—emblematically portrayed in psychoanalysis as the infant's Imaginary relation with the mother—and that which remains after the splitting of the subject, i.e., the desire that pushes us to seek what we have lost, but also that which, as desire, guarantees that we will never find it.

This, Lacan observes, is the crucial difference between the Aristophanic and Freudian accounts: according to the Platonic Aristophanes, subjects seek their "sexual complements"—but in psychoanalysis, they seek that which is gone forever (Lacan 1973: 211, 221, 223, 229; Žižek 1996: 192–93). Indeed, as Lacan reiterates on more than one occasion, "there is no sexual relation." There is no possibility of the perfect other who is able to restore us to fullness, because the originary lack that defines our desire (as Socrates and Diotima recognize 199d–e, 201e–202e) is in fact a retrospective reflection into the past of who we are now far more than it is a simple cause of what we are to become. For Lacan, following in the wake of Heidegger and Sartre,[31] the lack that constitutes the subject is a function of the very contingent relation of the subject to the world. It defines the necessary negativity of that relation,[32] and hence the subject's capacity to desire the other, to

---

30. The related English term, *lamella,* does not really translate the French *lamelle,* which retains the notion that it is the diminutive of *lame,* the blade of a knife or sword, as well as signifying a membrane between cells.

31. On Lacan's debt to Heidegger, see Shepherdson (2003: 149). On his complex debt to Sartre, see Copjec (2002: 208) and P. A. Miller (forthcoming).

32. I use the term here in its technical, philosophical sense, of that which introduces a change in the existing state of things, which negates what is. Hence, a better translation for

want more than what is. We are always from the moment we enter into language and self-consciousness in excess (*de trop*)[33] of both ourselves and the world: a half without a whole. We desire to be a whole, to return to a fantasized Aristophanic state of completion and continuity with the world before the perceived rupture of our specific difference. We desire to be not for ourselves—"pour personne, pour moi"—but in ourselves. Yet, as Lacan, Heidegger, and Sartre all perceived, such a nostalgic desire can only orient the subject toward a future that simultaneously creates, or better renders effective, the past (Renaut 1993: 53, 187–89). The nostalgia for a lost wholeness is always the desire for a different future.

> It is the future that decides if the past is living or dead. The past, in effect, is originally a project, as the present leaping forth of my being. And, in so far as it is a project, it is an anticipation; its sense comes from the future it sketches in advance. . . . The past's power comes only from the future: in whatever manner I live or appreciate my past, I can do so only in light of a pro-jection of myself into the future. (Sartre 1943: 556)

It is precisely this complex relation between the facticity of the present, the pro-ject of the future, and the etiological force of the past that defines the temporality of desire. The lack at the heart of being, like *das Ding,* is a retrospective construction from within the structures of the Symbolic, not a pre-empiric cause. Thus, Antigone could not exist without Creon. Indeed, she is already dead only with respect to the Law that he represents and the desire his edict necessarily projects. By the same token, Alcibiades could not exist without Socrates, nor could desire without the Law and its beyond. From a Lacanian perspective, these binary oppositions are always, at the same time, a function of difference, of language's division of the manifold of experience into categories and determinate entities (Eco 1976: 71–79), the annihilation of which would result in psychosis or Symbolic death. They are thus also a function of our entry into the realm of erotic substitution that constitutes the threshold of the pleasure and reality principles.[34]

Sartre's *Being and Nothingness* (*L 'être et le néant*) might well be *Being and Negating*. For a more complete discussion of the concept of the negative in its philosophical and specifically Hegelian dimensions, see P. A. Miller 1998.
   33. See the famous passage in *La nausée* (Sartre 1981c: 150–60).
   34. See Lacan (1973: 215; 1975: 53, 65, 76–80); Clément (1975: 16); Ragland-Sullivan (1986: 96); Copjec (1994: 207); Althusser (1996: 72); Roudinesco (1997: 369).

Lacan's rereading of Aristophanes' speech, however, is nothing more than a gloss on Diotima's own corrective: we do not desire our missing half (the past); we desire what is good (the future, that toward which we project ourselves; 205d–e). The Aristophanic fantasy of completion thus holds out a possibility that Eros, defined as a *philo-sophos* (lover of wisdom), can by nature never attain (Nightingale 1995: 126–27), a possibility that would represent the very end of philosophic desire, one that Socrates explicitly refuses in the *Apology*. We desire what is missing, but what is missing is not us, but precisely our own transcendence, that which is both in and beyond us: in us because as the *Lysis* (216d5–217a2) and the *Symposium* (202a–b) demonstrate, if we were wholly lacking in the good, we would have no basis for desiring it, since that which is completely evil cannot desire the good; beyond us because what we desire is ultimately the *prôton philon*,[35] according to the *Lysis*, or the form of the good and the beautiful, according to the *Symposium*.

Both sides of this complex equation are captured in a pun Diotima makes when she encourages Socrates to accept the possibility of substituting "the good" (*to agathon*) for the "beautiful" (*to kalon*) when answering the question what does the desiring one desire. The answer, we learn, is first to be happy and second that "it is in the possession of *tôn agathôn* [good things/ goods/Agathons] that happy ones come to be happy" (204e–205a1). The poet Agathon is of course the host of the party and portrayed as the object of attraction to both Socrates and Alcibiades. "Moreover, we must never forget that Agathon himself ('Mr. Good') is also the most beautiful (*kallistos*) person at his own party (e.g., 213c5)" (Hunter 2004: 87). The pun is made all the easier by the fact that the convention of marking proper names through capitalization did not yet exist in Plato's Greek. Lest we miss the erotic implications of the pun, it becomes clear immediately in Diotima's correction of Aristophanes when she says, "My *logos* says that desire is neither of the half or the whole, unless, my friend, in some way it happens to be Agathon/good." Thus the happy are happy to the extent they possess that which is good, but that which is immediately good is Agathon. We do not desire completion but the transcendence of the self in the possession of the object of desire. And the object of desire is at once that which corresponds to our own internal lack (our other half), that which we accept as one of the chain of substitutions in the endless

---

35. The *prôton philon* may seem to be first temporally when it appears in a narrative exposition, but its priority is in fact logical rather than temporal.

metonymy of desire under the reign of the pleasure principle (goods), and that which causes us to go beyond the very structure of our identity in the realization of our pure desire (the form of the good, the *prôton philon*). The poet Agathon, in turn, stands as an ironic metonymy for each of these.

What Lacan is investigating in his reading of the *Symposium*, however, is not merely desire or love. He is interested in a special kind of love, that which a patient feels for his or her analyst. The essence of the transferential relationship is the possibility of substitution or metaphor, and the fundamental model for this substitutive relationship, according to Lacan, can be found in the complex interplay between Socrates and Alcibiades. Two different, but complementary, levels of substitutability can be found in their relationship as defined in the *Symposium*'s final movement: the well known inversion of roles wherein *erastês* and *erômenos* exchange places, as Socrates becomes the object of Alcibiades' desire (Wohl 2002: 130–31, 163–64); and the potential of substituting Agathon for the object of desire of both Socrates and Alcibiades, so that each comes to occupy for the other the logically necessary, but empty, third position that makes Symbolic relationships of equivalence, and hence substitutability, possible.[36] This third position is precisely that occupied by the analyst in the typical psychoanalytic scenario. Nonetheless, transference is not a phenomenon limited to the analyst's couch. It is, as Lacan observes, in the nature of love and of Symbolic relationships per se (Julien 1990: 74, 120; Henderson 1993: 125–26). The psychoanalytic relationship is only a specific instance of this more general phenomenon.

The first level of substitution, that between the *erastês* and the *erômenos*, and hence between Socrates and Alcibiades, is the most apparent in Plato's text and the easiest to elucidate. Alcibiades tells us that it is well known that Socrates was his first lover, but when he sought for Socrates to affirm his desire for him directly, the philosopher always evaded him. Alcibiades therefore sets out on the path of seduction hoping to come to possess Socrates' wisdom—the *agalma* or image of divine essence locked inside his Silenic exterior—by allowing Socrates

---

36. On "triangular desire" as the essence of emotional identification with, and structural imitation of, Socrates, see Blondell (2002: 107). The logical necessity of a third position to make any determination of value, and hence comparison and exchange or substitutability, possible was first demonstrated in modern times by Hegel (1977: 58–66 and passim), and then specifically elaborated upon by Marx (1976: 125–77) in his notion of the universal equivalent. On the relation of these dialectical systems of thought to Freud and Lacan, see Goux (1990: 9–63).

to possess him in the more conventional pederastic sense. Yet theirs is anything but a normal pederastic relationship since the older lover has become the object of pursuit and the younger beloved, the pursuer (215a4–222a6). The unusual nature of this situation is highlighted by the fact that certain early commentators have felt that the eruption of the drunken Alcibiades on the scene of the *Symposium*'s orderly exchange of speeches in praise of Love constituted a breach in the stylistic and thematic unity of the dialogue. Indeed, Lacan remarks, the dialogue's first French translator, Louis Le Roy, chose to end his text with Socrates' recounting of the lesson of Diotima, believing that the Alcibiades passage was a joking coda that was neither integral to the dialogue nor appropriate reading matter for a Christian nation (1991: 30–31, 36; Lloyd-Jones 1996: 100–101; Le Roy 1558: 180r).

Yet, as Lacan also notes, the theme of substituting the lover for the beloved is present from the earliest speech in the dialogue, where Phaedrus praises both Alcestis' dying in place of Admetus and Achilles' taking the place of Patroclus after the latter's death (179b4–180b5). The first is an example of simple substitution along the lines of Alcibiades and Socrates. Alcestis assumes the role of Admetus, without any relationship to a possible third position that would make a more general equivalence possible. The case of Achilles, however, as Phaedrus observes, is worthy of greater praise and wins him the reward of spending the hereafter in the Isles of the Blessed. In it, the *erômenos* does not merely take the place of the *erastês* but actually becomes a subject of desire in his own right. "Achilles, having come to the aid of and having avenged his *erastês,* Patroclus, not only dared to prefer to die in place of, *but also in addition to,* the one whose life had already ended" (179e5–180a2; emphasis mine). In short, Achilles can occupy the vacant place of the *erastês* and die in turn, precisely because Patroclus himself has died, has moved to the vacant third position. It is the transformation of Achilles into a lover, into one who actually occupies the place of Patroclus, that is so miraculous (Lacan 1991: 69):

> Aeschylus talks nonsense when he says that Achilles desires Patroclus. He was more beautiful not only than Patroclus but than all the heroes, and he was still beardless, since he was much younger, as Homer says. Truly, this is why the gods greatly honored his virtue in love, moreover they wonder, admire, and esteem it more when the *erômenos* is fond of the *erastês* than when the *erastês* is fond of the boy: for such a boy is more godlike than the lover of boys; he is divinely inspired. On account of these things, the gods honored

Achilles more than Alcestis, sending him to the Isles of the Blessed. (180a4–b5)

Achilles does not simply mirror Patroclus, in the manner of Alcestis and Admetus, but actually assumes his position, suffers what he suffers. As Lacan shrewdly notes, such a transformation must assume that one of the two positions in the essentially dyadic love relationship has become vacant, so that the necessity of a third position (in this case death) must be posited (1991: 63). The existence of this more complex triadic love relationship, in turn, looks forward to that of Socrates, Alcibiades, and Agathon.

Alcibiades' attempt to seduce Socrates, of course, fails. The merely dyadic pattern of substitution comes up short. Socrates refuses to adopt the passive position because he refuses to admit the existence in himself of a positive substance that is the object of Alcibiades' desire (Lacan 1991: 185, 188). Rather he recognizes that what Alcibiades in fact desires is Socrates' desire, that is, to realize his own desire through the desire of the Other (Lacan 1991: 202–3; Julien 1992: 122). It is for this reason that Alcibiades must paradoxically seek signs of Socrates' love, while confessing that it is universally known that Socrates was his first lover. Why does he need signs of that which is already beyond question? He seeks not so much to confirm Socrates' love but to possess it as an object (Lacan 1991: 185). Socrates in his recognition that Eros is not a positive substance, as demonstrated in Diotima's speech, but rather a daimonic mediator between presence and absence, mortal and immortal, the ugly and the beautiful can truly grant Alcibiades' desire only by refusing him (201d1–204c6; Lacan 1991: 144; Clarke 1995: 13, 19–20; Carnes 1998: 115). This recognition of desire as a fundamental lack constitutes the essential kernel of Socrates' erotic mastery (Lacan 1991: 185–86). It represents the constitutive emptiness that through the intensely personal process of Socratic dialectic, with its characteristic erotic reciprocity, leads from attraction to the beautiful body to the "ecstatic contemplation" of beauty itself (210a–212a; Vlastos 1991: 78). This recognition of pure desire is in fact the *agalma* Alcibiades seeks and that Socrates, in refusing the latter's advances, grants, if only Alcibiades could recognize it (Žižek 1991: 7; see also Berger 1994: 107). It is the recognition of the constitutive lack at the heart of desire that makes substitution itself possible but also infinite, for as Diotima in the *Symposium* and Socrates in the *Phaedrus* demonstrate, what is desired in the individual beloved is not that which the individual possesses but the possibility of seeing in the individual that good which is lacking or lost from the self. The *agalma* for Lacan, thus, stands for the "lost" object (or *objet petit a*) whose absence is constitutive of both human desire and individual identity, and which itself stands as the embodiment of that more fundamental loss designated by *das Ding*.[37]

We are now in a better position to see how Socrates occupies the place of the analyst in the transferential relationship (Julien 1990: 118). The goal of Lacanian psychoanalysis, as we have already seen in Lacan's examination of its ethics through the figure of Antigone, is not to provide patients with interpretations or answers, but to allow them to realize their own desires as constituted in their ambivalent relation to the world of conventionally recognized goods (Lacan: 1991: 18; Schneiderman 1983: 94; Ragland-Sullivan 1986: 81–82). The end of analysis is not the acceptance of a single *sovereign good* to which the subject must submit or be labeled perverse, but the realization of one's own constitutive lack (Lacan 1986: 347). It is this empty place of desire, which is occupied and made visible by the analyst, that engenders the transferential relationship summed up by Lacan in the phrase "the desire of analyst." And it is here that the Socratic lesson is most to be taken to heart:

> It is not to say that the analyst ought to be a Socrates, or pure, or a saint. Without a doubt these explorers like Socrates . . . can give us some indications concerning the field in question. This is an understatement. . . . Rather it is exactly because they have done the exploration that we are able to define . . . the coordinates that the analyst ought to be able to recognize simply to occupy the place that is his, i.e., that vacant place that he ought to offer to the desire of the patient in order that he might realize himself as the desire of the Other. It is for this reason that the *Symposium* interests us.[38] (Lacan 1991: 128)

Thus it is through the empty space of Socrates' desire that Alcibiades can realize his own, but only insofar as Socrates presents himself as one who desires but does not yield to false satisfactions—that is, only insofar as Socrates remains an *erastês* and refuses the seduction of becoming Alcibiades' *erômenos,* something he could become only by declaring (paradoxically) his desires in the manner of a conventional *erastês.*

---

37. See the discussion of *das Ding* in chapter 3 as well as Lacan (1991: 163, 190–91, 201–2; 1986: 65, 71–72, 142–43; 1975: 58; 1973: 119, 283–84); Clément (1974: 70); and Julien (1990: 121–22).

38. The same could be said of the *Antigone*.

To return to the paradigm offered in Phaedrus' speech at the beginning of the dialogue, the challenge is for Alcibiades to become Achilles. He must transform himself from an *erômenos* into a true *erastês* by occupying the vacant place of the desire of the Other. It is this more complex, triadic substitutive relation—exemplified by Achilles—that is glimpsed in Alcibiades' relationship to Agathon (*to agathon*), as mediated through the desire of Socrates (222b4–223b2). Instead, what he has desired to this point is merely to remain at the level of Alcestis, who took the place of her lover while staying the beloved. He has fallen prey to the siren song of the Athenian *dêmos* and his own *philotimia,* and so remains within the subject positions allotted to him by the dominant Symbolic system. In the process, as we see, he has failed to serve both the *polis* and the good.

The *Symposium* leaves the actual consummation of Alcibiades' ultimate transformation an open question, since at the very moment when Socrates is to praise Agathon in front of Alcibiades, a second crowd of revelers bursts in, bringing the evening's orderly proceedings to a close. But, as Lacan notes:

> That Socrates should praise Agathon is the response not to a past, but a present demand of Alcibiades. When Socrates praises Agathon, he gives satisfaction to Alcibiades. He gives satisfaction through his actual act of public declaration, of putting on the plane of the universal Other that which happened between them behind the veils of shame. The response of Socrates is this—you can love the one I am going to praise because praising him I, Socrates, will know how to show the image of you as a lover, insofar as it through the image of you as a lover that you are going to enter onto the road of higher identifications that the way of beauty traces. (1991: 189–90)

In his evocation of the way of beauty and of the road of higher identifications, Lacan here clearly alludes to the central myth of the *Phaedrus,* which, as Phillipe Julien notes, features a perfect description of the mutual identification of *erastês* and *erômenos,* and the consequent possibility of a substitution of places through their recollection of, and identification with, a vacant third position, the lost realm of the forms (1991: 121).[39] The role of the analyst, like that of Socrates, is to be the midwife that makes this intellectual birth—through the power of

---

39. On the parallels between Plato's description of desire in the *Phaedrus* and Freud's, see Ferrari (1987: 156–61).

recollection in the field of desire—possible: for it is through the erotic reciprocity of the *elenchus*, that a pure desire beyond the pleasure and reality principles can be realized by one who, unlike Alcibiades in the end, has the courage not to cede on his or her desire.

4. Conclusion: Desire, Ethics, and the Other

> Now, some people are pregnant in body, and for this reason turn more to women and pursue love in that way . . . while others are pregnant . . . with what is fitting for the soul to bear and bring to birth. And what is fitting? Wisdom and the rest of virtue, which all poets beget, as well as all the craftsmen said to be creative. But by far the greatest and most beautiful part of wisdom deals with the proper ordering of cities and households, and what is called moderation and justice. When someone has been pregnant with these in his soul from early youth, while he is still a virgin, and having arrived at the proper age, desires to beget and give birth, he too will certainly go about seeking the beauty in which he would beget; for he will never beget in anything ugly. Since he is pregnant, then, he is much more drawn to bodies that are beautiful than to those that are ugly; and if he has the luck to find a soul that is beautiful and noble and well-formed, he is even more drawn to this combination; such a man makes him instantly teem with ideas and arguments about virtue—the qualities a virtuous man should have and the customary activities in which he should engage; and so he tries to educate him. (*Symposium* 208e–209c; Nehamas and Woodruff 1997: 491–92)

> Phaedrus: And you, my remarkable friend, appear to be totally out of place [*atopos*]. Really, just as you say, you seem to need a guide, not to be one of the locals. Not only do you never travel abroad—as far as I can tell, you never set foot beyond the city walls.
> Socrates: Forgive me my friend. I am devoted to learning; landscapes and trees have nothing to teach me—only people in the city can do that. (*Phaedrus* 230c–d; Nehamas and Woodruff 1995: 6)

Antigone, on Lacan's reading, seeks a good beyond the pleasure principle, beyond the compromises that our daily unreflective commerce with the world necessarily entails. In so doing, she, like Anouilh's heroine, chooses death before happiness or *le bonheur*. But where in Anouilh's case this is ultimately a form of pre-oedipal narcissism, Lacan's Antigone is the product of a specific, historically localizable narrative—and hence irretrievably implicated in the Other. Yet she cannot either be simply reduced to the terms of that historical narrative or assimilated to the dominant narratives of the present. As such, she can never be contained within the bounds of our own pre-Oedipal fantasy constructions, but must always stand as a point of difference, the marker of a form of enjoyment that cannot be encompassed within the dominant forms of Imaginary and Symbolic identification. An ethics founded on Lacan's Sophoclean Antigone will at once demand a commitment to unrepeatable historical specificity and to its necessary transcendence.[40]

Antigone may present the model of a psychoanalytic ethics for Lacan, but as the structure of Seminars 7 and 8 make clear, she represents only the first movement in the complex dance that the desire of and for the analyst entails. Alcibiades too seeks a good beyond all recognized goods, but what his and Socrates' example shows is that this desire need not lead to Haemon's bloody ejaculation on Antigone's cold, dead cheek. The Socratic model may lead to a kind of death to the world, as revealed by the image of the philosopher's discourse being a Siren song capable of holding Alcibiades immobilized. But as Diotima's speech in the *Symposium* and Socrates' great speech in the *Phaedrus* (as well as numerous statements in the *Phaedo*) make clear, this death to the manifold, contradictory, and ultimately unsatisfying goods of the dominant Symbolic system is but a prelude to a fuller life whose desire is embodied precisely in the pursuit of wisdom (*philosophia*), that is, the pursuit of the ideal and unreachable transcendence of the forms. The task of psychoanalysis, like that of philosophy, is not to impose a single vision of the object of that desire, not to substitute for it one particular fetish, but to come to a recognition of that desire through an encounter with one's own emptiness. We must not stop our ears, as Alcibiades says he must if he is to remain in the kingdom of recognized goods. We must not cede on our desire, as he did in his final decision to seek dominance within the existing structure of the *polis*. Alcibiades' choice to eschew the Siren song of Socratic desire is one that Plato's target audience, even more than Lacan's, knew would lead to the personal and political disasters of bad faith, self-betrayal, and collaboration.[41]

The desire of the analyst is then, as we have seen, the medium through which the analysand comes both to realize the nature of his desire and to have the ability not to cede on it. The analysand desires

---

40. This is not to say that Lacan's actual practice of historicization is in fact satisfactory or that it would come close to meeting the rigorous demands of professional classicists, to whom he did not presume to speak. It is rather a matter of formal recognition within a psychoanalytic context and relative to the theatrical practice of his modernist predecessors.

41. Witness the case of Brasillach (chapter 2) and, some would say, Sartre's own later compromises with the Stalinist PCF.

the analyst's desire, as Alcibiades does Socrates'. He wishes both to be the object of the analyst's desire and to desire what the analyst desires. In the same way, as Diotima notes, the young man whose psyche is burgeoning with desire seeks beauty first by desiring the beauty of another, and then by desiring that which the other desires. Through this process he enters into a ladder of substitutions that at once reveals to the youth the nature of his own desire and opens it out to the world beyond that of received opinion and sensual immediacy, disclosing that of wisdom and justice. Nor is that realm an asocial or apolitical space of personal virtue and solipsistic desire. As Diotima observes above, "by far the greatest and most beautiful part of wisdom deals with the proper ordering of cities and households, and what is called moderation and justice."

Socrates' estrangement from the city, then, should not be equated with a quietistic withdrawal. His *atopia* at once places him outside the bounds of the *polis,* but also enables him ultimately to have a more effective engagement with it. As Phaedrus notes paradoxically, Socrates' *atopia* is in fact founded on engagement. He is like a stranger in his own land, not because he is always abroad, but precisely because he never leaves. His constant engagement is with the citizens of the *polis,* for only they can teach him the nature of virtue and justice. But that teaching is not achieved through a simple process of unreflective imitation: it is the product of a direct and focused engagement with the nature of those citizens' desire and its relation to Socrates' own. That engagement, in turn, occurs precisely through the kind of elenctic testing exemplified in the *Lysis* and the *Apology,* as well as through the existential challenge of the forms as seen in the *Symposium,* the *Phaedrus,* and the *Republic.*

Socrates appears like a stranger because he is at once outside and inside the community. Indeed, he is so deeply embedded that he appears to have no place at all. He is the intimate other that reveals both what the community is and what it wants to be, without his ever being fully assimilable to the dominant Symbolic structures that define the *polis.* He is a true "thought from the outside" that is only receivable as such because of his deep interiority. Consequently, he is not only a fit emblem of Lacan's vision of psychoanalysis, but also of the privileged status of antiquity in general, and of Platonic philosophy in particular, for a truly postmodern spiritual practice.

Chapter 5

Writing the Subject
Derrida Asks Plato to Take a Letter

> Is it not first of all a significant fact that the truly new aspect that the dialectic takes on in the *Phaedrus,* with the preponderant importance of the method of division, in spite of certain anticipations in the *Republic,* is precisely what the *Sophist* and the *Statesman* develop, and what the *Philebus* insists on with so much force, concerning its profundity? (Robin 1985: xii)

> What is called "deconstruction" is undeniably obedient to an *analytic*[1] demand, which is simultaneously critical and analytical. It is always a question of the *undoing, unsedimenting, decomposing, deconstituting* of sediments, *artefacts,* presuppositions, institutions. And the insistence on disaggregation, disjunction or dissociation, on being *"out of joint"* as Hamlet would have said, on the irreducibility of difference is too overwhelming to need to be insisted upon. Insofar as this analytic dissociation should in deconstruction, at least as I understand and practice it, also be a critico-genealogical return to first principles, then we appear to have [in it] the two moments of any analysis [. . .]: the *archeological* or *anagogic* moment of the return to a prior state [*l'ancien*] as the arché-original; and the *philo-lytic* moment of dissociative—one could almost say dis-social—disaggregation. (Derrida 1996a: 41; emphasis in original)

THE PLATONIC corpus, particularly dialogues such as the *Phaedrus,* the *Symposium,* the *Lysis,* and the *Philebus* that interrogate the relationship between desire and truth, love and transcendence, and pleasure and knowledge, are a central concern for all the major figures in poststructuralism. These texts, along with those of Nietzsche, Heidegger, Freud, and Saussure, constitute if not a grid of intelligibility, then at least a finite set of philosophemes, out of which the interventions that we know today as postmodern theory emerged. Lacan's readings of the *Antigone* and the *Symposium* helped inaugurate a dialogic space that not only made poststructuralism possible but also anticipated the later investigations of antiquity that characterized the

---

1. As the context makes clear, "*psycho*-analytic."

works of Derrida and Foucault, as well as Gilles Deleuze, Luce Irigaray, Julia Kristeva, and Hélène Cixous.

In this light, it is unsurprising that the *Phaedrus* was a crucial text for Derrida, who was not only a frequent auditor of Lacan's seminars but also a student of Foucault's at the Ecole Normale Supérieure (Schneiderman 1983: 28). Derrida's and Lacan's readings of Plato are, to be sure, hardly identical. With Derrida, the lens through which Plato is read is no longer in the first instance psychoanalysis as a clinical practice, but philosophy as the formal possibility of thought, as the inauguration of the *logos*. And while these two disciplines' respective ventures are, as we have seen in the preceding chapter, inextricably intertwined, neither can ever be simply reduced to the other (Plotnitsky 2000: 275). Derrida's vocabulary and set of concerns are, as we shall see, far more conceptual than experiential. Unlike Lacan, his task is not to train the next generation of analysts, but to analyze the possible formations of the psyche and reason per se as they are instantiated in the textual tradition that constitutes western philosophy and that is formally inaugurated by those transmitted under the name of Plato. How are these terms inscribed? To whom are they addressed? And what are the assumptions they entail? These are Derrida's central questions.

Thus, in Derrida's 1972 essay on the *Phaedrus,* "Plato's Pharmacy," the ambiguous figure of the *pharmakos/pharmakon* functions as the instantiation of the problematic status of writing, intentionality, and meaning that Derrida sees as structuring the subsequent western metaphysical tradition. Plato's aversion to writing is here interpreted as symptomatic of a more general tendency in philosophy to banish the external and the material from the essence of meaning and value, to posit a realm of pure presence, an absolute origin (Derrida 1972a: 182–83).

This Platonic attempt at metaphysical closure, at the creation of a finite system of fixed meanings beyond the contingencies of the merely material letter, has its parallel in the system of preexisting interpretations and conventionally recognized goods that Lacan views as the antithesis of both the ethics of psychoanalysis and a truly psychoanalytic ethics. Both the potted analytic interpretation and the attempt to establish a closed logocentric universe are, in the last analysis, designed more to limit the realm of possible meanings than to create new possibilities of self-creation and understanding.[2] The fully present subject

2. Although, as we shall see, the question of to what extent this metaphysical closure is an actual product of the Platonic texts, and to what extent it is the product of the abstraction known as Platonism remains an open question.

is one without a history, a pure cogito that is always already given. Derrida and Lacan turn to Plato as a way of calling this subject into question by reexamining the inaugural gestures of western reason, and thereby making possible new forms of experience, new constructions of the subject, and new modes of enjoyment. The deconstruction of the closure of western metaphysics aims, then, at nothing less than a radical desedimentation and archeology of thought itself and hence of the logics by which we define ourselves, our relations with others, and our forms of collective engagement (Derrida 1994: 127–28; 1996a: 41–42). The axis defined by Plato and Freud (particularly in Lacan's reading of them both) is central to this project,

Nonetheless, despite these clear connections, on an initial examination, there is no obvious relation between Derrida's engagement with the *Phaedrus* and his readings of Freud and Lacan. Indeed, Lacan's name is never used in "La pharmacie de Platon."[3] Yet, if the relation between Derrida's reading of Plato and his conversation with psychoanalysis is less than fully explicit in "La pharmacie,"[4] such is not the case with Derrida's next extended engagement with the figures of Plato and Socrates in *La carte postale: de Socrate à Freud et au-delà*. The latter contains both Derrida's most extended response to Lacan, "Le facteur de la vérité," and an investigation of the debt owed by Freud's *Beyond the Pleasure Principle* (*Au-delà du principe de plaisir*)[5] to Plato's *Philebus* in "Spéculer—Sur «Freud»." This latter essay, as Derrida acknowledges, is both central to his own preoccupations and directly engages Lacan (Derrida 1980: 402–3; 1996a: 38–39; 1996b: 59).

By the same token, it would be a mistake to see "La pharmacie" as less than fully implicated in the problematics that would bring Derrida into dialogue and dispute with one of his most powerful interlocutors.[6] Indeed, this is explicitly acknowledged in the epistolary novel that makes up the first part of *La carte postale*. Here, a semi-fictional Derrida imagines a book he will write entitled *Legs de Freud* (*Legacy of*

---

3. For Derrida's defensive response to questions about why Lacan is missing from the citations in his early work see the extraordinarily long footnote in *Positions* (1972b: 112nn.19, 33).

4. Nonetheless, it takes no great hermeneutic acuity to see an implicit psychoanalytic framework behind Derrida's extensive investigation in "La pharmacie" of the figure of the father of the *logos* and his death or absence, both in relation to the written word, and to Plato's writing of the Socratic word (Derrida 1972a: 86–93, 177).

5. A key text, it will be recalled, in Lacan's reading of the *Antigone*.

6. Thus Derrida himself would argue in a later lecture that what is most disruptive and disturbing, and hence most authentic, in postmodern philosophy, psychoanalysis, and theory in general would have been impossible without Lacan (Derrida 1996b: 63–64).

Freud),[7] which, suspiciously like *La carte postale*, will feature Socrates and Plato on its cover. The content of that book, and hence the scene of this legacy—which concerns both Plato's bequest to Freud and Freud's "bequest" to Plato—is, as "Derrida" notes, merely a repetition of that already played out in another fashion some twelve years before in "La pharmacie de Platon" (Derrida 1980: 59). The comment may be rather cryptic, but for Derrida, as we shall see, the problem of writing, of material inscription, is inseparable from both the constitution of the unconscious in the Freudian sense and the institution of philosophy in the Platonic sense. Freud and Plato, and particularly the Plato of the *Phaedrus* and the *Philebus*, cannot, he argues, be thought separately from one another, and each in turn is central to the Derridean conception of power.

1. *Nabel* Gazing: Philosophy, Psychoanalysis, and Deconstruction

> First of all, there is the inexhaustible insistence of the text [*The Interpretation of Dreams*] on the texture of the interwoven threads, on the inseparable skein of knots: the *Geflecht,* the interlacing, a word whose warp and weft Heidegger followed through some of thought's decisive places; the *netzartige Verstrickung* [the tightly woven entanglement], the *Knävel* [knot], the *Nabel* [navel], etc. This density of the rhetoric of thread and knot interests us because what it calls for, and defies, is precisely analysis as a methodical operation of untying and as a technique of disaggregation. It is a question of knowing how to pull the strings, to pull on the strings, following the art of the weaver, whom Plato's *Statesman* casts as the royal paradigm: for analytic division (*diairesis*), for dialectic, for the royal science (*e basilikè tekhnè,* 311C) of politics. (Derrida 1996a: 28)

The symbiotic or parasitic relation between Plato and Freud is first explicitly noted by Derrida in "Freud et la scène de l'écriture," a lecture given in 1966 and published in *Tel Quel* that same year, before being republished in 1967's *L'écriture et la différence* (1967a: 293–340), the year before "La pharmacie de Platon" (1972a) first appeared in *Tel Quel* (1968). In this lecture, Derrida examines Freud's image of the "magic writing pad"[8] as an illustration of the way in which "memory

---

7. But also an explicitly acknowledged pun on *Les Deux Freud*, which in the context could refer to Freud's own self-division, Freud and Lacan, or Socrates and Plato.

8. The "magic writing pad" is a common children's toy that consists of a piece of cardboard spread with a thin layer of dark wax, two semi-transparent covering sheets one

traces" are inscribed in the unconscious. He draws an explicit connection between Freud's image of the wax tablet of memory and the *Phaedrus*'s contrast between philosophy's attempt to write on the soul and the more superficial and externalized inscriptions of sophistic rhetoric. The passage repays quotation, since it contains *in nuce* all the fundamental elements that will be explored in this chapter: writing, memory, the *psychê* or soul, the trace, the limit, and its beyond:

> A pure representation, a machine, never functions on its own. Such, at least, is the limit that Freud recognizes in the analogy of the magic pad. . . . [T]he gesture is very Platonic. Only the writing of the soul, the *Phaedrus* said, only the psychic trace has the power to reproduce and represent itself spontaneously. [. . .] "The analogy of such an apparatus must encounter at some point a limit. The magic pad is not able to 'reproduce' from its interior writing that has been effaced; it would be a truly magic pad if it were able to do this as our memory does." The multiplicity of the layered surfaces of the apparatus is left to itself, a dead complexity without depth. Life as depth only pertains to the wax of psychic memory. Freud, like Plato, continues to oppose writing as *hupomnêsis* [external reminder] to writing ἐν τῇ ψυχῇ, itself woven from traces, empirical memories of a truth present outside of time. (Derrida 1967a: 336)

Thus, two years before its initial publication, the basic theme of "La pharmacie de Platon" makes its first appearance in the context of Derrida's reading of Freud. Freud, like Plato, he argues, sees writing as something external and alien to true memory, a kind of auxiliary technique, an imitation that constantly threatens to be mistaken for the original (Derrida 1967a: 328).

True memory, however, as Plato and Freud both define it, is in fact never the pure recall of past perceptions, but the product of a forming of the soul from the disorganized heterogeny of those perceptions (*Theaetetus* 185c–e), and hence of difference.[9] It is a process of editing,

---

on top of the other, and a plastic or wooden stylus. The child writes on the pad making marks on the wax below, which are visible through the covering sheets. When the interior sheet is removed the marks cease to be legible on the top sheet but, as Freud notes, the impressions in the wax below remain, if only as traces.

9. I.e., a synthetic memory is by definition different from the set of perceptions to which it makes reference. There is no recall, no repetition that is not fundamentally different from the original. We leave aside for the moment the Kantian question of whether perception is not itself always already mediated, and hence synthetic.

inscription, and reformation that produces meaningful recollection from the flux of brute experience. Memory, thus, already contains the principle of its own necessary self-alienation,[10] and it is this fact that makes possible wrong opinion (*doxa pseudê*), and hence philosophy as its opposite (Gadamer 1991: 167–68): for if the soul, as both Plato and Freud claim, can be compared to a block of wax receiving impressions (*Theaetetus* 191c–e), that wax will be written over numerous times. Moreover, it will receive impressions from near and far, thus multiplying the possibilities of error and the need for therapeutic intervention (*Theaetetus* 193b–d; *Philebus* 38c–d; Oudemans and Lardinois 1987: 207). At the same time, the wax that some people possess will be more malleable and less subject to corruption than that possessed by others (*Theaetetus* 194c–d). Moreover, like Freud, Plato too recognizes that mere passive impressions cannot account for the spontaneous moment of recollection and synthesis that constitutes memory and consciousness, as well as the possibility of misprision that that moment necessarily brings with it. To accommodate this possibility, the model of the wax tablet, which Plato puts forward in the *Theaetetus,* is later in that same dialogue replaced by the more dynamic model of an imaginary aviary housing the *rarae aves* of knowledge that we capture over the course of our life and later attempt to retrieve, with all the attendant possibilities of reaching for a "pigeon" but grasping a "ring dove" (*Theaetetus* 197c–199b). As Plato makes clear, knowledge and memory are active processes in which the traces of past impressions must be transformed through the labor of the psyche into a writing of the soul and the creation of *logoi*—both "arguments" and "accounts"—that then require testing in the crucible of the dialectic, i.e., that demand analysis (*Philebus* 38e–39a).[11]

---

10. As Derrida notes in the following very dense opening observation from the lecture on the magic writing pad, the difference between the pleasure and the reality principles, which is fundamental to *Beyond the Pleasure Principle*, and hence to his reading of that text in *La carte postale*, represents the institution of the possibility of difference in life and hence inaugurates the economy of death (1967a: 295):

> Différance, the pre-opening of the ontico-ontological difference [. . .] and all the differences that furrow Freudian conceptuality, such as they are able to be organized—and it's only an example—around the difference between the "pleasure" and the "reality" principles or derive from them. The difference between the pleasure principle and the reality principle, for example, is not only nor primarily a distinction, an exteriority, but the originary possibility, in life, of a detour, of différance (*Aufschub*) and of the economy of death.

For the definition of *différance*, see note 16.

11. Derrida observes in part 2 of *La carte postale*, "Spéculer—Sur «Freud»," that the repetition compulsion, which forms Freud's object of investigation in *Beyond the Pleasure*

We are not simply passively written by our experience, then, but actively writing it. Yet, it is precisely this moment of internal spontaneity, which distinguishes genuine memory from its externalized, scriptural imitation, that always eludes representation, comprehension, and intelligibility, and thus transforms itself into a realm of absolute externality.[12] In addition, that moment when the absolute inside becomes the opaque, becomes that which eludes the snares of analytical reason, like the *Nabel* that Freud posits at the center of the dream (1965: 143n.2, 564), is also the moment when any concept of the fully present subject is itself *subjected* to the dictates of the intimate Other. Thus, every moment of writing is also one of being written. It too is inscribed, dictated. This doubly contradictory movement is the moment of undecidability—of Platonic, Derridian, and psychoanalytic *aporia*—from which the possibility of error, deviation, and wrong opinion, but also of *philosophia* (the love/desire for wisdom), is sprung (Derrida 1994: 21; Gasché 2002). Thus, even a Platonic writing on the soul is always the inscription of a trace, a moment of otherness, rather than of simple self-presence:

> The subject of writing is a system of relations between layers: of the magic writing pad, of the psyche, of society, of the world. Inside this scene, the punctual simplicity of the classical[13] subject cannot be found. To describe this structure, it does not suffice to recall that one always writes for someone. [. . .] One searches the "public," in vain for the first reader, that is to say the first author of the work. And "the sociology of literature" completely misses the conflict and the ruses—whose stakes are the origin of the work—between the first author who reads and the first reader who dictates. (Derrida 1967a: 335)

This last image of a first reader who dictates, of a primal receptor who precedes the author who reads, is not only a wonderful description of the dynamic of the intimate Other—of the origin of meaning as always different, deferred, alienated from itself—but it is also precisely that

---

Principle, is the effect of memory traces that can only be enacted not remembered, and hence seem to come from nowhere, unbidden like the Socratic *daimôn*. Compare Lacan on the structures of unconscious memory in the "Seminar on the Purloined Letter" (1966b).

12. Spontaneity is a word freighted with philosophical consequence and history. Derrida prefers the concept of the "decision," which he contends can never be accounted for by any theory of the subject, and which by definition is radically heterogeneous to all factual or theoretical determination (1994: 86–87, 247).

13. I.e., Cartesian.

duality captured in the reproduction of the frontispiece of a thirteenth-century fortune-telling book from the Bodleian Library that graces the cover of *La carte postale*. There, Plato dictates to a clearly labeled Socrates who writes, thus reversing the classical opposition between these two figures who stand at the origin of western philosophy.

What, however, does this mean? Is Derrida merely being perverse and promoting a bit of late medieval fantasy to the status of an interpretive concept? Or is there not a sense in which Socrates, at least the Socrates of the Platonic tradition, has always been taking dictation? For, in a real sense, Socrates is only who he is because he in fact figures forth Plato's image of him. He thus takes dictation from his disciple, even as he writes, inscribes, and produces that disciple. This is not only true because the Socrates we know in western philosophy is by and large the Socrates of the Platonic dialogues[14] and hence the literary creation of Plato (Hadot 1995b: 70; Zuckert 1996: 26; Nehamas 1998: 7), but it is also true on a more profound level. To the extent that Plato could ever be the disciple of Socrates he must have already in some sense been dictating who Socrates was; he must have been creating (and supplanting) a Socrates who was nonetheless already there, already forming Plato in his own self-relation (Blondell 2002: 110–11).

> Example: if one morning Socrates had spoken for Plato, if to Plato, his addressee, he had addressed a message, it is also that p. would have had to be able to receive, expect, desire, in brief, called for in a certain manner what Socrates will have said to him; and therefore what S., under dictation, seems to invent—writes, in fact. p. sent himself a post card (legend + image), he sent it back to himself from himself, or even he sent himself Socrates. (Derrida 1980: 35)

This first reversal of the relation between Plato and Socrates, master and disciple, writer and reader, is in turn also the image of Freud's relation to Plato as explored in Derrida's reading of the *Philebus*. Here not only is Freud's debt to his great predecessor plumbed, but we also come to the recognition that Freud's debt to Plato cannot but be read in terms of *Freud*'s own argumentative and discursive structures. We come to recognize that Freud too is a reader who dictates, and hence that Plato owes a debt to Freud (Derrida 1980: 120). Each discourse supplements the other and, therefore, simultaneously figures its own excessive character and the other's radical incompleteness. For Derrida, then, there is

---

14. Compare the very different image found in Xenophon's Socratic writings.

no point of pure origin from which meaning, memory, and consciousness flow in a unidirectional, univalent, or totalizable movement. There is no classical subject, but rather an endless series of contingent constructions: momentary gatherings and dispersions of meaning across time and between texts.

The Freudian unconscious on Derrida's reading is a text woven from "pure" traces. It unites the immanence of meaning (re-ferring) with the externality of force in an unstable, undecidable whole, like a stylus applied to the wax tablet of the Platonic soul. Psychic life begins precisely with these traces, with re-production, with the remembrance of things past. It is thus always already a deferred origin. The trace necessarily precedes the presence to which it refers. Without memory and its necessary repression, there can be no unconscious, no subjective depth, and no consciousness as the presence of self to self (Freud 1965: 575–607). There is only a pure and meaningless, undifferentiated immediacy. Thus past and present, auditor and receptor, reader and writer, inside and outside are constantly switching positions: each one necessarily positing, making room for, bearing the trace of, supplementing, and subverting the other (Derrida 1967a: 302, 314; 1972b: 45–46; 1980: 373; Kittler 1999: 33; Zuckert 1996: 213–14).

At the center of every psychic text, including that which marks the royal road to the unconscious, the dream, there is what Freud calls the "navel," the place where the tissue of meanings, the interweaving of trace upon trace, becomes so dense as to be unanalyzable. And yet it is this navel, the mark of psychic birth, which, as the principle of irreducible difference, articulates the weave of the text, its spacing and coherence, and therefore makes meaning, re-ferring, and hence analysis and interpretation, possible (Derrida 1996a: 23–24; 1972b: 38–39). Deconstruction, like psychoanalysis, is a form of archeology or genealogy (two terms that loom large in Foucault's historico-analytical lexicon).[15] It institutes an interminable analysis that seeks not to destroy, but precisely to touch the indestructible, the unanalyzable, from which analysis and interpretation necessarily begin and with which they invariably end (Derrida 1980: 249; 1996a: 48).

Thus, as Derrida notes, the basic methodology of Freudian analysis, like that of deconstruction, is the heir to two Greek terms that form the etymological and conceptual underpinnings of all modern concepts of the analytic per se: *analuein*, a return from the multiplicity of phenomena to that which is indivisible; and *lysis,* a simultaneous dissolution

---

15. See chapter 1.

of all aggregates into their component unities and subunities (1996a: 33). This double movement is, of course, exactly what Plato refers to in both the *Phaedrus* and the *Philebus* as the method of collection (*sunagôgê*) and division (*diairesis*). Unlike either its Freudian or Foucauldian analogues, however, deconstructive analysis according to Derrida presents a radicalization of this philosophical dialectic by not only calling into question the possibility of an original indivisibility, but also by subjecting "the desire or phantasm" of such an originary moment to this same double demand:

> It is a question in deconstruction of not only a counter-archeology, but also a counter-genealogy: the "genealogy" of the genealogic principle is no longer a matter of a simple genealogy. . . . What is the deconstruction of presence except the experience of this hyper-analytical dissociation of the simple from the originary? The trace, writing, the mark is at the heart of the present, at the origin of presence, a movement of return to the other, to some other, a reference as différance[16] that would resemble an *a priori* synthesis if it was of the order of judgment and the thetic.[17] But in a prethetic and pre-judgmental order, the trace is in fact an irreducible link (*Verbindung*). (Derrida 1996a: 41–42; emphasis in original)

Deconstruction is conceived of as an analytic genealogy and archeology that has been radicalized to the prethetic moment beyond all recognizable simples, that is precisely to the Platonic level of the unlimited or indeterminate (*apeiron*), which the *Philebus* posits.

Thus, for Derrida, the reading of Plato is not only a necessary moment in any archeology of western metaphysics, but also there can be no reading of Freud, Lacan, and Foucault that does not necessarily entail a response to Plato, and no response to Freud, Lacan, and Foucault that is not always already a reading of Plato (Derrida 1967a: 294; 1992: 266–67).

---

16. *Différance* is Derrida's term for the simultaneous movement of difference and deferral that makes signification, and hence consciousness as articulated experience, possible. To re-fer is to point to that which is other (the movements of referring to and of being referred to are always, at least analytically, separable) and to that which is not immediately present (even the statement, "I think," is always separated from the act to which it points by a necessary, if infinitesimal, interval).

17. The thetic is the moment of positing in which the undifferentiated continuum of experience is broken as consciousness and its object simultaneously come into being. It is thus analogous to the imposition of the limit (*peras*) on the unlimited (*apeiron*) described in the *Philebus*, which will be examined in more detail later in this chapter.

In this context, it is no surprise that Derrida in "La pharmacie de Platon" follows his reference text for the *Phaedrus*, Leon Robin's Budé with its monumental two hundred-page introduction, and sees an intimate connection between the *Phaedrus* and the *Philebus* (Derrida 1972a: 74n.3, 80).[18] In both of these dialogues, he observes, there is not only a focus on the relation between the dialectic of collection and division in relation to the cognate problems of Eros/desire and pleasure, but also each of them prominently features the Egyptian god Theuth (who appears nowhere else in the Platonic corpus). In both, he appears as the inventor of the alphabet. He is the divine figure who first imposed a limit (*peras*) or mark upon the undifferentiated continuum (*apeiron*) of sound and thereby made it possible to analyze language into letters that combine first into syllables and from there produce the signifiers that constitute the ground of consciousness, the signifiers that trace their way in the wax tablet of memory and so write us in the moment of our writing (Derrida 1972b: 187–88, citing *Philebus* 11d, 16c–17b, 18b–d).[19]

Thus from the essay on the magic writing pad (1967a), to "La pharmacie de Platon" (1972a), to *La carte postale* (1980), and to such late works as *Khora* (1993b) and the three essays on Freud (1996a), Lacan (1996b), and Foucault (1997) collected in *Résistances de la psychanalyse*, the problematic of the Platonic trace, mark, and limit has been integral to Derrida's conception of the possibility of thought in relation to both history and the unconscious, and hence to the ongoing dialogue he maintained with such contemporaries as Lacan and Foucault. The remainder of this chapter will consist of three movements. The first will examine Derrida's articulation of the relation of Plato's conception of writing in the *Phaedrus* to the history of western metaphysics. The second will explore the *Philebus* in relation to Derrida's reading of Freud and Lacan. The last section will consider how these two movements relate to Derrida's ongoing debate with Michel Foucault, which began with a 1963 lecture delivered by Derrida on Foucault's *Histoire de la Folie,* and which specifically engaged the question of whether the Socratic *logos* knew any opposite.

---

18. Derrida (1972a: 100 n.19, 191n.76) also displays a clear knowledge of the works of Festugière (1950) and Goldschmidt (2003) respectively.

19. In addition, as Peponi has demonstrated (2002: 143–44, 156–58), there is an elaborate system of erotic, medical, and lyric intertexts linking the *Phaedrus* and the *Philebus*.

2. Pharmakon/Pharmakos:
"Take two and call me in the morning."

> For Plato, writing is a part of the wider sphere of imitation, because it is only a copy. It is a copy of the word of the soul which is silent in the case of thought and vocal when the voice is used as a medium. In this case, as in all others, imitation tends to transgress its limits by presenting its copy as a complete reality. Thus Plato often goes to great lengths not to discredit writing completely—which would be a paradoxical attitude on the part of someone who makes such an important and remarkable use of it—but to remind us of its ambiguity. (Brisson 1998: 37)

> Derrida's analysis of the *pharmakon* avoids valorizing one "side" of this term against the other; writing—the *pharmakon* of Plato's *Phaedrus*—is not just a "poison" as such, and for that reason cannot simply be affirmed in the face of the phonocentric and logocentric "truth." Instead, it is the stability or the coherence of the very borderline between writing as poison and writing as cure that is seen as possible only through the intervention of the dead, external supplementarity of writing. (Stoekl 1992: 201)

The Derridean reading of the Platonic text is a multifaceted enterprise. On one level, Derrida sees in Platonism, and more specifically in the *Phaedrus*'s attempt to expel writing and imitation from, or at least strictly contain it within, the realm demarcated by the *logos*—i.e., by a finite, totalizable set of meanings, essences, and *eidê*—the chief instantiation of logocentrism. This in turn is the main dividing line between many contemporary interpreters of the *Phaedrus*[20] and Derrida himself: for, where, on this view, Derrida sees in the *Phaedrus* a necessarily failed attempt to create a closed system, many critics see a self-conscious acknowledgment of the necessity of that failure (Shankman 1994b: 8; Mara 1997: 246–51). In place of an unfulfilled monological striving for metaphysical closure, they see the dialogue's multileveled deployment of Socratic irony as a recognition of the ultimate openness of the dialectical process. Thus, while the basic logic of Derrida's reading of the dialogue as exemplifying the impossibility of metaphysical closure is hardly ever called into question, the real bone of contention is over whether Plato, in the words of David Halperin, can be viewed "as a kind of deconstructionist *avant la lettre*" (1994: 62; see also Ferrari 1987: 207, 220).

In point of fact, however, the issue is somewhat miscast since, as

---

20. At least those who are committed to a hermeneutic or textual reading of Plato, as opposed to those who would take a more strictly analytic approach that would seek to reduce the text to a finite set of argumentative propositions.

Berger and others have pointed out, Derrida's interest in making this claim is less in Plato the writer than in Platonism as a system (Berger 1994: 76, 97). His focus is on the role of the Platonic texts in the establishment of systematic western philosophy (Derrida 1972a: 182–83; Ferrari 1987: 214); the argument is that, if we are to grasp the subsequent history of occidental thought, we must first understand how the *logos* is constituted at philosophy's beginnings. Hence, whether or not the historical Plato was aware of the contradictions of reason in ways that his successors were not is from one perspective irrelevant. Indeed, as we shall see, it is precisely Foucault's failure to recognize the determining influence of the tradition of post-Socratic philosophy on the understanding of the nature of reason that constitutes one of Derrida's major critiques of *Histoire de la folie*.

Nonetheless, it would be a mistake to cast Derrida as a vulgar reader of Plato who naively assimilates the texts of the Platonic dialogues to the history of their reception and hence to the creation and consolidation of Platonism as a guiding force in the history of metaphysics. His position is far more nuanced. Indeed, by his own logic, the recognition of Platonic textuality forbids that it be reduced to a transcendental signified, to a regulative system of meaning that writes but is never written. Rather the deconstruction of Platonism occurs precisely by understanding it as a textual system, by foregrounding the Platonic text as text (Alliez 1992: 226; Derrida 1972a: 71). The self-subverting nature of the *pharmakon* (drug/poison) does not escape Plato on Derrida's reading—which is not to say Plato completely masters it either—but rather Socratic irony consists precisely in the self-conscious deployment of the *pharmakon*'s double-sided nature:

> Socratic irony precipitates out one *pharmakon* by bringing it into contact with another. Or rather it reverses the *pharmakon*'s powers and turns *its* surface—thus taking effect, being recorded and dated, in the act of classing the *pharmakon,* through the fact that the *pharmakon* properly consists in a certain inconsistency, a certain impropriety, this nonidentity-with-itself always allowing it to be turned against itself. (Derrida 1981: 119; 1972a: 136; emphasis in original)

The deconstruction of Plato and Platonism is neither an assault against nor an exclusive valorization of the Platonic text. Rather it is a strategic operation that takes place on the undecidable border between the Platonic project's self-conscious textuality and its equally self-conscious desire for closure, certainty, and transcendental guarantees (Derrida 1996a: 45).

Platonism as a system of metaphysical postulates and as a discourse of authority grounded upon them is neither an alien graft onto the open and free play of the Platonic text, nor is it its necessary and logical extension. Rather Platonism, according to Derrida, is something that haunts the Platonic/Socratic project: a somewhat sinister body, which is neither wholly foreign nor completely at home in the text of the dialogues. Like the "nocturnal council" of the *Laws*, it seeks to establish philosophy as a form of law whose function is to dominate other modes of discourse present in the text (Derrida 1993b: 83; Alliez 1992: 221). It posits a privileged experience of absolute presence, of access to a higher intelligible world that is both the double of the sensible and its ontological superior (Vlastos 1991: 78; Festugière 1950: 210). For Derrida, then, philosophy's first chapter is called Plato (Wolff 1992: 235), and Platonism itself is a force that infinitely continues, repeats, and disseminates itself across both the Platonic text and the history of philosophy, even in the moment of its transgression and negation (Loraux 1996: 169).

Yet, as the dialectical formulation of the last sentence indicates, Platonism as a metaphysical system is at most only half the story. It is in fact an abstraction from the Platonic texts, a logocentric reduction that seeks to deny their "written" quality and therefore the considerable energy deployed by them against any monolithic domain of sense separate from the sensibility, from the force of the material letter (Derrida 1993b: 81–82; Wolff 1992: 241–42; Berger 1994: 97). It is no accident that Plato never accepted the treatise as a mode of philosophical thought (Diès 1941: xvi). The love of wisdom was never reducible to a straightforward exposition of his thought as a set of abstract propositions on the world. Instead, Plato experimented relentlessly with a variety of narrative frames and forms of dialectical exchange, from the crisp question and answer of the *Ion*, to the alternating speeches of the *Symposium*, to the synthetic structure of a recited written dialogue within a framing oral dialogue of the *Theaetetus*, to the mixture of all these modes of exposition and argumentation found in the *Phaedrus* itself (Hunter 2004: 22–23).

There is, in fact, no stable place of truth within the Platonic text from which clear and unproblematic propositions can be deduced: each text is instead a place of dialectical tension, contradiction, negotiation, and exchange. As Nicole Loraux observes:

> In Plato everything is played out between *khôra* and *khôris*. Between

khôra, neither sensible nor intelligible and, hence, the principle of undecidability, and *khôris*, that which separates and isolates.[21] It happens—and it's no mere hazard—that *khôris* is found in etymological dictionaries *sub verbo khôra*, which already suggests that the game will be endless but ought not authorize any reader [. . .] to read *khôra* in Plato as "that which separates," but always as "that which receives"—and the tension between *dekhomai* and *khôris*, which develops for example in the *Phaedrus* between the soul that sees the beautiful object, receives it, and opens out, and the isolated soul, subject to pain, [can] be considered as constitutive of the Platonic concept of place. (1996: 169–70)

It is the great merit of Derrida's reading of the *Phaedrus* and of the figure of the *pharmakon* as the remedy/poison of writing, rhetoric, and the exteriorized material letter, to follow out these tensions in minute detail. Derrida deftly limns the dialectic of Platonism and textuality that constitute the Platonic corpus as we have received it and as it continues to structure the basic concepts and tropes of our entire philosophical and theoretical tradition.

Derrida begins his reading of the *Phaedrus* in an eminently philological fashion. He notes that the dialogue has been the topic of much debate concerning both its date and quality. The final disquisition on the origin and history of writing, he observes, has often been felt to be extraneous to the main argument of the dialogue and has hence been taken as a sign of either juvenile ineptitude or creeping senescence.[22] Thus the traditional understanding of both the quality and the date of the dialogue are shown to be dependent on the relationship of the final characterization of writing to the body of the work as a whole. Derrida's thesis is that this final section forms a crucial part of the dialogue and that writing and its metaphorical representation in the figure of the *pharmakon* represent the key philosophemes that simultaneously hold the dialogue together and divide it against itself (Derrida 1972a: 74–75; Halperin 1994: 66–67; Clarke 1995: 3).

The word *pharmakon* is first used to describe writing in the *Phaedrus* in reference to the copy of Lysias' speech that Phaedrus uses to lure Socrates beyond the walls of Athens (230d8; Derrida 1972a: 78–79). *Pharmakon* is also the term used by Theuth at the dialogue's end to

---

21. These two terms are comparable to the *Philebus*'s master terms, *peras* and *apeiron*, "the limit" and "the unlimited."

22. For more on the history of this debate and the issues involved, see Robin (1964: 53–55) and Santas (1988: 58–59, 64).

describe to Ammon his invention of writing (274e7) and again by Ammon in his reply (275a7). Derrida notes that Plato deliberately plays upon the inherent ambiguity of the word: for while Theuth presents writing as a remedy or beneficial drug, one meaning of *pharmakon*, Ammon says it is in fact just the opposite (*tou'nantion*, 275a2) and thus deploys the equally common meaning of poison or harmful drug. This play on the different senses of the word, as Derrida observes, is almost always lost in translation, where a choice must be made either to translate the same word two different ways, in which case Plato's "anagrammatic" jest is lost, or to accept only one of the two possible meanings, in which case the point of the repetition is lost (1972a: 109–11).[23] The use of the term *pharmakon* (poison/remedy/charm) to describe both Lysias' speech, which is an example of dishonorable writing, and the invention of the technology of inscription itself is, Derrida notes, not an accident. It shows that the same basic suspicion not only envelops both writing and medicine, but also that the fundamental ambiguity denoted by the equation of writing and the *pharmakon* is one of the most basic philosophemes structuring the dialogue (Derrida 1972a: 77, 81). Indeed, Plato's punning use of the word *pharmakon* is an illustration of the fundamental problem he is addressing in the *Phaedrus:* the divorce between the external inscription of the signifying substance in writing, rhetoric, and seduction and the presumed internality of meaning and love in relation to the *logos* itself.[24] The final discussion, then, on the origin, history, and value of writing is not merely an extraneous excrescence, or a mark of the dialogue's imperfection, but rather its fitting climax. In this context, Derrida observes that the question of what exactly is the nature of *logographia* or "speech-writing"—a term whose combination of *logos* with *graphê* neatly sums up the issues

23. As Nightingale has shown (1995: 135, 150–53, 163–66), Ammon/Thamus' speech is itself an intertextual rewriting or parody of a speech or speeches by Palamedes in Sophocles' and Euripides' tragedies of the same name (frgs. 479 Radt and 587 Nauck, respectively). Thus the "anagrammatic" jest Derrida perceives is raised to the second power, and Ammon's charge that writing is not a "remedy" (*pharmakon*) but a "poison" (*pharmakon*) for memory because it relies on eternalized and alien discourses, such as the speech of Lysias that Phaedrus carries with him, is itself shown to be predicated on an alien discourse that Plato has incorporated into his own. Thus Szlezák (1999: 29–30, 41) is correct when he argues that the *Phaedrus*'s critique of writing applies to Plato himself, but clearly oversimplifies when he and others posit a body of esoteric doctrine that would be purged of all such ambiguity, of externality, of writing as the presence of the material letter. Rather the *Phaedrus* itself recognizes the impossibility of such a discourse even as it imagines its desirability and, from a certain perspective, its necessity.

24. On the theme of internality versus externality, see Ferrari (1987: 38–39) and Berger (1994: 94). On the organic relationship between the topics of love and rhetoric in the dialogue, see Robin (1985: xxxix–xl).

evoked by the dialogue as a whole—is posed at the exact mathematical center of the work in terms of its total number of lines (257c–e; Derrida 1972a: 76).

These formal considerations are not the only indication of the importance of the figure of the *pharmakon* to the institution of the Platonic *logos*. Derrida remarks that in Socrates' jesting, rationalist accounting of the myth of the abduction of Oreithyia by Boreas, Oreithyia is said to be playing outside the city walls with another young girl named *Pharmakeia*, or "poisoner," at the time she is swept into the abyss (229c10; Derrida 1972a: 78). Thus, Derrida notes, the motifs of the *pharmakon*, externality, and death, as well as the opposition between a traditional *muthos* and a rationalizing *logos*,[25] are in play from the moment Socrates is enticed by the lure of Lysias' speech to come out of Athens into the Attic countryside.[26] Socrates' humorous account of the myth, which he himself promptly rejects, is reminiscent of the probabilistic manner of argument typical of the sophists. And they, like Lysias, are subsequently stigmatized as dealing only with the externalities or appearances of knowledge, in the same way that writing is criticized by Ammon as a mere simulacrum of the *logos* (Ferrari 1987: 10, 234n.12; Halperin 1994: 52–53).[27] Yet Socrates, as he proves in the great second speech, is himself an inveterate mythmaker, and frequently uses myth throughout the dialogues in places where the dialectic itself cannot produce certainty or at least where its mortal practitioners would be unable to follow it: i.e., those dealing with the nature of metaphysical reality and with the verities of the world beyond death (Brisson 1998: 129–30: Goldschmidt 2003: 104–6). As such, *muthos* designates the realm of discourse that has both yet to reach the scientific regularity of the *logos* and simultaneously transcends it. It is at once infra- and supralogical, like writing itself (Brisson 1998: 73–74, 103–4; Robin 1985: xcvi). Plato seeks not to do away with *muthos* but to break the monopoly of mythic discourse on the public consciousness. For this reason he strives to introduce a rigorous distinction between *muthos* and *logos*, writing and speech, even as he simultaneously demonstrates that in the last analysis each presupposes and depends upon the other (Derrida 1972a: 98; Brisson 1998: 87–88; Zuckert 1996: 218).

25. For a deconstruction of (and homage to) Vernant's reading of this opposition in Greek culture, see *Khôra*, Derrida's reading of the *Timaeus* (1993b).

26. "[J]ust this, I believe, is Plato's point in 'doing philosophy' in this dialogue through two distinct and strikingly juxtaposed verbal paths of myth and dialectic. He allows neither path to reach a satisfactory goal; rather one leads only to the other" (Ferrari 1987: 34).

27. On the sophists, like writing and the *pharmakon*, as being both inside and outside the charmed circle of Platonic philosophy, see Derrida (1972a: 123).

The nymph *Pharmakeia,* however, is not the only potential poisoner on the Platonic scene of writing. *Pharmakeios,* the masculine form of *Pharmakeia,* is applied to Eros in the *Symposium* (203d8). Elsewhere in the same dialogue, the verb *pharmattein* is used by Agathon of Socrates' attempt to charm, bewitch, or seduce him with the promise of the audience's expectations concerning the former's speech in praise of love (194a5; Derrida 1972a: 134–35). Writing, rhetoric, and the *pharmakon* in the Platonic corpus are clearly portrayed as simultaneously seductive and dangerous, attractive and disruptive. In the *Republic,* the word is used by Socrates of lies (*pseudê*) or fictions (*muthologiai*) that he qualifies as both potentially dangerous to the *polis* and useful (*khrêsimos*) when dealing with enemies or educating the young (382a–d, 387a–d; Berger 1994: 83; D. Allen 2000: 267). But, while Plato, according to Derrida, strives in the *Phaedrus* to create a clear opposition between writing and the Socratic dialectic of truth, the very ambivalence of the *pharmakon* and Socrates' status as mythologizing *pharmakeios* show this opposition in constant danger of collapsing. Socrates' speech both is and is not of the order of the *pharmakon* (Derrida 1972a: 105, 142–43; Oudemans and Lardinois 1987: 88; D. Allen 2000: 85), just as Plato both is opposed to writing and the author of beautifully crafted works.

What writing and the *pharmakon* have in common is that both belong to the realm of externality. They are supplements to the *logos* and the body respectively and as such represent their contamination by forces that are properly outside them (Derrida 1972a: 112–17; Stoekl 1992: 201). Like the *pharmakos* or scapegoat, they are the foreign agents that must be expelled if a realm of internal purity is to be established in both the person and the *polis* (Derrida 1972a: 149; Stoekl 1992: 204). Writing does not, Ammon responds to Theuth, actually improve memory but rather degrades it by substituting a mere facsimile of knowledge for its vital presence. In place of *mnêmê,* active recollection, we have *hupomnêsis,* the dead letter of the passive reminder (274e–275b3).[28] In place of the living *logos,* we have the mindless repetition of *muthos* (Derrida 1972a: 84, 98, 122, 126). Thus, as in the case of the *pharmakon,* what on one level appears to be a remedy, on another proves to be a poison.

28. On the homology of these two terms with the opposition between rhetoric and dialectic and their subsequent deconstruction in the dialogue, see Halperin (1994: 72n.18). On memory (especially of past lives) as an ascetic, purifying practice in the doctrines of Empedocles and the Pythagoreans, and a reading of the *Phaedrus*'s condemnation of writing as a threat to these practices, see Vernant (1965: 1.94–115).

Yet the externality of writing is ultimately indissociable from knowledge and memory per se (Stoekl 1992: 202). This is perhaps nowhere clearer than at the end of the *Phaedrus* when Socrates concludes that what dialectic demands is not the dead letter of *logographoi* [speech writers] like Lysias but a kind of writing on the soul, a direct interaction between, in the words of Robin, "master and student" (276a6–11, 278a3; Robin 1985: lxiv, lxvii; Halperin 1994: 51, 61–62). "After he complains at some length of the inferiority of the written word to the best kind of speech, he goes on to speak of the good discourse as 'another sort of writing' in which the dialectical speaker directly inscribes his auditor's soul [or psyche]" (Berger 1994: 76). The metaphor here is telling because, even at the level of the most profound internality, the presence of the *logos* in the soul can only be conceived of as a form of otherness or externality that has penetrated it (Derrida 1972a: 105). It alienates the soul from itself at the moment of its constitution. If that were not the case there would be no need for philosophy and dialectic, since the *logos* would be fully present to each and all of us, rather than a palimpsest that philosophy needs to uncover. A supplement is always required to realize the *logos*. It is for this reason, Derrida suggests, that *épistémè* or knowledge of the order of the *logos* is itself described as a *pharmakon* in both the *Critias* and the *Charmides* (106b5–6, 155d–157a; Derrida 1972a: 142–43). The status of the *logographoi*, whether writing on paper or the soul, is thus shown to be the central problem in the inauguration of western reason, and the subject it posits.

3. Beyond the Pleasure Principle: The *Apeiron*

> Part of the self-understanding of a life that is directed only at enjoyment is to set no limits and, for just that reason, to have to accept no end of pain, as well, which results in its necessarily failing in its own intention and not being able *to be*. So "measurelessness" is not, as Philebus thinks, the character of pleasure which positively enables it to be good but (on the contrary) a negative characteristic of it: that which makes it impossible for pleasure, on its own, to fulfill itself and to be an unvarying perspective from which to understand existence. (Gadamer 1991: 145; emphasis in original)

> The three terms—two principles plus or minus différance—are in fact one, the division of the same, since the second principle (that of reality) and différance are only "effects" of the modifiable pleasure principle.
> But by whatever *end* you take this structure in one-two-three terms, it's

death. *In the end,* and this death is not opposable, it is not different from, in the sense of being opposed to, the two principles and their différance. It's inscribed, although not inscribable, in the process of this structure [. . .] If death is not opposable, it is already life, death. (Derrida 1980: 304–5; emphasis in original)

In *La carte postale,* Derrida argues that Freud's *Beyond the Pleasure Principle,* the central text in Lacan's reading of the *Antigone,* owes an unacknowledged debt to Plato's *Philebus.* Indeed, any reader of the *Philebus*'s account of physical pleasure as the restoration of harmony in the psyche after a period of lack or disruption (31c–32b), and of Freud's description of the pleasure principle's being founded on the restoration of equilibrium after a period of heightened excitation cannot help but notice the resemblance (1961a: 1–5).[29] More specifically, Derrida contends that Plato establishes the centrality of the concept of limit to the calculus of pleasure, and so also makes possible the envisioning, or the positing, of a beyond of that limit (Derrida 1980: 425). In the same book, Derrida also contends that Lacan's reading of Poe's "Purloined Letter" founders on the psychoanalyst's logocentric claim that the "letter" is both material and ultimately indivisible, that it is possessed of an absolute limit of divisibility (Lacan 1966b: 23–24; Benstock 1991: 98–99). Moreover, he observes, Lacan owes to this his ability to claim that "the letter always arrives at its destination," that there is always the possibility of reconstructing its itinerary, if only as an absence and after the fact. In this section, I will claim that the *Philebus*'s complex meditation on the relations between pleasure and limit as well as between the good life and the dialectical method of collection and division is central to understanding Derrida's arguments. I shall also offer the subsidiary thesis that the *Philebus* has the potential to mediate between Derrida and Lacan through its own overdetermined vision of the relation between the competing claims of the dialectic and of practical ethical life, that is, between the philosopher as therapist and the therapist as philosopher.

La carte postale, in fact, stages a genealogical inquiry into the history of western thought as a series of passing-overs, transferences, letters, and estrangements to itself. The formation of the subject and the questions of origins, address, and identity are what's at stake in this inquiry. In this text, Derrida interrogates both Freud's debt to Platonic

---

29. This is especially the case if one is relying on Festugière's account of the *Philebus* (1950: 297–98), which reads as a virtual paraphrase of Freud and with which Derrida was familiar (1972a: 100n.19).

reason, and Plato's debt to Freud, in terms of both writing and a set of relays and mediations that he ironically dubs the "postal system" (1980: 190–91). A crucial passage for understanding this Platonic reading of psychoanalysis and its relation to "postality" is the following:

> Any history of postal *tekhnè* tends to join destination with identity. For a subject to arrive is to arrive at a self. Now a mark, whatever it may be, is coded to make an impression, be it only a scent. As soon as it is divided, *it is the equivalent of several instances in any one instance:* thus no more unique destination. That's why, on account of this divisibility (the origin of reason, the mad origin of reason and of the principle of identity), the *tekhnè* does not arrive at language—at that which I sing for you. (Derrida 1980: 207; emphasis in original)

The "techniques" of the postal system join destination with identity in a system of transmission and mediation. The postal system also constitutes the series of relays and *points de repères* whereby the potentially infinite dissemination of meaning at any given point is gathered up into an ostensibly coherent system of communication, of literal tradition, *traditio,* or handing from one point to the next. Postality is not a transcendental system but the very possibility of the transference of meaning from one relay point to the next. It is "a fold" or "crease" in signification, an endless series of substitutions that "re-ply to" or "fold back against" one another in a complex and endless network of transmissions, "sendings across," metaphors, transferences (Derrida 1980: 206). "The postal system is no longer a simple metaphor, it is also, as the site of all transfers and correspondences, the 'proper' possibility of all possible rhetorics" (1980: 73). It is from this perspective that Derrida argues for a double debt: of Freud's *Beyond the Pleasure Principle* to Plato's *Philebus* and of the *Philebus* to its temporally subsequent, but logically prior, Freudian reading.

The claim is at least a paradox. Traditional western reason assumes a univocal, irreversible system of transmission in which the subject is produced in a stable order of knowledge with a discernible origin. Socrates teaches Plato. Plato teaches Aristotle. Jesus teaches the disciples. The disciples and the church fathers found the church. And the western *logos* is established and handed down to us: a divine mixture of Hellenic wisdom and Hebraic faith, in which Freud, Matthew Arnold, and Charles Maurras all play their parts. Platonism's function has been to anchor that system of knowledge. Derrida's interrogation of Plato in relation to Freud and Lacan, however, serves to show not simply the debt of Freud to Plato, but the way in which debt per se is the condition of possibility for any investment, the way in which each step forward must recreate its own past in a movement of double conditioning that is always already decentered. Thus any given relay in the system of transmission of meaning that constitutes western reason must be radically historicized not only in terms of its debt to the past, but also in terms of the way that that past itself becomes an object of transmission and hence potentially of appropriation and misappropriation as a condition of entering that system, of becoming a project.

Moreover, every mark, every letter, to the extent that it is capable of being addressed to a specific identity, must be able to be reproduced, and hence to be divided from its originary unity: a fact that of necessity undermines that letter's relation to a unique destination. This divisibility is the origin of reason as demonstrated in the *Philebus*'s exposition of the "divine method" of collection and division as the foundation of philosophical dialectic. It is also the origin of writing itself. As Plato points out, it was only by analyzing words into their component sounds, their ultimately meaningless phonemes, that the Egyptian god Theuth was able to develop the art of writing (*Philebus* 17a–b, 18b–d).

Division is also the origin of madness: for there must be a limit to divisibility if reason is to produce intelligible language, if the letter is to arrive at its destination. Yet that limit cannot be stated as a principle separate from the process of division per se, outside of the categories of thought that division itself makes possible. Sense, then, depends on that very institution of difference or literal nonsense, and hence potential plurivocity, that Lacan labeled the insistence of the letter and origin of the Freudian unconscious (1966d). The mark of division that makes transmission, mediation, meaning, and transference possible is also that which necessarily derails both it and subjective identity. This is what Derrida means when he speaks of Freud's (and hence Lacan's) unacknowledged debt to Plato (Derrida 1980: 36, 70 180–81; Zuckert 1996: 233).[30]

The addresser and addressee of communication in Derrida's postal system represent positions in an infinitely disseminated web of significations, whose very constitution under the images of law and limit we see first elaborated in the Platonic corpus (1980: 60). The *Philebus*, inasmuch as it founds true knowledge on the dialectic of collection and

---

30. Derrida, far from contesting Lacan's basic reading of *Beyond the Pleasure Principle*, acknowledges it as "le plus intéressant et le plus spectaculaire" (1980: 402–3).

division (14a–20a), and inasmuch as the burden of Socrates' argument is to demonstrate the superiority of knowledge to pleasure,[31] must also posit a world beyond limit, beyond all division, and hence beyond all meaning, mixture, and exchange. The unlimited, *apeiron,* is that which does not contain any quantity, that which can never be reduced to a unity and hence to an entity that might be measured against another (24a–d; Gadamer 1991: 131).[32] The limit, *peras,* then, is the marker of division. It makes the delimitation of discrete logical or material entities possible and thus opens the world to exchange and classification, and hence to knowledge and culture (Lacan 1973: 169). Logical categories and rational entities are predicated on the concept of limit (25a; Boussoulas 1952: 171; Festugière 1950: 230). The conjunction of the limit and the unlimited, of continuity and its determinate negation, make possible, as Plato notes, rhythm, music, mathematics, and signification. This is the realm of the mixed (26a; Frede 1992: 428; Gadamer 1991: 138).

The pleasure principle in Freud, inasmuch as it represents the pursuit of the object of desire as delimited by the reality principle, which is itself a reflex of the pleasure principle and not its beyond, always operates within the realm of the mixed, of entities defined by the limit (Freud 1961a: 4; Lacan 1986: 29; Zuckert 1996: 233). It is for this reason that the Law, substitution, and transference are possible. The division of the subject instituted by its submission to the realm of law and language are the founding moments of desire, as recognized by both Aristophanes' speech in Plato's *Symposium* and by Lacan himself. This division is also the object of Derrida's own inquiry (1980: 36, 60; Ragland-Sullivan 1986: 270; Julien 1990: 151–52, 176, 231):

> La «détermination» c'est la limite—et d'abord du plaisir (du *Philèbe* à *Au-delà* . . .), ce qui lie l'énergie; elle identifie, elle décide, elle définit, elle marque les contours, et puis c'est la destination (*Bestimmung,* si on veut s'appeler comme ça), et la loi et la guêpe[33] (Sp)[34]

---

31. He ultimately shows knowledge to be a superior kind of pleasure, or more properly part of a mixed entity in which knowledge brings pleasure, since a life of knowledge without pleasure would offer no attraction (20b–23b; Frede 1992: 427–28). See also 66a8 in Diès's text along with the accompanying note. There he prints the marginal gloss in B, τινα ἥδιον, in place of the ungrammatical τὴν ἀίδιον found in the vulgate. His explication of the passage and defense of the reading in the introduction to the Budé edition both anticipates Derrida's (and Plato's) deconstruction of the opposition between pleasure and knowledge and provides a plausible rationale for this rather speculative piece of textual reconstruction (1941: lxxxix).

32. See Frede's helpful introduction and notes (1993).

33. A punning allusion to Aristophanes' *Wasps,* a satire on the law, and to the "gap."

34. In the context of the *La carte postale* uppercase S normally refers to Socrates

quand elle est pas folle, qu'elle veut savoir de qui de quoi: et moi donc qu'est-ce que je deviens dans cette affaire, faudrait encore que ça me fasse un peu retour, que la lettre revienne à sa destination, etc.

"Determination" is the limit—and first of all of pleasure (from the *Philebus* to *Beyond* [*the Pleasure Principle*]), it is what binds energy: it identifies, it defines, it marks the contours, and finally it's the destination (*Bestimmung* [regulation, purpose, destiny, setting, classification], if you want to call it that), it's both the law and the gap/Wasp (Sp), when it's not mad, that wants to know of whom and of what: and for me then, whatever I become in this affair, it will still be necessary that there be some small return for me, that the letter comes back to its destination, etc. (1980: 65)

Deconstruction, as Derrida defines his own project, seeks to touch upon the same space beyond the limit, beyond the pleasure principle, that Freud limns in his Phileban investigation of the pleasure and reality principles as relative goods. It does not seek to destroy this Platonico-Freudian opposition between desire/pleasure and knowledge/reality, but to move beyond it to the indestructible, which, as Lacan's reading of *Antigone* and Freud show, is indistinguishable from death (Derrida 1980: 249, 304–4, 425–27).[35] It is also precisely this space beyond the oppositions of change and rest, which embraces both being and becoming, that the Eleatic stranger in the *Sophist* denotes as the ultimate object of philosophical pursuit: "that which is" (249c–250c).

Freud's position as a psychoanalyst and scientist, rather than as a philosopher, is not, however, to embrace the beyond or death, but

---

and lowercase *p* to Plato. Printing them together treats them as a unit in reference to the law, its sting, and the "gap" or limit it imposes. Of course, *Sp* is also an English editorial abbreviation for spelling, thus drawing attention to the punning nature of the word *guêpe*.

There is, however, a deeper Freudian sense to all this. As Micaela Janan points out to me (*per litteras*), the letters *Sp* also refer to the Wolfman's Dream. "The Wolfman . . . tells Freud of having dreamed of a wasp (*Wespe*) that was missing its wings—and thus was 'truncated' into, he joked, an 'espe.' Then the Wolfman remarked in a sudden insight, 'That's me—S.P.!' His real name was, of course, Sergei Pankeiev, and thus 'S.P.' were his initials. The relevance of this incident is that it's often cited as part of the 'linguistic' concentration in Freud's early work that drew Lacan's attention: here's a dream that signifies, not by metaphor . . . but directly with the letter—or rather, the letters, 'S.P.' And I think this must have been on Derrida's mind, because he wrote the preface to Nicholas Abraham and Maria Torok's *The Wolfman's Magic Word*." See Freud (1955: 94).

35. In "La pharmacie," Derrida suggested that this aporetic space beyond all oppositions can be identified with the *khôra* in the *Timaeus* (1972a: 184–86).

rather the realm of the mixed entity defined by the limit. In *Beyond the Pleasure Principle,* he struggles constantly to articulate even the most radical of his metapsychological insights within the realm of the Law. For, on the one hand, the Law, as he acknowledges in *Civilization and Its Discontents* (1961b),[36] is the ultimate cause of our unhappiness; but on the other, it also marks the ground on which the pleasure principle finds its erection. The institution of language and culture constitutes the fundamental delimitation of the subject and the signifier that make transference, treatment, and psychoanalysis possible (Lacan 1966c: 412–18; Kristeva 1987: 21–38; Derrida 1980: 360–61, 409). It is this fundamentally aporetic structure of being both within and beyond the Law that accounts for what Derrida terms Freud's "athétique" style in *Beyond the Pleasure Principle,* his constant hesitation before the positing of a potential transgression of the very limits that enable his discourse (1980: 425). As the "Derrida" of *La carte postale*'s opening epistolary novel observes:

> Je relis *Au-delà* . . . d'une main tout y est merveilleusement *hermétique,* c'est-à-dire postal et *traînant*–souterrainement ferroviaire, mais aussi boiteux, trainant la patte: il ne nous dit RIEN, ne fait pas un pas qu'il ne retire au pas suivant.

> I am rereading *Beyond* [*the Pleasure Principle*]: on the one hand there is something marvelously *hermetic,* that is to say postal and *meandering*—like a subterranean railway, but also limping, dragging its paw: he says to us NOTHING, doesn't make one step that he doesn't take back with the next. (1980: 153; emphasis in original)

Freud, then, even as he searches to articulate its beyond, continues to work within the closure of western metaphysics and the bounded entities it discerns. The logocentric world of western reason that subtends the pleasure and the reality principles constitute a kind of subway on which one can only get transfers from one line to the next but never truly get off. The signifier as it moves from post to post in its infinite path of circulation and exchange traces the path of transferences, substitutions, and displacements that produce the talking cure.

Psychoanalysis consists of a series of relays through which meaning passes. It operates within the field of divisibility and the unit, not in the unmarked realm of the formless and limitless, which, like Plato, it must

---

36. See Lacan's reading (1986: 36, 44).

posit. Through these transfers of meaning, through the delimited places of desire, psychoanalysis continues to function within the postal system of western metaphysics. The repetition of the law and the limit insures that the possibility of meaning always remains, that the letter always arrives at its destination (1980: 50, 73, 190–91).

It is, in fact, Lacan's decision to continue to operate within this system of meanings that constitutes the burden of Derrida's indictment of him in the now famous essay also from *La carte postale,* "Le facteur de la vérité," or "The postman of truth" (1980: 455). As Derrida observes, the notion that the letter always arrives at its destination, is predicated on its final indivisibility, on there being a limit to delimitation (Lacan 1966b: 23–24). There is always in the last analysis a moment when the address can be reconstructed, even if only after the fact, even if that address is the site of a lack, the constitutive moment of the speaking subject's desire (1980: 464–65, 469).

Moreover, it is precisely the limits of the dialectic, of the philosophic practice of collection and division, in relation to pleasure and to the ethical question of the good life—that is to say, in relation to the desire of the analyst—that is the subject of the *Philebus*. The *Philebus* begins with Socrates advancing the thesis that knowledge is superior to pleasure. Philebus has been Socrates' eristic opponent but, at the beginning of the dialogue, Protarchus is asked to take over for him (11c). This much-debated move paves the way for the shift from the strict binary opposition between these two perspectives asserted at the dialogue's beginning to the more pragmatic, mixed position adopted at its end.

Socrates begins his questioning of Protarchus by asking whether the latter will grant that there are different kinds of pleasure or does he contend that pleasure is an undifferentiated unity (12d–13a). When Socrates subsequently concedes that knowledge too is a multifaceted thing, Protarchus becomes willing to admit the same of pleasure. This concession immediately leads into a discussion of the relation of the many to the one and to the introduction of the "divine method" of collection and division. This method, which was first identified as such in the *Phaedrus* and is explicitly pursued in the *Sophist* and the *Statesman* (Diès 1941: xix; Hampton 1990: 26; Brisson 1998: 112–13), represents nothing more than a formalization of the logical procedures already deployed in the dialectic of the *Phaedo* and the *Republic* (Gadamer 1991: 80–81). There follows a lengthy exposition (16c–17e) that points to the conclusion that in order to determine the unity of any given form or abstract universal, such as knowledge or pleasure, one would first need to follow the procedure of division till one reached the smallest possible constituent unit of that universal[37] and from there proceed back through its many genera and species in quest of its universal form: a unity which embraces all possible instances and thus is in itself without any necessary spatio-temporal limit.

> Socrates: A gift of the gods among men, as it seems to me, it was snatched from the gods by some Prometheus[38] along with the famous fire. And the men of old, who were greater than we are and lived nearer to the gods, handed down this pronouncement, that those things said to be are of the one and the many and have the limit and the unlimited as constituents of their original nature. And so since things have been arranged in this manner it is necessary that we always put ourselves to searching for one form for each thing at all times—for we will find it being present. And then after one, we should look for two, if that is how things are, but if not, then for three or another number, and the same for each one of these back again in the same manner until we reach the one in principle, not so that someone may see that there is only the one, the many, and the unlimited, but so that he may also know their quantity: lest someone apply the form of the unlimited to the many before he should know their full number as well as the unlimited and the one, then at that point he can bid adieu to each one of all these things, releasing them into the unlimited. (16c5–e2)

37. There is evidence that such exercises in logical division were a regular part of the Academy's curriculum (Goldschmidt 2003: 20, 95).

38. It is generally agreed that this Prometheus was Pythagoras. The terminology of the *peras* (the limit) and the *apeiron* (the unlimited) was a common part of Pythagorean vocabulary and describes the creation of the unit in relation to primal chaos (Gadamer 1991: 129–30). See the fragments 424–26 of Philolaus in Kirk, Raven, and Schofield (1983). As Gosling has shown (1975: xvi, 83, 89, 165–71, 203–4), the basic concept of the limit and the unlimited comes from the problem of incommensurables in Pythagorean harmonics. If we think of a string on a lyre as a continuum of possible sounds, we can then limit or subdivide it into articulated notes. These notes create a scale that can be expressed as set of ratios between whole numbers. But beneath this set of articulated limits or divisions the unlimited continuum of possible sounds continues to exist. Between each set of articulated points on the scale there is necessarily an infinity of other points that cannot be expressed in terms of ratios permitted by the scale. These points could only be represented as irrationals. It is precisely the problem of the irrationals, of those points in space or time that cannot be reduced to a system of articulated limits that requires the positing of the unlimited, of a continuum of existence that persists beneath the ontic. Eudoxus, a member of the Academy and a mathematician interested in the problem of irrationals, argued that pleasure was the highest good, the position advocated first by Philebus and then Protarchus in our dialogue. See also Aristotle, *Metaphysics* 1, 987b–988a.

All things, then, are of the one, the totality of what is, its unity as a one. And each thing, to the extent that it is that thing, participates in that one (Hampton 1990: 87–88).

Pleasure exists, but it is also many. There are a variety of pleasures: eating, evacuating, sex, listening to Puccini, solving mathematical problems, and pure philosophical contemplation. Yet while these all represent pleasure, it would be a vulgar oversimplification to reduce them to an undifferentiated one. This is what Protarchus must concede before a rational discussion can take place concerning which pleasures are to be preferred and how we should rank them in relation to the various forms of knowledge to create a good life. If we simply say that pleasure is one and many, or even unlimited, then we fall into a facile contradiction (Gadamer 1991: 98–99). This, as Socrates notes, is the error of the clever young men trained by the sophists who mistake the fact that contradictory predicates can be applied to the same entity for an actual, substantial contradiction.

This observation is also the reason for Socrates' emphasis on the necessity of intermediate quantification. We cannot simply pass directly from the infinity of the concrete to the singularity of the form (Festugière 1950: 165). For each phenomenon, we must first seek its unity, its status as a one, and only then proceed to discover how that one relates to others that can then be synthesized in relation to a more encompassing totality, and from there proceed toward the unity of the One (Diès 1966: xxiv–xxv; Hampton 1990: 31, 34; Gadamer 1991: 120). As Hampton observes, "In the *Philebus,* the emphasis is on the interrelations between the forms, conceived as wholes composed of parts which constitute a single unified system" (1990: 73). These complex wholes are both many and one without contradiction. Thus in the *Theaetetus* we find the following exchange:

> Socrates: Well now, if the complex is both many elements and a whole, with them as its parts, then both complexes and elements are equally capable of being known and expressed, since all the parts turned out to be the same thing as the whole.
> Theaetetus: Yes, surely.
> Socrates: But if, on the other hand, the complex is single and without parts, then complexes and elements are equally unaccountable and unknowable—both of them for the same reason.
> Theaetetus: I can't dispute that. (205d–e; Levett 1997: 228)

Form then presents itself in a complex that must be fully analyzed in order to determine that aspect of the complex that can be qualified as form, i.e., that which harmonizes and coordinates the elements of the complex (Goldschmidt 2003: 82–83). Only once we have fully articulated the relation of these subunities to one another can we proceed to the "One" and release each of these subunities, in the words of the *Philebus*, "into the unlimited." The concepts of the universal and the limit in the dialectic of collection and division then serve both to fragment the One as an undifferentiated and eternal whole, an unbroken immediacy, and to reconstitute it as an articulated and intelligible unity (Boussoulas 1952: 98–99; Diès 1966: xxii).

In the *Philebus*, and in such closely related dialogues as the *Parmenides*, the *Theaetetus*, the *Sophist*, and the *Statesman*, the forms are less ontologically separate beings than ideal patterns in nature, the conditions of possibility for the intelligibility of the world and human experience (*Parmenides* 130b–d, 132b–d; *Sophist* 259e).[39] They do not exist in bounded time and space any more than do scientific laws (where is the second law of thermodynamics?), the concept of the triangle, or causality per se. Moreover, sensible particulars are only intelligible, and hence can be said to exist as identifiable entities, to the extent that they are related to the forms. They are thus strictly relational entities and not things in themselves, and only rise to the level of the ontic to the extent that they can be assimilated to the world of complex and interpenetrating forms that constitute the intelligible world (Festugière 1950: 193; Boussoulas 1952: 8, 92–93; Diès 1966: xcv). A chair is a chair only because there is the idea of chairness, of being a chair, as opposed to being a stool, a table, or a mushroom. It is not a chair because it has four legs and I stumble over it in my dining room (like my cat), or even because I sit on it. The forms are thus ontologically prior to but not separate from their sensibles. The sensibles cannot in fact be recognized without the forms (*Sophist* 253d–e; Hampton 1990: 92).

From an existential perspective, then, there are indeed two "unlimiteds" or "infinities" operative in the *Philebus*. There is both that which is beyond the many particular instances, and hence the infinitely large, and that which is not yet limited or below the threshold of the defined entity, the realm of pure continuity, discussed earlier. Both can be characterized according to Frede's definition as "the kinds of things that have no definite degree in themselves" (1993: xxxiii–xxxiv).[40] We can neither quantify the pure form of harmony in itself and for itself, nor

---

39. See Gadamer (1988: 260; 1991: 97–98); Zuckert (1996: 73); and Goldschmidt (2003: 87–89).

40. For specific slippages in Plato's use of the term *apeiron*, see Frede (1992: 428–29).

the continuum of all possible sounds. Yet the first, the form of harmony, transcends and subsumes the limit. It must presuppose a mixed condition of existence—the continuum of the unlimited as defined by the imposition of the limit and hence the possibility of a quantitative relation—as the predicate of its transcendence of those specific limits per se (Gadamer 1988: 265; Boussoulas 1952: 65). Without the limits, definitions, formalizations imposed upon an undefined continuum, the defined ratios or proportions that constitute a harmonic relation cannot come into existence, but harmony itself can never be limited to any given set of relations occupying a defined moment in space and time. It therefore transcends those limitations precisely insofar as it is a universal. The harmonic, from the Platonic perspective, is both an immutable whole and a totalization of discrete existences that defines those existences as recognizable entities in themselves. In turn, as harmony in and for itself, the harmonic participates in, or enters into a proportional or "harmonic relation" with, the totalizing form of the world as an articulated cosmos, which is known variously as the One or the Good, depending on the dialogue (Boussoulas 1952: 143–44; Hampton 1991: 89–92; Goldschmidt 2003: 79–82).

The second form of the unlimited exists not beyond, but below the limit. This is the realm to which the term *apeiron* is properly applied in the *Philebus:*

> All unlimited entities consist in a continued flux (24d), so they are motions. These motions terminate when order is imposed; this imposition of a limit leads to the establishment of a definite being, the successful mixture (*genesis eis ousian,* 26d). Pleasures are motions of filling that are terminated by such an imposed order. (Frede 1992: 439)[41]

Characteristic examples of the *apeiron* are such continua as are expressed in concepts like hotter and colder, harder and softer, higher and lower, and bigger and smaller. None of these concepts has meaning in itself, but each instead reflects an endless and fundamentally incalculable oscillation between opposites such that a given point on the continuum can always be both hotter and colder, higher and lower, etc., in relation to two other points.

Even these examples, however, do not do full justice to the dizzying flux of the unlimited, since the moment a point is determined, let alone

---

41. Compare Diès (1941: xxvii–xxx).

triangulated with two other points, we are already operating within the realm of the limit and of potential quantification. It is for this reason that Plato expresses these continua using the grammatical dual.[42] Hotter and colder are both opposites and thereby emphasize the necessary undecidability of such binary judgments, owing to the lack of a mediator that is able to establish a definitive limit and hence create a stable mixed entity (*Philebus* 24a–d). The limit is precisely what puts a halt to such oscillations and thereby allows the demarcation of commensurable units, the formulation of rational judgments, the institution of fair exchanges, and the creation of a system of determined substitutions (Hampton 1990: 44)[43]:

> Socrates: We already attributed to the dryer and wetter, the more and less, the longer and shorter, and the greater and lesser, and everything that admits of the more and less one single nature.
> Protarchus: Do you mean the unlimited?
> Socrates: Yes. But mix into these things the coming to be of the limit.
> Protarchus: What coming to be?
> Socrates: That of the limiting, which we ought to have just now collected into a unity, as we did of the unlimited, but we did not. But perhaps with these two [the unlimited and the mixed] having been collected together, this too will become clear.
> Protarchus: What kind of thing do you mean?
> Socrates: That of the equal and the double, and however many things stabilize those others that are in opposition to one another, and by establishing a numerical relation render them symmetrical and harmonious. (*Philebus* 25d2–e2)

It will be recalled that in chapter 3 the grammatical dual in the *Antigone* was associated with the incestuous domain of Imaginary identification and with resistance to the imposition of Symbolic law, to the establishment of difference and limit, of relations of exchange and hence the pleasure principle.[44] Similarly, the flux of the *apeiron* represents a

---

42. Sayre (1983: 95–102, 112–17) thus relates the *apeiron* in the *Philebus* to Aristotle's account of Plato's doctrine of the "indefinite dyad" in *Metaphysics* 1 (987b–988a). See also Hampton (1990: 99).

43. Hampton, while a philosophically astute reader of the dialogue, is at times disturbingly sloppy. Among other things, she here refers to 26e when 25e is meant and on page 42 translates *poson* "quality" rather than "quantity."

44. For more on the duality of the Imaginary as opposed to the ternary or digital structure of the Symbolic, see also Lacan (1966e: 67); Kristeva (1980: 22); Jameson (1981:

constant alternation between more and less, excess and lack, becoming and dissolution that comes to stability only with the imposition of the law of measure, even as it must simultaneously continue to exist in its own self-same nature below the level of—and as the ground of—determination (Diès 1966: xxviii; Gosling 1975: 200). It is for this reason that the *apeiron* has also been compared by many readers to the *Timaeus*'s *khôra*,[45] which like the *apeiron* is associated by Plato with the formless and maternal, as opposed to the determining paternal impress of law, difference, and the eternal (*Timaeus* 50–51; Derrida 1993b: 30, 37, 95–96; Zuckert 1996: 236; Sallis 1998: 406–7; Copjec 2002: 33).

From a psychoanalytic perspective, however, these two forms of the infinite are ultimately the same. They are both beyond the pleasure principle. The realm of what is before and of what is beyond the law of limit are both worlds of continuity in which the one, the many, and the mixed have either been transcended or not yet come to exist. In such realms, there is possible neither knowledge, in the form of discrete information possessed by a knower, nor individual existence. There is only the pure and meaningless, undifferentiated immediacy of the *tabula rasa* of psychic existence before it has been creased by the least determination, limit, or trace; or the loss of self and hence the effacement of the wax tablet of the psyche that comes with subsumption into the eternal, and hence Symbolic death (Freud 1961a: 2; Bataille 1957: 20–27, 155n.1; Lacan 1991: 174–75; 1973: 159).

Protarchus, unlike Socrates, however, is not interested in the abstract verities of the dialectic of collection and division, nor in its ontological and psychic grounding. His questions are much more practical. The potentially infinite progression and regression involved in the practice of collection and division may be the only method on which true knowledge can be based. Yet how does it lead to a decision on which is the superior good: knowledge or pleasure?

> Protarchus: While it is a great thing for the wise man to know everything, the second best is not to be mistaken about oneself. . . . You Socrates have granted this meeting to all of us, and yourself to boot, in order to find out what is the best of all human possessions. . . . Since you . . . committed yourself to us, we therefore insist, like

---

175–76); Ragland-Sullivan (1986: 42, 56, 154); Goux (1990: 145); Julien (1990: 75, 193); Butler (1990: 82–83).

45. See Boussoulas (1952: 57–58); Gadamer (1988: 260); Hampton (1990: 43); and their respective bibliographies.

children, that there is no taking back a gift properly given. So give up this way of turning against us the discussion here.

Socrates: What way are you talking about?

Protarchus: Your way of plunging us into difficulties and repeating questions to which we have at present no proper answer to give you. But we should not take it that the aim of our meeting is universal confusion. (19c–20a; Frede 1993: 13)

The result is a sudden shift in direction. Socrates, unlike the philosopher but much like the psychoanalyst, responds to Protarchus' demand by recounting what may, he says, have been a dream (20b6): in it Socrates had learned that neither pleasure nor knowledge was the highest good, but there was a third unnamed thing. In this way, Socrates undoes the false binary of pleasure and knowledge and relativizes both to an unnamed third object to which each can stand in relation. By the same token, their rapport is now relational rather than oppositional so that pleasure and knowledge are no longer seen as pure unities but are now able to appear together in mixed entities (20b–23b). This last move allows the earlier discussion of the pure dialectic of collection and division to be transformed into the more pragmatic analysis of the unlimited, the limit and the mixed discussed above (23c–27c).

The rest of the dialogue consists, then, of an analysis and classification of the various forms of mixed pleasures and knowledges. It concludes with a series of recommendations on how a balanced life might be pursued. In short, while acknowledging the claims of the dialectic and the search for absolute knowledge, the *Philebus* also grants the existence of another realm of practical ethical action: the philosopher as therapist. True knowledge may be founded upon the method of collection and division, which provides the epistemological foundation for the late doctrine of the forms, but it is a foundation that simultaneously posits its own beyond, the *apeiron* or limitless world of pure continuity in which the law of limit, demarcation, property, and exchange makes its mark (Derrida 1980: 379). It is to this latter world, that beyond the closure of western metaphysics, beyond the field in which unity and the unit can be envisioned, that Derrida seeks the indestructible (Derrida 1980: 249). This, as he notes, is the same realm that Freud locates beyond the pleasure principle (1980: 304–5).

This is also the realm to which he gestures when Derrida argues that Lacan remains within the logocentric realm when the latter contends that the letter is ultimately indivisible and that it thus always arrives at its destination. Therefore, while the Lacanian letter may signal nothing more than absence or lack, that lack never lacks place. It is always localizable. It always traces a path through discourse and so can be endowed with a meaning and a relation to a speaking subject, even if only in the form of a negation or lack (Derrida 1980: 443, 472, 492–93). The letter always arrives at its destination (Lacan 1966b: 41). It is always decipherable, at least as the symptomatic presence of the indecipherable.

Yet, how can it be otherwise in psychoanalysis (Julien 1990: 147–48; Lacan 1973: 236, 276; Žižek 1989: 72, 174–75; Ragland-Sullivan 1986: 218)? The philosopher may and even must pursue the foundations of knowledge to and beyond the limitless realm in which meaning dissolves. He may and must conceive of the possibility of radical nonmeaning, of a pure contingency in which the letter may or may not arrive at its destination (Derrida 1980: 133–35; 1996a: 49). The psychoanalyst, however, is still faced with Protarchus, lying there on the couch wanting to know the value of pleasure. As Derrida himself recounts, when he first met Lacan at a conference at Johns Hopkins in 1967, Lacan remarked to René Girard after hearing Derrida speak, "Yes, yes, that's very good, but the difference between him and me, is that he doesn't have to deal with people who suffer" (1996b: 86).[46]

Lacan was always very clear that he was not a philosopher or literary theorist, but an analyst whose writings and teachings were in the first instance aimed at forming other analysts.[47] Derrida, in contrast, says that his goal is precisely to pose the philosopher's epistemological question to the psychoanalyst (1980: 261). Thus, he and Lacan represent two sides of the same postcard—the readable and the unreadable—that must always co-exist with and condition one another (1980: 88). The *Philebus* itself, in its very discontinuity between the dialectic and the calculus of pleasure (Gadamer 1991: 9–10; Frede 1992: 430–31), embodies this same double logic even as it offers the possibility of mediating between the needs of the philosopher and the demands of the analyst and his or her analysand.[48]

---

46. Derrida's response that he too has "to deal with people who suffer" hardly seems an adequate acknowledgement of what he admits to be his and Lacan's different institutional settings and the obligations that come with them.

47. Although as Derrida acknowledges, "Lacan's philosophical refinement, competence, and originality have no precedent in the tradition of psychoanalysis" (1996b: 65, see also 73–75).

48. The possibility of this mediation is signaled by Derrida's acknowledgment that some have argued that the Lacanian and Derridian positions are homologous. As both he and others have observed, this is an oversimplification, but not one with no basis (1980: 163). Žižek totally rejects such a move (Hanlon 2001: 13, but cf. Žižek 1992: 102–3), but

4. The Will to Power: Eros, Thanatos, Plato and Foucault

> It is by limiting the possible intensity of the pleasure or the displeasure that the PP[49] conquers its mastery. It only draws its benefits from a certain moderation. The problem for it to resolve—let one trace it back again to the *Philebus*—is that of pleasure's essential excess. (Derrida 1980: 427)
>
> As Freud's writing of the mastery (*Herrschaft*) of the pleasure principle and Ernst's getting pleasure from mastering his pain indicates, the drive which is irreducible to any other is a drive not for pleasure but for mastery. And that drive is essentially self-referential. "The drive to dominate must also be the drive's relation to itself: there is no drive not driven to bind itself to itself and assure mastery over itself as a drive." (Zuckert 1996: 233, citing Derrida 1980: 430)

As noted earlier in this chapter, the dialectic of collection and division is explicitly linked by Derrida both to psychoanalysis and to deconstruction's own radicalization of the practice of genealogy and archeology, two terms most clearly and commonly associated with the work of Michel Foucault. We shall in the next chapter take up in detail Foucault's relationship with both psychoanalysis and Lacan in the context of his later work's exploration of the problematics of power, self-mastery, and the care of the self in Plato and the Stoics. We shall also examine the late Foucault's own extensive response to and engagement with Derrida's reading of Plato. What concerns us in the final section of this chapter, however, is the way in which Derrida's reading of antiquity in general and of Plato in particular was a response not only to Lacan but also to Foucault and his conceptualization of power.

The roots of this dialogue run deep. As was noted above, "Plato's Pharmacy" was published by the journal *Tel quel* in 1968, four years after Lacan's revisiting of the *Symposium* in his eleventh seminar. This, however, was not the first time Derrida had raised the issue of the constitution of the interiority of Platonic reason in relation to a fallen, but logically necessary, externality that the *Phaedrus* associates with writing. In 1963, Derrida had addressed the *Collège philosophique*[50] concerning the recently published *Folie et Déraison, Histoire de la folie à*

Derrida himself portrays a much more complex and conflicted relationship between him and Lacan based on a profound mutual regard (1996b: 60–61, 70–71, 81–84). See also Ragland-Sullivan (1986: 254–55); Benstock (1991: 99); Lacan (1966a: 11); and Roudinesco (2003: 32).

49. Pleasure Principle.
50. A philosophical association headed by Jean Wahl.

l'âge classique, by his former teacher at the Ecole Normale Supérieure, Michel Foucault. The lecture, later revised and published as "Cogito et histoire de la folie," is a searching critique of the basic philosophical assumptions underlying Foucault's project.

Derrida's assault was wide-ranging and complex.[51] For our purposes, however, one main aspect of Derrida's argument is relevant: his charge that Foucault ignores the profound ties between reason as constituted in the seventeenth century—when Foucault argues that the modern concept of madness as rationality's opposite was first formed—and the *logos* of Socratic and Platonic philosophy. Foucault's claim, advanced in his preface, is that the Greek *logos* knew no opposite. As Derrida notes, such a reading is not only untrue to the text of Greek philosophy but a logical impossibility necessitated by Foucault's thesis that western reason was produced by the seventeenth century's mass internment of the mad and the socially marginal (Derrida 1967a: 62–66). In contrast, Derrida's position, as later elaborated in "La pharmacie de Platon," is that the history of western reason's relation to its other can only be understood in terms of its initial constitution from Platonic philosophy's opposition of *muthos* to *logos*—that is, in terms of the opposition of practices of mirroring and imitation to a rational discourse of measure, quantification, and categorical determination (1972a: 98).[52] Derrida's reading in this early lecture, as in "La pharmacie" and *La carte postale,* is therefore in accord with the Platonic claim that there is no intelligible realm outside the *logos*. Below the limit, the trace, the mark of measure—in the virgin wax of Freud's magic pad—there is no articulation, no regulated Symbolic exchange, no reasoned reflection, no subject.

Thus, Derrida contends that Foucault's argument that western reason constitutes itself through the exclusion of madness at the beginning of the seventeenth century is incorrect. In particular, he takes issue with Foucault's statement in the original preface to the book, which was dropped from subsequent editions, that in the Greek world there was no "other" of reason, since *hubris* was not excluded from but welcomed within the "reassuring" *logos* of Socratic dialectics. Yet, as Derrida points out, if that were the case, then the other of reason would have already been contained within reason itself, and the great

---

51. The following paragraphs are based on the account of the debate featured in Larmour et al. (1998b: 6–9).

52. On *muthos* versus *logos,* see Nadaff (1998: viii–x) and Brisson (1998: 66–70, 84, 121). On the *khôra* in the *Timaeus* as the formal putting into question of this opposition, see Derrida (1993b: 15–16) and Wolff (1992: 245).

confinement of the seventeenth century would have represented not the founding consolidation of western reason, but a historically determined fold in which a schism between reason and madness was created within the larger framework of reason as a whole. If, on the other hand, *hubris* were not so contained, then neither would the Socratic dialectic be so reassuring, nor would the split between reason and its other at the beginning of the modern world be unique or determining (Derrida 1967a: 62–63).

Foucault does not respond directly to these charges, except to note that Derrida's assertion of the inescapability of the *logos* is designed primarily to insure the preeminence of philosophy as the queen of the sciences and to promote a renewed emphasis on textuality rather than practical discursivity, with all the necessary archival and historical research the latter implies (1972). In this response, Foucault has been largely seconded by subsequent critical opinion.[53] Yet, as Roy Boyne notes, Foucault's later articulation of the inescapability of power at once effectively acknowledges "the correctness of Derrida's formulation" of the omnipresence of the normalizing *logos* and simultaneously transforms it into a means of analyzing practical-discursive complexes beyond the reach of an all-consuming textualism (Boyne 1990: 76, 118). Foucault moves it from the realm of pure philosophical analysis to that of a practical tool in the micropolitics of everyday life, though Derrida himself might say that such a move merely reveals the radical political implications that have been part of deconstruction all along.

It was in the 1970s that Foucault articulated his analytics of power, first in *Surveiller et Punir* (1975) and then in *La volonté de savoir* (1976). The latter, which was Volume 1 of the *Histoire de la sexualité,* also constituted Foucault's major rejoinder to psychoanalysis. There, Foucault argued that sexuality, far from being repressed in the eighteenth and nineteenth centuries, as commonly stated by certain forms of psychoanalysis and sexology, was actually formulated, consolidated, and incited into discourse by those very scientific and therapeutic practices. These practices were not something external to sexuality, an outside that came and distorted, perverted, or repressed its intrinsic inner nature. They were part and parcel of its ontological substance. If, as Foucault's genealogy of sexuality sought to demonstrate, sexuality could not be thought outside the practices that produced the claim of its repression, if in fact there is no outside of power, then this realization demanded of

---

53. Boyne (1990: 74–75); Kremer-Marietti (1985: 131); Frow (1986: 216). But see Spivak (1976: lx–lxii).

us a new understanding of power, one not predicated on a concept of Law, the state, or the sovereign as an external authority imposed upon a preexisting entity, but as immanent to and constitutive of the entity itself. Power is not repressive, but productive. It is for this reason that Foucault proposes that we replace a theory of law and repression with an "analytic of power," and shift our focus from sexuality to bodies and pleasures.

Such an analytic of power's self-constitution is reminiscent of the pleasure principle's own self-limitation and its constitutive relation to the drive for mastery that Derrida and Zuckert outline in the epigraphs to this section. That self-limitation is, in turn, expressly related by both Derrida and Zuckert to the *Philebus*'s meditation on the constitutive relation of the limit to the ontic and the calculus of pleasure. In this light, it is perhaps less than surprising that at the end of "Spéculer—Sur «Freud»," Derrida's reading of *Beyond the Pleasure Principle* in *La carte postale* (1980), we find the contention that the Freudian concept of *Bemächtigung*, "mastery, domination," actually precedes the death drive, and names that which is truly beyond the pleasure principle. To schematize, Derrida proposes that Thanatos be understood as a drive for domination, a drive for power, which as such knows no outside, no beyond:

> Now, if such a power drive exists [. . .] it is necessary to admit that it plays a primary role in the most "meta-conceptual" and "metalinguistic," precisely the most "dominant" organization of Freudian discourse. For it is exactly in the code of power—and not only metaphorically—that the problematic is installed. It is always a question of knowing who is the "master," who "dominates," who has the "authority," to what point does the PP exert power, how can a drive become independent of it or precede it, what are the respective functions of the PP and the rest, what we have called the prince and his subjects, etc. "Posts" are always posts of power. And power is exerted by means of a network of posts [positions, relays]. [. . .] In other words, the motive of power is more originary and more general than the PP, it is independent of it, it is its beyond. It should not be confused with the death drive or the repetition compulsion, it gives us the means to describe them and plays the role of transcendental predicate in relation to them [. . .]. Beyond the pleasure principle: power. (1980: 431–32)

In the years immediately following the publication of *La volonté de savoir* it is hard to believe that either Derrida or his readership could miss the Foucauldian resonances of the claim that power is in fact that which is beyond the pleasure principle.[54] He continues:

> Au-delà[55] de toutes les oppositions conceptuelles,[56] la *Bemächtigung* situe bien l'un des échangeurs entre la pulsion d'emprise, comme pulsion de pulsion, et la «volonté de puissance».[57] (Derrida 1980: 432)

> Beyond all the conceptual oppositions, *Bemächtigung* situates very precisely one of the exchanges between the drive for domination, as drive's drive, and the "will to power."

The juxtaposition of Freud, Lacan, and Foucault that we find in the three essays of 1996's *Résistances de la psychanalyse* is therefore already present in 1980. Moreover, in a typically Derridian move, the Foucauldian reply to Freud is already found in Freud himself. Their opposition is also a complicity. That opposition/complicity can, in turn, be traced to the originary moments of western reason in Plato, and more specifically to the *Philebus*. Indeed, it is not without reason that this penultimate section of "Spéculer—Sur «Freud»" is entitled "Platon derrière Freud."

Nor is this engagement with Foucault limited to this one section of *La carte postale,* however pivotal these passages may be to Derrida's reading of Freud, Lacan, and Plato.[58] Foucault's *History of Sexuality* is also clearly evoked in the context of a discussion by Derrida of

---

54. Derrida does not of course make direct reference to Foucault. Their relations were very tense after Derrida published his early lecture on *Histoire de la folie*. Instead, Derrida includes a note pointing to a 1978 work by François Laruelle, *Au-delà du principe du pouvoir*. Laruelle was hardly a household name in France in 1980, though he is associated with the Non-Philosophie movement and a prolific writer (now better known in French than he is in English). Foucault, however, was already a member of the Collège de France and his lectures regularly drew overflow crowds. He also gave regular interviews on the question of power.

55. *Beyond the Pleasure Principle* is frequently abbreviated simply *Au-delà* . . . in *La carte postale*.

56. The realm of the *apeiron*.

57. On Derrida's preference for the concept of "force" to that of "volonté de puissance," see "Nous autres Grecs" (1992: 268–69).

58. See also the "envoi" of August 25 1977 (1980: 46), where immediately following a discussion of how "Derrida" believes "Le facteur de la vérité" has been misread, we find a very Foucauldian evocation of the ways in which the discourse of desire itself comes to serve as a series of "dispositifs érotiques." *Dispositif* is the term Foucault uses in his later genealogical work to replace the earlier *épistémè* found in the archeologies.

scholarship on the Platonic letters, a reading of which he proposes to use as the introduction to *La carte postale*'s fictional counterpart, *Legs de Freud* (1980: 65–66, 95). In this passage, the controversy over the letters' authenticity is compared to that over whether sexuality per se exists (or whether, à la Foucault, it is a discursive construction and an effect of power).[59]

A less explicit allusion may also be found in the lengthy "envoi" of September 10, 1977, the day after the discussion of the authenticity of Plato's letters and their transmission. Here, following a detailed reading of the image on the postcard of Plato dictating to Socrates, the problem of postality is explicitly linked to the problematics of psychoanalysis, sexuality, and power:

> La Prospective Postale, voilà le lieu de la problématique psych. et po[60] désormais (la question des femmes, de la psychanalyse et de la politique, ça ramasse tout); la question de Le Pouvoir, comme ils disent encore, c'est d'abord les postes et télécommunications, bien connu. (1980: 113)

> Postal Futurism, this is the place of the psychoanalytic and political problematic henceforth (the question of women, psychoanalysis, politics, it brings together everything); the question of Power, as they still say, it is first of all a matter of the postal service and telecommunications, as everyone knows.

The capitalization of power alerts us to the fact that a specific, technical usage of the term is being evoked,[61] while the connection with

---

59. It is perhaps not coincidental, then, as we shall see in the next chapter, that Foucault in the course of his 1983 lectures at the Collège de France chooses to make one of his most direct retorts to Derrida in the course of a reading of Plato's seventh letter. For Derrida's comments on this letter in *La carte postale*, see the *envoi* of September 9, 1977 (1980: 91). While there is not room to deal with it here, Derrida's extensive and learned, if unconventional, discussion of the letters and their authenticity, has not received the attention it deserves (1980: 65–66, 91–102, 148–49, 273).

60. *Psychanalyse et Politique*, often abbreviated *Psych. et Po*, was one of the first feminist political groups in France (Moi 2002: 95–96). Derrida, by using the abbreviation without capitalization, at once signals his solidarity with the group and at the same time broadens the problematic from that of the actual organization to the entire field of the conjunction of psychoanalysis and politics.

61. On the next page (1980: 114), "Derrida" recounts how he had agreed to give a series of taped interviews critical of the media in order to boost the sales of his book. His agreement was conditional upon his being allowed "to improvise freely" on the role of the postal in the Iranian revolution. It will be remembered that the Ayatollah Khomeini ("l'ayatollah telekommeiny") was living in France during the Iranian uprising against

psychoanalysis, feminism, and politics at once points us toward the series of problematics in which the *History of Sexuality* proposed to intervene and toward a famous lacuna in that intervention, the absence of feminist theory and the failure to engage questions of gender. Finally, the recontextualization of this intervention within the larger field of postality and in relation to the specific question of the authenticity and transmission of the Socratico-Platonic *logos* points to the same basic historical and philosophical problem that Derrida alleged in his response to *Histoire de la folie:* Foucault's failure to escape from the confines of the dominant and dominating structures of western reason, and the consequent need to produce a radicalized or counter-genealogy of this very discourse.

As we shall see in the next chapter, this is precisely what Foucault himself did, after his own fashion, when he too turned to antiquity at the very time when *La carte postale* was being published. Derrida would later recognize the kinship and continuing antagonism between their respective projects in a moving and subtle tribute to Foucault at the end of his *La politique de l'amitié* (1994). There, Derrida concludes his investigation of the concepts of friendship, kinship, enmity, and the state with a reading of Blanchot's *Michel Foucault tel que je l'imagine* (1986). He chooses a passage devoted to Foucault's late work on self-fashioning and friendship in ancient philosophy. It concludes with Blanchot asserting:

> By testifying on behalf of a work that needs to be studied (read without bias) rather than praised, I hope to remain faithful, however clumsily, to the intellectual friendship that his death, which was very painful for me, permits me today to declare to him: at the same time, I remember the saying attributed by Diogenes Laertius to Aristotle: "Oh my friends, there is no friend."[62] (Derrida 1994: 332–33)

Blanchot's declaration of friendship—out of respect, out of discretion, out of love—can come only after Foucault has died and only in the form

---

the Shah. He largely communicated with his followers through taped sermons that were smuggled into the country. Foucault, like many French intellectuals of the period, supported the revolution, which seemed to offer an authentic indigenous response to a corrupt autocracy installed as the result of a CIA coup and thus a real alternative to both American imperialism and Soviet totalitarianism. He wrote a number of well-known articles on the subject in 1978 and 1979 (1994n–1994aa), including one specifically on the role of these taped messages in the uprising (1994u).

62. On Montaigne's citation of this formula, see chapter 1, page 24.

of a declaration addressed to friends that declares the impossibility of that friendship, the necessary absence, ambivalence, and aggression that lies at the heart of the most genuine affections. Derrida's choice of this passage is revealing: for, it is precisely through the reading of Foucault, and not his praise, that Derrida too has testified to the powerful bond between the student and his former teacher.

> "Oh my friends, there is no friend."

This apocryphal declaration by Aristotle opens every chapter of *La politique de l'amitié*. By choosing to conclude his book with this passage from Blanchot, Derrida transforms the whole work retrospectively into a declaration of friendship for a now absent Foucault. Of course, Aristotle's (and Blanchot's) formula does not simply assert friendship ("Oh my friends"), but also its impossibility ("there is no friend"), and takes that impossibility as a gage of authenticity. Blanchot too seeks that same complex authenticity. He comes not to praise Foucault but to read him. By the same token, Derrida in this work occupies himself precisely with Aristotle's writings on friendship, *philia,* which, as he notes, Foucault passed over in his final turn to antiquity (1994: 334). Thus Derrida's declaration of friendship is also an implicit critique, a correction, a reading.

Yet when the book ends, Derrida leaves no doubt that Blanchot's words are also his, that his continuing engagement with Foucault, his debates, his criticisms—always in the context of both the immediate intellectual moment and a continuing engagement with antiquity—were also a homage, a simultaneous declaration of friendship and its impossibility. Derrida writes:

> Will one have ever punctuated with more rigor, economy, reserve, while leaving open the hypothesis, but let's not stop there, that, perhaps, no one is there anymore for anyone, and there is precisely death, that dying of which Blanchot complains so often, so profoundly, not that it might be fatal but that it might remain impossible? Like friendship perhaps: "I hope to remain faithful, however clumsily, to the intellectual friendship that his death, which was very painful for me, permits me today to declare to him: at the same time, I remember the saying attributed by Diogenes Laertius to Aristotle: 'Oh my friends, there is no friend.'" Which is demonstrated (performatively), by the fact attested here that this

friendship could not have been declared with the friend still living. It is death that "permits me today" to "declare" this "intellectual friendship," ": at the same time." Thanks be to death. It is *thanks* to death that friendship can declare itself. Never before, never otherwise. And never except by remembering (so long as, thanks to it, the friend remembers that there are no friends). And when friendship is declared to friends who are alive, it confesses at bottom the same thing, it confesses the death thanks to which the chance of declaring itself, although never lacking, finally came.

Without trying to hide it, one will have understood, that I would like to speak here about those to whom I am bound by a rare friendship, that is to say that I want also to speak *to them*. Be it across the rare friendships that I name and which never lodge within me without admiration and gratitude. (Derrida 1994: 335; emphasis in original)

Amen.

5. Conclusion: Writing Death, Writing *Philia*

The high ones die, die. They die. You look up and who's there?
—Easy, easy, Mr. Bones. I is on your side.
I smell your grief.
—I sent my grief away. I cannot care
forever. With them all again & again I died
and cried, and I have to live. (John Berryman, "36," *The Dream Songs*)

Phaedo: I had no feeling of pity, such as would seem natural in my sorrow, nor indeed of pleasure, as we engaged in philosophical discussion as we were accustomed to do—for our arguments were of that sort—but I had a strange feeling, an unaccustomed mixture of pleasure and pain at the same time as I reflected that he was just about to die. (*Phaedo* 59a; Grube 1997: 51)

And so we return via Socrates and Plato, Freud and Foucault to the necessary relation between death and *philia*. We first saw this relation in the *Antigone* where the only real possibility of a *philia* beyond the conventions of Creon's social contract—of a *philia* grounded in kinship, friendship, and shared being—was found in death: for death is beyond the pleasure principle, beyond the compromises, exchanges, and substitutions that make intercourse possible. Death (both the first and the second) is like the unlimited in the *Philebus*. It is that which is both before and beyond the ontic, before and beyond the possibility of recognized goods, before and beyond self and other. As such, it is simultaneously the predicate of *philia* and the desire that fuels it. It is the moment before the Aristophanic androgyne is split in the *Symposium*, before desire becomes the rubric of our being, and it is the posited reunion with our other, better half that is desire's telos: a reunion that, as Diotima observes, can only ultimately be conceived as the totalization of the forms of phenomenal existence in the One, the Good, or the Beautiful. Beyond the pleasure principle lies the unchanging.

The self-conscious desire for that totalization, the desire that recognizes itself as the desire for that totalization, is precisely, according to Plato, *philo-sophia*. As the lover of wisdom proceeds through the logic of collection and division to plumb the realms of the limited, the unlimited and the mixed, s/he seeks a kind of mastery which both encompasses that totalization and is predicated on its divisions, the cuts, the marks that forever defer the possibility of either obtaining a final totalization or of reaching an absolute origin of division: the virginal wax tablet before the trace, before the incision of writing. As Diotima reminds the young Socrates, only the gods possess wisdom. Mortals possess the desire for it, and seek it through the mediation of Eros, the *daimôn* who is neither good nor bad, neither mortal nor immortal, neither beautiful nor ugly. The desire/love of wisdom, then, as Plato, Lacan, and Derrida all recognize, is always already predicated on a primal lack, an initial cut, a limit or division.

Philosophia, then, as a kind of desire, is a form of the drive for mastery, both of the self and the other. This drive for mastery, in turn, according to Derrida—who is drawing upon intellectual resources whose roots stretch beyond and through Foucault, Lacan, and the existentialists to the dawn of formalized western thought in Plato—is "the place of the psychoanalytic and political problematic . . . the question of Power." Power, however, from a Derridean perspective, cannot be separated from the question of the ontic, of division and writing. Nor can it be separated from the soul and its analysis, from the internalized writing that both creates the psyche and forever alienates it from itself.

Thus every politics is for Derrida a politics of friendship, of *philia*. The question of power is made possible by the prior question of division that the prospect of shared being, kinship, *concitoyenité*, and friendship must presume. And yet the practice of division, the drive to spilt, to cut, to dismember so as to re-member, can only be viewed as a function of the larger drive for mastery: *la volonté de puissance, la volonté de savoir.* It is thus the predicate and the manifestation of power. This drive can only be fully achieved and *philia* fully forged, however, in the moment of death, in the moment beyond the pleasure principle, in the moment when division itself is mastered and overcome. "Oh friend, there are no friends." Thus for Derrida, a politics of friendship is always predicated on a true spiritual practice and that practice is inconceivable outside the continuous movement of a certain form of analysis, of collection and division, that traces its genealogy to Plato's debt to Freud, and whose telos must forever be deferred, but whose desire is not to be ceded upon.

Chapter 6

The Art of Self-Fashioning, or Foucault on the *Alcibiades*

Caring for the Self and Others

> Socrates: I'm sure you've noticed that when a man looks into an eye his face appears in it, like in a mirror. We call this the 'pupil,' for it's a sort of miniature of the man who's looking.
> Alcibiades: You're right.
> Socrates: Then an eye will see itself if it observes an eye and looks at the best part of it, the part with which it can see.
> Alcibiades: So it seems.
> Socrates: But it won't see itself if it looks at anything else in a man, or anything else at all, unless it's similar to the eye.
> Alcibiades: You're right.
> Socrates: So if an eye is to see itself, it must look at an eye, and at that region of it in which the good activity of an eye actually occurs, and this, I presume, is seeing.
> Alcibiades: That's right.
> Socrates: Thus, if the soul, Alcibiades, is to know itself, it must look at a soul, and especially at that region in which what makes a soul good, wisdom, occurs, and at anything else similar to it. (*Alcibiades* 133a–b; Hutchinson 1997: 592)

MICHEL Foucault began his 1982 course at the Collège de France, *L'herméneutique du sujet*, with a meticulous reading of the *Alcibiades* (2001).[1] This dialogue, which is considered by some today to be pseudo-Platonic,[2] was widely appreciated in antiquity and universally accepted as genuine. One reason for its wide popularity was its theme: the necessity of caring for the self (*epimeleisthai heautou*),

---

1. See also his résumé of the dialogue in his unpublished lecture of February 16, 1983, in the course "Le gouvernement de soi et des autres" (1983a), tapes of which are available at the Institut Mémoires de l'Édition Contemporaine.
2. For a survey of the problem and a persuasive argument for the dialogue's authenticity, see Denyer (2001: 14–26). For a brief survey of the latest stylometric research, see Brandwood (1992: 112). And for Foucault's position and an updated bibliography on the status of the controversy in France, see Foucault (2001: 71, and Gros's accompanying note). Croiset's Budé edition (1960: 49–53), which would have been Foucault's reference volume, emphatically rejects all questions concerning the dialogue's authenticity.

defined as caring for the soul, as a propaideutic to entering into the affairs of state. For this reason, in late antiquity when the study of philosophy had predominantly become an exercise in textual commentary, and when the reading of the Platonic corpus proceeded through a structured curriculum, the *Alcibiades* was generally the first text read just as the *Philebus* was often the last (see chapter 5). The *Alcibiades,* in particular, was thought to provide both a protreptic admonition to turn to philosophy, as a means of caring for the self, and a general overview of Platonic philosophy (Foucault 2001: 164; Denyer 2001: 14; Hadot 1995b: 238–40).

In the dialogue, Socrates encounters Alcibiades on the cusp of maturity and declares his love for him. He recognizes that Alcibiades has had and shunned many suitors in the past, believing that his good looks, fortune, and social station permitted him to turn up his nose at such plebeian blandishments. Now, however, those suitors have deserted him and he has reached an age when boys were no longer considered attractive. Unlike others, Socrates had been silent about his love until now, at the behest of his famous *daimôn.* But Alcibiades is about to address the Athenian assembly for the first time a few days hence, and Socrates approaches him with the proposition that he can now be of more service to Alcibiades than all his previous lovers, and more than even his famous guardian, Pericles himself. Alcibiades is charmed by the declaration of Socrates' affection and intrigued by his offer. He agrees to enter into a series of questions and answers with Socrates so that the latter can make clear to him the nature of his services. In the course of the ensuing dialogue, Socrates is able to demonstrate that Alcibiades has neither expert knowledge on the matters of state that he presumes to advise the Athenian people on, nor a fundamental knowledge of the good and the just. It is precisely the revelation of this aporia at the heart of Alcibiades' self-understanding that is the service Socrates presumes to offer. The result of this initial dialectical interchange is an agreement between Socrates and Alcibiades on the necessity to care for themselves before they presume to offer their services to the city. A man who does not know that which is best in himself cannot know how to make his fellow citizens better.

This recognition leads to a final series of questions and answers concerning the nature of the self and how it is to be cared for. The self as seen in the passage cited at the beginning of this chapter is identified with the soul, and the soul, we learn, is only made visible in the soul of one's interlocutor, i.e., through the practice of the dialectic. The dialogue concludes with Alcibiades agreeing to pursue this form of caring for himself. Therefore, we can picture the prospect of many future such dialogues as the young man sees his soul reflected in his lover's and as the truth is pursued through the practice of Socratic intercourse.[3] In the final lines of the dialogue, however, Socrates voices his concern that Alcibiades' conversion may only be temporary and that he may once more be seduced away from him and philosophy by the allure of the *polis*. We conclude, therefore, by looking forward to the end of the *Symposium,* where an older but not wiser Alcibiades is shown precisely to have succumbed to the seductions of the unreflective life while nonetheless continuing to be smitten by Socrates' unfathomable charms.[4]

For Foucault, as for late antique philosophy, the *Alcibiades* constituted, to paraphrase Olympiodorus, "the gateway of the temple." Foucault saw in it the first and fullest theorization of an ethic of self-relation that was to constitute his primary object of interest in the last years of his life (2001: 46; 1994c: 615). For him, the *Alcibiades* provided not only an explicit theorization of one of the guiding threads of the Platonic corpus, it also represented a model of self-relation that made possible the Stoic ethic of the care of the self in the first two centuries of the Roman imperial period (2001: 65).[5] It was this latter form of self-constitution and cultivation that Foucault would directly contrast with the Christian model of confession and self-renunciation that he saw at the heart of modern technologies of disciplining and normalizing the self (2001: 242, 247; Gros 2001: 490–93, 507; Sennellart 2003: 157). The Stoics, starting from Plato's initial model, offered an alternative form of self-relation both to the Christian archetype and to that described later and implicitly denounced in Foucault's middle works such as *Surveiller et punir* and *La volonté de savoir*. It was this alternative model on which Foucault concentrated during the final years of his life (Foucault 1994f: 364; J. Miller 1993: 322, 340).

In this chapter, we shall examine Foucault's reading of the *Alcibiades* as part of his wider understanding of Plato and ancient philosophy

---

3. Foucault notes that the conversion preparatory to the pursuit of self-knowledge is the province of what he terms, following Pierre Hadot, "spirituality." Spirituality has two main forms in the west, *erôs* and *askesis* (2001: 17). The *Alcibiades* combines these two forms.

4. The dating of the *Alcibiades*, assuming its genuineness, is notoriously problematic. Denyer argues for a late composition (2001: 11–14). Foucault accepts Weil's thesis that the dialogue was first drafted early in Plato's career and later rewritten (2001: 71–72). Croiset (1960: 49–53) without much real evidence thinks it early. In any case, dramatically it is set prior to the last scene in the *Symposium*.

5. In his final course in 1984, Foucault lectured on the care of the self in the *Laches, Apology, Crito* and *Phaedo*. See Nehamas (1998: 163).

as a whole. We shall do so first as part of his continuing dialogue with Deleuze, Derrida, and Lacan on the importance and interpretation of Plato in contemporary philosophy. We shall then look in more detail at the relation between his reading of the *Alcibiades* and his overall political and ethical project, before examining a number of passages from the dialogue itself.

1. Genealogy of the Ethical Turn: Foucault's Platonic Dialogues

a. Deleuzean Dialogues

> You aren't unpracticed in detecting crooked conduct,
> What the wise Portico, bedaubed with trousered Medes,[6]
> Teaches, the things the sleepless and close-shaven youth
> Stays up to study, fed on pods and proud polenta.
> (Persius 3.52–55; Lee and Barr 1987: 29)

Among the postmodern authors we have been examining, it is Foucault's turn to antiquity that has received the most notice among theorists and professional classicists. His work in many ways represents the telos of the trajectory we have been tracing throughout this book. The final Foucault not only addresses the relation of ancient philosophy in general, and Platonism in particular, to the philosophical understanding of the subject in postmodern France, it also constitutes a deliberate and measured response to the problematics outlined by Lacan and Derrida in their respective readings of Plato.

We can provisionally date the origins of Foucault's ethical turn to 1970 and his praise of Deleuze's 1969 *Logique du sens*.[7] Deleuze in this idiosyncratic work launches an attack on the insidious Platonism that he sees infecting western thought. Using Stoic logic's distinction between bodies and events, as well as Lewis Carroll's *Alice in Wonderland* and *Through the Looking Glass*, he sets out to undermine Platonism's doctrines of the representation, recollection, and imitation of an ideal

---

6. Zeno, the founder of Stoicism taught at the *Stoa Poikile* ("Painted Portico") in Athens. It was adorned with a fresco depicting the defeat of the "trousered Medes" at the battle of Marathon.

7. See also Miriam Leonard's important reading of a series of lectures Foucault gave in Brazil in 1973, "La vérité et les formes juridiques," on the *Oedipus Tyrannos* (Leonard 2005: 68–95). The lectures were translated and published in Portuguese in 1974, but were never published by Foucault himself in French (Foucault 1994dd).

original, in the hopes of uncovering an alternative philosophical tradition that privileges surface over depth and event over essence (Benatouïl 2003: 20). For Deleuze, Stoic doctrine represents the logical inverse of Platonic metaphysics. In Stoic logic, the ideal, precisely because it is an "incorporeal," is always only an effect of a body's surface rather than the ultimate guarantor of its essential identity. No longer representing the realm of strict determination, as we saw in Derrida's reading of the *Philebus*, the ideal is now associated with the world of becoming and the unlimited, "The realm of becoming and the unlimited becomes the event itself, ideal, incorporeal, with all the reversals that are proper to it" (Deleuze 1969: 17). For Deleuze, Stoic logic is an open system of expanding and multiplanar surfaces, as opposed to the closed system of Platonic metaphysics. It represents the possibility of new lines of flight, rather than the consolidation of an ideal identity that is thought to subtend and determine the world of becoming (Alliez 1992: 221).

Foucault in his laudatory review argues that Deleuze's method of reconstructing this system is "rigorously Freudian." It is based on a careful symptomatic reading of the omissions, displacements, and repressions that constitute the history of western philosophy, offering a restoration not of a lost depth, but of a lost surface. The upshot of the review is a call not only for a return to ancient philosophy, but to precisely those texts and events from antiquity that are the least read and most frequently neglected:

> We should not scorn Hellenistic confusion or Roman platitudes, but listen to those things said on the great surface of the empire; we should be attentive to those things that happened in a thousand instances, dispersed on every side: fulgurating battles, assassinated generals, burning triremes, queens poisoning themselves, victories that invariably led to further upheavals, the endlessly exemplary Actium, the eternal event. (Foucault 1977a: 172)

Although Foucault's eventual reading of the Stoics would be very different from Deleuze's—focusing on the elaboration of an art of existence rather than a counter-Platonic logic—and although Foucault and Deleuze would later take their distances from one another philosophically and politically, nonetheless, even at this early date we can see Foucault's interest in the Stoics, as well as the Cynics, and such ostensibly marginal figures as Diogenes Laertius.

More importantly, we can also see in this same review his emerging conviction that the opposition to the classic metaphysics of "Platonism," which he, Derrida, Deleuze, and Irigaray all saw as subtending western thought, can be found in Plato himself: for he contends that a counterdiscourse to metaphysical Platonism can be found not only in the later Stoics, but also in the pre-Socratics, the figure of Socrates himself, and in Plato's *Sophist* (Foucault 1977a: 166–69; Flynn 1991: 112; Wolff 1992: 241–42; Benatouïl 2003: 24, 30–31, 36). In Foucault's later work, this perception of the inherent heterogeneity of the Platonic oeuvre will lead to his reading the dialogues as an interconnected web of individual texts rather than attempting to subordinate them to a single overarching vision (Castel-Bouchouchi 2003: 176, 186–87).[8] In the manner of Pierre Hadot—one of the main intellectual influences on the late Foucault (Davidson 1997)—he reads Plato less as an abstract theorist than as an advocate for a specific mode of reflective life (Hadot 1997: 211–12; 1995b: 102–3).[9]

b. Derridean Dialogues

> This sort of madness is given us by the gods to ensure our greatest good fortune. (*Phaedrus* 245b; Nehamas and Woodruff 1995: 29)

This pragmatic reading is in many ways separate from the mainstream of philosophical Platonism in early twentieth-century France, as represented by the works of people like Festugière (1950),[10] Robin (1929, 1985), Diès (1941), and Boussoulas (1952). This latter tradition was that to which Derrida's reading of the *Phaedrus* and *Philebus* in chapter 5 was both an heir and a response. This observation is important because Foucault, in his return to Plato at the end of his life, is not simply carrying forward his ongoing dialogue and later debate with Deleuze, nor is he merely grafting a reading of Hadot onto his own concerns with the body and sexuality; he is also continuing a polemic with Derrida that has its origins in the latter's 1963 lecture on his *Histoire de la folie*. Indeed, the Platonic subtext remains one of the most lasting

---

8. For a defense of this approach to the dialogues, see Kenney (2003: 8–27).

9. It is interesting to note that Foucault, presaging his own later interest in the topic, labeled Deleuze and Guattari's *Anti-Oedipe* "a book of ethics" in the "Preface" he wrote to the English edition (Foucault 1983b: xiii). See Leonard (2005: 86).

10. Nonetheless, it would be wrong to underestimate the influence of these earlier more traditional French Platonists on the later postmodernists' thought. Thus Festugière defines philosophie as "le soin de l'âme" ("care of the soul") and opens his chapter on "La vie intérieure" with a citation from the *Alcibiades*, τί ἐστιν τὸ ἑαυτοῦ ἐπιμελεῖσθαι; ("what is the care of the self?") (1950: 61, 130).

threads in the set of discussions, debates, and dialogues that constitute French poststructuralist thought.

That Derrida's criticism of Foucault had struck a nerve can be seen in the fact that he waited over nine years to respond and that, when he did, he ignored those parts of Derrida's argument that dealt directly with the constitution of western reason through the Socratic dialectic.[11] Instead, he silently dropped from the 1972 edition of the book the original preface in which he had made the claim that the Greek *logos* knew no opposite (Boyne 1990: 74–76, 118). There was no longer a place for such sweeping generalities about ancient philosophy. As Foucault admitted at the beginning of volume 2 of the *History of Sexuality*, it had become clear to him that his genealogies of modernity could only be valid if their difference from and grounding in antiquity were solidly established (1984a: 11–14).

Nonetheless, neither the *History of Sexuality* nor Foucault's courses at the Collège de France during the eighties should be seen as a concession to Derrida; rather they constitute a continuing rejoinder to his criticisms.[12] In his initial response to Derrida's essay, Foucault had argued that Derrida's perspective was too exclusively philosophical, that it sought to reduce history to a system enclosed within the Socratic *logos*, and that it treated socially and historically embedded discursive practices as mere textual traces (1972: 584, 602). Twelve years later when volumes 2 and 3 of the *History of Sexuality* were published, the more strictly philosophical discourses of Plato, Aristotle, and Seneca were consistently read in the light of ancient medicine, manuals of domestic conduct such as Xenophon's *Oikonomikos,* and the correspondence of the younger Pliny. Thus while Foucault granted Derrida's contention that it was impossible to do a genealogy of western reason without a thorough consideration of its earliest exemplars, he refused to grant philosophical texts any special status. They were always examined as part of a larger ensemble of related discursive practices as opposed to the disembodied texts of traditional philosophy, of which he saw Derrida as the latest and "most decisive representative" (1972: 602).[13]

In fact, Foucault's later readings of Plato remain deeply implicated in his polemic with Derrida on the origins and constitution of western reason. The range of his response is multileveled and often quite subtle. But the significance of this ongoing debate is not to be underestimated

---

11. See chapter 5.
12. By all evidence, the debate continued to fascinate Derrida as well. See his analysis of the ambivalent place of Freud in *Histoire de la folie* and Foucault's later work (1997).
13. See Kremer-Marietti (1985: 131) and Boyne (1990: 75).

if we are not to miss both the philosophical stakes of Foucault's evolving understanding of the Socratic *logos* and the centrality of Plato to the debates that shaped the French intellectual scene in the last half of the twentieth century. Thus, at the start of his 1982 course on *L'herméneutique du sujet,* before his actual reading of the *Alcibiades,* Foucault sketches the historical importance of the concept of the "care of the self"—in both its Socratic and its later Hellenistic and imperial versions. The practice of the care of the self is contextualized in the history of western philosophy in relation to that of "knowing the self." In the ancient world, he argues that self-knowledge was predicated on a preliminary "spiritual" transformation, which he defines as "the research, the practice, the experience through which the subject effects upon itself the necessary transformation to have access to the truth" (2001: 16). These practices range from physical and dietary regimens to the repeated engagement of Socratic dialectic or, in the later Stoic tradition, the keeping of notebooks and journals for recording both one's own spiritual progress and the discourse of others. By contrast, Foucault argues, in the modern world the act of knowing oneself is predicated solely on the pursuit of the proper intellectual method, and the attainment of certain necessary conditions. Here, he pointedly refers to Descartes's exclusion of madness from his first meditation as an example of the way in which the conditions for the subject's access to truth come to be increasingly defined from within the domain of knowledge in the modern period, as opposed to knowledge being predicated on the subject's having already gained access to truth through his or her own spiritual transformation, in those periods when the ethic of the care of the self is predominant. Philosophy, like poetry, may be a form of divine madness in the *Phaedrus* but not in Descartes. In this allusion to Descartes's first *Meditation,* the editor of *L'herméneutique du sujet* immediately picks up on a reference to the earlier polemic with Derrida in an accompanying note (Foucault 2001: 19).

The topic is returned to later in the course. There it is a question of whether Descartes's *Meditations* constituted actual spiritual exercises, in the antique mode, or purely textual investigations. Again the reference escaped neither the editor nor, one imagines, Foucault's auditors (Foucault 2001: 340–41). The understanding of Descartes's practice as an actual meditation was crucial to Foucault's response to Derrida (1972: 591), since one who dreams can still think and hence meditate, but one who is *demens* cannot engage in this methodical practice of thought. For Foucault, then, the practice of being a subject can never be disarticulated from its relation to specific conceptions and practices of knowledge and truth, even though the relative priority or secondariness of those technologies of self-constitution in relation to the domain of knowledge may be radically historically variable.

The stakes, then, of Foucault's reading of Plato could not be higher. The reasons are three. First, for Foucault, the "care of the self" is a crucial feature in determining the history of the subject's relation to truth in western philosophy: he demands that we ask the question, is philosophy, both for us and for Plato, an abstract set of propositions, a theoretical structure, or something we do, an activity whereby we come to form and re-form ourselves. Clearly, these are not mutually exclusive propositions, but it makes a great deal of difference on which formulation we place the accent, on whether we pursue the study of ancient philosophy primarily in the manner of analytic ancient philosophers such as Terrence Irwin[14] and Gail Fine or that of more practice-oriented and hermeneutic philosophers, such as Pierre Hadot and Alexander Nehamas.[15] Second, this concept of the subject's practice of the self is integral to Foucault's personal polemic with Derrida, arguably the other, single most influential French philosopher of the postmodern period.[16] Third, this polemic and its corollary issues are central to understanding Foucault's conception of reason as defined by the foundational texts of western philosophy.

Indeed, evidence of a subtle retort to Derrida's reading of Plato's *Phaedrus* and the latter's suspicion of writing can be seen in Foucault's privileging of the Stoics throughout his later work.[17] Foucault

14. See Roochnik's indictment of Irwin's methods (1988) and Irwin's reply (1988).
15. In this particular division of the philosophical field, as Foucault understands it, Derrida winds up more as the uncomfortable bedfellow of his analytic confrères Irwin and Fine than of Foucault and Hadot.
16. Carlos Lévy (2003) thus has argued that Foucault's exclusion of ancient Skepticism, as embodied in the work of both Pyrrho and later Sextus Empiricus, from his genealogy can best be understood in light of his polemic with Derrida on Descartes and the nature of radical doubt. Lévy argues that Foucault inadvertently repeats the totalizing gesture that Derrida had earlier seen (wrongly in Lévy's view) to characterize his reading of Descartes. See also Gros (2001: 502 n.21).
17. Evidence of Foucault's counterdiscourse to Derrida can be seen already in *Les mots et les choses*. Where Derrida had argued in his early work *De la grammatologie* (1967b), *L'écriture et la différence* (1967a), and *La voix et la phénomène* (1967c) that western metaphysics was constituted by the systematic exclusion of writing in favor of the voice and consciousness's immediate self-presence to itself, Foucault in *Les mots et les choses* argued for an alternative tradition of Renaissance philosophy that privileges writing (1966: 53). This theme would be picked up in the 1982 course at the Collège de France where Montaigne is specifically seen as the heir to the late antique tradition of the care of the self (2001: 240; 1994c: 410), a theme that is later repeated by Hadot (1995b: 395, 413) and Nehamas (1998). Foucault's *Les mots et les choses* was published the year before Derrida published his three books, but the latter's ideas had been in circulation for some time in the

observes that in the Stoics, and indeed all the philosophers of the imperial period, the exclusion of writing is completely discarded (Foucault 1994f: 361). Philosophical pedagogy had changed, he notes, following Hadot (1995b: 271–72). "The Platonic culture of the dialogue cede[d] its place to a culture of silence" predicated on the written word, and an "art of listening" (Foucault 1994g: 796). In making this case, Foucault implicitly argues that there is an alternative philosophical tradition to the (neo-)Platonic one from which Derrida derives, a tradition whose primary focus is ultimately on practice rather than the *logos,* and whose chief concern is the ethics of self-fashioning rather than the metaphysics of meaning as the presence of consciousness to itself (Spivak 1976: xvi–xl; Zuckert 1996: 213–14).

Indeed, while Derrida is never mentioned, the careful reader of Foucault's *Dits et écrits* can discover a careful rebuttal of all the major points made in "La pharmacie de Platon," beginning with the *pharmakon* itself.[18] The *pharmakon,* it will be recalled, symbolizes writing's suspect status as something outside, yet also integral to, the *logos* itself. Thus Plato in the *Phaedrus* has Ammon argue that writing is a *pharmakon* that allows people to appear to know more than they do by repeating the discourses of others, as Phaedrus does in the case of Lysias, rather than coming to real knowledge through an active engagement in dialectic. In contrast, Foucault points out, even a Platonist such as Plutarch recommends learning the discourses of others *as a pharmakon,* or drug, that guards the soul against illness (Foucault 1994f: 360; 2001: 310). *Aretê* on this model comes from study and prescribed spiritual exercises. Socratic *epimelia heatou* ("care of the self") as outlined in the *Alcibiades* has, in imperial philosophy, become indissociable from the practice of writing (Vernant 1965: 1.112).

Thus what Plato on Derrida's reading sees as harmful, imperial philosophy according to Foucault views as beneficial. Where Plato rejects writing,[19] according to Derrida, as mere *hupomnêsis* instead of *mnêmê,* the philosophers of the empire, Foucault observes, directly advocated the keeping of *hupomnêmata,*[20] or notebooks, not as a substitute for

---

form of lectures and conference papers.

18. In at least one case, Foucault's interviewers clearly invite him to situate his work relative to the problematic investigated by Derrida in "La Pharmacie." Foucault's response is to switch immediately to a discussion of the history and technical status of *hupomnêmata,* a move that appears to refuse the engagement with Derrida while simultaneously accepting it on his own terms (Foucault 1994c: 624–25).

19. For a discussion of the bibliography surrounding the issue of writing, orality and Plato, see note 33.

20. The importance of the *hupomnêmata* as a genre of philosophic writing that was

memory—conceived of by Plato as vital and interior to the soul—but as a form of practice, a technology of the self (Foucault 1994d: 417–19; 1994f: 361–61; 2001: 343). Writing, rather than undermining the presence of the *logos* to itself or representing a form of discourse whose author is never present to defend the integrity of his intentions, actually renders the absent party present, according to Seneca (Foucault 1994d: 425). The grapheme is not the foreign element that threatens the interiority of the soul, but rather the technology that makes interiority possible. Foucault states:

> The *hupomnêmata* ought to be resituated in the context of a very palpable tension during this period: inside this culture that was so affected by tradition, by the recognized value of the quotation, by the recurrence of discourse, by the practice of "citation" under the seal of age and authority, an ethics was in the process of developing that was very openly oriented by the care of the self toward some very precise objects: the retreat into oneself; the interior life; independence; the taste for oneself. Such is the objective of the *hupomnêmata*: to make the memory of a fragmentary *logos* transmitted by teaching, listening or reading, a means of establishing a relation with oneself as adequate and as perfect as possible. (1994c: 625–26)

Thus Foucault carefully and unobtrusively takes up each of Derrida's major themes with regard to the role of writing in the constitution of western philosophical reason—the *pharmakon, mnêmê* versus *hupomnêsis,* presence versus absence, interiority versus exteriority—and demonstrates the existence of a countertradition that Derrida ignores. That countertradition, like Foucault himself in his response to Derrida's attack on *Histoire de la folie,* privileges practice over the abstractions of pure reason, and self-fashioning over textuality in a vacuum. Thus it is no surprise that immediately following his discussion of Descartes in *L'herméneutique du sujet,* Foucault returns to a discussion of the practice of philosophy in the first and second centuries CE, where he demonstrates that reading, through the practice of meditation, is directly linked in Stoic practice to writing, and thus that writing was central to the care of the self (2001: 341).

The final and most explicit proof of the validity of this reading of

---

designed to serve as a spiritual exercise, and hence a technology of the self, was first discussed by Pierre Hadot in reference to Marcus Aurelius' *Meditations* (1992: 40–49; Davidson 1995: 10–11).

Foucault's interpretation of Plato in light of his continuing engagement with Derrida can be heard in the recordings of his 1983 course on Le gouvernement de soi et des autres. This course is devoted to an in-depth examination of *parrhêsia*, the Greek term for truth-telling or frank speech.[21] It chronicles the changing sense of the word as it evolves from a primarily political term in fifth-century BCE Athenian politics and culture to one that refers to the courage of the philosopher to tell the truth, in the first instance to his prince, and ultimately to his disciple who, in the very different world of first- and second-century CE imperial Rome, would often be his social superior and patron.[22] In the latter instance, it was a tool of the philosophical director of conscience to produce a self-relation of ideal transparency in the consciousness of his charge.[23] In line with this investigation, the course features an

---

21. For a discussion of the concept, see Flynn (1991). For Foucault's knowledge of Philodemus' surviving treatise *Peri Parrhêsias* at a time when it had yet to be translated into any modern language, see Foucault (2001: 372) and Konstan (2004: 27). Philodemus' text is now available in English (Konstan et al.: 1998). For the changing meanings of *parrhêsia* from classical Athens to the Hellenistic period, see Konstan (1996).

22. For a full review of *parrhêsia* in its political and philosophic contexts as well as Foucault's 1982–83 lectures on it at the Collège de France, see Monoson (2000: 51–63, 154–80) and P. A. Miller (2006).

23. See *L'herméneutique du sujet* as well (2001: 232, 357–63, and 382–89). There are places in these discussions where Foucault's historical and philological expertise lets him down. On page 363 in a discussion of Plato's critique of flattery (the opposite of *parrhêsia*), the *locus classicus* of which, as noted by the editor is *Gorgias* 463a, Foucault claims that "la flatterie dont parle Platon, et à laquelle il oppose le véritable rapport du philosophe au disciple, est une flatterie qui est essentiellement celle de l'amoureux à l'égard du garçon" ("the flattery about which Plato is speaking, and to which he opposes the true relationship of the philosopher to the disciple, is a flattery that is essentially that of the lover in regard to the boy"). The context, here, however is not erotic, but a description of rhetoric as a form of flattery addressed to the Athenian people in the assembly (463d2; see Dodds 1959: 224–25). Gros in his accompanying note also briefly mentions *Phaedrus* 240B, which is in an amorous context. But far from opposing *kolakeia* to philosophical *parrhêsia*, this passage occurs in Lysias' speech, an example of the very kind of rhetoric Socrates exposes to critical examination in the *Gorgias*. Moreover, as noted by the editors of the Budé text, which both Gros and Foucault use as their primary reference, the flatterer and the courtesan, who is the next figure evoked in the speech, are traditional comic types (Moreschini and Vicaire 1985: ad loc). It is precisely at the conjunction of the erotic and the political that, as Foucault recognizes, the *Alcibiades* is set (1994g: 790).

On pages 382–83, Foucault equates *parrhêsia* with the Roman concept of *libertas*, which is often translated "freedom of speech." He cites Seneca's letters 29, 38, 40, and 75. Foucault argues that Seneca opposes philosophical *libertas* to popular *oratio* or diatribe as practiced by itinerant cynic preachers (40.3). This is an oversimplification. *Libertas* is a value term that traditionally refers to aristocratic freedom of speech. The image of the Roman orator addressing the *populus Romanus* in *contio* or the popular assembly was precisely the ideal image of *libertas* promoted by writers such as Cicero. Seneca, in fact, both cites the example of the *contio* (38.1) and Cicero's authority in these letters and contrasts the measured nature of Roman oratory with Greek excess (40.11). Thus rather than a

extensive, detailed, and at times brilliant reading of Euripides' *Ion* (January 12, 19, 26, and February 2) as well as shorter interpretations of the *Phoenician Women,* The *Bacchae,* and the *Orestes* (February 2). There are, in addition, examinations of specific passages from Polybius (January 12), Thucydides (February 2), and Isocrates (February 2). The rest of the course is focused on Plato and features explications of passages from the *Republic* (February 9), the *Laws* (February 9), and the letters (February 9).

The key discussion for our purposes comes in the course of a lengthy reading of Plato's seventh letter on February 16, 1983. After an examination of the authenticity of the letters in the preceding meeting, a question that, as we have seen, Derrida addresses in his own manner in *La carte postale* (chapter 5), and which has been a matter of intense philological dispute since the early nineteenth century,[24] Foucault turns his

---

simple opposition between the private frankness of the director of conscience and the public rhetoric of the popular preacher, we have a complex negotiation concerning different styles of rhetoric (Greek versus Roman, Ciceronian measure versus oriental excess), different ideological contexts (republican versus imperial), and the changing definitions of what constitutes the freedom (*libertas*) of the aristocrat (*magnus vir,* 29.2) in a context where real political oratory is no longer possible. The irony of Seneca's having also served as Nero's tutor only makes the conflicting ideological messages in these letters all the more complex. The extent of Foucault's lack of sensitivity to the political resonances of these terms in Latin becomes even clearer in the 1983 course where he suggests that *licentia* is a possible Latin translation of *parrhêsia* without realizing that it represents a stigmatized form of excessive freedom of speech that is opposed to *libertas.* Seneca, in fact, uses it in this sense in letter 40.11. On these terms and the debates surrounding them, see Cicero, *De Sua Domo* 130–31; *Pro Cluentio* 118; *Ad Familiares* 12.16; Tacitus *Annales* 1.2; *Dialogus* 40; Wirszubski (1950); Syme (1960: 155); Lafleur (1981); Ste Croix (1981: 366); Corbeill (1996: 16–20, 105–6); Roller (2001: 213–87); P. A. Miller (2005a).

24. He contends that 6, 7, and 8 are authentic, while the others are more likely to be forgeries. His position, while not uncontroversial, is in line with the most common views expressed in French and English in the twentieth century. It is also less important for Foucault that Plato actually wrote the seventh letter than that it represent a genuinely Platonic position. Thus, Cooper (1997: 1635) indicates that the seventh letter is "the least unlikely to have come from Plato's pen" and certainly dates from the period and shows a thorough acquaintance with Plato's personal history and philosophy. Irwin (1992: 51) rejects it as spurious, but agrees that it must date from the period and be by the hand of "someone who knew Plato well." His note contains a good English bibliography on the question. Julia Annas notes that such forgeries were a common rhetorical genre exercise throughout antiquity. Brandwood, however, indicates that the seventh letter is stylometrically consonant with the late dialogues (1992: 111–13), and Penner notes its thematic and tonal continuities with these same works (1992: 130). Souilhé, the editor of the Budé edition of the letters, which was Foucault's reference text, has both an excellent history of the controversies surrounding the letters in general (1960: v–xxxi) and what is to my mind a convincing defense of the authenticity of the seventh letter (1961: xxxiii–lviii). See also Morrow's defense of the authenticity of the seventh and eighth (1935: 11–22) and Festugière on the seventh (1950: 61n.1). More recently, Brumbaugh offers an intriguing defense of the letter based on the congruence of its philosophical and expository methods

attention to the twin problems of the nature of philosophical knowledge and the refusal of writing, as those problems are formulated in the seventh letter. The letter itself is addressed to the followers of Dion of Syracuse after the latter's death. They are seeking advice on how to prosecute their continuing opposition to the tyranny of Dionysius II. In the course of his response, Plato outlines the circumstance under which he undertook his second visit to Dionysius II at the urging of Dion and his friends in an attempt to convert the young tyrant to philosophy and convince him to rescind Dion's banishment. Plato had tried to instruct Dionysius once before and had met with little success. Nonetheless, Dionysius had claimed a continuing interest in philosophy during Plato's absence and held dialogues with the members of his court. Plato thus decided to test him on his return. He discussed with him a number of issues that were apparently at a great level of abstraction and probably included such difficult notions as the forms of justice and the good as first principles of nature (344d). The goal was to expose to Dionysius the difficulty of the philosophical pursuit and to see if he would be inspired to undertake the strenuous labor necessary to live the life of a philosopher. "Those who are really not philosophers but have only a coating of opinions, like men whose bodies are tanned by the sun, when they see how much learning is required, and how great the labor, and how orderly their lives must be to suit the subject they are pursuing, conclude that the task is too difficult for their powers" (340d; Morrow 1997: 1658).[25] Unsurprisingly, the young tyrant failed the test (345a). But Dionysius, Plato notes, was rumored to have later written a book based on their discussions. It is in this context that Plato launches into a brief digression on the nature of philosophical knowledge and its relation to writing.

Dionysius or any other writer, he argues, could not have been serious if he attempted to set down Plato's essential doctrine, or that of any other philosopher, in writing. Such an exclusion of writing, of course, would seem to provide direct evidence for the Derridean thesis of the phonocentric nature of the *logos* at the dawn of occidental philosophy. The seeming contradiction, moreover, of Plato's contention with the manifest fact that he himself did write would appear to be an example of precisely the kind of aporia and undecideability that Derrida

---

with those found in the late and middle dialogues (1988). For a position that in its essence is congruent with Foucault's both on the seventh letter and what it reveals about the roles of writing and *sunousia* in the practice of philosophy, see Sayre (1988).

25. Plato only once tried to lecture on the Good. Aristotle tells us it was completely incomprehensible (*Metaphysics* A.6).

traces in his examination of the term *pharmakon* and its peregrinations throughout the Platonic corpus.

Foucault, however, constructs a different reading of the letter. He notes that Plato argues there are five aspects to the knowledge of any real object: name, definition, image, the acquaintance our minds have with the object (scientific knowledge, reasoning, and right opinion), and the object itself in its abstract ideality (342). Inasmuch as the first two elements are language-dependent and hence mutable, and inasmuch as the third is dependent upon individual material instantiations, which is made clear in Plato's discussion of the example of a circle, while these three elements are necessary to the formation of the fourth element, they can never be adequate to a true *epistêmê* of the object in itself. Hence, "no sensible man will venture to express his deepest thoughts in words, especially in a form which is unchangeable, as is true of written outlines" (343a; Morrow 1997: 1660).

The problem is not, according to Foucault, one of writing per se, but of philosophy as a practice rather than as a set of "formulas"[26] (see also Hadot 1995: 106). According to the seventh letter, we arrive at the knowledge of "real" objects not through direct sense perception, nor through the memorization of discrete formulas, but through the process of approximation, refutation, and reformulation that characterizes what has become known as the Socratic-Platonic *elenchus* (Irwin 1992: 65–66, 68–69; Penner 1992: 139–47; Fine 1992: 203–11; Nehamas 1998: 82–87).[27] The dialectic of Socratic conversation, moreover, is pursued in the intense erotic relationship between master and disciple evoked by Socrates at the beginning of the *Alcibiades* (Souilhé 1960: liv–lv; Kenney 2003: 28–90)[28] when he confesses his love for the young

26. Foucault seems to be paraphrasing Souilhé (1961: 1), but see also Festugière (1950: 191).

27. Foucault makes this clear at the conclusion of the course on April 9, 1983 in a discussion of the *elenchus* and the *Gorgias*. On problems with abstracting the concept of *elenchus* from the larger context of Socratic conversation or dialectic, Charles Platter comments (*per litteras*), "I have to admit I grit my teeth every time I see the word *elenchus* used as a synonym for Socratic conversation. It's an organic process, not a formula. Nor do I see what is gained even heuristically by using it. So I view it as a kind of anachronistic terminology that doesn't pay its way. For me it represents another way that professional philosophers get away from the dialogues and begin creating their own formulaic para-text where the complex issues brought into play by the dialogue form can be discarded."

28. Foucault notes that the term for this relationship is *sunousia* ("being with"), which often has an erotic sense; he then asserts that it has does not have that sense in the context of the seventh letter while admonishing us not to "overinterpret." It is difficult to know how seriously to take this admonition. On the one hand, it could be a deliberate attempt to innoculate his audience against a premature or facile psychoanalytic reading (on Foucault's complex relationship with psychoanalysis, see below). On the other, Foucault is well aware

man, and described by Lacan in his reading of the *Symposium*.²⁹ The seventh letter is clear.

> There is no writing of mine about these matters, nor will there ever be one. For this knowledge is not something that can be put into words [*rhêton*] like other sciences; but after long continued intercourse [*sunousias*] between teacher and pupil in joint pursuit of the subject, suddenly [*exaiphnês*],³⁰ like the light flashing forth when a fire is kindled, it is born in the soul and straightaway nourishes itself. (341c–d; Morrow 1997: 1659)

Lest Foucault's audience miss the larger importance of his highlighting this passage to his understanding of the role of writing and speech at the origins of western formal reason (and consequently of his entire rereading of Plato in terms of the practice of the care of the self), Foucault pauses to invoke directly Derrida's reading of this same problematic as a foil to his own. To paraphrase, Foucault says, "You see the Platonic exclusion of writing, therefore, has nothing to do with the birth of logocentrism in western philosophy." "Logocentrism" is of course Derrida's term for the constitution of western reason under the sign of the self-presence of the transcendental signified to itself, which in turn is manifest in a phonocentrism that privileges speech over writing as the immediate transparence of meaning to consciousness itself (see chapter 5 and Derrida 1967b: part 1).

Foucault continues by noting that Plato does not in fact contrast writing with the *logos* in 342 but rather asserts the inadequacy of the *logos* to the thing itself in its abstract ideality (compare Sayre 1988: 95–97). The problem of writing, then, is not one of its difference from or deferral of full meaning, but of its rigidity, its removal from the question and answer of the dialectical process that leads to the flash

---

of the erotic frame of the *Alcibiades* and its relation to Alcibiades' drunken entrance in the *Symposium*, which is the crux of Lacan's reading of this latter dialogue. By calling attention to the possibility of the erotic reading of *sunousia* before an audience of non-Hellenists, while simultaneously warning against it, Foucault both calls our attention to the intense affective relationship between master and disciple and cautions us against an overhasty assimilation of it to a purely genital one. Of course, the ancient satiric texts reveal that this assimilation was as common in a pre-Freudian era as it is today. See Juvenal 2 and *Satyricon* 85–87 as well as McGlathery (1998). On erotics as an essential protreptic strategy in Plato, see Kenney's excellent reading (2003).

29. See *Symposium* 211 a–b. For a comparison of this passage with the seventh letter, see Robin (1929: xci).

30. On the centrality of this concept in Platonic metaphysics, see Boussoulas (1952: 77–82).

of insight in the intense relation between master and student. He concludes by summarizing 344b, a passage that I quote here in full:

ἅμα γὰρ αὐτὰ ἀνάγκη μανθάνειν καὶ τὸ ψεῦδος ἅμα καὶ ἀληθὲς τῆς ὅλης οὐσίας, μετὰ τριβῆς πάσης καὶ χρόνου πολλοῦ, ὅπερ ἐν ἀρχαῖς εἶπον· μόγις δὲ τριβόμενα πρὸς ἄλληλα αὐτῶν ἕκαστα, ὀνόματα καὶ λόγοι ὄψεις τε αἰσθήσεις, ἐν εὐμενέσιν ἐλέγχοις ἐλεγχόμενα καὶ ἄνευ φθόνων ἐρωτήσιν καὶ ἀποκρίσεσιν χρωμένων, ἐξέλαμψε φρόνησις περὶ ἕκαστον καὶ νοῦς, συντείνων ὅτι μάλιστ' εἰς δύναμιν ἀνθρωπίνην·

> For it is necessary to learn these things together, the true and the false of all being, with work and much time, as I said at the beginning. With each of these things worked hard against the others—names, accounts, observations, perceptions—being tested in well-intentioned disputations and using without envy questions and answers, wisdom and intelligence shine out concerning each thing, extending to the limits of human power.

From his reading of this passage, Foucault concludes that, "The refusal of writing is not made in the name of the *logos,* but of something positive. It is made in the name of *tribê,*[31] exercise, work, and a laborious relation of the self to itself. It is the western subject itself that is engaged in this simultaneous rejection of writing and the *logos."* Just as in 1972 when Foucault published his response to Derrida's 1963 lecture, in 1983 he continues to see the latter as the "decisive" representative of a certain tradition of teaching philosophy in France, a tradition that emphasizes systems, categories and metaphysics as opposed to the relations, technologies, and practices that were Foucault's central focus (Gros 2001: 506; Flynn 1994: 29).

There are, of course, a number of potential weaknesses in Foucault's response to "La Pharmacie de Platon," some more apparent than real. The first is the seeming contradiction between Plato's rejection of writing in favor of the direct, interpersonal practice of dialectic and the fact that Plato nonetheless not only wrote, but wrote voluminously and with great care.[32] For Derrida, as noted above, this contradiction

---

31. As Dodds notes in his commentary on *Gorgias* 463b4, on rhetoric as *empeiria kai tribê, tribê* can refer to an unscientific *bricolage,* an "empirical knack," as opposed to methodical scientific inquiry (1959: ad loc). That seems to be the opposite of the meaning here, which refers to the acquisition of philosophic knowledge through the hard labor of the dialectic, through wearing words and perceptions out by rubbing them against one another (Places 1964: 509). But the emphasis in each case is on cumulative effect of the labor.

32. Of course, even then, he wrote dialogues.

is embodied in the ambivalence of the word *pharmakon* and of writing itself both in the *Phaedrus* and throughout the Platonic corpus. Foucault's response to this problem, while not logically mutually exclusive with Derrida's, is convincing and shifts the ground firmly back from theory to practice. He begins by drawing our attention to passage 344c in the seventh letter, "What I have said comes, in short, to this, whenever we see a book, whether the laws of a legislator (*nomothetes*) or a composition on any other subject, we can be sure that if the author is really *serious,* this book does not contain his best thoughts; they are stored away with the fairest of his possessions" (Morrow 1997: 1661; italics mine). Foucault is quick to note the seeming contradiction with *The Laws* and *The Republic,* in which Plato appears to play precisely the role of the *nomothetes* or lawgiver. He then notes that Plato also invents and relates a variety of myths, such as Aristophanes' tale of the androgyne in the *Symposium,* the chariot procession in heaven of Socrates' great speech in the *Phaedrus,* or the story of Er that concludes the *Republic.* These myths, he argues, are also not "serious" in the sense that they are not to be taken literally. Rather they are a provocation to thought and thus to a reexamination of our relation to ourselves, and hence of our capacity to govern both ourselves and others. Foucault then asks if this is not the real philosophical work of the *Laws* and the *Republic* as well: not to provide prefabricated recipes and formulas for the perfect state, but to prompt readers to question the nature of how they govern themselves and others and to seek what may be the best laws for each.[33] In this regard, he cites the admittedly fictive fifth letter, which he believes nonetheless reflects Platonic if not Plato's thought (see Souilhé 1960: lxxxix–xci). It contends that the philosopher's job as counselor to the state is not to impose a constitution, but to listen to each particular constitution's voice, and to help it come to speak "its own language to gods and men" (321d–e; Morrow 1997: 1645). If we accept this, as well as the seventh letter's judgment that philosophy cannot be reduced to "formulas" and that what we must seek instead is a system where men can live under freedom and the best laws, then the notion that the *Republic* and the *Laws* constitute actual blueprints for a real state becomes absurd. Thus, Foucault concludes that these dialogues are not to be taken "seriously," but are to be read in a fashion analogous to the myths themselves.[34]

The *Republic* in fact explicitly supports this claim when Socrates

---

33. Compare Gadamer (1991: 44–45), who sees the shared pursuit of collective understanding as the animating spirit of the Platonic dialectic from the aporetic dialogues through the *Philebus, The Laws,* and the seventh letter.

34. See Asmis (1992: 338).

states that he wishes not to discuss the possibility of putting his plan in practice but rather to indulge his "fancy like an idle daydreamer out for a solitary walk" (458a–b; Lee 1987: 178–79). Later, when he and Glaucon are discussing whether the ideal philosopher would actually take part in politics, we find the following exchange:

> Glaucon: You mean that he will do so in the society which we have been describing and which we have theoretically founded; but I doubt if it will ever exist on earth.
> Socrates: Perhaps . . . it is laid up as a pattern in heaven, where he who wishes can see it and found it in his own heart. But it does not matter whether it exists or will ever exist. . . . (592a–b: Lee 1987: 358).[35]

The philosopher is to be the new artist who faithfully reproduces (*mimeisthai*) the harmonic forms of beauty and justice in themselves (500c–501b), rather than copies of copies like the mimetic artists who are expelled in Book 10. His is a fiction that points beyond the limits of the means of representation and actualization as in the myth of Er. As the Athenian says in the *Laws,* responding to an imaginary petition on behalf of tragedians, "Our entire state has been constructed to be a 'representation' of the finest and noblest life. . . . So we are poets like yourselves" (817a–b; Saunders 1997: 1483–84; see also Asmis 1992: 338; Nightingale 1995: 88).

A more weighty objection to Foucault's critique of Derrida is to be found in his focus on the seventh letter: for, while it is possible to argue that the letter's text does not discount writing in favor of the *logos* as the transcendental guarantor of meaning, but rather focuses on philosophy as an interpersonal practice of subject formation, one cannot say the same of the *Phaedrus,* which is the primary focus of Derrida's exposition. The myth of Theuth makes clear that writing itself is seen as opposed to *epistêmê* and *mnêmê,* for Ammon does not condemn writing as part of a broader denunciation of the reduction of philosophy to verbal formulas as Plato does in the seventh letter, but he condemns the invention of writing per se as leading to a neglect of memory (*mnêmês ameletêsiai*).[36] *Mnêmê* and *epistêmê,* as in the *Meno* (Hamilton 1973: 55n.2), are equated with one another in the myth

---

35. On the translation, see the note in Lee and Adam's (1963) important discussion *ad loc.*

36. *Ameletêsia* is an alpha-privative form of the word *meletaô* ("to care for"), which gives us the *epimelia* of Foucault's *epimelia heautou* or "care of the self."

recounted in Socrates' great speech. The forms, as is made clear there, provide the transcendental guarantee of meaning, and it is our immediate recollection of the forms that constitutes real knowledge and sparks our love of wisdom (*philosophia*):

> For the soul that has never seen the truth will not assume human form. For it is necessary that a person understand what is spoken (*legomenon*) according to the form (*eidos*), a language which goes from the multitude of sense impressions to bringing them together by reasoning (*logismôi*) into a unity (*hen*). (249b–c)[37]

Writing here, therefore, suffers from the same degree of ontological inferiority that poetry does in book 10 of the *Republic* and that the lover who physically consummates his desire for the beautiful boy in Socrates' great speech does, and each must be expelled from the realm of pure presence constituted by the forms, if only to return in the guise of Eros as mediator in the *Symposium*, the writing on the soul of the *Phaedrus*, or the myth of Er at the end of the *Republic*.

Of course, Foucault, after such a provocative gesture as singling out Derrida for criticism, does not dare to neglect the *Phaedrus*. He turns to it two weeks later on March 2 as part of a larger discussion of the relation between philosophy and rhetoric. This lecture contains no direct acknowledgment of Derrida. Foucault's first two texts for this lesson are taken from the *Apology*. In one, he says that Socrates announces that he will not use a speech produced by a *logographos*, but will address the court in his usual manner (17–18a). Foucault contends that Socrates contrasts his *etumos logos*[38] ("true, genuine speech") with the false or fictive rhetorical speech that the jurors have just heard

---

37. The translation is my own. The passage is much controverted. For three very different translations see Moreschini and Vicaire (1985: ad loc); Nehemas and Woodruff (1995: ad loc); and Hamilton (1973: ad loc). Nehemas and Woodruff adopt Badham's emendation of *iont'* for *ion*, which changes the subject of the last clause. This is in line with their overall interpretation of the dialogue as moving from the transcendental vision of the forms found in the *Republic* to a more immanent, almost Aristotelian vision, found in the *Philebus* (1995: xlii–xliii).

38. In point of fact, the adjective *etumos* appears nowhere in the *Apology*, although the phrases *ton t'alêthê legonta* ("speaking the truth") (17b4–5), *pasan tên alêtheian* ("the whole truth") (17b8), and *t'alêthê legein* ("to speak the truth") (18a6) do. The phrase *etumos logos* does, however, occur in the *Phaedrus*, where it is attributed to Stesichorus and serves to introduce Socrates' great speech (243a9). It is impossible to tell whether the conflation is deliberate and Foucault is anticipating his argument on the *Phaedrus* or a simple slip, given that we are dealing with oral teaching and do not yet have access to an official transcript.

(17a1–4) and which, he implies, is the kind usually heard in the courts (17c7–d3). In the second passage, Socrates explains why, if he claims to speak the truth, he nonetheless does not speak in the assembly (31c–32). His answer is that he would not be heeded and would have certainly been put to death before now. In both passages, as Foucault reads them, the emphasis is on Socrates as parrhesiast and on philosophy as truth-telling. Foucault then turns his attention to Socrates' great speech in the *Phaedrus* as another example of an *etumos logos*. His argument is that in the *Phaedrus* Socrates' true speech is directly contrasted with Lysias' attempt at a rhetorical *tour de force* in the speech Phaedrus reads. Lysias is later in the dialogue explicitly referred to as a *logographos* and Phaedrus, now converted to what he thinks to be Socrates' point of view condemns him for that reason. Nonetheless, as Foucault notes, Socrates reproves Phaedrus on this point and indicates that the question is less if one's *logos* is *graphos* ("written") than if it is *aischros* ("shameful") (258d). Lest we miss the Derridean resonances to these passages, Foucault underlines the fact that *logos* is used by Plato for both written and oral speech.

Socrates concludes, then, by arguing that Phaedrus says that for a speech to be good, the person who delivers it must be someone who knows the truth. But Socrates is not satisfied with this. Rhetoric on this model is conceived of as an add-on and ornament, a mere externality. Knowledge of the truth, however, is not given in advance, but is a function of discourse as it is practiced through the *elenchus* as discussed in the seventh letter.[39] From here he concludes that the true art of rhetoric is nothing other than *psychagogia,* that is, the ability to "lead souls." Dialectic, not rhetorical set speeches in the manner of Lysias, is the true example of this art. The tricks of rhetoric found in the manuals are only valuable to the extent that they are subordinated to the dialectic (and its *etumos logos*). Dialectic, in fact, makes a double demand, the knowledge of being and *psychagogia*. These are two faces of the same coin. It is by the movement of the soul that one comes to know being, and it is through knowing the nature of being that one knows the nature of the soul. Thus, according to Foucault, Socrates' great speech has only the function of giving an example of the *etumos logos*, that is, of anticipating the discussion of rhetoric in the dialogue's final part and hence of showing the link that exists between access to the truth and the soul.

39. This is a reasonable deduction, but Foucault does not cite a specific passage and I know of nowhere in the *Phaedrus* where Socrates actually says this.

Foucault's reading is a *tour de force*. It offers an interpretation of the dialogue that at once unifies the two sections and recasts the *Phaedrus* not as meditation on writing's relation to the *logos,* and hence to the soul, but as rhetoric's relation to philosophy's vocation to speak the truth and to lead others to the truth. Nonetheless, while valid in its own terms and offering important insights into how the *Phaedrus* can be read in terms of philosophy—viewed as a set of practices that are aimed in the first place at the relation of self to self and then of self to truth—it is not clear that Foucault's performance invalidates the reading of Derrida. First, Foucault never offers a counterreading of the myth of Theuth, which is Derrida's strongest piece of evidence. Second, he never addresses the way in which the vocabulary of writing as a *pharmakon* relates to the myth of Pharmakeia that opens the dialogue or to the nature of Eros as depicted in the competing speeches, nor, in spite of Foucault's assertions to the contrary, can the discourse on love be reduced to a mere illustration of the problem of true speech as opposed to rhetoric (see Ferrari 1992).[40] Third, Foucault oversimplifies what Derrida means by writing. As Derrida's critique of Husserl in *La voix et le phénomène* makes clear, there can be no meaning without some form of inscription (1967c). All language represents a materialization of thought, an encoding of the conceptual in the signifier whether its medium be that of vibrations in the air, synaptic firings in the brain, or paper and ink. But thought has no reality outside that materialization; thus, as Derrida famously claims in *De la grammatologie,* writing always precedes speech (1967b). Linguistic formalization is not merely the medium of thought, but that which makes thought possible. Writing in Derrida stands for that formalization, which is at once inescapable and yet always alienates thought as pure meaning from itself (Stoekl 1992: 201; Zuckert 1996: 201–16). This is why Theuth's invention must be banished because it threatens to make manifest the fact that the *logos* is always internally divided, always carrying its own other within itself. The attempt to expel writing from western metaphysics is the attempt to recover a lost origin, a realm of pure meaning, that like the forms is always posited, but never present. Thus Foucault's observation that Plato uses *logos* of both speech and writing in a sense falls wide of the mark. It represents an overliteralization of Derrida, a reduction of writing to the practice of the letter, and hence a rereading of Derrida's text not from the standpoint of the history of metaphysics, but precisely from that of the genealogy of philosophy as a practice.

---

40. Which is not to say that it does not also serve as such an illustration.

In the end, in spite of Foucault's polemical jibes, and the strong evidence that it was at least in part the challenge of Derrida that led Foucault to return to Plato, it is not clear that the two levels of analysis are mutually exclusive. While Foucault is undoubtedly right to refocus us on the problematic of the care of the self in ancient philosophy and the relation of the subject to truth as a set of practices, nonetheless we cannot neglect the fact that it *is* with Plato's dialogues that the very possibility of formulating in a rigorous manner questions about the nature of the good, the just, and the relative merits of pleasure and knowledge comes into formal existence in occidental thought (Grant 1866: 45). Plato is the founder of western metaphysics, and the conceptual and epistemological foundation of this ontology was from the beginning, as any reader of the *Ion* must know,[41] linked to a break with the predominantly oral and poetic structures of thought that dominated Greek education and culture until at least the middle of the fifth century BCE.[42]

Plato's relationship with writing is problematic and the fact that this problematization is linked to a conception of philosophy as a spiritual practice pursued through the Socratic dialectic does not exclude it from also being a theoretical conundrum. Writing's relationship to thought and the fundamental realities that make rigorous conceptual investigation possible is fraught with ambivalence and contradiction. The problem of externality and inscription, whether in the case of poetry, as in the *Republic*'s doctrine of mimesis; of sexual attraction, as formulated in the *Phaedrus* and the *Symposium;* or of writing's relation to thought and the real, as defined in the *Phaedrus* and the seventh letter, is central to Plato's concerns. The doctrines of recollection and spiritual purification that Plato describes in the great middle dialogues and integrates

---

41. For a discussion of recent readings of the *Ion* in relation to the *Republic*'s "banishment" of the poets and the elaboration of Plato's mature metaphysical theories, see Ledbetter (2003: 78–99), who accepts a rigorous distinction between the early Socratic dialogues and the later Platonic dialogues.

42. It was Havelock (1963) who most decisively, if somewhat monochromatically, demonstrated this. His text remains fundamental (Nadaff 1998: xiv–xv; Brisson 1998: 37–38; Nightingale 1995: 17; Thomas 1989: 34; Foley 1988: 62; Svenbro 1993: 1; Gentili 1984: 53; Asmis 1992: 361 n.1; Rose 1992: 337), even if its more extreme claims, particularly about alphabetic literacy and the direct causal effects of literacy are today questioned (Nadaff 1998: xvii; Thomas 1989: 3, 17n.2, 26; 1992: 17; Harris 1989: 50n.23; Rose 1992: 116–17). See also Luria (1976) for empirical verification of many of his cognitive claims, as well as Zumthor (1983: 34, 46); Goody and Watt (1968: 53); Berger (1994: 82); Thomas (1992: 18); and Graff (1987: 5).

On poetry as the dominant form of *paideia*, and the lack of any significant form of book trade until the end of the fifth century BCE, see Grant (1866: 50); Snodgrass (1980: 174); Harris (1989: 57–59, 84–93); Graff (1987: 26); Thomas (1992: 8, 13, 51; 1989: 21); Kurke (1991: 88); Nagy (1990a: 38; 1990b: 404).

directly into his general theory of knowledge certainly have their roots, as Vernant (1965: 1.92–117; 2001: 24–25) and Morgan (1992) have shown, in traditional Greek religious and Pythagorean practices. But spiritual practice is ultimately inseparable from its theoretical values, however informal, unconscious, or provisional.

c. Psychoanalytic Dialogues: Foucault, Lacan, and Alcibiades on the Couch

> It is less a matter of calling into question the apparent knowledge one thinks one possesses than of calling into question oneself and the values that direct our own lives. For in the final analysis, after having been in dialogue with Socrates, his interlocutor no longer knows why he does what he does. He becomes conscious of the contradictions of his discourse and of his own internal contradictions. He doubts himself. He, like Socrates, comes to know that he knows nothing. But in so doing, he takes a certain distance from himself, he doubles himself, with part of him identifying henceforth with Socrates in the mutual accord that Socrates demands of his interlocutor at each step of the discussion. A certain self-consciousness arises in him; he puts himself into question. (Hadot 1995b: 55)

The philosophical practice of dialectic is an interpersonal essay inscribed within an overdetermined complex of individual, technological, and cultural factors. As an ongoing exercise, it is dependent upon self-examination, the probing of the incoherence of one's own beliefs and of one's own self-relation in an intense prolonged dialogue with a master or director of conscience who is bound to one by the deep affective and erotic ties that Socrates cites at the beginning of the *Alcibiades*: "I was the first man to fall in love with you, son of Clinias, and now that others have stopped pursuing you I suppose you're wondering why I'm the only one who hasn't given up" (103a; Hutchinson 1997: 558; Halperin 1990a: 270). These encounters, which, as Plato describes in the seventh letter, lead over time to the spark of enlightenment, ideally produce both cognitive aporia and a resulting desire to pursue wisdom as modeled in the person of Socrates or his heirs (Hadot 1995b: 105). Eros thus leads both to the love of wisdom, *philo-sophia* (*Symposium* 204b; Kenney 2005), and a desire to know oneself as reflected in the soul of the interlocutor (*Alcibiades* 133a–b; Zuckert 1990: 148).

> Such will be the definition of the philosopher, of the man who desires wisdom, in Plato's *Symposium*. And this sentiment comes from the

fact that one has encountered a personality, Socrates, who by his very presence obliges whoever approaches to put themselves into question. This is what Alcibiades lets us understand at the end of the *Symposium*. (Hadot 1995b: 56–57)

Yet while the *Alcibiades* in antiquity was considered "the gateway to the temple," it also reminds us of how uncertain the journey could be. Alcibiades, the person and the literary character, may have shown great promise as a student of Socrates, but in the end, as the *Symposium* and his own checkered history show, he was seduced by the lure of the *dêmos:* by its promises of glory, power, and adulation (Kenney 2003: 28–44; J. Allen 2005; Wohl 2002).

The desire for wisdom is alluring, but of uncertain consequence. Diotima in her great speech in the *Symposium* says the true philosopher seeks to beget intellectual offspring in beauty (206b–207a, 208e6–209e5). Yet, as the *Theatetus* reminds us, such intellectual labors often miscarry. Moreover, the philosopher as midwife, who tries to bring the fertile young mind to issue, must test the result to see if the offspring is viable or abortive.

> Socrates: So the work of midwives is a highly important one, but it is not so important as my own performance. And for this reason, that there is not in midwifery the further complication, that the patients are sometimes delivered of phantoms and sometimes of realities, and that the two are hard to distinguish [. . .]. the most important thing about my art is the ability to apply all possible tests to the offspring, to determine whether the young mind is being delivered of a phantom, that is an error, or a fertile truth. (*Theaetetus* 150a–c; Levett 1997: 167)

This testing is the role of the *elenchus* as described in the seventh letter, the free and open process of question, answer, and refutation. Yet, as the case of Alcibiades demonstrates, the results were not always happy. Those who seem most fertile will not always stay until the testing program is complete: sometimes they depart in mid-travail:

> But it is I, with God's help, who deliver them of this offspring. And a proof of this may be seen in the many cases where people who did not realize this fact took all credit to themselves and thought that I was no good. They have then proceeded to leave me sooner than they should, either of their own accord or through the influence of

others. And after they have gone away from me they have resorted to harmful company, with the result that what remained within them has miscarried; while they have neglected the children I helped them to bring forth, and lost them, because they set more value upon lies and phantoms than upon the truth; finally they have been set down for ignorant fools, both by themselves and by everybody else. [. . .] Sometimes they have come back, wanting my company again, and ready to move heaven and earth to get it. (*Theaetetus* 150d–151a; Levett 1997: 167–68)

The reminiscences of Alcibiades' speech at the end of the *Symposium,* in the figure of those who have left Socrates' company and seek to regain it, are too obvious to need to be belabored. This passage clearly aims in part to answer the question, why did Socrates' favorite pupil come to such a bad end: treason, sacrilege, murder. Yet, what remains crucial in the *Alcibiades,* for the later ancient tradition and for Foucault, is not philosophy's ultimate failure to convert the brilliant ward of Pericles, but the model the dialogue establishes of the intense emotional relationship between lover and beloved, teacher and student, master and disciple that is at the heart of the Socratic dialectic as exemplified in the dialogue, but also in such other texts as the *Phaedrus,* the seventh letter, and the *Theaetetus*. There are never, however, as the Socratic midwife is at pains to explain, any guarantees. *Philo-sophia* is an activity of the soul, not a formula capable of producing invariable, predictable results. It is not a commodity that can be bought, sold or exchanged, but an interpersonal essay.

The Socratic care of the self is not a solitary project. It requires reflection through the figure of the *philosophos,* who in his care for his charges makes possible a doubling, a reflexivity, and hence an externalization of the self, which is the image of his "disinterested" love for them (Foucault 2001: 58).[43] That reflection, however, cannot be a simple sublimation of the self into the other or the concept. There is a

---

43. "Le maître, c'est celui qui se soucie du souci que le sujet a de lui-même, et qui trouve, dans l'amour qu'il a pour son disciple, la possibilité de se soucier du souci que le disciple a de lui-même. En aimant de façon désintéressée le garçon, il est donc le principe et le modèle du souci que le garçon doit avoir de lui-même en tant que sujet." ("The master is he who cares for himself with the care that subject has for himself, and who finds, in the love that he has for his disciple, the possibility that the disciple has of caring for himself. In loving the boy in a disinterested fashion, he is thus the principle and the model for the care the boy ought to have for himself insofar as he is a subject.") This formulation parallels closely Robin's paraphrase of Phaedrus' speech in the *Symposium* (1929: xxxix), a source Foucault was no doubt familiar with.

necessary opacity and remainder. The discourse and person of the Socratic philosopher must always in the end escape finality and full comprehension if it is to serve as the surface upon which the self catches sight of itself and thus comes to know and care for itself (Hadot 1995b: 57, 110; Nehamas 1998: 87). As Alcibiades says of Socrates, he never quite says what he means. "He has deceived us all: he presents himself as your lover, and before you know it, you're in love with him yourself" (*Symposium* 222b; Nehamas and Woodruff 1997: 503). Socratic irony, as Alcibiades learns when he arises from Socrates' couch the next morning as pure as the night before, is in fact not a riddle to be solved, a Silenus box to be opened and its contents immediately possessed (222b). Rather it is the ground for the establishment of a complex reflective relationship whereby the subject comes to understand and possess the truth of its desire as reflected by the other who eludes full comprehension (Nehamas 1998: 61).

This interpersonal relationship is of course precisely what Lacan speaks of in his reading of the *Symposium* in the *Seminar on Transference* (chapter 4). Such a responsion between Foucauldian and Lacanian interpretations of the erotic ties that bind Socrates and Alcibiades should not surprise us. Indeed, it would be hard to imagine how Foucault's *History of Sexuality* and his lectures at the Collège de France could not take place in the shadow of Lacan's work on ethics in his commentaries on the *Antigone* and the *Symposium* (Davidson 1994: 117–18).

In fact, Foucault's engagement with psychoanalysis in general and Lacan in particular was substantial and ongoing. Nor, despite assertions to the contrary, was the relationship simply a negative one (Halperin 1995: 121; Dean 2003: 238–52). Foucault not only underwent analysis himself in the late forties, but he attended Lacan's seminars in the 1950s and later read the *Ecrits* (Lane 2000: 312–13, 324; Eribon 1994: 251). Moreover, he explicitly cites Lacan along with Lévi-Strauss and Dumézil in interviews throughout the sixties and as late as 1978 as among his major influences in combating what he saw as the oppressive and ahistorical reign of Sartrean phenomenology in postwar France (Eribon 1994: 234–49). Far from seeing Lacanian analysis as a normalizing human science,[44] in *Les mots et les choses* he specifically

---

44. See Eagleton (1996: 141), "Equally serious is the complaint that psychoanalysis as a medical practice is a form of oppressive social control, labeling individuals and forcing them to conform to arbitrary definitions of 'normality.' This charge is in fact more usually aimed against psychiatric medicine as a whole: as far as Freud's own views on 'normality' are concerned, the accusation is largely misdirected. Freud's work showed, scandalously,

exempts Freud from this charge, as well as those like Lacan who, rather than seeking to install the normalized ego of psychology and/or American psychoanalysis,[45] search "for something that exists with the mute solidity of a thing," a clear echo of Lacan's emphasis on *das Ding* in the seminar on the *Antigone* (Foucault 1966: 372, 385–86; Lane 2000: 344; Dean 2003: 238, 244).

Indeed, the task Foucault set for himself in *Les mots et les choses* was in many ways quite Lacanian. It was nothing less than to uncover the "positive unconscious of knowledge" (Foucault 1970: xi; Bannet: 1989: 157; Lane 2000: 316; Shepherdson 2003: 150 n.13). By the same token, in *L'archéologie du savoir*, Foucault explicitly compared his project to similar modes of inquiry in contemporary psychoanalysis. Its role was not to "dissipate oblivion," nor to reconstruct the primal scene of history, but "to make differences," to open a space for new "countermemories" and new practices (Foucault 1969: 268–70). Thus, Charles Shepherdson summarizes the relationship between the two thinkers in his aptly titled "History and the Real: Foucault with Lacan" as follows:

> In short, unlike the "new historicism" with which Foucault is so often confused, genealogy is not *an elaboration of knowledge* that admits to having a perspective, in the sense that it may one day prove to be inadequate, or to be only one point of view, but rather *an act* that bears on the present, on what Lacan calls the position of enunciation. The same holds for psychoanalysis: its aim is not to uncover the truth about the past, contrary to many commentators; it does not seek to discover "what really happened," as if a realist view of the past could address the questions proper to psychoanalysis. On the contrary, it is directed at what Lacan calls imaginary and symbolic elements, at the narrative which, however

---

just how 'plastic' and variable in its choice of objects libido really is, how so-called sexual perversion forms part of what passes as normal sexuality, and how heterosexuality is by no means natural or self-evident."

45. On Lacan's opposition to the normalizing protocols of American ego psychology (to which Foucault also alludes) and to the hegemony of those protocols in the IPA, headed by Anna Freud, from which Lacan was expelled, see Lacan (1973: 143); Julien (1990: 14–15); Malone (2000); Gherovici (2000: 97); Liu (2000: 129–30). On psychoanalysis's opposition to biopower (Copjec 2002: 29–30).

One of the difficulties in judging Foucault's attitudes toward psychoanalysis is determining to which form he is referring in a given statement. While his attitudes to psychoanalysis as a whole seem to have fluctuated (see 19941: 683, where he treats psychoanalysis as an instance of "pouvoir médical" ["medical power"]), he always treated Lacan with respect and considered him a worthy interlocutor.

real or fabricated, has brought the client into analysis. (1995: ¶ 51; emphasis in original)

Far, then, from being fundamentally opposed, Foucault and Lacan, by Foucault's own explicit admissions, are in many ways involved in what can be conceived of as complementary, or at least certainly not mutually exclusive, projects.

Foucault's opinion of Lacan did not change radically over time. In an interview given on the occasion of Lacan's death in 1981, he declared that the latter "searched in psychoanalysis not for a procedure to normalize behaviors, but for a theory of the subject" (1994e: 204). More importantly, for our purposes, in the middle of his 1982 course at the Collège de France, after his extensive reading of the *Alcibiades,* one of the auditors posed the question of whether in fact the logical operators in Foucault's discourse were not essentially Lacanian. Foucault responded by noting that whether the categories of his discourse were in essence Lacanian was more for the audience than for him to judge, but nonetheless he would say this much, that there were only two thinkers in the twentieth century who had posed the question that ultimately interested him in his reading of Plato and the Stoics—i.e., what is the relationship of the subject to truth? And what is the cost and nature of that relationship? They were "Heidegger and Lacan." Thus, any reader of Foucault's late ethics who does not see this work as in important ways a response to Lacan's own efforts in this same field, is not only misjudging the nature of Foucault's relation with Lacan throughout his career, but also ignoring the former's direct acknowledgment of a profound affiliation (Foucault 2001: 180–82; Castel-Bouchouchi 2003: 188–89).

The relationship was mutual. Lacan himself recognized the importance of Stoic ethics and saw them as anticipating those he sought to outline for psychoanalysis (1973: 283).[46] He also repaid Foucault's interest in his teaching with a lively admiration for the latter's work (Lacan 1966e; Julien 1990: 13n.3; Eribon 1994: 251–54). He was particularly appreciative of the importance Foucault had accorded his "return to Freud" in the philosopher's 1969 lecture, "Qu'est-ce qu'un auteur," and he evoked Foucault several times in his seminar of that same year. Often these evocations came in the context of recalling his seminar a decade earlier on the *Ethics of Psychoanalysis,* which not only included his

---

46. Deleuze in *Logique du sens* had also offered a rapprochement between Stoicism and psychoanalysis (1969: 245–52; Benatouïl 2003: 23).

reading of the *Antigone,* but also laid the intellectual groundwork for the following year's interpretation of the *Symposium* (Rabaté 2003a: 7–8; Foucault 1994m).

Nonetheless, as should hardly be surprising in the case of two such original thinkers, there were substantial differences between them, and their mutual regard did not entail a homogeneity of views. Indeed, one common reading of the *History of Sexuality* is as a critical genealogy of psychoanalysis. The three volumes together and the accompanying lectures at the Collège de France pose in part the following question: what are the structures of discourse, of subjectivity, and of the self's relation to truth that make the talking cure possible (Eribon 1994: 255; Dean 2003: 241–42). Foucault saw in the Christian practice of confession—in its positing of the subject's identity as a hidden truth that must be ferreted out from within, and exposed by and to the confessor—a set of structures and assumptions that laid the foundation for the psychoanalytic clinic.[47] To establish the historically variable, and hence contingent, nature of these structures, in turn, required an investigation of the alternative modes of self-relation found in the Stoic and Platonic philosophy that had preceded Christianity (Foucault 2001: 170–71, 208; 1994f: 364; Benatouïl 2003: 29; Gros 2003: 12; Sennellart 2003: 157). Such a reading of psychoanalysis as a historically contingent structure also required Foucault to elaborate a way of thinking about the history of sexuality that did not rely, at least implicitly, on a Freudian model (Foucault 1994c: 610; 1994i: 215; Butler 1990: 72–73; Jameson 1991: 12; Black 1998).

If we examine the *History of Sexuality,* there are numerous echoes between Foucault's and Lacan's texts. Two brief examples will illustrate the phenomenon. First, in the opening pages of the seminar on the *Antigone,* Lacan anticipates Foucault's arguments in volume 1 of the *History of Sexuality* when he contends that "genitality" is an ideological construction, not a biological reality, and that psychoanalysis, in striving to produce a *scientia sexualis,* has neglected the establishment of an *ars erotica* (Lacan 1986: 17–19, 182; see also 1973: 213; Foucault 1976: 71–98, 204–5). Second, in the seminar on the *Symposium,* we find a discussion of how the ethics of pederasty differed from one community to the next in ancient Greece, immediately followed by a comparison of the *erômenos* to the beloved in the medieval courtly

---

47. For the controversy on the extent to which Foucault saw psychoanalysis as an instrument of disciplinary power, and on the degree to which he overestimates the kinship between the confessional and the analytic couch, see Leonard (2005: 88) and Armstrong (2005: 130–31, 184).

tradition.[48] Both ideas are closely paralleled by a series of passages in Foucault's *L'usage des plaisirs* (Lacan 1991: 42; Foucault 1984a: 211–12, 216–17, 235–36). In fact, a number of the concepts that Foucault would later develop in more detail and from the standpoint of a different philosophical agenda can already be found in embryonic form in the seminars of Lacan. Thus Foucault's assertion of the relative insignificance of the gender of one's sexual object choice in ancient concepts of eros is anticipated by Lacan's comment that the ancients concentrated on the drive itself (Eros, Amor) rather than the traits of the object (Lacan 1986: 117).

Most important from our perspective, however, is that Foucault chooses to close volume 2 of the *History* with his own extended reading of the *Symposium*. Where Lacan focuses on transference, the problematics of desire, and the nature of erotic substitution, Foucault argues that the Platonic text represents a historical mutation in the development of Greek pederastic discourse, wherein the seeker of truth is described as the *erastês* and the role of the *erômenos* disappears (Foucault 1984a: 266; Carnes 1998: 110; Nicholson 1998: 26–28). In its place, a regime of erotic symmetry is instituted based on a new discourse concerning the ontology of love, as opposed to the more traditional debates on the proprieties of the pederastic relationship that focused on questions such as to whom, how often, and under what circumstances a boy should grant his favors to a suitor (Foucault 1984a: 259–64). What Socrates introduces is not the figure of the desire of the analyst but that of the master of truth who reduces others to amorous slavery in their pursuit of wisdom and who wins this position through the power that he exercises over himself as demonstrated in his relation to Alcibiades (Foucault 1984a: 265). Foucault's reading of the *Symposium* thus differs from Lacan's in two crucial fashions. First, Foucault historicizes Lacan's reading by recontextualizing the *Symposium* within the larger discourse of pederasty in classical Greece. Second, the gesture of historicization renders impossible any easy identification with the figure of Socrates. Hence, while for Lacan Socrates serves as a precursor for the psychoanalyst, Foucault himself explicitly rejects both the role of *maître de la vérité* and the very notion that the fundamental structures of the subject's relation to desire can be translated directly from antiquity to the present (Stoekl 1992: 197; Poster 1989: 34–52; Macey 1993: 458, 468).

The Lacanian response as given by Žižek is telling on both counts.

---

48. Both seem to derive from a passage in Robin (1929: xlv).

Žižek argues that Lacan's and Foucault's visions of the subject are not as mutually exclusive as they appear. Each of them sees subjectivity as a construction undertaken outside the guarantees offered by a universal reason, that is, in the realm of history and practice. Yet there remains a central difference. The late Foucault wants to reserve the possibility that, through a contemporary reconstitution of a culture of the self, there could be a successful subjectivation, i.e., "the formation of the self qua esthetic whole." It is this theoretical possibility of absolute self-coincidence or self-harmony that constitutes for Foucault the utopian ideal of ancient *parrhêsia* or truth telling as a philosophical practice governing the relations between master and disciple.

> I speak the truth, I speak the truth to you. And that which authenticates the fact that I speak the truth to you is that effectively I am, as subject of my conduct, absolutely, integrally, and totally identical with the subject of the enunciation that I am when I say to you that which I say to you. (Foucault 2001: 389, see also 132 and 305)

For Lacan, however, the project of constituting a self-consistent, coherent subject is an impossible dream (Žižek 1992: 183–84).

The necessary failure of such a project, from the Lacanian perspective, is predicated precisely upon a differing view of the relation between sex and sexuality, as they are historically constituted, from that found in Foucault. For as Foucault famously argues at the end of volume 1 of the *History of Sexuality,* sex itself is a discursive construction that groups together a disparate group of practices, sensations, and organs. Its origins can be traced in the scientific and medical literature to the end of the seventeenth century. Sexuality in turn is a secondary formation that seeks to found an individual identity (normal, perverse, heterosexual, homosexual, transvestite, pedophile, fetishist, etc.) on this initial factitious heterogeneity (Foucault 1976: 204–8). For Lacan, however, sex never was a unity or the ground of an identity, but precisely the point at which all such constructions failed. It named not a neutral positivity, nor a contingent construction, but the historically variable, yet never escapable limit of identity constructions, the traumatic cut or core from which, as Aristophanes in the *Symposium* saw, desire emerges (Žižek 1992: 123–24; Rabinovich 2003: 208).[49]

---

49. Moreover, as Laurent Jaffro argues, it is precisely in an effort to construct a theory of self-formation, i.e., an ethics, that is not in the last instance founded on the self's necessary alienation or division from itself, that Foucault downplays the role of rhetorical manipulation in ancient Stoicism, as opposed to the frankness of *parrhêsia*. His emphasis

The ultimate difference between Foucault and Lacan, then, is not, as often charged, that psychoanalysis accepts the repressive hypothesis, and Foucault rejects it. For Lacan never posits the unconscious as an inner realm of instinct that needs to find expression, nor does he accept the possibility of liberation from oppression through the production of a "more open and honest discourse about sexuality" (Lacan 1973; 142, 167; Žižek in Hanlon 2001: 5). When Foucault sets his sights on the repressive hypothesis, it is the ideology of Marcuse, Reich, sixties free love, and Dr. Ruth that he has in mind (Foucault 1976: 25–67; Lane 2000: 320–21; Butler 1990: 72; Eribon 1994: 256–57; Nehamas 1998: 174; Armstrong 2005: 269). For Foucault and Lacan both, law and desire are not opposed to, but consubstantial with, one another (Foucault 1976: 108). There is no desire per se before the institutions that seek to regulate and limit it, and yet bid us to speak, confess, and shape it (Dean 2003: 241). Nor is the ultimate difference, as is sometimes alleged, that Lacan and psychoanalysis[50] are homophobic, while Foucault's call for an emphasis on "bodies and pleasures" is the basis for modern queer theory (Foucault 1976: 211; Dean 2003: 241; Feher-Gurewich 2003: 203–4). Lacan rejected all attempts to "normalize" or "cure" homosexuals in his clinical practice and had strong words for those who brought homosexuals to psychoanalysts "for their own good" (Lacan 1991: 75; Roudinesco 1997: 224; Liu 2000: 128). As early as 1938, he had rejected any notion of a "natural family" (Luepnitiz 2003: 223), and his later dictum that "there is no sexual relation" explicitly rejects the notion of heteronormative complementarity (Dean 2003: 243–44). Finally, as Roudinesco notes, Lacan's use

---

on the absolute self-transparency of the discourse of *parrhêsia*, as opposed to the opacity of rhetorical trickery, allows him to diminish the degree to which Stoic conversion involves a necessary rupture of, or violence to, the self, in order to then (re)form the self so as to maintain a new harmonious relation to the truth (2003: 64–68). Even here, one must beware of overstatement and a lack of nuance. Foucault elsewhere readily admits that there are fundamental ambiguities within Hellenistic and Roman thought concerning the self, including whether the self is a plenitude that is recovered through systematic practice, or an object that is laboriously constructed and thus never given wholly in advance, and consequently never completely coincident with its own history (2001: 205). Nonetheless, Laurand has observed that Foucault seems deliberately to avoid any discussion of *pothos* or "desire" in the Stoic Musonius Rufus' writings on marriage (2003: 97–99).

50. Freud of course does regard homosexuality as a perversion, but in that sense he does not see it as different from any other formalized sexual practice, including heterosexuality (Feher-Gurewich 2003: 191–92; Gherovici 2000: 363; Copjec 1994: 109–11). Freud chastised Ernest Jones for trying to exclude known homosexuals from becoming practicing analysts (Luepnitz 2003: 234). Lacan's concept of perversion is to this extent strictly Freudian (Leonard 2005: 174–75). He did, however, criticize Freud's reading of paranoia as a defense against homosexuality (Roudinesco 1997: 288).

of the Socratic model of transference as presented in his reading of the *Symposium* was a direct challenge to the psychoanalytic establishment, which by and large in the late fifties and early sixties continued to reject homosexual candidates who wanted to become training analysts (1997: 254).⁵¹

The true difference between Lacan and Foucault concerns the way in which they view the relationship of power to the law. Foucault charges that Lacanian psychoanalysis still sees power as essentially negative and limiting—that is to say, as a kind of legal stricture—whereas he is elaborating a model of power that sees it as essentially positive and productive (Foucault 1976: 109–14; Dean 2003: 242; Eribon 1994: 258; Butler 1990: 72–73). I have written extensively elsewhere about Foucault's exclusion of the negative, his attempt to elaborate a purely positive model of history, and the difficulties this implies for any concept of historical change, and the contrast between it and a Lacanian historicism of the Real. Thus there is no need to recapitulate those arguments in detail here (P. A. Miller 1998; 2004: chap. 1).⁵² What we do need to realize, however, is that positivity and negativity are themselves relative terms that ultimately cannot avoid implying a dialectical relation. A positive production is always also a determination and hence a negation. A given regime of power relations necessarily produces A rather than B. Thus the distinction Foucault draws between positive productive power and the negative law is one that is hard to maintain with absolute logical rigor (Žižek 1993: 22–24, 98, 109, 122–24, 263; Derrida 1967a 380; Stoekl 1992: 180–82; Copjec 2002: 94–96).

Nonetheless, as we argued in chapter 1, while Lacan's concept of the Real, in its function as the negation of the Symbolic, makes historical explanation possible, he himself often fails to deal fully with the

51. It is true that at one point Lacan calls the *Symposium* a reunion of old "fags" and "queens," but he is there speaking explicitly from the perspective of a Greek peasant (1991: 54). This is not to say there is nothing to object to in Lacan's treatment of same-sex attraction, but these are by and large not objections Foucault would have made. There is, for one thing, no explicit theorization of homoeroticism per se in Lacan (Restuccia 2000: 359). The centrality of the phallus to Lacanian thought also makes the articulation of a truly female homosexuality difficult (Blévis 2000; Pommier 2000: 83). Lastly, many practicing Lacanian analysts are a good deal less open to the radical implications of Lacan than was the master himself (Feher-Gurewich 2000: 376). As Leonard notes, Lacan's treatment of ancient pederasty still seems to take place within what are predominantly heterosexist categories (Leonard 2005: 173–76). Yet in late fifties France, it would be hard to find any major intellectual figure of Lacan's generation who did not assume, at least implicitly, a heterosexist norm, even if they were not personally and politically actively homophobic. This certainly would include Lacan's contemporary, Sartre.

52. See also our discussion of History, historicism, and the Real in chapter 1 of the present volume.

concrete historicity of the texts he examines (Butler 1990: 29, 55, 76; Irigaray 1977b: 97). Thus, even though he makes it clear that the Symbolic and the subject's insertion into it are open to historical modification,[53] he does not speak in requisite detail of how that modification happens and the nature of its consequences. One result of this failure is that Lacan's description of the Symbolic, particularly in relation to gender, can appear to be a prescription (Ragland-Sullivan 1986: 277). This is the gist of Luce Irigaray's feminist critique of her former teacher: not that his description of Woman's exclusion from the Symbolic, as constituted by patriarchal reason, is inaccurate, but rather that his failure to posit an alternative to this situation implies that it is unalterable and perhaps even desirable (Irigaray 1977b: 92, 99; 1977c: 205; Weed 1994: 87, 99, 100–102). Lacan, then, may make historicization possible, as Jameson recognized, but he does not himself fully historicize. Foucault, on the other hand, does historicize, but his refusal of any explicit conception of historical negation in favor of a purely positive analytics of power is not only impossible to maintain strictly, but, were it possible, would render the historical succession of different Symbolic regimes or "*dipositifs*" logically inexplicable. But this, as just noted, is ground we have already covered.

What is more important for the present inquiry is to recognize the urgency Foucault felt to elaborate a theory of power that could be conceived as a positivity and hence would imply the necessity of resistance in its very foundation (Foucault 1976: 121–35; Halperin 1995: 59–60; Rouse 1994: 108–9). The conception of power as a series of differentials in positive force always demands that the resistance to power be conceived as immanent to the very nature of the differential that articulates it. Negation, however, at least from the point of view of practice, does not require us to imagine power as this ever shifting field of countervailing forces that constantly contains the potential of its own tactical rearticulation as an ontological given (Bannet 1989: 94). Negation figures itself as a pure gap (*not A*).

Foucault, in fact, recognized only too well the omnipresence of the law. In the 1960s he argued that the law is the outside or limit that envelops all behaviors and empties them of interior determination. At that time, he saw literature as a way to make the law visible and thus as a means of being able to posit an outside or *dehors* to its reign (Foucault 1986: 33–34; Lane 2000: 334). By the eighties, he had come to

---

53. See Lacan (1986: 118–19); Ragland-Sullivan (1986: 299–300, 305); Jameson (1981: 153); Žižek in Hanlon (2001: 12).

see the law as only one mode of power in a vast productive system, which creates the fabric of its resistance in the very moment that a given regime of power relations comes into being (2001: 109). The outside, to the extent that it still existed, became visible precisely in the genealogical analysis of the difference between various systems of power, and the forms of self-relation and subjectivation they made possible (1994h: 721; 2001: 303). Lacan's fault ultimately, from a Foucauldian point of view, was to fail to account precisely for these changing positive regimes of self-relation and power, and by focusing on the negative, to assume an identity of structure, if not content, from one regime to the next.[54] It is in this context that Foucault's reading of the *Alcibiades* looms large.

2. Ethics, Politics, and the Care of the Self

> "You handle the people's business?" Picture the bearded master,
> whom a grim dose of hemlock carried off, saying these things.
> "With what qualification? Speak up then, ward of great Pericles."[55]
> (Persius 4.1–3)

In the last two volumes of the *History of Sexuality* and in his lectures at the Collège de France from the same period, Foucault sought to elaborate an ethics founded not on the juridical, authoritarian, or disciplinary structures of modernity but on what he refers to as an "art" or "stylization" of existence (J. Miller 1993: 322–23, 340, 346–47; Larmour et al. 1998b: 22–33; Vizier 1998: 67–68, 71).[56] In particular, Foucault saw in the work of such philosophers as Seneca, Epictetus, and Plutarch a turn to the self that, through various practices of examination and study, sought to fashion a beautiful existence in which the subject attained perfect mastery over itself (Foucault 1994f: 356)[57]:

   54. Thus Lacan in his reading of pederasty in the *Symposium* asserts that the only thing that separates its ancient from its modern practice is that modern boys have bad skin and lack culture. "C'est toute la différence. Mais la structure, elle, n'est en rien à distinguer" (1991: 43). No one who has read the *History of Sexuality* could accept the truth of this statement. For Foucault's attempt to historicize the death drive, see Dean (2003: 250–51).
   55. The bearded master (*magister*) is Socrates, and the ward of Pericles is Alcibiades.
   56. On the relation between Foucault's late ethical thought and Anglo-American "virtue ethics," see Levy (2004), who fails to emphasize sufficiently the importance of aesthetics in the final Foucault, but nonetheless notes some important points of meeting between these two bodies of thought.
   57. On the convergence of the various philosophical schools of the imperial period in their focus on philosophy as an *askesis,* or technology of the self, see Davidson (1995:

> In the philosophical tradition inaugurated by Stoicism, *askesis,* far from denoting self-abnegation, implies the progressive consideration of the self, the mastery of the self—a mastery one attains not by renouncing reality, but by acquiring and assimilating the truth. The ultimate goal of the *askesis* is not to prepare the individual for another reality, but to permit him to accede to the reality of this world. In Greek, the word that describes this attitude is *paraskeuazô* ("to prepare oneself"). The *askesis* is a set of practices by means of which the individual is able to acquire, to assimilate the truth, and to transform it into a permanent principle of action. *Alétheia* becomes *êthos*. It is a process of intensifying subjectivity. (Foucault 1994g: 800)

Stoic *askesis*—as opposed to later Christian practice, which borrows many of the same techniques of self-surveillance—is not designed to root out hidden desires, nor to decipher the reality of who we are beneath appearances, but as a device to mold behavior. This self-surveillance is less disciplinary, in the sense of being designed to make the individual conform to a single pre-established end, than shaping. It is a technology of the self that seeks to allow the subject to attain mastery over its thoughts, feelings and reactions to external events (Foucault 1994c: 610, 615, 626–27; 1994f: 359, 364–65; P. A. Miller 1998: 184–88). Stoic *askesis,* as such, conforms to Foucault's definition of ethics as the "mindful practice of freedom" (1994h: 711–12). It is less a purely cognitive activity than a practice, or in the words of Pierre Hadot, a "spiritual exercise" (1987: 15–16; 1995: 82–83).[58]

The course Foucault offered in 1982 on the *Alcibiades* and the care of the self in many ways takes up where the *History of Sexuality* leaves off. It was originally conceived of as the draft of a book that was projected to accompany the final three volumes of the *History* (Gros 2001: 489, 496–97). Unfortunately, Foucault died before he could bring this project to fruition and before he could publish the final volume of the *History of Sexuality,* on early Christian practices.

Volumes 2 and 3 of the *History of Sexuality* famously have very

---

30–31) and Hadot (1987: 206; 1995a: 59). Hadot 1995a is a revised English translation of Hadot 1987. The revisions, however, are in some cases quite extensive and the reader is advised to consult both texts.

58. On Hadot's importance to Foucault's project, see Davidson (1994: 121–23; 1995: 1). On Hadot's subsequent criticism of Foucault's reading of the Stoics as too narrowly focused, see Davidson (1995: 24–25) and Hadot (1987: 229–33; 1995a: 206–13). For a good in-depth discussion of the practice of Stoic *meditatio,* see Newman (1989).

little actual sex in them[59] (Macey 1993: 358; Edwards 1993: 75). It was not Foucault's intention "to reconstitute the history of sexual comportments" (Foucault 1994b: 578). By the time these volumes were published, his concerns had shifted from the thesis announced in volume 1, that sexuality was the product of a certain practico-discursive *dispositif*[60] established at the end of the seventeenth and beginning of the eighteenth century, to how the subject constitutes itself in relation to itself, i.e., as an ethical subject (Davidson 1994: 117–18; Elden 2005). Sexual practices and desire would be central to any such account, but only insofar as they contributed to the larger project. As Foucault himself observed, his goal was to "study the game of truth implicated in the relation of the self to the self and in the constitution of itself as subject, in taking as [his] domain of reference and field of investigation what we might call the 'history of the desiring man'" (1984a: 12). The revised *History of Sexuality* was to be a "history of self-reflection, -knowledge, -examination, and -interpretation" conceived as the means or the technologies for constituting the self as the subject of its own formation (1984a: 35–36). Volumes 2 and 3 of the *History of Sexuality* were, in fact, far more the first installments in a new history of the subject, than they were a mere modification of the program announced in *La volonté de savoir* (Kremer-Marietti 1985: 251–52).

It was this study of different forms of the subject's relation to itself that led Foucault to his final turn to the ancient world far more than an interest in pederasty or other sexual practices per se (Jaffro 2003: 78; Gros 2001: 511). Antiquity served as the ground for a fundamentally new conception of the self as the subject of ethical action (Foucault 1994h: 711–12). It was through the historicization of the subject, not simply as the object of knowledge in the mode of the human sciences or as a responsible agent in the Sartrean mode, but as a historically specific form of self-relation that Foucault came to be able to "think differently" about the subject and the possibility of effective ethical action

---

59. And what there is is mostly male. The Greek texts themselves say relatively little about women and Foucault readily acknowledges their oppression (1994c: 612).

60. "The actual term dispositif [. . .] is borrowed from Gaston Bachelard, who employed it to counter the reigning philosophy of phenomenology. Bachelard proposed instead the study of 'phenomeno-*technology*,' believing that phenomena are not given to us directly by an independent reality but are rather constructed (cf. Greek *technê*, 'produced by a regular method of making rather than found in nature') by a range of practices and techniques that define historical truth" (Copjec 1994: 20). On the specifics of Foucault's use of the term see Macey (1993: 355); Dreyfus and Rabinow (1982: 121); and Elden forthcoming.

(Foucault 1984a: 14; 1994c: 617; Kremer-Marietti 1985: 277–78). On the philosophical, moral, and political levels, the encounter with antiquity in general, and the concept of the self's relation to itself as defined in the *Alcibiades* in particular, offered the possibility of what only literature had promised in the 1960s, "une pensée du dehors"[61]:

> So long as Foucault confined himself to the study of the eighteenth and nineteenth centuries, the subject, as if by a natural path, found itself reflected as the objective product of systems of knowledge and power, the alienated corollary of these *dispositifs* of power/knowledge in which the individual sought and exhausted an imposed exterior identity, outside of which there was no salvation save madness, crime or literature. Beginning in the eighties, while studying the techniques of existence promoted in Greco-Roman antiquity, Foucault allows us to see another image of the subject, which is no longer constituted but self-constituting through regulated practices. The study of the modern west had hidden from him for a long time the existence of these techniques, hidden as they were in the archive by systems of knowledge and *dispositifs* of power. (Gros 2001: 494–95)

Foucault thus came to see his work in the eighties as a series of studies on the "arts of the self," that is to say, on both "the aesthetics of existence and the government of the self and others" (1994d: 415). In doing so he returned to the Nietzschean roots of his philosophy and ultimately to Nietzsche's roots in ancient philology (Nehamas 1998: 142; Foucault 1994j: 703–4; Benatouïl 2003: 32–33). Life itself could become an aesthetic object, and ethics the means and name of this project (1994c: 617).

The purpose of this stylization of existence was not self-absorption, but to offer new means of resistance to the normalizing structures of the market, scientific and social institutions, and the state (Žižek 1992: 180–81; Gros 2001: 524–25). To know oneself, the injunction of the Delphic oracle, had, under the conditions of modern society, become a means of discipline, adaptation, and control rather than freedom. Self-knowledge had become the internalization of the modern means of observation and control, which Foucault had evoked emblematically in the image of Bentham's Panopticon in *Surveiller et punir* (1975: 228–64):

---

61. See chapter 1.

Subjects don't consume enough anymore: they're depressed. Subjects don't vote anymore: they lack confidence. Subjects destroy property and steal: they lack a strong paternal role model. Every social problem today is cast in terms of the psychology of the subject. Every problem, no matter how small, ought still to find its resolution in a knowledge of this same psychological subject. Every good psychology is in addition without qualification a psychology of the good consumer, the good worker and the good citizen. . . . The specialists of self-knowledge teach us once more how to work, to buy, and to vote. (Gros 2003: 12; compare Shepherdson 1995: ¶ 29)

Foucault, as we have seen, thus rejoins Lacan, who in his own version of ethics as aesthetics also explicitly used the turn to antiquity to construct a model of resistance to the normalizing and adaptive structures of modern ego/industrial psychology, whose motto he sums up in the phrase, "Continuons à travailler, et pour le désir, vous repasserez" ("Back to work, and as for desire, better luck next time!") (1986: 367).[62] It is small wonder that Foucault mentions Lacan approvingly at the beginning of his reading of the *Alcibiades* as the first since Freud to have sought to "recenter" psychoanalysis on the relation between the subject and truth (2001: 31–32). An ethics and aesthetics of existence, founded on the history of subjectivation, thus becomes a means of resistance to the commodified and normalized subject of capitalist modernity, *une pensée du dehors* (Davila 2003: 207).[63]

We see, then, that Foucault's turn to the self is hardly a matter of narcissism, but just the opposite. It is the recognition that all forms of governmentality—i.e., the reversible field of power relations that founds both the state and the subject—must pass through a defined form of self-relation:

> If we take the question of power, of political power, and place it under the larger question of governmentality—governmentality understood as a strategic field of relations of power, in the largest sense of the term and not simply political power—then, if we understand by governmentality a strategic field of relations of power, insofar as they are mobile, transformable, reversible, I believe that reflection on this notion of governmentality cannot not

---

62. I owe this translation to Pierre Zoberman. See also Žižek (1989: 117).
63. On the relation between disciplinary practices and capital, see Foucault (1994g: 785; 1994k: 466–70); Dreyfus and Rabinow (1982: 135); and Sakolsky (1992).

pass through, both theoretically and practically, the element of a subject that would be defined by its self-relation. While political theory as an institution ordinarily is based on a juridical concept of the legal subject, it seems to me that the analysis of governmentality ought to be based on an ethic of the subject defined by the relation of the self to the self. This means that [. . .] relations of power—governmentality—government of self and others—self-relation, all this constitutes a chain, a network, and it is there, around these notions, that we ought to be able, I think, to articulate the question of politics and the question of ethics. (Foucault 2001: 241–42)

The study of ethics and the history of the self's self-relation is an "urgent task" that is "fundamental" and "politically indispensable," therefore, inasmuch as the self's relation to itself is "the first and last" point "of the resistance to political power" (Foucault 2001: 241). In this way, through a critical genealogy of the self, new forms of self-relation may be created, new relations of power, and new possibilities of resistance (Foucault 1994c: 612; 1994h: 711; Sawicki 1994: 294). Consequently, Foucault's reading of the *Alcibiades* and its relation to later Greco-Roman philosophy was not only part of his continuing dialogue with the most important thinkers of his day (Deleuze, Lacan, and Derrida), but was also a matter of immediate political and cultural actuality, as testified to by the hundreds of auditors who crowded into the halls of the Collège de France to hear him lecture on Plato, Seneca, and Marcus Aurelius (Gros 2001: 502–3).

What Foucault offered them was not a history of ideas or philosophy, but a critical genealogy of the subject. For his argument is that conventional intellectual histories fail to recognize that the ancient axes of self-knowledge and self-constitution differ fundamentally from those found in the modern world. For where modern philosophy and the human sciences have fixated on the Delphic oracle's injunction "to know thyself" and have seen the care of the self as a secondary matter of disciplining the self in accord with that knowledge and the law—the self being taken as an object of positive knowledge—in ancient philosophy this order was precisely reversed (2001: 442–43). The care of the self was the practice necessary for knowledge of the self to be produced; it was the means of the subject's access to a truth inseparable from the ethical work necessary for its production. Thus in the *Alcibiades*, once Socrates, through the practice of the *elenchus*, has elicited the admission from Alcibiades that he neither knows that on which he presumes to advise the Athenian assembly, nor in the final analysis what he himself is saying, the conversation then turns not to what a positive knowledge of either one of these phenomena might be, but to what it might mean to care for oneself and what is the nature of the self (127d6–128a3).

> Schematically, let us say the following: where we moderns understand the question [of self-knowledge as] "the possible or impossible objectification of the subject in a field of empirical knowledge," the Ancients of the Greek, Hellenistic and Roman period understood: "the constitution of a knowledge about the world as the spiritual experience of the subject." And where we moderns understand "the subjection of the subject to the order of the law," the Greeks and the Romans understood "the constitution of the subject as an end for himself, through and by the exercise of truth." There is here a fundamental heterogeneity that ought to warn against all retrospective projection. (Foucault 2001: 304–5)

It is precisely this spiritual dimension—defined as the practico-discursive regime of self-transformation that makes possible access to the truth—that is, according to Foucault, neglected in most modern treatments of ancient philosophy. That neglect, in turn, creates distortions as concepts are abstracted from the practical contexts in which they were deployed (Foucault 2001: 16–17; Hadot 1995b: 21–22, 412). In the process, those same concepts are robbed of their ability to posit an outside to modern regimes of power and subjectivation, to "make differences."

A critical history of thought, in contrast, implies an analysis of the historical conditions according to which discrete "relations to truth, to rule and to self were constituted" as "singularities" transformable though the "work of thought on itself" (1994b: 580). By examining the knowledge of the self within different regimes of caring for the self, Foucault claims that one comes to see that self-knowledge has meant different things under different regimes of self-formation. In fact, one must address the different forms of caring for the self to understand the different forms of self-constitution that are to be known (Foucault 2001: 443–44). Foucault's critical genealogy of the subject aims at nothing less than the reconstitution of a lost body of knowledge that had been obscured by the triumph of the punctual subject of post-Cartesian thought: the normative subject of classical economics, game theory, and the social sciences (Foucault 2001: 13–15).

3. Reading the *Alcibiades*

> Socrates: Was the person who put up the injunction on the temple at Delphi a fool, and knowing oneself is an easy thing, or is it difficult and not for everyone?
>
> Alcibiades: Often it has seemed to me to be for everyone, and often very difficult.
>
> Socrates: But, Alcibiades, whether it is easy or not, all the same, the situation for us is as follows: when we know what that thing is, then we should know how to care for ourselves, but not knowing it, we should never know how. (*Alcibiades* 129a2–9)

The passage just cited poses the question of the relation of the care of the self to self-knowledge with particular acuity. On the one hand, it seems to contradict Foucault. It claims that the condition of possibility for the self to care for itself is knowing the self. On the other, it makes it quite clear that the self as conceived here is not the pure consciousness, the punctual self of Cartesian and post-Cartesian thought. It is a self the knowledge of which is not available to all and is difficult to attain.[64] That knowledge, as the remainder of the dialogue makes clear, can only be attained through a deliberate effort of reflection, of self-examination, and of labor by and on the self undertaken with an interlocutor, a master, and/or lover in dialogue with whom one's soul becomes visible to oneself. The knowledge of oneself that permits one properly to care for oneself is therefore dependent upon a kind of spiritual practice or care that makes that knowledge possible. This knowledge and care, in turn, as the frame of the *Alcibiades* makes clear, is the predicate for any reasoned and constructive engagement with the political institutions of the democratic *polis*, to the extent that such an engagement is achievable at all. The seduction of the unreflective exercise of power over oneself and others, however, as both the conclusion of this dialogue and of the *Symposium* makes clear, remains ever alluring. The unrefracted love of the approbation of the *polis* leads one to become a slave to its changing whims, a flatterer to its vanities, and a traitor to oneself (Foucault 1994h: 712–16; *Gorgias* 500e–501c, 502d–503b, 521a–522a; *Theaetetus* 175e).

---

64. As Charles Platter points out to me (*per litteras*), the attribution of self-knowledge to the Delphic oracle is made doubly problematic by *Phaedrus* 244a9–b6, where Socrates notes that it is only reliable when the priestess is mad (*maineisai*). Of course, love and poetry are themselves later termed forms of madness in this same dialogue, and philosophy too, since it is the highest form of love (245a, 246e6, 249d4–e4, 250b7, 252e). This obviously renders problematic any notion of philosophy as the triumph of a disembodied reason.

The *Alcibiades* for Foucault provides the first and most comprehensive account of this complex relationship between the knowledge and the care of the self, a relationship that is less a vicious circle than a mutually enriching and co-constituting dialectic in both the Platonic and the Hegelian senses of that term (Foucault 2001: 46). The dialogue is the starting point for his history of the "care of the self" as a self-conscious practice. That practice in turn is understood to constitute a crucial nexus for both "a history of subjectivity and an analysis of the forms of governmentality" (1994i: 213–14). Consequently, this dialogue, regardless of its actual provenance, represents the emergence of an "event" in thought. It represents the theorization of a form of self-relation that for the first time explicitly problematizes the nature of the subject (Foucault 2001: 11, 242, 247). The soul or psyche was no longer a shadowy substance that was evacuated from the body at death, as it was in archaic poetry, but had now become a self-consciously theorized vehicle for, and a repository of, truth (Davidson 1994: 126; Havelock 1963: 198–200; Snell 1953: ix, 5–20).

As the *Alcibiades* makes clear, the care of the self requires a conversion of one's gaze from the world of externals to the self and a meditation on its nature. In fact, it requires nothing less than the constitution of subjective interiority as a form of practice (Foucault 2001: 12). This practice, in turn, requires the isolation of what constitutes the self in itself. Thus, in the passage immediately following the one cited at the beginning of this section, Socrates continues:

> Socrates: Come then, in what manner would this very thing itself [*auto to auto*] be found? For in this manner we would quickly find what we ourselves [*autoi*] are, but if we remain in ignorance, then we would be unable [to discover this]. (129b1–3)

As Foucault notes, on one level, Socrates' question is purely methodological and formal, but on another it is the telos toward which the whole dialogue has been moving and explains why the *Alcibiades* occupies the crucial place Foucault assigns it in his genealogy of the modern subject. Socrates does not ask Alcibiades, "what sort of animal are you, what is your nature, how are you composed," but "what is this relationship that is designated by the reflexive pronoun *heauton*, what is this element which is the same on the side both of the subject and the object" (Foucault 2001: 52).

The answer to Socrates' question, while definitively offered only after another considerable passage of dialectical exchange, is implicit in what immediately follows:

Socrates: With what are you now in conversation (*dialegêi*)? Is it anything other than me?
Alcibiades: You're right.
Socrates: And I with you?
Alcibiades: Right.
Socrates: Is Socrates in conversation?
Alcibiades: Absolutely.
Socrates: And Alcibiades listening?
Alcibiades: Yes.
Socrates: And so does Socrates engage in conversation by means of speech [*logôi*]?
Alcibiades: What else?
Socrates: Do you call conversation [*dialegesthai*] and the use of speech the same thing [*t'auton*]?
Alcibiades: Yes.
Socrates: But the one using and what he uses is there not any difference between them?
Alcibiades: How do you mean?
Socrates: Just as the leather cutter cuts with a cutter and knife and other tools.
Alcibiades: Yes.
Socrates: And so the one cutting and using is one thing, and the things the one cutting uses are another.
Alcibiades: Could it be otherwise? (129b5–c12)

This is a passage of great subtlety. On the one hand, it prepares a logical distinction between the agent of an action and the means by which that action is accomplished. This will be the basis for Socrates' later definition of the self as equated with the soul. It is, as Foucault notes, a definition of the subject as that toward which the activity of reflection, of the return toward the self, ought to be oriented, not of the soul as a prescriptive nature that in itself dictates the law of our behavior (Foucault 2001). On the other, it establishes on the connotative level the means by which that reflective activity is be pursued: in a dialogue (*dialegesthai*) between Alcibiades (the student, disciple, beloved) and Socrates (the teacher, master, lover), using reason/speech (*logos*) to reveal the nature of the thing itself (*auto to auto*) that makes use of, and is only made manifest by, these means. What we see, then, is nothing less than, in capsule form, the ideal cognitive and affective working of the dialectic as described in the seventh letter and elaborated in the *Symposium*.

The next step in the argument is to acknowledge that if the cobbler or leather cutter (*skutotomos*) uses tools, he also uses his hands and eyes, and since these body parts have the same relation of instrumentality to the cobbler as does his knife, then, insofar as the agent of an action and the means by which the action is accomplished are distinguished, the self of the cobbler cannot be identified with his body. The self of the cobbler, then, and of any other human being would not be that which is used but that which uses, and this is what we call the soul.

> Socrates: What then is a human being (*anthrôpos*)?
> Alcibiades: I am not able to say.
> Socrates: You are able to say that it is what uses the body.
> Alcibiades: Right.
> Socrates: Does anything else use this than the soul?
> Alcibiades: Nothing else.
> Socrates: And so it is in the position of command?
> Alcibiades: Yes. (129e10–130a4)

The soul, as defined in this dialogue, as opposed to its tripartite conception found in the *Republic* and the *Phaedrus,* is less a substance than a relationship. The self that we must care for is the soul as self-constituting subject, as that which acts through and upon itself, more than a discrete entity among others with definable positive qualities (Foucault 2001: 56).[65] And it is precisely insofar as we possess the capacity to know and act upon ourselves, as revealed through our interactions with others, that the care of the self becomes both a necessary quality in defining ourselves as human (*anthrôpos*) and a prerequisite to any meaningful exercise of power over oneself (i.e., ethical power) and over others (i.e., political power). Care, then, becomes the ground of all authentic interaction with both ourselves and others (Silverman 2000: 32–33).[66]

Thus, when Alcibiades' other suitors claimed to love him, it was not him they loved, but his accidental attributes: his looks, his fortune, and his political connections. Socrates, however, loves *him* and manifests this love, first, through revealing Alcibiades' lack of self-

---

65. The theorizations of the soul found in Plato represent less a consistent doctrine than a series of fertile metaphors. See, for example, the passage in *Symposium* where Diotima seems to indicate that the soul's make-up is in constant flux, just like the body itself (207e2–208a7).

66. On the Heideggerian roots of Foucault's conception the care of the self and its technologies, see Jaffro (2003: 71–72) and Gros (2001: 505).

knowledge, and then through reflecting the true nature of the self to him, by means of their dialectical intercourse, so that Alcibiades may care for it and become as beautiful as possible, in the only sense that belongs inherently to Alcibiades:

> Socrates: This is then the cause: I was your only lover; the others loved your possessions. Your possessions are now passing out of season, but you are just beginning to bloom. And I will not leave you lest the people of Athens corrupt you and you become ugly. For this I truly fear, that you should become a lover of our people [*dêmerastês*] and so be corrupted. For many good men have already suffered this at the hands of the Athenians. For the people of greathearted Erechtheus are good looking, but it's necessary to see them naked. Keep well what I am saying to you.
> Alcibiades: What do you mean?
> Socrates: First of all strip down and train hard [*gumnasai*], blessed man, and learn what is needed to attend to the affairs of the city, so that you go in already having an antidote and will therefore suffer no harm.
> Alcibiades: You seem to me to speak well, Socrates, but try to explain how we should take care of ourselves.
> Socrates: We explained this before—for what we are was agreed upon—but I feared lest weakening we should forget this and care for something other than ourselves.
> Alcibiades: That's it.
> Socrates: And then we agreed that it was necessary to care for the soul and that we must look to this. (131e10–132c2)

In this passage, the language of love, pederastic desire, political power, self-mastery, and self-fashioning all become inextricably intertwined (Foucault 1984a: 82–88, 96, 232–37; 2001: 80–81). Alcibiades must not be seduced into becoming a lover of the city (*dêmerastês*), as his guardian Pericles had recommended in his famed funeral oration (Thucydides 2.43; Wohl 2002).[67] Such a seduction, Plato insinuates, implies a reversal of normal subject/object relations since the *erastês* is normally the pursuer and not the pursued, and thus in the active position, but the lover of the city is seduced by the love of unreflected power and the need for the city's approbation and so becomes passive

---

67. Of course, these may not represent Pericles' exact words, but a discourse typical of the period.

in regard to its wishes. To disabuse himself of its seductive powers, Alcibiades must see the city as it is, naked (*gumnos*), and stripped of all pretensions. He will achieve this by himself stripping down (being naked to himself) through training hard and caring for his soul,[68] a practice which will ultimately culminate in an insight into the nature of the good and the just, as described in the seventh letter. The place where hard training is done in the classical *polis* is the *gumnasium*, which is where one sees, and is seen by, others naked. It is also the primary place for pederastic encounters both philosophical and otherwise (see the *Lysis*). There, through the practice of Socratic intercourse one comes to see oneself unadorned and is thus prepared to protect oneself from the blandishments of the people or *dêmos* and in turn to offer it what is needed. The real question, as Socrates intimates at the dialogue's end, is whether Alcibiades is prepared to undergo the hard training necessary to see himself naked in the eyes of his philosophic lover.

4. Conclusion

> The phrase, "return to," designates a movement with its proper specificity, which characterizes the initiation of discursive practices. If we return, it is because of a basic and constructive omission, an omission that is not the result of accident or incomprehension.... It follows naturally that this return, which is part of the discursive mechanism, constantly introduces modifications and that the return to a text is not a historical supplement that would come to fix itself upon the primary discursivity and redouble it in the form of an ornament which after all, is not essential. Rather, it is an effective and necessary means of transforming discursive practice. A study of Galileo's work could alter our knowledge of the history, but not the science of mechanics; whereas, a reexamination of the books of Freud or Marx can transform our understanding of psychoanalysis or Marxism. (Foucault 1977b: 134–36)

Thirteen years after Foucault pronounced these words in 1969, he would add Plato's name to that of Marx and Freud. His return to Plato, like Lacan's to Freud and Althusser's to Marx, was not designed simply to reproduce what was already there, but to probe the silences and gaps in Plato. It sought, as all authentic returns must, to transform our understanding not only of Plato, but also of ourselves. The method

---

68. Compare *Theaetetus* 162b.

of that transformation was not merely to appropriate a set of models and impose an ill-fitting classicism on a very different age, but to historicize both our contemporary understanding of what it means to be a subject and our readings of the foundational texts upon which that understanding inescapably rests.

The return to Plato is not a conservative move, but one of surpassing radicality. It seeks not a return to the past, nor an allegorization of the present, but a true thought from the outside, *une pensée du dehors*. It seeks the moment when the now naked Alcibiades comes to recognize the nature of his own grimace as reflected in his lover's eyes and the movement of the soul that lies behind it. It seeks to achieve self-knowledge in a Platonic epistle sent to us from antiquity, a letter that never quite reaches us, and yet that in its very failure always arrives at its destination. It seeks a return to the cave with a vision of the outside that will cause us and others to see anew, and hence to create an authentic self that does not cede on its desire, a desire which, in the end, can be realized only in the eyes of the other.

Chapter 7

Searching for a Usable Past

A la fin tu es las de ce monde ancien
Bergère o tour Eiffel le troupeau des ponts bêle ce matin
Tu en as assez de vivre dans l'antiquité grecque et romaine
Ici même les automobiles ont l'air d'être anciennes

In the end you are tired of this ancient world
Shepherdess, Eiffel tower, your flock of bridges bleats this morning
You've had enough of living in Greco-Roman antiquity
Here even the automobiles seem ancient. (Apollinaire 1983: "Zone" 1–4)

The past, in effect, is originally a project, as the present leaping forth of my being. And, in so far as it is a project, it is an anticipation; its sense comes from the future it sketches in advance. . . . (Sartre 1943: 556)

THE QUESTION of modernity, and *a fortiori* of postmodernity, cannot be posed except in an explicit relation to the past it creates. Apollinaire in his 1912 ode to the triumph of the future, "Zone," cannot sing the glories of the modern except by envisioning Paris as a vast pastoral landscape with the Eiffel Tower as a shepherdess and the bridges across the Seine as her bawling flock. Even this futurist profession of faith is not intelligible without reference to the conventions of pastoral, to Vergil and Theocritus, to Hellenistic sophistication. We may have had enough of living in the past, but as Sartre recognizes, there is no future that does not project its own past, and no past that does not imply a relation to the present and the future.

Given the inescapability of the past, given the necessary antiquity that pervades even our modern machines, as Apollinaire himself reminds us, the question remains of how we should be oriented to the past. Is the past the authorization of the present? Should we seek in it the models of our behavior? In Victorian England, schoolboys read Cicero and Horace to prepare them to administer the empire. In the antebellum American South, the sons of South Carolina planters read Thucydides at the newly opened Carolina College (later the University of South Carolina, my home institution) while their slaves bearing names such as Brutus, Cassius, and Caesar died in the rice and indigo plantations of the tidewaters round Charleston. In Napoleonic France, the first consul of the newly established French republic crowned himself emperor in explicit imitation of Augustus. The models of antiquity do not necessarily, in and of themselves, always have a lot to recommend them.

It is important, therefore, that we not delude ourselves about the inherently liberatory nature of the classical tradition. The allegory of the present in terms of the past that produced such powerful pieces of Resistance drama as Sartre's *Les mouches* also produced the far more ambivalent, if not directly "fascist," *Antigone* of Anouilh, as well as Mussolini's experiments with both tragic form and with rewriting the Roman empire in blood. Yet the power that these appropriations tap into is undeniable. They recognize that the past not only defines us, but is defined by us. And mere ignorance cannot free us from its grip—in spite of many of my fellow citizens' best efforts.

The postmodern turn to antiquity, then, is an effort to find a past that is usable for the needs of the present. It does not seek legitimation, but difference. Lacan's reading of the *Antigone* asks us not to become like her, not to die in the tomb, but to pursue an ethics that, in going beyond the pleasure principle, also goes beyond good and evil, beyond the self-satisfied relation to the present that sees it as the fulfillment of the past (Shepherdson 1995: ¶ 27). It asks us to recognize and not cede on our desire through a deliberate investigation of that desire's necessary relation to the Other by means of a Socratic engagement with its ontological grounds.

The Other and the past it incarnates, then, are not in opposition to our subjectivity, nor are they a mirror that forever reflects ourselves back to ourselves. They represent neither the object that must be overcome, eliminated, or sublimated, nor—what amounts to the same thing—the mere reflection and confirmation of our self-identity. Rather the Other is always the intimate other, that which makes us who we are without ever being assimilable to our identity. The Other thus becomes a way ultimately of refashioning the self through a recognition of the self's own constitutive emptiness, its primal lack, the Aristophanic cut that drives it to seek an ever absent completion.

The past of postmodernism is, then, the past of the Derridean trace: the mark or incision that both institutes the ontic, the entity on which identity is predicated, and forever separates it from itself. The first and in many ways fullest theorization of that mark, and at the same time the first and fullest theorization of the desire to efface, contain, and master it, can be found, according to Derrida, in the dialectic of Plato and Platonism. *Philo-sophia*, the desire for wisdom, is precisely the self-conscious desire to master the trace, to place a limit on division, and thus to insure that the letter always arrives at its destination, in the full realization that such a desire can never reach fulfillment except in its own self-extinction. The practice of *philia*, for Derrida, i.e., the pursuit of friendship and shared being, is dependent upon this practice of *philo-sophia*: the self-conscious practice of both collection and division; the refusal to accept the decreed range of the ontic as the limits of our political, economic, and erotic life, and the simultaneous refusal to annihilate difference in the name of a more primal unity whose very existence and articulation must assume the marks, cuts, and divisions it would seek to deny.

In this light, Foucault's final turn to ancient philosophy in general, and Plato in particular, is neither surprising nor announces a major break. It is rather part of an ongoing and productive dialogue. This is a dialogue that is pursued on a variety of levels and is extraordinarily rich. On the first level, it is the dialogue that defines itself as the ongoing dialectical interchange that constitutes philosophy in the West, which regardless of national tradition sees its origins in Greece and in the figures of Socrates and Plato. On a second level, it is a dialogue with the whole of French culture, which defines itself to this day explicitly in terms of its classical heritage and which in its highest formal educational institution, the Ecole Normale Supérieure, still features a Plato-centered syllabus. On a third level, it is a dialogue with the previous generation of modernist philosophers and writers, who not only couched their theatrical work in terms of the models of antiquity, but who also explicitly sought to define an ethics and practice of the subject, which, like Foucault's, was post-Nietzschean and so beyond good and evil. Finally, and this is the most intense level, but one which is not fully comprehensible without the other three, it is a focused and precise dialogue with Lacan and Derrida about specific Platonic texts and their relation to the earliest manifestations of our contemporary understandings of thought, philosophy, ethics, and the subject.

This book has been an effort both to uncover this dialogue and to think, in a sustained fashion, its implications. The study of classics and the classical tradition has a choice to make (which is not exactly new) and an examination of the postmoderns' relation to classical antiquity can help us think through that choice. Will the study of the ancient world be hagiographic and self-congratulatory or will it be genealogic and self-critical? The Platonic model adopted by the postmoderns clearly points to the latter.

An authentic spiritual practice, as Plato tells us, will never consist in a strictly imitative relation, which ultimately seeks to domesticate the other by rendering it a model of the same, but will use the testing and the probing of the other to engage in a sustained and protracted *elenchus* with the self. The obligations we have to self and other will then be seen not only as the products of our desire, as Diotima tells us, but also as that which is not to be ceded. Foucault's reading of the *Alcibiades,* as a response to Plato and to Lacan's and Derrida's own powerful readings of the Platonic text, is an example of how such a critical practice of the self's relation to itself, and thence to the other, might be undertaken with the requisite rigor, diligence, and care.

Appendix

Queering Alcibiades

Persius on Foucault and Halperin

You handle the people's business?" Picture the bearded master, whom a grim dose of hemlock carried off, saying these things. "With what qualification? Speak up then, ward of great Pericles. . . .

Socrates: But if all oiled up you should be relaxing and fixing the rays of the sun in your skin, there is a stranger nearby who touches you with his elbow and bitterly spits out, "What morals! To show the people both how you weed round your cock and the hidden part of your groin, your shriveled asshole. But when you comb the balsamed wool on your cheeks, why does a shaven little worm stand out from your groin. Though five official oilers and depilators should pluck those seedlings and shake your boiled buttocks with hooked tweezers, nonetheless that hedge would not be tamed by any plow."[1] (Persius 4.1–3, 33–41)

THE FOURTH satire of Persius, itself a creative rereading of the *Alcibiades* (Miller 2005; Ramage 1974: 121–25), provides a particularly useful comparandum to Foucault's interpretation of the *Alcibiades*. First, Persius himself was a Stoic as his ancient *vita* attests. Second, Foucault clearly indicates that he has read him (2001: 74). More significantly, Persius is a poet, a category of writer that, as Konstan notes, Foucault self-consciously excludes from his archive (Foucault 1984a: 18). Foucault privileges philosophic and scientific discourse in his reading of the ancient world just as he had in his early work on seventeenth-, eighteenth-, and nineteenth-century Europe. His reasoning, Konstan points out, is that these forms constitute the primary normalizing and orthopedic discourses that have produced the modern disciplinary subject. It stands to reason, therefore, that if one wishes to investigate whether similar forms of subjectivation existed in the ancient world, one would turn to similar forms of discourse. Yet, as Konstan observes, this may well have been a mistake: poetry played a much stronger socially regulative role in the ancient world than it does today and was

---

1. On the attribution of this passage to Socrates, see P. A. Miller (2005a).

arguably more important than medicine or philosophy in its impact on the lives of all but a small minority (2002).² Persius' reading of the *Alcibiades* is thus particularly important because it allows us to test both what Foucault says about ancient regimes of subjectivation and ethics, and perhaps more importantly, the philosophical and political conclusions drawn by theorists from his work.

Beyond doubt one of the most influential aspects of Foucault's interest in the care of the self has been its impact on queer theory. His tracing of different modalities of self-relation is, as we have seen, explicitly aimed at providing new possibilites of resistance to the normalized, disciplinary subject of late capitalism and exposing the roots of that subject in a specific mode of self-relation that can be traced to the Christian confessional (1994c). The Stoic and Platonic models of the care of self offer crucial resources to all marginal groups that seek to fashion new forms of subjectivity, experience, and resistance to the dominant forms of governmentality.³ Nonetheless, Foucault's claims have been subject to two forms of falsification. On the one hand, his own arguments about ancient sexual norms have been called into question. On the other, some of his most vocal advocates have drawn distorted and illegitimate claims from his work.

Foucault's major claims, on which subsequent extrapolations have been based, are as follows. First, ancient moral philosophy contains "no trace of normalization." It is based not upon obedience to a preexisting law or code, but upon a self-conscious mode of shaping oneself. Consequently, the ancient mode of *khrêsis aphrodisiôn,* or the "use of pleasure," escapes the repressive hypothesis that Foucault had attacked in volume 1 of the *History of Sexuality* (1994c: 610; 1994i: 215). If we grant the accuracy of this hypothesis, then it is clear that sexual identities such as homo- and heterosexual did not exist as such in the ancient world, but are the product of the modern sexual *dispositif* and the invention of sex per se as a unitary phenomenon (see our discussion of Foucault's relation to Lacan).⁴ Foucault's claim is not that there was no same-sex eroticism, but rather that people's personal identities were not determined by the gender of their sexual object choice. In short, Socrates may have loved Alcibiades, but it would be absurd to say that Socrates was "gay."

Although the details of Foucault's reading of the ancient evidence

---

2. See also Goldhill (1995: 44–45, 110–11, 161).
3. See also Hocquenghem (1978: 36).
4. See also Davidson (1987) and Katz (1995).

have been contested,[5] its general thrust has given rise to a broad and important body of work. In *One Hundred Years of Homosexuality* (1990b) David Halperin provides a detailed exposition of Foucault's theories and uses them for wide-ranging discussions of Greek sexual and discursive practices, as well as for a series of hard-hitting polemics against Boswell (1980) and other historians of homosexuality who do not share his strict constructionist line.[6] John J. Winkler's highly regarded *The Constraints of Desire: The Anthropology of Sex and Gender in Ancient Greece* (1990) likewise starts from the position that sexuality (including homosexuality) is a social construction, rather than an essence. The volume of essays, *Before Sexuality: The Construction of Erotic Experience in the Ancient World* (1990), edited by Halperin, Winkler, and Froma Zeitlin, discusses a variety of aspects of ancient erotic culture against a broadly Foucauldian horizon. All these works, as well as those more indirectly inspired by Foucault, such as Hallett and Skinner's *Roman Sexualities* (1997), have made important contributions to our understanding of ancient erotic culture and modern sexual identities.

Nonetheless, it is largely in Halperin's later work that Foucault's ethics have been read as a specific program for the creation of a queer identity (Dean 2003: 239; Halperin 1995: 107). In his *Saint Foucault*, Halperin argues that the destabilization of normative sexual identities leads to the possibility of a utopian politics based on the invention of new modes of self-relation founded upon radical sexual practices such as sado-masochism and fistfucking. "The shattering force of intense bodily pleasure, detached from its exclusive localization in the genitals and regionalized throughout various zones of the body, decenters the subject and disarticulates the psychic and bodily integrity of the self to which a sexual identity has become attached" (1995: 96–97).[7] Self-transformation and self-fashioning are political acts in which the most intimate of personal practices strikes a blow against an oppressive heteronormative culture. On this view, the care of the self is seen to

---

5. See Cohen (1991: 171–202); Cohen and Saller (1994); Richlin (1993); and Larmour et al. (1998b: 22–33).

6. Constructionism argues that gender and sexual identities are social constructs rather than natural and universal. The Foucauldian position that sees sex itself as a discursive construct clearly falls within this camp.

7. As Eribon notes, Halperin seems to accept all of J. Miller's most sensationalistic depictions of Foucault's private life but changes the valences from negative to positive. The problem, he observes, is not whether or not Foucault performed this or that sex act, but what happens when his vast and complex life's work is reduced to an allegory of those acts (Eribon 1994: 49–54).

underwrite everything, from piercing, to gay body builders, to "shopping for the right outfit" (1995: 32, 115–18). It is hard to argue that drag queens and leather bars do not represent a transgression of, and hence a challenge to, the dominant culture of compulsive heterosexuality, but it is quite another to see these phenomena as the necessary, or even desirable, consequences of Foucault's reading of the *Alcibiades* and its *Nachleben*.

While Foucault certainly viewed a return to the culture of the self as a means of resistance to the normalizing disciplinary culture he saw at the heart of modernity (Kremer-Marietti 1985: 278–79), it is at best reductive to reduce Foucault's complex and variegated reading of the Platonic enterprise to a fashion statement ("shopping for the right outfit"), however politically charged that statement may be. Such an interpretation fails to do justice to the specificity and nuance of his reading, to his engagement with the Socratic dialectic as a means of shaping the soul. It also fails to acknowledge the overdetermined dialogic situation in which that reading transpired. If Foucault's study of ancient philosophy was in part inspired by a desire to provide a new set of tools to fashion queer and other resistant forms of identity, it was also equally designed as a response to the work of Deleuze, Derrida, and Lacan, and as an archeology of the subject per se.

Finally, as the passages from Persius quoted above makes clear, Foucault overstated the case when he declared that there was no trace of normalization in ancient philosophical discourse. We know that sexual encounters between males at Rome, while certainly permitted in some cases and not regulated along the same axes as they would be in modern societies, were nonetheless subject to both legal and moral restrictions, and that the penalties for soldiers who violated those strictures and fraternized with one another, could include death (Grimal 1986: 103–6; Edwards 1993: 75, 188–89; Nippel 1995: 11; Corbeill 1996: 145; Walters 1997; Parker 1997). Indeed, in our second quoted excerpt from Persius, we have Socrates, or a figure meant to recall him, attacking Alcibiades for precisely the kind of fashion statement that Halperin seems to read Foucault and the Stoics as underwriting. Alcibiades in this poem is portrayed as a young effeminate who exposes himself to the public both politically and erotically, and thus effectively disqualifies himself from any claim to political power. His practice of anal depilation is stigmatized precisely as inviting penetration and degradation. It represents not the care for the self, but a care for one's possessions. Alcibiades in Persius' poem has clearly not learned the distinction between the leather cutter and his tools. He is neglecting his soul, and thus as the opening lines of the poem make clear, just like the opening of the Platonic dialogue, has no right to presume to handle the affairs of the state. Nor, despite his caustic wit, was Persius an isolated crank. Neither for the Socrates of the *Alcibiades* nor for the Stoic Persius could the care of the self be found in shopping for the right outfit or fistfucking.

Of course, Foucault's position is more complex than it is often given credit to be, even by (or especially by) his most ardent admirers. Despite the occasional incautious statement, he clearly rejected any simplistic contrast between ancient tolerance and modern repression (Gros 2001: 503; Nehamas 1998: 178). He explicitly recognized that in the imperial period the sexual act was viewed as a time of profound danger, not freedom (1984b: 135), and that Greek sexual ethics, far from constituting a model, were fraught with anxiety (witness Socrates' *daimôn* forbidding him to approach Alcibiades until he was on the cusp of maturity) and predicated on necessary asymmetries of power between the pursuer and pursued, the lover and the beloved, the penetrator and the penetrated (Foucault 1994c: 614; 1984a: 56; Gros 2001: 512–13; Konstan 1994: 116, 121; Macey 1993: 458, 468; Kremer-Marietti 1985: 256). The genealogy of the modern subject may well have created new possibilities of resistance to our dominant forms of subjectivation, but neither did it create models to be emulated nor did it authorize (let alone mandate) specific behaviors (Veyne 1997: 226). Only the tough work of self-reflection and the rigors of philosophical dialogue, undertaken in the context of profound affection, could lead to the discovery of the soul and the fashioning of a self that one found beautiful and authentic. It is in this labor of unflinching examination that the real nucleus of resistance and the real urgency of Foucault's reading of ancient philosophy can be found.

Works Cited

Ackroyd, Peter. 1984. *T. S. Eliot: A Life*. New York: Simon & Schuster.
Adam, James. 1963. *The Republic of Plato*. 2nd ed. Cambridge: Cambridge University Press.
Adorno, Theodor. 1983. *Negative Dialectics*. Trans. E. B. Ashton. New York: Continuum.
Allen, Danielle S. 2000. *The World of Prometheus: The Politics of Punishing in Democratic Athens*. Princeton: Princeton University Press.
Allen, Joel. 2005. "Was Alcibiades Self-Absorbed and Irresponsible, Caring Little for the Interests of Athens?" *Classical Studies and the Ancient World. History in Dispute*. Vol. 21. Eds. Paul Allen Miller and Charles Platter. Detroit: Thomson Gale. 65–71.
Allen, Paula Gunn. 1992. "'Border' Studies: The Intersection of Gender and Color." *Introduction to Scholarship in Modern Languages and Literatures*. Ed Joseph Gibaldi. 2nd ed. New York: The Modern Language Association. 303–19.
Alliez, Eric. 1992. "Ontologie et logographie. La pharmacie, Platon et le simulacre." *Nos Grecs et leurs modernes*. Ed. Barbara Cassin. Paris: Seuil. 211–31.
Althusser, Louis. 1968. *Lire le capital*. Vol. 1. Paris: Maspero.
———. 1971. "Ideology and Ideological State Apparatuses (Notes towards an Investigation) (*January–April 1969*)." *Lenin and Philosophy and Other Essays by Louis Althusser*. Trans. Ben Brewster. New York: Monthly Review Press, 127–86.
———. 1996. *Writings on Psychoanalysis: Freud and Lacan*. Eds. Olivier Corpet and François Matheron. Trans. Jeffrey Mehlman. New York: Columbia University Press.
Annas, Julia. 1993. *The Morality of Happiness*. New York: Oxford University Press.
———. 1996. "Plato." *The Oxford Classical Dictionary*. 3rd ed. Eds. Simon Hornblower and Antony Spawforth. Oxford: Oxford University Press. 1190–93.
Anzieu, Didier. 1966. "Oedipe, avant le complexe ou de l'interprétation psychanalytique des mythes." *Les temps modernes* 245: 675–715.
Anouilh, Jean. 1942. *Eurydice. Pièces noires*. Paris: Calmann-Lévy. 363–505.
———. 1946a. *Antigone. Nouvelles pièces noires*. Paris: La Table Ronde. 131–212.

———. 1946b. *Roméo et Jeannette. Nouvelles pièces noires.* Paris: La Table Ronde. 213–354.
———. 1963. "Préface." *Oeuvres complètes de Robert Brasillach,* tome 4. Ed. Maurice Bardèche. Paris: Club de l'Honnête Homme. ix–xiii.
Apollinaire, Guillaume. 1983. "Zone." *Alcools.* Ed. Bernard Lecherbonnier. Paris: Fernand Nathan. 33–40.
Appel pour le latin et le grec, document page. 2005. Sauver les lettres. February 3, 2005 'http://www.sauv.net/latingrec2004.php'.
Appel pour le latin et le grec 2004: 70,000 signataires. 2004. Paris: Les Belles Lettres.
Archer, Marguerite. 1971. *Jean Anouilh.* New York: Columbia University Press.
Armstrong, Richard. 2005. *A Compulsion for Antiquity: Freud and the Ancient World.* Ithaca: Cornell University Press.
Aronson, Ronald. 1980. *Jean-Paul Sartre: Philosophy in the World.* London: Verso.
Asmis, Elizabeth. 1992. "Plato on Poetic Creativity." *The Cambridge Companion to Plato.* Ed. Richard Kraut. Cambridge: Cambridge University Press. 338–64.
Auerbach, Erich. 1953. "L'Humaine Condition." *Mimesis: The Representation of Reality in Western Literatures.* Trans. Willard R. Trask. Princeton: Princeton University Press. 285–311.
Aviram, Amittai. 2001. "Lyric Poetry and Subjectivity." *Intertexts* 5: 61–86.
Bannet, Eve Tavor. 1989. *Structuralism and the Logic of Dissent: Barthes, Derrida, Foucault, Lacan.* Urbana: University of Illinois Press.
Bataille, Georges. 1957. *L'érotisme.* Paris: Minuit.
Bayrou, François. 2004. "Discours de François Bayrou." *Appel pour le Latin et le Grec 2004: 70,000 signataires.* Paris: Les Belles Lettres. 115–18.
Benardete, Seth. 1999. *Sacred Transgressions: A Reading of Sophocles' Antigone.* South Bend, IN: St. Augustine's Press.
Benatouïl, Thomas. 2003. "Deux usages du stoicisme: Deleuze, Foucault." *Foucault et la philosophie antique.* Eds. Frédéric Gros et Carlos Lévy. Paris: Kimé, 2003. 17–49.
Benjamin, Walter. 1969. "The Work of Art in the Age of Mechanical Reproduction." *Illuminations.* Ed. Hannah Arendt. Trans. Harry Zohn. New York: Schocken Books. 217–51.
Bennett, William J. 1992. *The De-Valuing of America : The Fight for Our Culture and Our Children.* New York: Touchstone.
Benstock, Shari. 1991. *Textualising the Feminine: On the Limits of Genre.* Norman: University of Oklahoma Press.
Benveniste, Emile. 1969. *Le vocabulaire des institutions indo-européennes,* Paris: Minuit.
Berger, Harry, Jr. 1994. "*Phaedrus* and the Politics of Inscriptions." Shankman 1994a. 76–114.
Bernstein, Richard. 1990. *Fragile Glory: A Portrait of France and the French.* New York: Knopf.
Berryman, John. 1981. *The Dream Songs.* New York: Farrar, Straus, and Giroux.
Black, Joel. 1998. "Taking the Sex out of Sexuality: Foucault's Failed History." Larmour et al. 1998a. 42–60.
Blanchot, Maurice. 1955. *L'espace littéraire.* Paris: Gallimard.

———. 1986. *Michel Foucault tel que je l'imagine*. Paris: Tata Morgana.
Blévis, Marcianne. 2000. "On Female Homosexuality: A Lacanian Perspective." *Lacan in America*. Ed. Jean-Michel Rabaté. New York: The Other Press. 379–97.
Blondell, Ruby. 2002. *The Play of Character in Plato's Dialogues*. Cambridge: Cambridge University Press.
Bloom, Allan. 1987. *The Closing of the American Mind*. New York: Simon and Schuster.
Boswell, John. *Christianity, Tolerance, and Homosexuality: Gay People in Western Europe from the Beginning of the Christian Era to the Fourteenth Century*. Chicago: University of Chicago Press.
Boucris, Marie-Odile, Agnès Guinchard, Vianella Guyot, eds. 1998. *Jean Giraudoux: Electre*. Paris: Larousse.
Boussoulas, Nicolas-Isidore. 1952. *L'être et la composition des mixtes dans le «Philèbe» de Platon*. Paris: Presses Universitaires de France.
Boyne, Roy. 1990. *Foucault and Derrida: The Other Side of Reason*. London: Unwin Hyman.
Brandwood, Leonard. 1992. "Stylometry and Chronology." *The Cambridge Companion to Plato*. Ed. Richard Kraut. Cambridge: Cambridge University Press. 90–120.
Braunstein, Nestor A. 2003. "Desire and Jouissance in the Teachings of Lacan." *The Cambridge Companion to Lacan*. Ed. Jean-Michel Rabaté. Cambridge: Cambridge University Press. 102–15.
Brée, Germaine, and Alexander Y. Kroff, eds. 1969. *Twentieth Century French Drama*. Toronto: MacMillan.
Brisson, Luc. 1998. *Plato the Mythmaker*. Trans and Ed. Gerard Nadaff. Chicago: University of Chicago Press.
Brumbaugh, Robert S. 1988. "Digression and Dialogue: The *Seventh Letter* and Plato's Literary Form." *Platonic Writings, Platonic Readings*. Ed. Charles L. Griswold, Jr. New York: Routledge. 84–92.
Buci-Glucksman, Christine. 1992. "Lacan devant Aristote: De l'esthétique." *Nos Grecs et leurs modernes: Les stratégies contemporaines d'appropriation de l'antiquité*. Ed. Barbara Cassin. Paris: Seuil, 1992. 363–82.
Burian, Peter. 2004. "Seminar on *Antigone*." Venice International University. February.
Butler, Judith. 1990. *Gender Trouble: Feminism and the Subversion of Identity*. New York: Routledge.
———. 1999. *Subjects of Desire: Hegelian Reflections in Twentieth-Century France*. 2nd ed. New York: Columbia University Press.
———. 2000. *Antigone's Claim: Kinship Between Life and Death*. New York: Columbia University Press.
Caldwell, Richard S. 1994. "Aeschylus' *Suppliants*: A Psychoanalytic Study." *Modern Critical Theory and Classical Literature*. Eds. Irene J. F. de Jong and J. P. Sullivan. Mnemosyne Supplement. Leiden: Brill. 75–102.
Camus, Albert. 1962a. *Caligula. Théâtre, Récits, Nouvelles*. Ed. Roger Quilliot. Bibliothèque de la Pléiade. Paris: Gallimard. 3–108.
———. 1962b. *La peste. Théâtre, Récits, Nouvelles*. Ed. Roger Quilliot. Bibliothèque de la Pléiade. Paris: Gallimard. 1217–1474.
———. 1965a. *Lettres à un ami allemand. Essais*. Eds. R. Quilliot and L. Faucon. Bibliothèque de la Pléiade. Paris: Gallimard. 213–43.

———. 1965b. *Le mythe de Sisyphe. Essais.* Eds. R. Quilliot and L. Faucon. Bibliothèque de la Pléiade. Paris: Gallimard. 87–211.

———. 1965c. "Sur «Les îles»." *Essais.* Eds. R. Quilliot and L. Faucon. Bibliothèque de la Pléiade. Paris: Gallimard. 1157–61.

———. 1965d. "Essai sur la musique." *Essais.* Eds. R. Quilliot and L. Faucon. Bibliothèque de la Pléiade. Paris: Gallimard. 1200–1203.

———. 1965e. *L'envers et l'endroit. Essais.* Eds. R. Quilliot and L. Faucon. Bibliothèque de la Pléiade. Paris: Gallimard. 5–50.

———. 1965f. *Noces. Essais.* Eds. R. Quilliot and L. Faucon. Bibliothèque de la Pléiade. Paris: Gallimard. 52–88.

Carnes, Jeffrey S. 1998. "This Myth Which is Not One: Construction of Discourse in Plato's *Symposium*." Larmour et al. 1998a. 104–21.

Castel-Bouchouchi, Anissa. 2003. "Foucault et le paradoxe du platonisme." *Foucault et la philosophie antique.* Eds. Frédéric Gros et Carlos Lévy. Paris: Kimé, 2003. 175–93.

Chaitin, Gilbert D. 1996. *Rhetoric and Culture in Lacan.* Cambridge: Cambridge University Press.

Champigny, Robert. 1982. *Sartre and Drama.* N.c.: French Literature Publications Company.

Clarke, Bruce. 1995. *Allegories of Writing: The Subject of Metamorphosis.* Albany: SUNY Press.

Clément, Cathérine. 1975. "La Coupable." *La jeune née.* Paris: Union Générale d'Edition. 8–113.

Cohen, David. 1991. *Law, Sexuality, and Society: The Enforcement of Morals in Classical Athens.* Cambridge: Cambridge University Press.

———, and Richard Saller. 1994. "Foucault on Sexuality in Greco-Roman Antiquity." *Foucault and the Writing of History.* Ed. Jan Goldstein. Oxford: Oxford University Press. 35–59.

Cohen-Solal, Annie. 1987. *Sartre: A Life.* Trans. Anna Cacogni. Ed. Norman Macafee. New York: Pantheon Books.

Contat, Michel, ed. 2005. "Préface." *Jean-Paul Sartre: Théâtre complet.* Bibliothèque de la Pléiade. Paris: Gallimard, 2005. xi–xliv.

———, en collaboration avec Ingrid Galster. 2005. "*Les mouches:* Notice." *Jean-Paul Sartre: Théâtre complet.* Ed. Michel Contat. Bibliothèque de la Pléiade. Paris: Gallimard, 2005. 1255–82.

Cooper, John M., ed. 1997. *Plato: Complete Works.* Assoc. ed. D. S. Hutchinson. Indianapolis: Hackett.

Copjec, Joan. 1994. *Read My Desire: Lacan against the Historicists.* Cambridge, MA: MIT Press.

———. 2002. *Imagine There's No Woman: Ethics and Sublimation.* Cambridge, MA: MIT Press.

Corbeill, Anthony. 1996. *Controlling Laughter: Political Humor in the Late Roman Republic.* Princeton: Princeton University Press.

Croiset, Maurice, ed. and trans. 1960. *Platon: Introduction, Hippias Mineur, Alcibiade, Apologie de Socrate, Euthyphron, Criton.* 9th ed. Paris: Société d'Edition «Les Belles Lettres». First published 1920.

Culler, Jonathan. 1975. *Structuralist Poetics: Structuralism, Linguistics, and the Study of Literature.* Ithaca: Cornell University Press.

Curtis, Anthony. 1948. *New Developments in the French Theater.* London: The Curtain Press.

Davidson, Arnold. 1987. "Sex and the Emergence of 'Sexuality.'" *Critical Inquiry* 14: 17–49.
———. 1994. "Ethics as Ascetics, Foucault, the History of Ethics, and Ancient Thought." *The Cambridge Companion to Foucault.* Ed. Gary Gutting. Cambridge: Cambridge University Press. 115–40.
———. 1995. "Introduction: Pierre Hadot and the Spiritual Phenomenon of Ancient Philosophy." Hadot 1995. 1–45.
———. 1997. "Introductory Remarks to Pierre Hadot." *Foucault and His Interlocutors.* Ed. Arnold I. Davidson. Chicago: University of Chicago Press. 195–202.
Davila, Jorge. 2003. "Ethique de la parole et jeu de la vérité." *Foucault et la philosophie antique.* Eds. Frédéric Gros et Carlos Lévy. Paris: Kimé. 195–208.
Dean, Tim. 2003 "Lacan and Queer Theory." *The Cambridge Companion to Lacan.* Ed. Jean-Michel Rabaté. Cambridge: Cambridge University Press. 238–52.
Deleuze, Gilles. 1969. *Logique du sens.* Paris: Minuit.
———. 1988. *Foucault.* Trans. Seán Hand. Minneapolis: University of Minnesota Press,
Denyer, Nicholas. 2001. *Plato: Alcibiades.* Cambridge: Cambridge University Press.
Derrida, Jacques. 1967a. *L'écriture et la différence.* Paris: Seuil.
———. 1967b. *De la Grammatologie.* Paris: Minuit.
———. 1967c. *La voix et le phénomène.* Paris: Presses Universitaires de France.
———. 1972a. "La pharmacie de Platon." *La dissémination.* Paris: Seuil. 74–196.
———. 1972b. *Positions.* Paris: Minuit.
———. 1976. *Of Grammatology.* Trans. Gayatri Spivak. Baltimore: Johns Hopkins University Press.
———. 1980. *La carte postale: de Socrate à Freud et au-delà.* Paris: Aubier-Flammarion.
———. 1981. "Plato's Pharmacy." *Dissemination.* Trans. Barbara Johnson. Chicago: University of Chicago Press. 61–171.
———. 1992. "Nous autres Grecs." *Nos Grecs et leurs modernes.* Ed. Barbara Cassin. Paris: Seuil. 251–73.
———. 1993a. *Spectres de Marx.* Paris: Galilée.
———. 1993b. *Khôra.* Paris: Galilée.
———. 1994. *Politiques de l'amitié, suivi de L'oreille de Heidegger.* Paris: Galilée.
———. 1996a. "Résistances." *Résistances de la psychanalyse.* Paris: Galilée. 11–53. First published 1992.
———. 1996b. "Pour l'amour de Lacan." *Résistances de la psychanalyse.* Paris: Galilée. 55–88. First published 1992.
———. 1997. "'To Do Justice to Freud': The History of Madness in the Age of Psychoanalysis." Trans. Pascale-Ann Brault and Michael Naas. *Foucault and His Interlocutors.* Ed. Arnold I. Davidson. Chicago: University of Chicago Press. 57–96. First published 1992, later republished in *Résistances de la psychanalyse.* Paris: Galilée, 1996. 90–146.
Descombes, Vincent. 1980. *Modern French Philosophy.* Trans. L. Scott-Fox and J. M. Harding. Cambridge: Cambridge University Press.
Diès, Auguste. 1941. "Notice." *Platon: Philèbe.* Paris: Société d'Edition «Les Belles Lettres». vii–cxii.

Dodds, E. R. 1959. *Plato: Gorgias, Revised Text with Introduction and Commentary.* Oxford: Oxford University Press.
Dover, Kenneth. 1980. *Plato: Symposium.* Cambridge: Cambridge University Press.
Dowling, William C. 1984. *Jameson, Althusser, Marx: An Introduction to the Political Unconscious.* Ithaca: Cornell University Press.
Dreyfus, Hubert L., and Paul Rabinow. 1982. *Michel Foucault: Beyond Structuralism and Hermeneutics.* Chicago: University of Chicago Press.
Eagleton, Terry. 1976. *Criticism and Ideology: A Study in Marxist Literary Theory.* London: New Left Books.
———. 1996. *Literary Theory: An Introduction.* 2nd ed. Minneapolis: University of Minnesota Press.
———. 2003. *After Theory.* New York: Basic Books.
Eco, Umberto. 1976. *A Theory of Semiotics.* Bloomington: Indiana University Press.
Edwards, Catherine. 1993. *The Politics of Immorality in Ancient Rome.* Cambridge: Cambridge University Press.
Elden, Stuart. 2005. "The Problem of Confession: The Productive Failure of Foucault's *History of Sexuality*" *Journal for Cultural Research* 9.
———. Forthcoming. "Discipline, Health and Madness: Foucault's *Le pouvoir psychiatrique.*"
Eliot, T. S. 1957. "What is a Classic?" *On Poetry and Poets.* London: Faber and Faber. 53–71.
Eribon, Didier. 1994. *Michel Foucault et ses contemporains.* Paris: Fayard.
Fagles, Robert, trans. 1982. *Sophocles: The Three Theban Plays.* New York: Penguin.
Fazia, Alba della. 1969. *Jean Anouilh.* New York: Twayne.
Feher-Gurewich, Judith. 2000. "The Philanthropy of Perversion." *Lacan in America.* Ed. Jean-Michel Rabaté. New York: The Other Press. 361–77.
———. 2003. "A Lacanian Approach to the Logic of Perversion." *The Cambridge Companion to Lacan.* Ed. Jean-Michel Rabaté. Cambridge: Cambridge University Press. 191–207.
Ferrari, G. R. F. 1987. *Listening to the Cicadas: A Study of Plato's Phaedrus.* Cambridge: Cambridge University Press.
———. 1992. "Platonic Love." *The Cambridge Companion to Plato.* Ed. Richard Kraut. Cambridge: Cambridge University Press. 248–76.
Festugière, A. J. 1950. *Contemplation et vie contemplative selon Platon.* 2nd ed. Paris: Vrin. Original, 1935.
Fine, Gail. 1992. "Inquiry in the *Meno.*" *The Cambridge Companion to Plato.* Ed. Richard Kraut. Cambridge: Cambridge University Press. 200–26.
Flynn, Thomas. 1991. "Foucault as Parrhesiast: His Last Course at the *Collège de France* (1984)." *The Final Foucault.* Eds. James Bernauer and David Rasmussen. Cambridge, MA: MIT Press. 102–18.
———. 1994. "Foucault's Mapping of History." *The Cambridge Companion to Foucault.* Ed. Gary Gutting. Cambridge: Cambridge University Press. 28–46.
Foley, John Miles. 1988. *The Theory of Oral Composition: History and Methodology.* Bloomington: University of Indiana Press.
Foucault, Michel. 1961. *Folie et déraison, Histoire de la folie à l'âge classique.* Paris: Plon.

———. 1966. *Les mots et les choses*. Paris: Gallimard.
———. 1969. *L'archéologie du savoir*. Paris: Gallimard.
———. 1970. "Foreword to the English Edition." *The Order of Things: An Archeology of the Human Sciences*. Trans. Alan Sheridan. New York: Pantheon. ix–xiv.
———. 1972. "Mon corps, ce papier, ce feu." *Histoire de la folie à l'âge classique suivi de Mon corps, ce papier, ce feu et La folie, l'absence de l'oeuvre*. Paris: Gallimard. 583–603.
———. 1975. *Surveiller et Punir: Naissance de la Prison*. Paris: Gallimard.
———. 1976. *La volonté de savoir*. *Histoire de la sexualité*, vol. 1. Paris: Gallimard.
———. 1977a. "Theatrum Philosophicum." *Language, Counter-Memory, Practice: Selected Essays and Interviews*. Trans. Donald F. Bouchard and Sherry Simon. Ed. Donald F. Bouchard. Ithaca: Cornell University Press. 165–96. First published 1970, reprinted under the same title in *Dits et écrits: 1954–1988*, vol. 2. Eds. Daniel Defert and François Ewalt. Paris: Gallimard, 1994. 75–99.
———. 1977b. "What is an Author?" *Language, Counter-Memory, Practice: Selected Essays and Interviews*. Trans. Donald F. Bouchard and Sherry Simon. Ed. Donald F. Bouchard. Ithaca: Cornell University Press. 113–38. Originally published as Foucault 1994m.
———. 1983a. Le gouvernement de soi et des autres: Cours au Collège de France. 1982–83. Recordings housed at the Institut Mémoires de l'Edition Contemporaine.
———. 1983b. "Preface" to Gilles Deleuze and Félix Guattari. *Anti-Oedipus: Capitalism and Schizophrenia*. Trans. Robert Hurley, Mark Seem, and Helen R. Lane. Minneapolis: University of Minnesota Press. xi–xiv. Originally published in English 1977.
———. 1984a. *L'usage des plaisirs*. *Histoire de la sexualité*, vol. 2. Paris: Gallimard.
———. 1984b. *Le souci de soi*. *Histoire de la sexualité*, vol. 3. Paris: Gallimard.
———. 1986. *La pensée du dehors*. Paris: Fata Morgana.
———. 1994a. *Dits et écrits: 1954–1988*, vol. 4. Eds. Daniel Defert and François Ewalt. Paris: Gallimard.
———. 1994b. "Préface à l'«Histoire de la sexualité»." Foucault 1994a. 578–84.
———. 1994c. "A propos de la généalogie de l'éthique: un aperçu du travail en cours." Foucault 1994a. 609–31.
———. 1994d. "L'écriture de soi." Foucault 1994a. 415–30.
———. 1994e. "Lacan, le «libérateur» de la psychanalyse." Trans. A. Ghizzardi. Foucault 1994a. 204–5.
———. 1994f. "L'herméneutique du sujet." Foucault 1994a. 353–65.
———. 1994g. "Les techniques de soi." Foucault 1994a. 783–813.
———. 1994h. "L'éthique du souci de soi comme pratique de la liberté." Foucault 1994a. 708–29.
———. 1994i. "Subjectivité et vérité." Foucault 1994a. 213–18.
———. 1994j. "Le retour de la morale." Foucault 1994a. 696–707.
———. 1994k. "La société punitive." *Dits et écrits: 1954–1988*, vol. 2. Eds. Daniel Defert and François Ewalt. Paris: Gallimard. 456–70.

———. 1994l. "Le pouvoir psychiatrique." *Dits et écrits: 1954–1988*, vol. 2. Eds. Daniel Defert and François Ewalt. Paris: Gallimard. 675–86.

———. 1994m. "Qu'est-ce qu'un auteur." *Dits et écrits: 1954–1988*, vol. 1. Eds. Daniel Defert and François Ewalt. Paris: Gallimard. 789–821.

———. 1994n. "L' Armée, quand la terre tremble." *Dits et écrits: 1954–1988*, vol. 3. Eds. Daniel Defert and François Ewalt. Paris: Gallimard. 662–69.

———. 1994o. "Le chah a cent ans de retard." *Dits et écrits: 1954–1988*, vol. 3. Eds. Daniel Defert and François Ewalt. Paris: Gallimard. 679–83.

———. 1994p. "Téhéran: la foi contre le chah." *Dits et écrits: 1954–1988*, vol. 3. Eds. Daniel Defert and François Ewalt. Paris: Gallimard. 683–88.

———. 1994q. "A quoi rêvent les Iraniens?" *Dits et écrits: 1954–1988*, vol. 3. Eds. Daniel Defert and François Ewalt. Paris: Gallimard. 688–94.

———. 1994r. "Une révolte à mains nues." *Dits et écrits: 1954–1988*, vol. 3. Eds. Daniel Defert and François Ewalt. Paris: Gallimard. 701–04.

———. 1994s. "Défi à l'opposition." *Dits et écrits: 1954–1988*, vol. 3. Eds. Daniel Defert and François Ewalt. Paris: Gallimard. 704–06.

———. 1994t. "Réponse de Michel Foucault à une lectrice iranienne." *Dits et écrits: 1954–1988*, vol. 3. Eds. Daniel Defert and François Ewalt. Paris: Gallimard. 708.

———. 1994u. "La révolte iranienne se propage sur les rubans des cassettes." *Dits et écrits: 1954–1988*, vol. 3. Eds. Daniel Defert and François Ewalt. Paris: Gallimard. 709–13.

———. 1994v. "Le chef mythique de la révolte de l'Iran." *Dits et écrits: 1954–1988*, vol. 3. Eds. Daniel Defert and François Ewalt. Paris: Gallimard. 713–16.

———. 1994w. "L'esprit d'un monde sans esprit." *Dits et écrits: 1954–1988*, vol. 3. Eds. Daniel Defert and François Ewalt. Paris: Gallimard. 743–55.

———. 1994x. "Une poudrière appelée islam." *Dits et écrits: 1954–1988*, vol. 3. Eds. Daniel Defert and François Ewalt. Paris: Gallimard. 759–61.

———. 1994y. "Michel Foucault et l'Iran." *Dits et écrits: 1954–1988*, vol. 3. Eds. Daniel Defert and François Ewalt. Paris: Gallimard. 762.

———. 1994z. "Lettre ouverte à Mehdi Bazargan." *Dits et écrits: 1954–1988*, vol. 3. Eds. Daniel Defert and François Ewalt. Paris: Gallimard. 780–82.

———. 1994aa. "Inutile de se soulever?" *Dits et écrits: 1954–1988*, vol. 3. Eds. Daniel Defert and François Ewalt. Paris: Gallimard. 790–94.

———. 1994bb. "Nietzsche, la généalogie, l'histoire." *Dits et écrits: 1954–1988*, vol. 2. Eds. Daniel Defert and François Ewalt. Paris: Gallimard. 136–56.

———. 1994cc. "La vie: l'expérience et la science." *Dits et écrits: 1954–1988*, vol. 4. Eds. Daniel Defert and François Ewalt. Paris: Gallimard. 763–76.

———. 1994dd. "La vérité et les formes juridiques," *Dits et écrits: 1954–1988*, vol. 2. Eds. Daniel Defert and François Ewalt. Paris: Gallimard. 538–646.

———. 2001. *L'Herméneutique du sujet: Cours au Collège de France. 1981–82.* Ed. Frédéric Gros. Paris: Gallimard/Seuil.

Fowler, Don. 1994. "Postmodernism, Romantic Irony, and Classical Closure." *Modern Critical Theory and Classical Literature*. Eds. Irene J. F. de Jong and J. P. Sullivan. Mnemosyne Supplement. Leiden: Brill. 231–56.

Fowlie, Wallace. 1960. *Dionysus in Paris: A Guide to Contemporary French Theater.* New York: Meridian Books.

Frank, Jill. 2005. *A Democracy of Distinction: Aristotle and the Work of Politics.* Chicago: Chicago University Press.
———. 2006. "The *Antigone*'s Law." *Law, Humanities, Culture* 2: 336–40.
Frede, Dorothea. 1992. "Disintegration and Integration: Pleasure and Pain in Plato's *Philebus.*" *The Cambridge Companion to Plato.* Ed. Richard Kraut. Cambridge: Cambridge University Press. 425–63.
———, trans and ed. 1993. *Plato: Philebus.* Indianapolis: Hackett.
Freeman, Edward. 1971. *The Theatre of Albert Camus.* London: Methuen.
Freiberger, Erich D. 2000. "'Heads I Win, Tails You Lose': Wittgenstein, Plato and the Role of Construction and Deconstruction in Psychoanalysis and Ethics." *Lacan in America.* Ed. Jean Michel Rabaté. New York: The Other Press. 223–46.
Freud, Sigmund. 1955. *From the History of an Infantile Neurosis.* Trans. James Strachey and Anna Freud. The Standard Edition. London: Hogarth Press.
———. 1961a. *Beyond the Pleasure Principle.* Trans. James Strachey. The Standard Edition. New York: Norton.
———. 1961b. *Civilization and Its Discontents.* Trans. James Strachey. The Standard Edition. New York: Norton.
———. 1965. *The Interpretation of Dreams.* Trans. James Strachey. New York: Avon Books.
Frow, John. 1986. *Marxism and Literary History.* Cambridge, MA: Harvard University Press.
Gadamer, Hans-Georg. 1988. "Reply to Nicholas P. White." Trans. Roger C. Norton and Dennis J. Schmidt. *Platonic Writings, Platonic Readings.* Ed. Charles L. Griswold Jr. New York: Routledge, 258–66.
———. 1991. *Plato's Dialectical Ethics: Phenomenological Interpretations Relating to the Philebus.* Trans. Robert M. Wallace. New Haven: Yale University Press.
Gasché, Rodolphe. 2002. "L'expérience aporétique aux origines de la pensée. Platon, Heidegger, Derrida." *Etudes françaises* 38: 103–21.
Gates, Henry Louis. 1992. "'Ethnic and Minority' Studies." *Introduction to Scholarship in Modern Languages and Literatures.* Ed Joseph Gibaldi. 2nd ed. New York: The Modern Language Association. 288–302.
Gentili, Bruno. 1984. *Poesia e pubblico nella Grecia antica: Da Omero al V secolo.* Rome: Editori Latera.
Gherovici, Patricia. 2000. "Psychoanalysis: Resistible and Irresistible." *Lacan in America.* Ed. Jean-Michel Rabaté. New York: Other Press, 2000. 93–105.
Gignoux, Hubert. 1946. *Jean Anouilh.* Paris: Editions du Temps Présent.
Giraudoux, Jean. 1982. *Electre. Théâtre complet.* Eds. Jacques Body et al. Bibliothèque de la Pléiade. Paris: Gallimard. 593–685.
Goldhill, Simon. 1986. *Reading Greek Tragedy.* Cambridge: Cambridge University Press.
———. 1995. *Foucault's Virginity: Ancient Fiction and the History of Sexuality.* Cambridge: Cambridge University Press.
———. 2006. "Antigone and the Politics of Sisterhood." *Laughing With Medusa: Classical Myth and Feminist Thought.* Eds. Vanda Zajko and Miriam Leonard. Oxford: Oxford University Press, 141–62.
Goldschmidt, Victor. 2003. *Le paradigme dans la dialectique platonicienne.* Paris: Vrin. First Vrin ed. 1985. Originally published 1947, P.U.F.

Goody, Jack, and Ian Watt. 1968. "The Consequences of Literacy." *Literacy in Traditional Societies*. Ed. Jack Goody. Cambridge: Cambridge University Press. 27–68.
Goold, John. 1988. "The Language of Oedipus." *Sophocles' Oedipus Rex*. Ed. Harold Bloom. New York: Chelsea House. 143–60.
Gosling, J. C. B. 1975. *Plato: Philebus, Translated with Notes and Commentary*. Oxford: Clarendon Press.
Goux, Jean-Joseph. 1990. *Symbolic Economies: After Marx and Freud*. Trans. Jennifer Curtiss Gage. Ithaca: Cornell University Press.
Graff, Harvey J. 1987. *The Legacies of Literacy: Continuities and Contradictions in Western Culture and Society*. Bloomington: University of Indiana Press.
Grant, Alexander. 1866. *The Ethics of Aristotle Illustrated with Essays and Notes*. Vol. 1. London: Longman's.
Greene, Thomas. 1982. *The Light in Troy: Imitation and Discovery in Renaissance Poetics*. New Haven: Yale University Press.
Grene, David. 1992. "Antigone." *The Complete Greek Tragedies. Volume II: Sophocles*. Centennial ed. Eds. David Grene and Richmond Lattimore. Chicago: University of Chicago Press. 161–12.
Grenier, Roger. 1987. *Albert Camus: Soleil et ombre*. Paris: Gallimard.
Griffith, Mark. 1999. *Sophocles: Antigone*. Cambridge: Cambridge University Press.
Grimal, Pierre. 1986. *Love in Ancient Rome*. Trans. Arthur Train Jr. Norman: University of Oklahoma Press.
Gros, Frédéric. 2001. "Situation du Cours." In Michel Foucault, 2001, *L'Herméneutique du sujet: Cours au Collège de France. 1981–82*, ed. Frédéric Gros (Paris: Gallimard/Seuil). 487–526.
——. 2003. "Introduction." *Foucault et la philosophie antique*. Eds. Frédéric Gros and Carlos Lévy. Paris: Kimé. 7–13.
Gross, Nicholas. 1988. *Sophocles' Antigone: Commentary*. Bryn Mawr, PA: Bryn Mawr College.
Grossvogel, David I, ed. N.d. "Introduction." In Jean Anouilh, *Antigone*. Cambridge, MA: Integral Editions. Original 1946.
Grube, G. M. C., trans. 1997. "Phaedo." Cooper 1997. 49–100.
Guyomard, Patrick. 1992. *La jouissance du tragique: Antigone, Lacan et le désir de l'analyste*. Paris: Aubier.
Hadot, Pierre. 1987. *Exercices spirituels et philosophie antique*. 2nd ed. Paris: Etudes Augustiniennes.
——. 1992. *La citadelle intérieur: Introduction aux* Pensées *de Marc Aurèle*. Paris: Fayard.
——. 1995a. *Philosophy as a Way of Life: Spiritual Exercises from Hadot to Foucault*. Ed. Arnold I. Davidson. Trans. Michael Chase. Oxford: Blackwell.
——. 1995b. *Qu'est-ce que la philosophie antique?* Paris: Gallimard.
——. 1997. "Forms of Life and Forms of Discourse in Ancient Philosophy." Trans. Arnold I. Davidson and Paula Wissing. *Foucault and His Interlocutors*. Ed. Arnold I. Davidson. Chicago: University of Chicago Press. 203–24.
Hallett, Judith P., and Marilyn Skinner, eds. 1997. *Roman Sexualities*. Princeton: Princeton University Press.
Halperin, David M. 1990a. "Why is Diotima a Woman? Platonic *Erôs* and the

Figuration of Gender." *Before Sexuality: The Construction of Erotic Experience in the Ancient Greek World*. Eds. David M. Halperin, John J. Winkler, and Froma Zeitlin. Princeton: Princeton University Press. 257–308.

———. 1990b. *One Hundred Years of Homosexuality*. New York: Routledge.

———. 1994. "Plato and the Erotics of Narrativity." Shankman 1994a. 43–75.

———. 1995. *Saint Foucault: Towards a Gay Hagiography*. Oxford: Oxford University Press.

Halperin, David, John J. Winkler, and Froma Zeitlin, eds. 1990. *Before Sexuality, The Construction of Erotic Experience in the Ancient World*. Princeton: Princeton University Press.

Hamilton, Walter, ed and trans. 1973. *Plato: Phaedrus and Letters VII and VIII*. London: Penguin.

Hampton, Cynthia. 1990. *Pleasure, Knowledge and Being: An Analysis of Plato's Philebus*. Albany: SUNY Press.

Hanlon, Christopher. 2001. "Psychoanalysis and the Post-Political: An Interview with Slavoj Žižek." *New Literary History* 32: 1–22.

Hanson, Victor Davis, and John Heath. 1998. *Who killed Homer?: The Demise of Classical Education and the Recovery of Greek Wisdom*. New York: Free Press.

Harris, William V. 1989. *Ancient Literacy*. Cambridge, MA: Harvard University Press.

Hartog, François. 2004. "Un truchement." *Appel pour le latin et le grec 2004: 70,000 signataires*. Paris: Les Belles Lettres. 51–54.

Havelock, Eric A. 1963. *Preface to Plato*. Cambridge, MA: Harvard University Press.

Hegel, G. W. F. 1977. *Hegel's Phenomenology of the Spirit*. Trans. A. V. Miller. Oxford: Oxford University Press.

Heidegger, Martin. 1962. *Being and Time*. Trans. John Macquarrie and Edward Robinson. San Francisco: Harper Collins.

Henderson, John. 1993. "Persius' Didactic Satire: The Pupil as Teacher." *Ramus* 20: 123–48.

Highet, Gilbert. 1949. *The Classical Tradition: Greek and Roman Influences on Western Literature*. Oxford: Oxford University Press.

Hocquenghem, Guy. 1978. *Homosexual Desire*. London: Allison and Busby.

Holquist, Michael. 1990. *Dialogism: Bakhtin and His World*. London: Routledge.

Hubbard, Thomas K., ed. 2003. *Homosexuality in Greece and Rome: A Sourcebook of Basic Documents*. Berkeley: University of California Press.

Hunter, Richard. 2004. *Plato's Symposium*. Oxford: Oxford University Press.

Hutchinson, D. S., trans. 1997. "Alcibiades." Cooper 1997. 557–95.

"Informations Diverses" document page. 2005. Association pour la défense des Langues Anciennes dans l'Académie d'Aix-Marseille. Université de Provence, Aix-Marseille 1. February 3, 2005 'http://www.univ-mrs.fr/wagapinfos.htm'.

Irigaray, Luce. 1974. *Speculum, De l'autre femme*. Paris: Minuit.

———. 1977a. "Le marché des femmes." *Ce sexe qui n'en est pas un*. Paris: Minuit. 167–85.

———. 1977b. "Cosi Fan Tutti." *Ce Sexe qui n'en est pas un*. Paris: Minuit. 83–102.

———. 1977c. "Quand nos lèvres se parlent." *Ce sexe qui n'en est pas un*. Paris: Minuit. 205–17.
Irwin, Terrence. 1977. *Plato's Moral Theory: The Early and Middle Dialogues*. Oxford: Clarendon Press.
———. 1988. "Reply to David L. Roochnik." *Platonic Writings, Platonic Readings*. Ed. Charles L. Griswold, Jr. New York: Routledge. 194–99.
———. 1992. "Plato: The Intellectual Background." *The Cambridge Companion to Plato*. Ed. Richard Kraut. Cambridge: Cambridge University Press. 51–89.
Jaffro, Laurent. 2003. "Foucault et le stoïcisme: Sur l'historiographie de *L'herméneutique du sujet*." *Foucault et la philosophie antique*. Eds. Frédéric Gros et Carlos Lévy. Paris: Kimé. 51–83.
Jameson, Fredric. 1971. *Marxism and Form*. Princeton: Princeton University Press.
———. 1972. *The Prison-House of Language: A Critical Account of Structuralism and Russian Formalism*. Princeton: Princeton University Press.
———. 1981. *The Political Unconscious: Narrative as a Socially Symbolic Act*. Ithaca: Cornell University Press.
———. 1988. "Imaginary and Symbolic in Lacan." *The Ideologies of Theory*, vol. 1. Minneapolis: University of Minnesota Press. 75–115.
———. 1991. *Postmodernism, or the Cultural Logic of Late Capitalism*. London: Verso.
Janan, Micaela. 1994. *"When the Lamp is Shattered": Desire and Narrative in Catullus*. Carbondale: Southern Illinois University Press.
Jebb, Richard. 1900. *Sophocles The Plays and Fragments with Critical Notes, Commentary, and Translation in English Prose. Part III. The Antigone*. 3rd ed. Cambridge: Cambridge University Press.
Johnson, Patricia. 1997. "Woman's Third Face: A Psycho/Social Reconsideration of Sophocles' *Antigone*." *Arethusa* 30: 369–98.
Johnson, W. R. 1982. *The Idea of Lyric: Lyric Modes in Ancient and Modern Poetry*. Berkeley: University of California Press.
Julien, Phillipe. 1990. *Pour Lire Jacques Lacan*. 2nd ed. Paris: E. P. E. L.
Kamerbeek, J. C. 1978. *The Plays of Sophocles: Commentaries. Part III: Antigone*. Leiden: Brill.
Kaplan, Alice. 2000. *Collaborator: The Trial and Execution of Robert Brasillach*. Chicago: University of Chicago Press.
Katz, Jonathan Ned. 1995. *The Invention of Heterosexuality*. New York: Penguin.
Kenney, Matthew. 2003. "Seducing the Soul: Erôs and Protreptic in the Platonic Dialogues." Ph.D. Dissertation. University of South Carolina.
———. 2005. "*Erôs* as Institution: A Consideration of Why Plato Wrote the *Symposium*." *Plato Redivivus: Studies in the History of Platonism*. Eds. John Finamore and Robert Berchman. New Orleans: University Press of the South. 53–64.
Kirk, G. S., J. E. Raven, and M. S. Schofield. 1983. *The Presocratic Philosophers*. 2nd ed. Cambridge: Cambridge University Press. Originally published 1957.
Kittler, Friedrich A. 1999. *Grammaphone, Film, Typewriter*. Trans. Geoffrey Winthrop-Young and Michael Wutz. Stanford: Stanford University Press.

Knox, Bernard. 1982. "Introduction" to *Antigone. Sophocles: The Three Theban Plays*. Trans. Robert Fagles. Penguin: New York. 35–53.
———. 1988. "Sophocles' Oedipus." *Sophocles' Oedipus Rex*. Ed. Harold Bloom. New York: Chelsea House. 5–22.
Konstan, David. 1994. *Sexual Symmetry: Love in the Ancient Novel and Related Genres*. Princeton: Princeton University Press.
———. 1996. "Friendship, Frankness, and Flattery." *Friendship, Flattery, and Frankness of Speech: Studies of Friendship in the New Testament World*. Ed. John T. Fitzgerald. Leiden: Brill. 7–19
———. 1997. *Friendship in the Classical World*. Cambridge: Cambridge University Press.
———. 2002. "The Prehistory of Sexuality: Foucault's Route to Classical Antiquity." *Intertexts* 6: 8–21.
———. 2004. "PARRHÊSIA: Ancient Philosophy in Opposition." *MYTHOS and LOGOS: How to Regain the Love of Wisdom*. Eds. Albert A. Anderson, Steven V. Hicks, and Lech Witkowski. Amsterdam: Rodopi. 19–33.
Konstan, David, Diskin Clay, Clarence E. Glad, Johan C. Thom, and James Ware, eds. and trans. 1998. *Philodemus: On Frank Criticism: Introduction, Translation and Notes*. Atlanta: Scholars Press.
Koyré, Alexandre. 1962. *Introduction à la lecture de Platon, suivi de Entretiens sur Descartes*. Paris: Gallimard.
Kraut, Richard. 1992. "The Defense of Justice in Plato's *Republic*." *The Cambridge Companion to Plato*. Ed. Richard Kraut. Cambridge: Cambridge University Press. 311–37.
Kremer-Marietti, Angèle. 1985. *Michel Foucault: Archéologie et généalogie*. 2nd ed. Paris: Livre de Poche.
Kristeva, Julia. 1969. *Σημειωτικὴ: Recherches pour une sémanalyse*. Paris: Seuil.
———. 1979. "Le temps des femmes." *Cahiers de recherché de S. T. D. Paris* VII 5: 5–18.
———. 1980. *Pouvoirs de l'horreur: Essai de l'abjection*. Paris: Seuil.
———. 1983. *Histoires d'amour*. Paris: Denoël.
———. 1987. *Tales of Love*. Trans. Leon S. Roudiez. New York: Columbia University Press.
Kurke, Leslie. 1991. *The Traffic in Praise: Pindar and the Poetics of Social Economy*. Ithaca: Cornell University Press.
Lacan, Jacques. 1966a. "Présentation." *Ecrits I*. Paris Seuil. 7–12.
———. 1966b "Le Séminaire sur «La lettre volée»." *Ecrits*. Paris: Gallimard. 11–60.
———. 1966c. "La chose freudienne ou Sens du retour à Freud en psychanalyse." *Ecrits*. Paris: Gallimard. 401–36.
———. 1966d. "L'Instance de la lettre dans l'inconscient ou la raison depuis Freud." *Ecrits*. Paris: Gallimard. 493–528.
———. 1966e. "De nos antécedents." *Ecrits*. Paris: Gallimard. 65–72.
———. 1966f. "Kant avec Sade." *Ecrits*. Paris: Gallimard. 765–90.
———. 1966g. "La science et la vérité." *Ecrits*. Paris: Gallimard. 855–77.
———. 1966h. "Fonction et champ de la parole et du langage en psychanalyse." *Ecrits*. Paris: Gallimard. 237–322.
———. 1973. *Le séminaire livre XI: Les quatre concepts fondamentales de la psychanalyse*. Ed. Jacques-Alain Miller. Paris: Seuil

———. 1975. *Le séminaire livre XX: Encore*. Ed. Jacques-Alain Miller. Paris: Seuil.
———. 1982. "Seminar of 21 January 1975." *Feminine Sexuality: Jacques Lacan and the école freudienne*. Eds. Juliet Mitchell and Jacqueline Rose. Trans. Jacqueline Rose. New York: Pantheon. 162–71.
———. 1986. *Le séminaire livre VII: L'éthique de la psychanalyse*. Ed. Jacques-Alain Miller. Paris: Seuil.
———. 1991. *Le séminaire livre VIII: Le transfert*. Ed. Jacques-Alain Miller. Paris: Seuil.
———. 1992. *The Seminar of Jacques Lacan. Book VII: The Ethics of Psychoanalysis, 1959–60*. Ed. Jacques-Alain Miller. Trans. Dennis Porter. New York: W. W. Norton.
Lafleur, Richard A. 1981. "Horace and *Onomasti Komodein*: The Law of Satire." *Aufstieg und Niedergang der römischen Welt*. Vol. 31.4. Ed. Wolfgang Haase. Berlin: De Gruyter. 1790–1826.
Lane, Christopher. 2000. "The Experience of the Outside: Foucault and Psychoanalysis." *Lacan in America*. Ed. Jean-Michel Rabaté. New York: The Other Press. 309–47.
Larmour, David H. J., Paul Allen Miller, and Charles Platter, eds. 1998a. *Rethinking Sexuality: Foucault and Classical Antiquity*. Princeton: Princeton University Press.
Larmour, David H. J., Paul Allen Miller, and Charles Platter. 1998b. "Introduction: Situating the *History of Sexuality*." Larmour et al. 1998a. 3–41.
Laruelle, François. 1978. *Au-delà du principe du pouvoir*. Paris: Payot.
Laurand, Valéry. 2003. "Souci de soi et marriage chez Musonius Rufus: Perspectives politiques de la *krâsis* stoïcienne." *Foucault et la philosophie antique*. Eds. Frédéric Gros and Carlos Lévy. Paris: Kimé. 85–116.
Ledbetter, Grace M. 2003. *Poetics before Plato: Interpretation and Authority in Early Greek Theories of Poetry*. Princeton: Princeton University Press.
Lee, Desmond, ed. and trans. 1987. *Plato: The Republic*. 2nd rev. ed. London: Penguin.
Lentricchia, Frank. 1980. *After the New Criticism*. Chicago: Chicago University Press.
Leonard, Miriam. 1999. "Irigaray's Cave: Feminist Theory and the Politics of French Classicism." *Ramus* 28: 152–68.
———. 2000a. "Creating Dawn: Writing through Antiquity in the works of Helene Cixous." *Arethusa* 33: 121–48.
———. 2000b. "The 'Politiques de l'amitié': Derrida's Greeks and a National Politics of Classical Scholarship." *Proceedings of The Cambridge Philological Society* 46: 45–78.
———. 2003. "Antigone, The Political and the Ethics of Psychoanalysis." *Proceedings of The Cambridge Philological Society* 49: 130–54.
———. 2004. "Classics." *Encyclopedia of Modern French Thought*. Ed. Christopher John Murray. New York: Fitzroy Dearborn. 142–46.
———. 2005. *Athens in Paris: Ancient Greece and the Political in Post-War French Thought*. Oxford: Oxford University Press.
———. 2006. "Oedipus in the Accusative. Derrida and Levinas." *Comparative Literature Studies* 43: 224–51.
Le Roy, Louis, ed. and trans. 1558. *Le Sympose de Platon, ou de l'Amour et de Beauté*. trans. *Loys Le Roy*. Paris: J. Longis & R. Le Mangnyer.

Levett, M. J., trans. 1997. *Theaetetus*. Rev. Myles Burnyeat. Cooper, 1997. 157–234.
Lévy, Carlos. 2003. "Michel Foucault et le scepticisme: Réflexions sur un silence." *Foucault et la philosophie antique*. Eds. Frédéric Gros et Carlos Lévy. Paris: Kimé. 119–35.
Levy, Neil. 2004. "Foucault as Virtue Ethicist." *Foucault Studies* 1: 20–31.
Liu, Catherine. 2000. "Lacanian Reception." *Lacan in America*. Ed. Jean-Michel Rabaté. New York: Other Press, 2000. 107–37.
Lloyd-Jones, Hugh. 1985. "Psychoanalysis and the Study of the Ancient World." *Freud and the Humanities*. Ed. Peregrine Horden. London: Duckworth. 152–180.
Lloyd-Jones, Kenneth. 1996. "'*Cest exercice de traduire* . . .': Humanist Hermeneutic in Louis Le Roy's Translations of Plato." *Recapturing the Renaissance: New Perspectives on Humanism, Dialogue and Texts*. Eds. Diane S. Wood and Paul Allen Miller. Knoxville, TN: New Paradigm. 85–106.
Loraux, Nicole. 1987a. *Tragic Ways of Killing a Woman*. Trans. Anthony Foster. Cambridge, MA: Harvard University Press.
———. 1987b. "La main d'Antigone." *Mêtis* 1 (1987): 165–96.
———. 1996. *Né de la terre: Mythe et politique à Athènes*. Paris: Seuil.
———. 2002. *Sophocle: Antigone*. Paris: Les Belles Lettres.
Loraux, Nicole, Gregory Nagy, and Laura Slatkin. 2001. "Introduction." *Antiquities*. Eds. Nicole Loraux, Gregory Nagy, and Laura Slatkin. *Postwar French Thought*, vol. III. Ed. Ramona Naddaff. New York: The New Press. 1–16.
Lucid, Daniel P., ed. and trans. 1977. *Soviet Semiotics*. Baltimore: Johns Hopkins University Press.
Luepnitz, Deborah. 2003. "Beyond the Phallus: Lacan and Feminism." *The Cambridge Companion to Lacan*. Ed. Jean-Michel Rabaté. Cambridge: Cambridge University Press. 221–37.
Luria, A. R. 1976. *Cognitive Development: Its Cultural and Social Foundations*. Trans. Martin Lopez-Morillas and Lynn Solotaroff. Ed. Michael Cole. Cambridge, MA: Harvard University Press.
Lyotard, Jean François. 1984. *The Postmodern Condition*. Trans. Geoff Bennington and Brian Massumi. Minneapolis: University of Minnesota Press.
Macey, David. 1993. *The Lives of Michel Foucault*. New York: Pantheon.
Malone, Kareen Ror. "The Place of Lacanian Psychoanalysis in North American Psychology." *Lacan in America*. Ed. Jean-Michel Rabaté. New York: The Other Press, 2000. 3–24.
Mara, Gerald M. 1997. *Socrates' Discursive Democracy: Logos and Ergon in Platonic Political Philosophy*. Albany: State University of New York Press.
Marcel, Gabriel. 1959. *L'heure théâtrale: De Giraudoux à Jean-Paul Sartre*. Paris: Plon.
Marx, Karl. 1976. *Capital*. Vol. 1. Trans. Ben Fowkes. New York: Vintage.
Maulnier, Thierry. 1933. *Nietzsche*. Paris: Librairie de la Revue Française.
McCredie, Wendy J. 1998. "Exploring the Text: Adorno, Lacan, and Literature" *Intertexts* 2: 74–82
McIntyre, H. G. 1981. *The Theatre of Jean Anouilh*. Totowa, NJ: Barnes and Noble Books.
McGlathery, Daniel. 1998. "Reversals of Platonic Love in Petronius's *Satyricon*." Larmour et al. 1998a. 204–27.

McLuhan, Marshall. 1962. *The Gutenberg Galaxy.* Toronto: University of Toronto Press.

Michon, Pascal. 2003. "On the Contemporary Disintegration of Cultural Meaning." *Intertexts* 7 (2003): 117–29.

Miller, James. 1993. *The Passion of Michel Foucault.* New York: Simon & Schuster.

Miller, J. Hillis. 1981. "The Ethics of Reading: Vast Gaps and Parting Hours." *American Criticism in the Poststructuralist Age.* Ed. Ira Konigsberg. Ann Arbor: University of Michigan Press. 19–41.

Miller, Paul Allen. 1998. "Catullan Consciousness, the 'Care of the Self,' and the Force of the Negative in History." Larmour et al. 1998a. 171–203.

———. 1999. "The Classical Roots of Poststructuralism: Lacan, Derrida, and Foucault." *International Journal of the Classical Tradition* 5: 204–25.

———. 2004a. *Subjecting Verses: Latin Love Elegy and the Emergence of the Real.* Princeton: Princeton University Press.

———. 2004b. "Dumézil, Georges." *Encyclopedia of Modern French Thought.* Ed. Christopher John Murray. New York: Fitzroy Dearborn. 189–91.

———. 2004c. "Vernant, Jean-Pierre." *Encyclopedia of Modern French Thought.* Ed. Christopher John Murray. New York: Fitzroy Dearborn. 637–39.

———. 2005a. *Latin Verse Satire: A Critical Anthology and Reader.* London: Routledge.

———. 2005b. "Lacan le con: Luce Tells Jacques Off." *Intertexts* 9: 139–51.

———. 2006. "Truth-Telling in Foucault's 'Le gouvernement de soi et des autres' and Persius 1: The Subject, Rhetoric, and Power." *Parrhesia* 1: 27–61.

———. Forthcoming. "It Don't Mean a Thing if it Ain't Got das *Ding*: or What is Literature." *The Desire of the Analysts: Psychoanalysis and Cultural Criticism in the New Millennium.* Eds. Greg Forter and Paul Allen Miller. Albany: SUNY Press.

MLA International Bibliography. 2005. http://web24.epnet.com.pallas2.tcl.sc.edu.

Moi, Toril. 1994. *Simone de Beauvoir: The Making of an Intellectual Woman.* Oxford: Blackwell.

———. 2002. *Sexual/Textual Politics: Feminist Literary Theory.* 2nd ed. London: Routledge. Original 1985.

Monoson, S. Sara. 2000. *Plato's Democratic Entanglements: Athenian Politics and the Practice of Philosophy.* Princeton: Princeton University Press.

Montaigne, Michel de. 1972. *Essais.* Tome 1. Ed. Pierre Michel. Paris: Librairie Générale Française.

Moreschini, Claudio, and Paul Vicaire, eds. 1985. *Platon: Phèdre.* Paris: Société d'Edition «Les Belles Lettres».

Morgan, Michael L. 1992. "Plato and Greek Religion." *The Cambridge Companion to Plato.* Ed. Richard Kraut. Cambridge: Cambridge University Press. 227–47.

Morrow, Glenn R., trans. 1997. "Letters." In Cooper 1997. 1634–76.

———. 1935. *Studies in the Platonic Epistles: With a Translation and Notes.* Urbana: University of Illinois Press.

Morson, Gary Saul, and Caryl Emerson. *Mikhail Bakhtin: Creation of a Prosaics.* Stanford: Stanford University Press, 1990.

Moxey, Keith P. F. "Semiotics and the Social History of Art." *New Literary History* 22 (1991): 985–99.
Nadaff, Gerard. 1998. "Translator's Introduction." Luc Brisson. 1998. *Plato the Mythmaker*. Trans and Ed. Gerard Nadaff. Chicago: University of Chicago Press. vii–liii.
Nagy, Gregory. 1979. *The Best of the Achaeans: Concepts of the Hero in Archaic Greek Poetry*. Baltimore: Johns Hopkins University Press.
———. 1990a. *Greek Myth and Poetics*. Ithaca: Cornell University Press.
———. 1990b. *Pindar's Homer: The Lyric Possession of an Epic Past*. Baltimore: Johns Hopkins University Press.
Nauck, A. 1964. *Tragicorum Graecorum Fragmenta*, with a supplement by Bruno Snell. Hildesheim.
Nectoux, François. 2004. "Vidal-Naquet, Pierre." *Encyclopedia of Modern French Thought*. Ed. Christopher John Murray. New York: Fitzroy Dearborn. 639–40.
Nehamas, Alexander. 1998. *The Art of Living: Socratic Reflections from Plato to Foucault*. Berkeley: University of California Press.
Nehamas, Alexander, and Paul Woodruff, eds. and trans. 1995. *Plato: Phaedrus*. Indianapolis: Hackett = Cooper 1997. 506–56.
———. 1997. "Symposium." Cooper 1997. 458–505.
Neveu, Valérie. 2004. "Langues anciennes et patrimoine écrit. Le latin, les fonds anciens et le bibliothécaire." *Appel pour le latin et le grec 2004: 70,000 signataires*. Paris: Les Belles Lettres. 79–85.
Newman, Robert J. 1989. "*Cotidie meditare*. Theory and Practice of the *meditatio* in Imperial Stoicism." *Aufstieg und Niedergang der römischen Welt*. II 36.3. Eds. Hildegard Temporini and Wolfgang Haase. Berlin: Walter de Gruyter. 1473–517.
Newton, K. M. 1997. *Twentieth-Century Literary Theory*. 2nd ed. London: St. Martin's.
Nicholson, Nigel. 1998. "The Truth of Pederasty: A Supplement to Foucault's Genealogy of the Relation between Truth and Desire in Ancient Greece." *Intertexts* 2: 26–45.
Nightingale, Andrea Wilson. 1995. *Genres in Dialogue: Plato and the Construct of Philosophy*. Cambridge: Cambridge University Press.
Nippel, Wilfred. 1995. *Public Order in Ancient Rome*. Cambridge: Cambridge University Press.
Ormand, Kirk. 1999. *Exchange and the Maiden: Marriage in Sophoclean Tragedy*. Austin: University of Texas Press.
Oudemans, Th. C. W., and A. P. M. H. Lardinois. 1987. *Tragic Ambiguity: Anthropology, Philosophy, and Sophocles' Antigone*. Leiden: Brill.
Palmer, Bryan. 1990. *Descent into Discourse*. Philadelphia: Temple University Press.
Parker, Holt. 1997. "The Teratogenic Grid." *Roman Sexualities*. Eds. Judith P. Hallett and Marilyn B. Skinner. Princeton: Princeton University Press. 49–65.
Penner, Terry. 1992. "Socrates and the Early Dialogues." *The Cambridge Companion to Plato*. Ed. Richard Kraut. Cambridge: Cambridge University Press. 121–69.
Peponi, Anastasia-Erasmia. 2002. "Mixed Pleasures, Blended Discourses:

Poetry, Medicine, and the Body in Plato's *Philebus* 46–47c." *Classical Antiquity* 21: 135–60.
Places, Edouard des, S.J. 1964. *Lexique de la langue philosophique et religieuse de Platon*. Paris: Société d'édition «Les Belles Lettres».
Platter, Charles. 2005. "Was Plato the Founder of Totalitarianism." *Classical Studies and the Ancient World. History in Dispute*. Vol. 21. Eds. Paul Allen Miller and Charles Platter. Detroit: Gale. 154–63.
Plotnitsky, Arkady. 2000. "On Lacan and Mathematics." *Lacan in America*. Ed. Jean-Michel Rabaté. New York: The Other Press. 247–76.
Pommier, Gérard. 2000. "New Resistances to Psychoanalysis." *Lacan in America*. Ed. Jean-Michel Rabaté. New York: The Other Press. 71–91.
Poster, Mark. 1989. *Critical Theory and Poststructuralism*. Ithaca: Cornell University Press.
Quilliot, Roger, ed. 1962. "*Caligula*: Notes et Variantes." *Théâtre, Récits, Nouvelles*. Bibliothèque de la Pléiade. Paris: Gallimard. 1733–87.
Rabaté, Jean-Michel. 2003a. "Lacan's Turn to Freud." *Cambridge Companion to Lacan*. Ed. Jean-Michel Rabaté. Cambridge: Cambridge University Press. 1–24.
———. 2003b. "Chronology of Lacan's Life." *Cambridge Companion to Lacan*. Ed. Jean-Michel Rabaté. Cambridge: Cambridge University Press. xix–xxviii.
———. 2003c. "Preface." *Cambridge Companion to Lacan*. Ed. Jean-Michel Rabaté. Cambridge: Cambridge University Press. ix–xv.
Rabinovich, Diana. 2003. "What is a Lacanian Clinic?" *Cambridge Companion to Lacan*. Ed. Jean-Michel Rabaté. Cambridge: Cambridge University Press. 208–20.
Race, William H. 1983. *Plato's Lysis*. Bryn Mawr: Bryn Mawr College.
Radt, S. 1977. *Tragicorum Graecorum Fragmenta*. Vol. 4, *Sophocles*. Göttingen: Vanhoeck and Ruprecht.
Ragland-Sullivan, Ellie. 1986. *Jacques Lacan and the Philosophy of Psychoanalysis*. Urbana: University of Illinois Press.
Ramage, Edwin S. 1974. "Persius, The Philosopher-Satirist." *Roman Satirists: The Fine Art of Criticism in Ancient Rome*. Eds. Edwin S. Ramage, David L. Sigsbee, and Sigmund C. Fredricks. Park Ridge, NJ: Noyes Press, 1974. 114–35.
Renaut, Alain. 1993. *Sartre: Le dernier philosophe*. Paris: Grasset.
Restuccia, Frances L. 2000. "The Subject of Homosexuality: Butler's Elision." *Lacan in America*. Ed. Jean-Michel Rabaté. New York: The Other Press. 349–60.
Richlin, Amy. 1993. "Not Before Homosexuality." *Journal of the History of Sexuality* 3: 523–73.
———. 1998. "Foucault's *History of Sexuality*: A Useful Theory for Women?" Larmour et al. 1998a. 138–70.
Roazen, Paul. 2000. "What is Wrong with French Psychoanalysis? Observations on Lacan's First Seminar." *Lacan in America*. Ed. Jean-Michel Rabaté. New York: The Other Press. 41–60.
Robert, Jean-Noël. 2004. "Les langues et la culture classiques sauvées par l'Europe." *Appel pour le latin et le grec 2004: 70,000 signataires*. Paris: Les Belles Lettres. 95–107.

Robin, Léon. 1929. "Notice." *Platon: Le Banquet.* Paris: Société d'Edition «Les Belles Lettres». vii–cxxi.

———. 1964. *La théorie platonicienne de l'amour.* 2nd ed. Paris: Presses Universitaires de France. Originally published 1933.

———. 1985. "Notice." *Platon: Phèdre.* Paris: Société d'Edition «Les Belles Lettres». vii–ccv. Originally published 1933.

Roller, Matthew B. 2001. *Constructing Autocracy: Aristocrats and Emperors in Julio-Claudian Rome.* Princeton: Princeton University Press.

Romilly, Jacqueline de. 2004. "Allocution de Madame Jacqueline de Romilly." *Appel pour le latin et le grec 2004: 70,000 signataires.* Paris: Les Belles Lettres. 15–18.

Roochnik, David L. 1988. "Terrence Irwin's Reading of Plato." *Platonic Writings, Platonic Readings.* Ed. Charles L. Griswold, Jr. New York: Routledge. 183–93.

Rose, Peter W. 1992. *Sons of the Gods, Children of Earth: Ideology and Literary Form in Ancient Greece.* Ithaca: Cornell University Press.

Ross, W. D., trans. 2001. *Ethica Nicomachea. The Basic Works of Aristotle.* Ed. Richard McKeon. New York: The Modern Library. 927–1112.

Roudinesco, Elisabeth. 1997. *Jacques Lacan.* Trans. Barbara Bray. Columbia University Press.

———. 2003. "The Mirror Stage: An Obliterated Archive." *Cambridge Companion to Lacan.* Ed. Jean-Michel Rabaté. Cambridge: Cambridge University Press. 25–34.

Rouse, Joseph. 1994. "Power/Knowledge." *The Cambridge Companion to Foucault.* Ed. Gary Gutting. Cambridge: Cambridge University Press. 92–114.

St. Aubyn, F. C., and R. G. Marshall, eds. 1963. *Jean-Paul Sartre: Les mouches.* New York: Harper & Row.

Sakolsky, Ron. 1992. "'Disciplinary Power,' the Labor Process, and the Constitution of the Laboring Subject." *Rethinking MARXISM* 5.4: 114–26.

Sallis, John. 1998. "Daydream." *Revue internationale de philosophie* 52: 397–410.

Santas, Gerasimos. 1988. *Plato and Freud.* Oxford: Basil Blackwell.

Sartre, Jean-Paul. 1943. *L'être et le néant: essai d'ontologie phénoménologique.* Paris: Gallimard.

———. 1981a. *L'âge de raison. Jean-Paul Sartre: Oeuvres romanesques.* Eds. Michel Contat et Michel Rybalka. Bibliothèque de la Pléiade. Paris: Gallimard. 391–729.

———. 1981b. "L'enfance d'un chef." *Le Mur. Jean-Paul Sartre: Oeuvres romanesques.* Eds. Michel Contat et Michel Rybalka. Bibliothèque de la Pléiade. Paris: Gallimard. 314–88.

———. 1981c. *La nausée. Jean-Paul Sartre: Oeuvres romanesques.* Eds. Michel Contat et Michel Rybalka. Bibliothèque de la Pléiade. Paris: Gallimard. 1–210.

———. 1981d. *L'âge de raison. Jean-Paul Sartre: Oeuvres romanesques.* Eds. Michel Contat et Michel Rybalka. Bibliothèque de la Pléiade. Paris: Gallimard. 391–729.

———. 2005a. "Entretien avec Yvon Novy (*Comoedia*, 24 avril 1943)." "Autour des *Mouches.*" Eds. Michel Contat and Ingrid Galster. *Jean-Paul Sartre: Théâtre complète.* Ed. Michel Contat. Bibliothèque de la Pléiade. Paris: Gallimard. 76–77.

———. 2005b. *Les mouches. Jean-Paul Sartre: Théâtre complet.* Ed. Michel Contat. Bibliothèque de la Pléiade. Paris: Gallimard. 1–70.

———. 2005c. "Ce que fut la création des *Mouches* (*La Croix,* 20 janvier 1951)." "Autour des *Mouches.*" Eds. Michel Contat and Ingrid Galster. *Jean-Paul Sartre: Théâtre complet.* Ed. Michel Contat. Bibliothèque de la Pléiade. Paris: Gallimard. 78.

———. 2005d. "Discussion autour des *Mouches* (*Verger* 5, 1948)." "Autour des *Mouches.*" Eds. Michel Contat and Ingrid Galster. *Jean-Paul Sartre: Théâtre complet.* Ed. Michel Contat. Bibliothèque de la Pléiade. Paris: Gallimard. 81–85.

———. 2005e. *Huis clos. Jean-Paul Sartre: Théâtre complet.* Ed. Michel Contat. Bibliothèque de la Pléiade. Paris: Gallimard. 89–128.

———. 2005f. *Les mains sales. Jean-Paul Sartre: Théâtre complet.* Ed. Michel Contat. Bibliothèque de la Pléiade. Paris: Gallimard. 147–200.

Saunders, Trevor J. 1997. *Laws.* Cooper 1997: 1318–1616.

Sawicki, Jana. 1994. "Foucault, Feminism, and Questions of Identity." *The Cambridge Companion to Foucault.* Ed. Gary Gutting. Cambridge: Cambridge University Press. 286–313.

Sayre, Kenneth M. 1983. *Plato's Late Ontology: A Riddle Resolved.* Princeton: Princeton University Press.

———. 1988. "Plato's Dialogues in Light of the *Seventh Letter.*" *Platonic Writings, Platonic Readings.* Ed. Charles L. Griswold, Jr. New York: Routledge. 93–109.

Schaerer, René. 1969. *La question platonicienne: Étude sur les rapports de la pensée et de l'expression dans les Dialogues.* Neuchâtel: Secrétariat de l'université.

Schmidt, Joël. 2004. "De mes études d'histoire latine et ancienne à mes ouvrages et à l'édition, trois diagnostics pessimistes." *Appel pour le latin et le grec 2004: 70,000 signataires.* Paris: Les Belles Lettres. 87–93.

Schneiderman, Stuart. 1983. *Jacques Lacan: The Death of an Intellectual Hero.* Cambridge: Harvard University Press.

Scholes, Robert. 1992. "Canonicity and Textuality." *Introduction to Scholarship in Modern Languages and Literatures.* Ed Joseph Gibaldi. 2nd ed. New York: The Modern Language Association. 138–58.

Segal, Charles. 1988. "The Music of the Sphinx: The Problem of Language in *Oedipus Tyrannus.*" *Sophocles' Oedipus Rex.* Ed. Harold Bloom. New York: Chelsea House. 127–42.

———. 1990. "*Antigone:* Death and Love, Hades and Dionysus." *Modern Critical Views: Sophocles.* Ed. Harold Bloom. New York: Chelsea House. 161–206.

———. 1995. *Sophocles' Tragic World: Divinity, Nature, Society.* Cambridge, MA: Harvard University Press.

Sennellart, Michel. 2003. "La practique de la direction de conscience." *Foucault et la philosophie antique.* Eds. Frédéric Gros and Carlos Lévy. Paris: Kimé. 153–74.

Shankman, Steven, ed. 1994a. *Plato and Postmodernism.* Glenside, PA: Aldine Press.

———. 1994b. "Plato and Postmodernism." Shankman 1994a. 3–28.

Shantz, Jeffrey. 2004. "Maurras, Charles." *Encyclopedia of Modern French Thought.* Ed. Christopher John Murray. New York: Fitzroy Dearborn. 468–70.

Sharpe, Matthew. 2005. "'Critique' as Technology of the Self." *Foucault Studies* 2: 97–116.
Shepherdson, Charles. 1995. "History and the Real: Foucault with Lacan." *Postmodern Culture* 5.2. http://muse.jhu.edu/journals/postmodern_culture/toc/pmc5.2.html.
———. 2003. "Lacan and Philosophy." *The Cambridge Companion to Lacan*. Ed. Jean-Michel Rabaté. Cambridge: Cambridge University Press. 116–32.
Shields, J. G. 2004. "Bardèche, Maurice." *Encyclopedia of Modern French Thought*. Ed. Christopher John Murray. New York: Fitzroy Dearborn. 43–46.
Silverman, Kaja. 2000. *World Spectators*. Stanford: Stanford University Press.
Snell, Bruno. 1953. *The Discovery of the Mind in Greek Philosophy and Literature*. Trans. T. G. Rosenmeyer. New York: Dover Press.
Snodgrass, Anthony. 1980. *Archaic Greece: The Age of Experiment*. Berkeley: University of California Press.
Souilhé, Joseph, ed. and trans. 1960. *Platon: Lettres*. Paris: Société d'Edition «Les Belles Lettres».
Spivak, Gayatri Chakavorty. 1976. "Translator's Preface." In Derrida, 1976. ix–xc.
Sprintzen, David. 1988. *Camus: A Critical Examination*. Philadelphia: Temple University Press.
Ste. Croix, G. E. M. de. 1981. *The Class Struggle in the Ancient Greek World: From the Archaic Age to the Arab Conquests*. Ithaca: Cornell University Press.
Steiner, George. 1984. *Antigones*. Oxford: Oxford University Press.
Stoekl, Allan. 1992. *Agonies of the Intellectual: Commitment, Subjectivity and the Performative in the 20th Century French Tradition*. Lincoln: University of Nebraska Press.
Sussman, Henry. 1993. *Psyche and Text: The Sublime and Grandiose in Literature, Psychopathology, and Culture*. Albany: SUNY Press.
Svenbro, Jesper. 1993, *Phrasikleia: An Anthropology of Reading in Ancient Greece*. Trans. Janet Lloyd. Ithaca: Cornell University Press.
Syme, Ronald. 1960. *The Roman Revolution*. Oxford: Oxford University Press. Original 1939.
Szlezák, Thomas A. 1999. *Reading Plato*. Trans. Graham Zanker. London: Routledge. Original 1993.
Taylor, Charles. 1989. *Sources of the Self*. Cambridge, MA: Harvard University Press.
Thomas, Rosalind. 1989. *Oral Tradition and Written Record in Classical Athens*. Cambridge: Cambridge University Press.
———. 1992. *Literacy and Orality in Ancient Greece*. Cambridge: Cambridge University Press.
Todorov, Tzvetan. 1984. *Mikhail Bakhtin: The Dialogical Principle*. Trans. Wlad Godzich. Minneapolis: University of Minnesota Press.
Todd, Olivier. 1996. *Albert Camus: Une vie*. Paris: Gallimard.
Tort, Michel. 2000. "Lacan's New Gospel." *Lacan in America*. Ed. Jean-Michel Rabaté. New York: The Other Press, 2000. 153–87.
Tyrrell, William Blake, and Larry J. Bennett. 1998. *Recapturing Sophocles' Antigone*. Lanham, MD: Rowman and Littlefield.

Vandromme, Pol. 1972. *Jean Anouilh: Un auteur et ses personnages. Essai suivi d'un recueil de textes critiques de Jean Anouilh*. Paris: La Table Ronde.
Vernant, Jean-Pierre. 1965. *Mythe et pensée chez les Grecs*. 2 vols. Paris: Maspero.
———. 2001. "The Spiritual Universe of the *Polis*." Trans. Janet Lloyd. *Antiquities*. Eds. Nicole Loraux, Gregory Nagy, and Laura Slatkin. *Postwar French Thought*, vol. III. Ed. Ramona Naddaff. New York: The New Press. 19–30.
Vernant, Jean-Pierre, and Pierre Vidal-Naquet. 1981. *Tragedy and Myth in Ancient Greece*. Trans. Janet Lloyd. Atlantic Highlands, NJ: Humanities Press, 1981.
Veyne, Paul. 1997. "The Final Foucault and His Ethics." Trans. Catherine Porter and Arnold I. Davidson. *Foucault and His Interlocutors*. Ed. Arnold I. Davidson. Chicago: Chicago University Press. 225–33.
Vizier, Alain. 1998. "*Incipit Philosophia*." Larmour et al. 1998a. 61–84.
Vlastos, Gregory. 1970. "The Individual as an Object of Love in Plato." *Platonic Studies*. Princeton: Princeton University Press. 3–42.
———. 1991. *Socrates, Ironist and Moral Philosopher*. Ithaca, NY: Cornell University Press.
Voloshinov, V. N. 1986. *Marxism and the Philosophy of Language*. Trans. Ladislav Matejka and I. R. Titunik. Cambridge, MA: Harvard University Press.
Wallace, Robert W. 1991. "Introduction." Hans-Georg Gadamer. 1991. *Plato's Dialectical Ethics: Phenomenological Interpretations Relating to the Philebus*. Trans. Robert M. Wallace. New Haven: Yale University Press. ix–xxiii.
Walters, Jonathan. 1997. "Invading the Roman Body: Manliness and Impenetrablity in Roman Thought." *Roman Sexualities*. Eds. Judith P. Hallett and Marilyn B. Skinner. Princeton: Princeton University Press. 29–43.
Watling, E. F., trans. 1947. *Sophocles: The Theban Plays*. London: Penguin.
Weed, Elizabeth. 1994. "The Question of Style." *Engaging with Irigaray*. Eds. Carolyne Burke, Naomi Schor, and Margaret Whitford. New York: Columbia University Press. 79–109.
Winkler, John J. 1990. *The Constraints of Desire: The Anthropology of Sex and Gender in Ancient Greece*. New York: Routledge.
Wirszubski, Ch. 1950. *Libertas as a Political Idea at Rome during the Late Republic and Early Principate*. Cambridge: Cambridge University Press.
Witt, M. A. F. 2001. *The Search for Modern Tragedy: Aesthetic Fascism in Italy and France*. Ithaca: Cornell University Press.
Wohl, Victoria. 2002. *Love among the Ruins: The Erotics of Democracy in Classical Athens*. Princeton: Princeton University Press.
———. Forthcoming. "Sexual Difference and the Aporia of Justice in Sophocles' *Antigone*." *Authorizing Sexual Difference: Greek Tragedy and the Formation of the Polis*. Eds. D. McCoskey and E. Zakin.
Wolff, Francis. 1992. "Trios. Deleuze, Derrida, Foucault, historiens du platonisme." *Nos Grecs et leurs modernes*. Ed. Barbara Cassin. Paris: Seuil. 232–48.
Woodruff, Paul, trans. 2001. *Antigone*. Indianapolis: Hackett.
Zalloua, Zahi. 2002. "Alterity and 'Care of the Self' in Montaigne's Essay 'Of Friendship.'" *Intertexts* 6: 20–36.
Zeitlin, Froma. 1990. "Thebes: Theater of Self and Society in Athenian Drama." *Nothing to Do with Dionysos: Athenian Drama in Its Social Context*. Eds.

John J. Winkler and Froma I. Zeitlin. Princeton: Princeton University Press. 130–67.

Žižek, Slavoj. 1989. *The Sublime Object of Ideology.* London: Verso.

———. 1991. *Looking Awry: An Introduction to Jacques Lacan through Popular Culture.* Cambridge, MA: MIT Press.

———. 1992. *Enjoy Your Symptom: Jacques Lacan in Hollywood and Out.* New York and London: Routledge.

———. 1993. *Tarrying with the Negative: Kant, Hegel, and the Critique of Ideology.* Durham, NC: Duke University Press.

———. 1996. *The Invisible Remainder: An Essay on Schelling and Related Matters.* London and New York: Verso.

———. 2004. "From Antigone to Joan of Arc." *Helios* 31: 51–62.

———. Forthcoming. "Lacan's Four Discourses: A Political Reading." *The Desire of the Analysts: Psychoanalysis and Cultural Criticism in the New Millennium.* Eds. Greg Forter and Paul Allen Miller. Albany: SUNY Press.

Zoberman, Pierre. Forthcoming. "Queer(ing) Pleasure: Having a Gay Old Time in the Culture of Early-Modern France." *The Desire of the Analysts: Psychoanalysis and Cultural Criticism.* Eds. Greg Furter and Paul Allen Miller. Albany: SUNY Press.

Zuckert, Catherine H. 1996. *Postmodern Platos: Nietzsche, Heidegger, Gadamer, Strauss, Derrida.* Chicago: University of Chicago Press,

Zumthor, Paul. 1983. *Introduction à la poésie orale.* Paris: Seuil.

Zupancic, Alenka. 2003. "Ethics and Tragedy in Lacan." *Cambridge Companion to Lacan.* Ed. Jean-Michel Rabaté. Cambridge: Cambridge University Press. 173–90.

Index

absolute, 23, 37, 45, 51
absurd, 31, 43–51, 54–56, 58, 60, 96
Achilles, 69n10, 126–27, 129
Action Française, 27, 30
Admetus, 126–27
Aegisthus, 22, 34, 37–40, 42, 54
Aeschylus, 22, 33, 35, 38, 39, 80n31, 82n33, 126
aesthetics, 19, 23, 28–31, 45, 52, 55, 58, 66, 72, 84, 213n56, 216–17
agalma, 71–72, 96, 98, 119–21, 125, 127–28
Agamemnon, 33–35, 39, 41
Alcestis, 126–27, 129
Alcibiades, 23–24, 60, 64, 71, 96, 98–99, 107, 110, 116, 118–21, 123–32, 178–81, 193n28, 201–4, 208, 213n54, 218–26, 231–32, 234–35
allegory, 18, 22–23, 34–35, 44, 51, 53, 75, 228, 233n7
Althusser, Louis, 14n23, 19, 225
Anglo-American scholarship, 2–4, 7, 9–10, 17, 213
Annas, Julia, 68–69, 72n13, 108n11, 190n24
Anouilh, Jean, 17–18, 23, 30–32, 36, 46n25, 51–60, 61, 65–68, 96–97, 101, 130, 228
anti-semitism, 27, 30
apeiron, 142–43, 147n21, 151, 155, 159–65, 171n56

Apollinaire, Guillaume, 227
aporetical dialogues, 112, 117, 195n33
aporia, 114, 117, 139, 156n35, 157, 179, 191, 207
archeology, 17, 133, 135, 141–42, 171, 205, 234
Aristophanes, 121–24, 155, 176, 195, 209, 228
Aristotle, 6, 20–21, 61, 67–68, 71–72, 85, 111, 153, 159n38, 163n42, 173–74, 184, 191n25
Armstrong, Richard, 15, 97, 98n52, 207n47
askesis, 1, 99, 180n3, 213n57, 214
atê, 80–81, 87, 91–92, 94–95
atopia, 16, 24, 64, 98, 103, 132
Augustine, 6, 45, 67
autadelphon, 87–91
authenticity, 28, 40, 43, 56, 59, 81, 174
autonomos, 63, 88, 91
auto to auto, 221–22

Bachelard, Gaston, 215n60
bad faith, 35, 37–39, 41–42, 59–60, 72n12, 74, 95, 97, 131
Bardèche, Maurice, 31
Barthes, Roland, 5
Bataille, Georges, 5, 6
Baudelaire, Charles, 6, 32
Bayrou, François, 8
beauty, 24, 59, 66, 72–74, 80, 81,

· 261 ·

83–85, 95–96, 101, 103, 105, 107, 118, 127, 129–30, 132, 196, 202
Beauvoir, Simone de, 16n28, 44
Benardete, Seth, 78–79, 88, 93, 95
Benjamin, Walter, 101
Bennett, William, 7
Bentham, Jeremy, 216
Benveniste, Emile, 42, 93
Berger, Harry, 127, 145, 148n24, 150, 151
Berryman, John, 175
bien, le, 37, 59, 70–71, 94, 96, 103, 108, 121
Blanchot, Maurice, 5, 11, 12n19, 15n26, 23, 51, 173–74
Blondell, Ruby, 108, 111, 113n18, 117–18, 125n36, 140
Bloom, Allan, 7
Bloom, Harold, 5
bonheur, 30, 36, 57, 71, 74, 86, 97, 130. See also *eudaimonia;* happiness
Boussoulas, Nicolas-Isidore, 161–62, 164n45, 183, 193n30
Boyne, Roy, 169, 184n13
Brasillach, Robert, 30–31, 44, 48, 131n41
Brecht, Bertold, 5
Butler, Judith, 5n8, 72n12, 79–83, 88, 102, 104

Caligula, 22–23, 32, 43–53, 55, 57–58, 70, 96–97
capitalism, 28, 69, 217, 232
Camus, Albert, 17–18, 22, 30–32, 36, 43–51, 52, 55–56, 58, 70, 96
Carnes, Jeffrey, 121–22, 208
Carroll, Lewis, 181
catharsis, 32, 56, 67
Catullus, 4, 110n13
Céline, Louis-Ferdinand, 51
Chirac, Jacques, 8
Cicero, 6, 21n46, 62n3, 189–90n23, 227
Cixous, Hélène, 1, 15, 134
Classics in France, 9–10
classical tradition, 1–3, 7–8, 10, 17, 21–22, 27–33, 37–38, 42, 45–46, 48, 52, 56, 60, 228–29
Claudel, Paul, 63
Clément, Cathérine, 15
Clytemnestra, 33n8, 39, 42, 54
Cocteau, Jean, 27n32, 32, 33
collaboration, 23, 30–31, 35, 44, 51, 54, 59, 131. See also Vichy
collection, 119, 142–43, 152, 154, 158, 161, 164–65, 167, 176–77, 229
Collège de France, 7n10, 13n20, 18, 19, 26, 60, 171n54, 172n59, 178, 184, 186n17, 189n22, 204, 206, 207, 213, 218
commodification, 2, 27–28, 32, 42, 70, 203, 217
communism, 27, 31. See also Marxism; Parti Communiste Français; Stalinism
comparative literature, 5
confession, 26, 180, 297, 232
contingent, the, 6, 13, 38n14, 39, 43, 85, 122, 141
Copjec, Joan, 34, 61, 66–67, 70, 75n18, 84n35, 122n31, 205n45, 210n50, 215n60
Corneille, Pierre, 30, 32
countertransference, 69, 106–8
Creon, 16, 23, 31, 32, 53–55, 57–58, 65–66, 70, 75–86, 88, 91, 93–95, 97–98, 101–2, 123, 175
Croiset, Maurice, 178n2, 180n4
Culler, Jonathan, 4, 5
Cynics, 182, 189n23

dadaists, 27n2, 103
daimôn, 80n30, 112, 121, 139n11, 176, 179, 235
Davidson, Arnold, 64n5, 183, 118n20, 204, 213n57, 214n58, 215, 232n4
death drive, 52, 73, 101, 170, 213n54. See also Freud; pleasure principle; reality principle
deconstruction, 2, 4, 6, 12, 16, 45n21, 133, 135–45, 149n25, 150n28, 155n31, 156, 169

Deleuze, Gilles, 1, 12n19, 25, 26, 134, 181–83, 206n46, 218, 234
Delphi, 109, 216, 218, 220
de Man, Paul, 4, 5, 23, 51
democracy, 2, 16–18, 27–28, 77n23, 94, 98, 120n26, 220
Demosthenes, 94
Denyer, Nicholas, 178n2, 179, 180n4
Derrida, Jacques, 1–8, 9n14, 10–12, 13n20, 15–18, 24–26, 32, 44–45, 60, 64, 96, 99, 133–37, 138n10, 139–58, 165–77, 181–91, 193–97, 199–200, 218, 228–30, 234
Descartes, René, 11, 21, 67n7, 89n45, 138n13, 185–88, 219–20
desire, 2, 13, 16, 21, 23–24, 41–43, 48, 50, 52, 57, 59–60, 62–72, 75–77, 79–86, 90–91, 95–111, 115–16, 118, 120–33, 139, 140, 142, 143, 155–56, 158, 171n58, 176–77, 197, 201–2, 204, 208–10, 214–15, 217, 224, 226, 228–30; of the analyst, 24, 68, 106, 131, 208; of the Other, 59, 98, 106–7, 127–29; pure, 63–64, 67, 75, 83–84, 95–96, 100, 109, 125, 127, 130
dialectic (Hegelian), 18–19, 42, 44–45, 107n10, 125n36, 211, 221, 229, 234
dialectic (Platonic), 21, 71, 108–16, 119, 121, 127, 133, 136, 138, 142–44, 146–47, 149–52, 154, 158, 161, 164–69, 179, 184–85, 187, 192–95, 198, 200–201, 203, 221–22, 228–29
Diès, Auguste, 146, 155n31, 158, 160–61, 162n41, 164, 183
difference, 17, 19, 72n12, 133, 138n10, 139, 142n16, 154, 163, 229
différance, 4, 138n10, 142n16, 151
Ding, das, 72, 81, 100, 105, 123, 128, 205. *See also* Thing
Diogenes Laertius, 173–74, 182
Dion of Syracuse, 191
Dionysius II of Syracuse, 191
Diotima, 107, 110, 112, 113n18, 116, 118–19, 121–22, 124, 126–27, 131–32, 176, 202, 223n65, 230
dispositif, 171, 215–16, 232
division, 119, 123, 136, 142–43, 151–55, 157–59, 161, 164–65, 167, 176–77, 229
dual, 91–92, 163
Dumézil, Georges, 3, 204

Eagleton, Terry, 9n13, 32, 40, 73, 204n44
Ecole Normale Supérieure, 8, 15n26, 30, 33, 134, 168, 229
ekhthros, 93, 113
Electra, 22, 32–33, 36–41, 54, 82n33
elenchus, 24, 60, 108–9, 111, 113, 116–17, 130, 192, 198, 202, 218, 230
Eliot, T. S., 27–29
Empedocles, 80n30, 150n28
emptiness, 38, 55, 67, 97, 107, 109–11, 127–28, 131, 228
Epictetus, 213
Epicureanism, 96–97
epistêmê, 68, 192, 196
erastês, 113n17, 125–26, 128–29, 208, 224
Eribon, Didier, 204, 206–7, 233n7
erômenos, 126, 128–29, 207–8
erôs, 68, 78, 107, 110, 116, 118, 121, 180n3
Eros, 63n2, 73, 79n29, 112, 124, 127, 143, 150, 167, 176, 197, 199, 201, 208
Eteocles, 76, 88, 90
ethics, 2, 12–17, 19, 23–26, 42, 44–45, 55–56, 58–60, 64, 66–76, 79, 81, 83–86, 95–97, 99–108, 119, 128, 131, 134, 152, 158, 165, 180–81, 183, 185, 187–88, 204, 206–7, 209n49, 213–18, 223, 228–29, 232–33, 235
eudaimonia, 68, 105n7. *See also bonheur;* happiness
Euripides, 13, 22, 33, 35, 38n15, 39, 77n23, 82n33, 148n23, 190

existentialism, 13, 21–22, 31, 33, 40, 42, 56, 57, 60
exchange, 28, 45, 58, 70, 73, 94, 98, 102, 116, 120, 125, 155, 157, 163, 165, 168, 175, 203

facticity, 43–44, 123
fascism, 8, 17, 22–23, 27–32, 34, 42–43, 45, 51–52, 54, 57, 59, 61, 65, 97, 101–2, 228
feminism, 1, 7, 9, 15, 103, 172n60, 173, 212
Ferrari, G. R. F., 129n 39, 144–45, 148n24, 149, 199
Festugière, A. J., 100, 117, 143n18, 146, 152n29, 155, 161, 183, 190n24, 192n26
Fine, Gail, 3, 186
finitude, 14, 40, 69, 84
forms, 99, 118–20, 124–25, 129, 132, 158–62, 165, 191, 196–97, 199
Foucault, Michel, 1–3, 4, 6–13, 16–19, 21, 22, 25–26, 32, 42–44, 55, 60, 64, 67, 72n13, 84, 96, 99, 134, 141–43, 145, 167–76, 178–201, 203–35; *L'herméneutique du sujet,* 13n20, 26, 178–80, 185, 188, 189n23, 203, 206–7, 209, 213–14, 217–24, 230; "Le gouvernement du soi et des autres," 13n20, 178n1, 189–201. See also *pensée du dehors*
Frank, Jill, 68n9, 69
Frede, Dorothea, 155, 161–62, 164–65, 166
freedom, 22–23, 32–33, 35, 37, 39–41, 49, 56–58, 70, 77, 83, 96, 190n23, 195, 214, 216
Freiberger, Erich, 108
Freud, Sigmund, 1, 6, 9n14, 24, 25, 61, 63–67, 97, 98n52, 100, 106, 122, 125n36, 129n39, 133, 135–43, 154, 168, 172, 175, 177, 182, 184n12, 204n44, 205, 206, 210n50, 217, 225; *Beyond the Pleasure Principle,* 24, 52, 64, 73–74, 76, 79, 83–84, 95, 100, 102, 110, 116, 120, 130, 135, 151–57, 164–65, 167, 170–71, 175–77, 228. See also death drive; pleasure principle; reality principle
Furies, 33–36, 41n19
futurism, 27n2, 28, 172, 227

Gadamer, Hans-Georg, 120, 138, 151, 155, 158, 159n38, 160, 161n39, 162, 164n45, 166, 193n33
gender, 16n28, 54, 90, 96n50, 173, 208, 232–33
genealogy, 2, 7, 11, 16–17, 29, 60, 63, 133, 141–42, 152, 167, 169, 171, 173, 177, 181, 184, 186, 199, 205, 207, 213, 218–19, 221, 235
Girard, René, 166
Giraudoux, Jean, 27n2, 32, 33, 35–37
Goethe, Johann Wolfgang von, 75–76, 94n49
Goldhill, Simon, 69, 93, 232n2
Goldschmidt, Victor, 143n18, 149, 159n37, 161–62
good, the, 2, 13, 23, 37, 59, 66–70, 73, 76, 81, 84, 86, 95, 99, 100–1, 107, 113–14, 118–19, 121, 124–25, 128–29, 159n38, 162, 176, 179, 191, 200, 225
Gosling, J. C. B., 159n38, 164
governmentality, 217–18, 221, 232
Grene, David, 78, 87
Grenier, Jean, 45–46
Griffith, Mark, 77, 78, 79n28, 82, 88, 90, 92n48, 93, 94
Gros, Frédéric, 178n2, 180, 186n16, 189n23, 194, 214–18, 223n66, 235
Gross, Nicholas, 86n40, 89
Guyomard, Patrick, 83, 101–2

Hades, 63, 66, 78–79, 101
Hadot, Pierre, 11n17, 20, 25, 64n5, 108–10, 180n3, 183, 186–87, 192, 201–2, 214

Haemon, 78–79, 82, 101, 131
Halperin, David, 9–10, 144, 150n28, 231–34
Hampton, Cynthia, 160–63, 164n45
hamartia, 95
Hamlet, 63, 133
Hanson, Victor Davis, and John Heath, 7
happiness, 30, 36, 51, 53, 57, 65, 67–69, 71, 74, 97, 100, 130
Hartman, Geoffrey, 5
Hegel, G. W. F., 5, 58, 67, 75–77, 105, 125, 221
Heidegger, Martin, 20, 22–23, 39–40, 44, 51, 60, 72n12, 80, 84n37, 122–23, 136, 206, 223n66
Hippothales, 111–16
historicism, 18–19, 205, 211
historicity, 23, 41–42, 44, 69, 212
historicization, 2, 10–11, 16–17, 32, 131, 154, 208, 212, 213n54, 215
history, 11–15, 118–19, 21–23, 39–40, 42, 44–45, 57–58, 60–61, 65–67, 98, 143, 184, 205–6, 209, 211, 215, 217–18, 221, 225
Homer, 93, 126
homosexuality, 16n28, 18, 35n12, 103–4, 209–11, 233. *See also* pederasty; queer theory
Horace, 4, 227
humanism, 21, 30, 46n24, 66

Imaginary, 13, 69–70, 72, 90, 93, 101, 106, 108, 122, 131, 163, 205. *See also* Lacan; Real; Symbolic
inhuman, 43–44
Irigaray, Luce, 1, 4, 7, 9n14, 15n27, 45n21, 62n2, 64, 96n50, 105n6, 134, 183, 212
irony, 105n6, 113, 120, 144–45, 204
Irwin, Terrence, 3, 186, 190n24
Ismene, 68, 76–77, 84n38, 86–87, 89–93
Isocrates, 190

Jaffro, Laurent, 209n49, 215, 223n66

Jameson, Fredric, 5n7, 13–15, 18, 28n3, 163n44, 212
Janan, Micaela, 65, 103, 105n6, 116n23, 156n34
Jebb, R. C., 77–78, 81, 86n40, 87, 90
Joan of Arc, 30–31
Jocasta, 62n2, 76n22, 96n50
Johnson, Patricia, 75–76
jouissance, 24, 34–35, 40, 100–5, 110, 116
Julien, Philippe, 68, 69–70n11, 74, 83, 106, 107, 121, 125, 127–29, 155, 205n45
Jupiter, 22, 34, 37–39
justice, 36–37, 43, 47, 50, 100, 130, 132, 191, 196

Kamerbeek, J. C., 77–78, 81–82, 88, 90
Kant, Immanuel, 68, 72n14, 83, 115, 137n9
Kaplan, Alice, 27n1, 30–31, 41
khôra, 146–47, 156n35, 164, 168n52
Kojève, Alexandre, 5
Konstan, David, 93, 189n21, 231
Kremer-Marietti, Angèle, 169n53, 184n13, 215, 234
Kristeva, Julia, 1, 4, 5n7, 6–7, 15, 64, 72n12, 103, 105, 134, 163n44

Labdacids, 66, 80, 82, 90–92, 95, 97
Lacan, Jacques, 1–3, 4n5, 5–7, 9n14, 10–18, 19n34, 22, 24–26, 32, 38n14, 42, 44, 45, 57, 61–62, 89–90, 98n52, 99, 103n4, 104, 106n8, 116, 134–35, 136n7, 142, 143, 154, 155, 156n34, 158, 163n44, 165–67, 171, 176, 181, 204–13, 217, 218, 225, 229, 230, 232, 234; Seminar VII (*Ethics*), 23, 51–52, 55, 58–60, 63–81, 83–86, 87n42, 94–97, 100–102, 105, 106n7, 130–31, 133, 152, 156, 204–5, 207, 217,

228; Seminar VIII (*Transference*), 24, 98, 106–7, 117, 121–33, 193, 204, 208, 213n54; *Seminar on the Purloined Letter,* 139n11, 152, 166. *See also* Imaginary; Real; Symbolic
Lentricchia, Frank, 5.
Leonard, Miriam, 1n2, 3n4, 10nn15–16, 13–14, 16n28, 18, 62n2, 63, 64, 75n18, 96n50, 105n6, 106, 181n7, 183n9, 207n47, 210n5, 211n51
Levinas, Emmanuel, 1
Lévi-Strauss, Claude, 10, 204
Lévy, Carlos, 186n16
limit, 25, 66, 69, 81, 95, 108, 137, 142–43, 152–65, 168, 170, 176, 212, 229
logic, 42, 46–48, 51, 56, 69–70n11, 91, 105, 125, 135, 144–45, 155, 158–59, 166, 181–82, 206
logocentrism, 25, 134, 144, 146, 152, 157, 165, 193
logos, 25, 68, 108–9, 111–12, 114–15, 120, 124, 134–35, 143–45, 148–51, 153, 168–69, 173, 184–85, 187–88, 191, 193–94, 196–99, 222
Loraux, Nicole, 10, 78n27, 91n47, 146–47
Lukács, Georg, 5
Lysias, 118, 147–49, 151, 187, 189n23, 198

Marcel, Gabriel, 31, 39, 40–41, 47, 57
Marcus Aurelius, 188n20, 218
Marx, Karl, 14, 125n36, 225
Marxism, 5, 14, 18–19, 42, 58–59, 120n26, 225. *See also* communism; Parti Communiste Français; Stalinism
Maulnier, Thierry, 29–30, 48, 52, 53
Maurras, Charles, 27, 29–31, 153
May 1968, 15n26
megalopsychos, 68–69n10

memory, 15, 49, 136–39, 141, 143, 148n23, 150–51, 187–88, 196
Miller, J. Hillis, 3, 4, 6n9
Miller, Jacques Alain, 62–63n3
Miller, James, 180, 213, 233n7
modernists, 17–19, 21–23, 27–60, 65, 97, 102, 131, 229
Moi, Toril, 15, 16n28, 64n4, 172n60
Molière, 32
Montaigne, Michel de, 19–21, 173n62, 186n17
Montherlant, Henri de, 30
Morgan, Michael L., 201
Morrow, Glenn, 190–91n24
Musonius Rufus, 210n49
Mussolini, Benito, 28, 29, 101n2, 228
muthos, 149–50, 168

Nagy, Gregory, 10, 200n42
Nazi (National Socialism), 28, 41, 44, 47
negative, 11, 14, 39, 41–42, 45, 66–67, 103, 107, 122, 123n32, 146, 155, 166, 204, 211–13
Nehamas, Alexander, 180n5, 186, 204
neoclassicism, 17, 22, 27, 33, 35–38, 42, 48, 52–53, 60
neo-Kantianism, 39
Nero, 45n22, 190n23
Nietzsche, Friedrich, 20, 22, 29–30, 44, 46, 48, 50–52, 55, 60, 65, 133, 216, 229
Nightingale, Andrea, 116, 120, 124, 148n23
Niobe, 83, 85, 95–96, 101
normalization, 26, 69, 95, 98n52, 108, 169, 180, 205–6, 216–17, 231–34

Oedipus, 45n23, 63, 67, 71, 74, 80, 87–92, 96n50, 104, 181n7
oikos, 75–76, 77n23
Orestes, 22, 32–33, 35–43, 46, 49, 54, 56–57, 59–60, 70, 97, 190

Oudemans, Th. C. W., and A. P. M. H. Lardinois, 75, 77, 79–81, 83n34, 84n35, 94, 138
Ovid, 62n3, 80, 114

parrhêsia, 189–90, 198, 209–10
Parti Communiste Français, 8, 58–59, 131n41. *See also* communism; Marxism; Stalinism
Patroclus, 126–27
Pausanias, 22, 39
pederasty, 112, 125–26, 207–8, 211n51, 213n54, 215, 224–25
pensée du dehors ("thought from the outside"), 11–13, 16–17, 21, 23, 51–52, 99, 104, 132, 216–17, 226
peras, 142n17, 143, 147n10, 155, 159n38
Pericles, 77n23, 179, 203, 213, 224, 231
Persius, 26, 181, 213, 233–35
Pétain, Maréchal Philippe, 35
Phaedrus, 118, 126–27, 129, 132, 148n23, 187, 198, 203n43
phallus, 103, 105–6, 122, 211n51
pharmakon, 24, 134, 144–51, 187–88, 192, 195, 199
philia, 93–94, 97, 105, 112–14, 174–77, 229
Philodemus, 189n21
philotimia, 98, 110, 129
Picasso, Pablo, 74
Plato, 1–3, 4, 6–10, 13, 16–18, 20, 21, 23–26, 60, 64–65, 68, 71, 72n13, 77n23, 82n13, 96, 99, 108, 111–20, 122–73, 175–204, 206–8, 211, 216–26, 228–32, 234–35; *Alcibiades,* 9n14, 13, 25–26, 110, 113n18, 178–81, 183n10, 185, 187, 189n23, 192, 193n28, 201–3, 206, 213, 214, 216–26, 230, 231–32, 234–35; *Apology,* 109, 110n14, 115, 117, 120, 124, 132, 180n5, 197–98; *Critias,* 117, 151; *Euthydemus,* 113n18; *Euthyphro,* 117; *Gorgias,* 111, 112n16, 113n18, 189n23, 192n27, 194n21, 220; *Hippias Major,* 113n18; *Hippias Minor,* 111; *Ion,* 13n20, 113n18, 117, 146, 200; *Laches,* 180n5; *Laws,* 117, 146, 190, 195, 196; *Lysis,* 24, 111–17, 124, 132, 133, 225; *Menexenus,* 77n23; *Meno,* 113n18, 196; *Parmenides,* 161; *Phaedo,* 108, 131, 158, 175, 180n5; *Phaedrus,* 6, 12, 16, 34, 60, 65, 82n33, 113n18, 117–20, 127, 129n39, 130–37, 142–51, 158, 167, 183, 185–88, 189n23, 195–200, 203, 220n64, 223; *Philebus,* 9, 12, 16, 25, 60, 113n18, 117, 119, 120, 133, 135, 136, 138, 140, 142–43, 147n21, 151–56, 158–67, 170–71, 175, 179, 182, 183, 195n33, 197n37; *Republic,* 108, 112n16, 117, 118, 132, 133, 150, 158, 190, 195–97, 200, 223; seventh letter, 60, 113n18, 120, 172n59, 190–202, 222, 225; *Sophist,* 117, 133, 156, 158, 161, 183; *Statesman,* 117, 133, 136, 158, 161; *Symposium,* 6, 12, 14, 16, 22, 23–24, 59, 60, 64–66, 68, 71, 96, 98–99, 106–7, 110–12, 113n18, 116–32, 133, 146, 150, 155, 167, 176, 180, 193, 195, 197, 200–4, 207–8, 209, 211, 213n54, 220, 222, 223n65; *Theaetetus,* 117, 137–38, 146, 160–61, 202–3, 220, 225n68; *Timaeus,* 9, 117, 149n25, 156n35, 164, 168n52
Platter, Charles, 120n26, 192n27, 220n64
pleasure principle, 12, 24, 52, 59, 64, 68, 70, 73–74, 76–77, 79, 83–85, 94–95, 97, 100, 102–3, 110–11, 116, 120, 123, 125, 130, 138n10, 152, 155–57, 163–67, 170–71, 175–77, 228. *See also* death drive; Freud; reality principle
Plotinus, 6–7, 45.
Plutarch, 213.
polis, 16, 24, 54, 64, 75, 77n23, 88, 98–99, 101, 103, 105, 110, 129, 131–32, 150, 180, 220, 225

politics, 2, 13–17, 22, 26–31, 34–35, 37, 43, 44–45, 51, 53, 56, 58, 68, 96, 102, 104, 119, 136, 169, 172–73, 176–77, 189n23, 196, 213, 216–18, 220, 223–24, 229, 232–33
Polybius, 190
Polynices, 76–77, 80, 82, 88, 90, 93–94
Popper, Karl, 120
postality, 25, 153–54, 157–58, 170, 172–73
postmodernism, 1–4, 7–11, 13, 17–19, 21–25, 32, 42–43, 51, 58, 60, 64, 103, 132–33, 135n36, 181, 183n10, 227–29
poststructuralism, 4–5, 7, 37, 29, 44–45, 60, 61, 133, 184
Pound, Ezra, 28
power, 2, 17, 21, 23–25, 28, 34–35, 38, 43–44, 46, 49, 52, 61, 63, 69, 70, 77n23, 80, 97, 101, 106n7, 108, 136, 167, 169–72, 176–77, 194, 202, 205n45, 207n47, 208, 211–13, 216–20, 223–24, 225, 228, 234–35
Protarchus, 158–60, 163–66
prôton philon, 115–16, 118, 121, 124–25
psyche, 99, 132, 134, 137–39, 151, 152, 164, 176, 221
psychoanalysis, 3–5, 7, 13–15, 19, 23–25, 55, 58, 60–70, 72n12, 73n15, 75–76, 83–85, 97–99, 104–8, 121–25, 128, 131–36, 139–41, 152–53, 156–58, 164–67, 169, 172–73, 176, 192n28, 201, 204–11, 217, 225
Puhvel, Jan, 4
purity, 17, 24, 29, 48, 51–53, 55–58, 64–66, 83, 103, 150
Pyrrho, 39, 186n16
Pythagoras, 150n28, 159n38, 201

queer theory, 9, 26, 96, 104, 210, 231–34

Rabaté, Jean Michel, 62, 67, 104n5, 207
Racine, Jean, 30, 32
Ragland-Sullivan, Ellie, 17n30, 69–70n11, 72n12, 106nn7–8, 212
Real, 13–14, 18, 45, 67, 69n11, 70, 72, 106, 211n52. *See also* Imaginary; Lacan; Symbolic.
reality principle, 67, 73, 76, 84–86, 94–97, 100, 102, 130, 138n10, 155–57. *See also* death drive; Freud; pleasure principle
Renaissance, 19, 21, 186n17
Renaut, Alain, 40n17, 42, 44, 84n37, 123
resistance, the, 30–31, 33n9, 35, 41, 44, 47, 54, 59
rhetoric, 38, 74, 111, 118–19, 137, 147–48, 150, 153, 189–90n23, 190n24, 194n31, 197–99, 209–10
Rhode, Erwin, 65
Richlin, Amy, 9n14, 233n5
Robin, Leon, 112, 114, 121, 133, 143, 147n22, 148n24, 149, 151, 183, 193n29, 203n43, 208n48
Romilly, Jacqueline de, 8
Rorty, Richard, 4
Rose, Peter, 120n26
Roudinesco, Elisabeth, 61n1, 62–63n3, 104n5, 167n48, 210–11
Rousseau, Jean-Jacques, 6

Sade, Marquis de, 68
Santas, Gerasimos, 93, 100, 147n22
Sartre, Jean-Paul, 5, 15n26, 16n28, 17–19, 22, 30–45, 46n25, 52, 55, 56, 58–59, 62n2, 67n7, 70, 71–72n12, 74, 84n37, 96, 122–23, 131n4, 204, 211n51, 215, 227–28
Saussure, Ferdinand de, 5, 6, 133
Sayre, Kenneth M., 163n42, 191n24, 193
Schmitt, Carl, 20
Segal, Charles, 76n20, 79, 85, 87–88, 91, 102

self, 1–2, 10, 13, 17, 19–21, 26, 42–43, 50–51, 56–57, 60, 66, 67, 70, 73–75, 81, 83–85, 88, 91–93, 97, 99, 103, 105–6, 109–10, 120–23, 128, 131, 138–39, 141, 151, 164, 167, 176, 178–80, 181n5, 183n10, 185–89, 193–94, 196n36, 199–204, 207, 209–10, 213–26, 228, 230, 232–34. *See also* psyche; soul; spiritual exercises; spiritual practices; subject
self-creation, 24, 25, 31, 42–45, 131
self-improvement, 68–69
self-fashioning, 19, 25–26, 42, 57, 173, 178, 187–88, 224, 228, 233
self-knowledge, 48, 109–10, 185, 215–20, 226
self-mastery, 89n45, 167, 214, 224
self-transcendence, 69, 84, 95, 124
self-transformation, 37, 50, 68, 219, 233
Seneca, 6, 30, 184, 188, 189–90n23, 213, 218
Serres, Michel, 1
sexuality, 16n28, 169–70, 172–73, 183–84, 205n44, 207, 209–10, 233
Sextus Empiricus, 39, 186n16
Shankman, Steven, 144
Shepherdson, Charles, 18, 65, 122n31, 205–6, 217, 228
Silenus box, 118–19, 204
Slatkin, Laura, 10
Socrates, 1, 23, 24, 60, 64, 67n7, 96, 98–99, 103, 107–32, 135, 136, 140, 147, 149–51, 153, 155, 158–60, 163–65, 172, 175, 176, 178–80, 183, 189n23, 192, 195–98, 201–4, 208, 213n55, 218, 220–25, 229, 231–32, 234–35
sophists, 38n15, 117n17, 114, 137, 149, 160
Sophocles, 6n9, 16, 22–23, 33, 35, 39, 45n23, 63, 56, 66, 68, 148n23; *Antigone,* 12–14, 16, 22–24, 51, 54, 57–59, 62n2, 63–68, 69n10, 70, 72–98, 100–6, 110, 116, 123, 128, 130–31, 133, 135n5, 152, 156, 163, 175, 204–5, 207, 228
Souilhé, Joseph, 190n24, 192, 195
soul, 1, 43, 53, 68–69n10, 77, 80n30, 98, 99, 130, 137–39, 141, 144, 147, 151, 176, 178–80, 183, 187–88, 197, 198–99, 201, 203, 220–26, 234–35. *See also* psyche; self; spiritual exercises; spiritual practices; subject
spiritual exercises, 180n3, 185–88, 214. *See also* psyche; self; soul; spiritual practices; subject
spiritual practices, 2, 9, 11, 45, 96, 132, 177, 185, 200–201, 219–20, 230. *See also* psyche; self; soul; spiritual exercises; subject
Stalinism, 28, 59, 131n41. *See also* communism; Marxism; Parti Communiste Français
Steiner, George, 53, 75, 91n47, 102
Stesichorus, 197n38
Stoics, 9, 13, 25–26, 76n22, 167, 180–83, 185–88, 206–7, 209–10n49, 214, 231–35
structuralism, 5
subject, 2, 4, 7, 10, 12, 16–17, 20–21, 23, 25, 39, 45, 59–60, 63, 66, 68 69–70n11, 72n12, 74, 84, 98, 99, 103, 105, 107, 120, 122–23, 126, 128–29, 134–35, 139, 151, 152–53, 155, 157, 181, 185, 194, 196, 200, 204, 206, 209, 213–15, 217–19, 221–22, 226, 232–35. *See also* psyche; self; soul; spiritual exercises; spiritual practices
subjectivation, 209, 213, 217, 219, 231–32, 235
sublime, 28, 72–73, 80–81, 85–86, 95–96, 101, 105
substitution, 94, 107, 116, 123–27, 129, 132, 153, 155, 163, 175, 208
Suetonius, 45–46, 50–51
suicide, 52–53, 76–77, 83, 101
surrealism, 5, 27n2, 32, 57, 103
Symbolic, 13–16, 23, 45, 59, 66, 69–70, 72–74, 77, 79–95, 98n52, 100, 102–6, 116, 118, 123,

125, 129, 131–32, 163–64, 168, 211–12. *See also* Imaginary; Lacan; Real
Szlezák, Thomas, 114n18, 148n23

Taylor, Charles, 2
Tel quel, 136
temporality, 40, 123
Theocritus, 227
theory, 3–7, 9–10, 14, 19, 26, 133, 135, 173, 209, 210, 212, 218, 219, 232
Theuth, 143, 147–48, 150, 154, 196, 199
Thing, the, 72–74, 80, 116, 120–21. See also *Ding, das*
thrownness, 39–40, 43. *See also* Heidegger
Thucydides, 77n23, 190, 224, 227
Tiresias, 95
trace, 137, 139, 141–43, 168, 176, 229
tragedy, 21–24, 29–36, 46, 48, 52–56, 58, 60, 61n2, 63, 65–67, 76n19, 78n27, 84, 85, 93, 102, 228
transference, 24, 59–60, 64–65, 68, 98n52, 100, 106–8, 125, 152–57, 208, 211
tribê, 194
two-deaths, 79–80

unlimited, the, 142, 147n21, 155, 157, 159–66, 175–76, 182

utopian, 36, 52, 102–3, 209, 233

Vergil, 20–21, 28–30, 227
Vernant, Jean-Pierre, 8, 10, 61–62n2, 79n29, 80, 82, 85, 89n45, 90, 149n25, 150n28, 201
Vichy, 27, 35, 53. *See also* collaboration
Vidal-Naquet, Pierre, 10, 61–62n2, 79n29, 80, 82, 85, 90

Watkins, Calvert, 4
Wolfman, 97, 156n34
Witt, Mary Ann Friese, 23, 29–31, 33n9, 34–35n12, 45, 51, 52–54, 57, 101
Wohl, Victoria, 86, 88, 91, 110n15, 125, 202, 224
Woodruff, Paul, 78n25, 87
Wray, David, 38n15, 76n22, 106n7
writing, 2, 16, 20, 24–25, 134, 136–39, 142–44, 147–51, 153–54, 176, 186–200

Zeitlin, Froma, 83n34, 233
Zeus, 22, 37–38, 87, 90, 94, 122
Žižek, Slavoj, 14n24, 15, 38n14, 72n12, 73, 80, 84n35, 102n3, 104–5, 107, 166, 208–9, 217n62, 211
Zuckert, Catherine, 24, 154, 161n39, 167, 170, 187, 199, 201

www.ingramcontent.com/pod-product-compliance
Lightning Source LLC
Chambersburg PA
CBHW032002220426
43664CB00005B/117